essential
COMMUNICATION

essential
COMMUNICATION

Ronald B. Adler
Santa Barbara City College

George Rodman
Brooklyn College, City University of New York

Athena du Pré
University of West Florida

New York   Oxford
OXFORD UNIVERSITY PRESS

Oxford University Press is a department of the University of Oxford.
It furthers the University's objective of excellence in research,
scholarship, and education by publishing worldwide.

Oxford   New York
Auckland   Cape Town   Dar es Salaam   Hong Kong   Karachi
Kuala Lumpur   Madrid   Melbourne   Mexico City   Nairobi
New Delhi   Shanghai   Taipei   Toronto

With offices in
Argentina   Austria   Brazil   Chile   Czech Republic   France   Greece
Guatemala   Hungary   Italy   Japan   Poland   Portugal   Singapore
South Korea   Switzerland   Thailand   Turkey   Ukraine   Vietnam

For titles covered by Section 112 of the US Higher Education Opportunity
Act, please visit www.oup.com/us/he for the latest information about
pricing and alternate formats.

Published by Oxford University Press
198 Madison Avenue, New York, NY 10016
www.oup.com

Oxford is a registered trademark of Oxford University Press.

Library of Congress Cataloging-in-Publication Data
Adler, Ronald B. (Ronald Brian), 1946–
Essential communication / Ronald B. Adler, Santa Barbara City College;
George Rodman, Brooklyn College, City University of New York; Athena DuPré,
University of West Florida.
     pages cm
ISBN 978-0-19-934236-5
1. Communication. 2. Interpersonal communication.
I. Rodman, George R., 1948– II. DuPré, Athena. III. Title.
   P90.A313 2015
   302.2—dc23   2014028837

Printing number: 9 8 7 6 5 4 3

Printed in the United States of America
on acid-free paper

BRIEF CONTENTS

CONTENTS

CHAPTER **3**   Communication and Culture   50

PART TWO   COMMUNICATION ELEMENTS

CHAPTER **4**   Language   74

CHAPTER **5**   Listening   100

CHAPTER **6**   Nonverbal Communication   124

PART THREE INTERPERSONAL COMMUNICATION

PART FOUR   PROFESSIONAL COMMUNICATION

CHAPTER 10   Communicating for Career Success   224

CHAPTER 11   Communicating in Groups and Teams   260

PART FIVE   PUBLIC COMMUNICATION

CHAPTER 12 Preparing Speeches 288

CHAPTER 13 Presenting Speeches 316

CHAPTER 14 Speaking to Inform, Persuade, and Entertain 340

The French theologian Francois Fénelon might have been thinking of college students when he observed, "The more you say, the less people remember." This statement provides the rationale for our approach in writing *Essential Communication*. We've worked hard to make this introduction to the academic study of communication comprehensive, succinct, clear, and engaging. *Essential Communication* aims to present the essential scholarship of the field in a straightforward way without being simplistic.

The title *Essential Communication* also reflects the truth that effective communication is indispensable in both successful personal relationships and the wider world. While this may be obvious to those of us who have dedicated our professional lives to the subject, it bears emphasizing to readers who are new to the discipline.

Essential Communication includes several distinctive features. First, it offers considerable coverage of interpersonal relationships (Chapter 7) and highlights contexts that professors and students have told us they care most about: friendships, families (Chapter 8), and romantic relationships (Chapter 9). Just as important, this book covers professional relationships in the context of workplace communication. Chapter 10 is loaded with practical advice on how to find, get, keep, and ultimately leave a job in a professional manner.

Finally, *Essential Communication* avoids the duplication and overlap that characterize the treatment of informative and persuasive speaking in many introductory textbooks. True to its title and approach, *Essential Communication* combines informative and persuasive speaking in a single chapter to stress the differences between these two types of speeches. We believe this not only reduces redundancy, but it also allows instructors to focus more on skill development and speech presentations.

KEY FEATURES

"Real world" focus   *Essential Communication* is full of practical examples and guidance that link theory and research to everyday life. Photos from films, television shows, and popular culture help relate the material to students' experiences and concerns. Special attention is devoted to friendships, family, and romantic relationships—the contexts that matter most to many students.

Integrated coverage of social media   Because social media play a central role in virtually every dimension of communication, coverage is integrated throughout the book.

Focus on culture   In an increasingly diverse world, awareness of cultural and cocultural differences is an important part of communicative competence. Along with a dedicated chapter on this topic, cultural factors are addressed throughout the book.

Career emphasis   In a challenging economy, students need all the help they can get to find and excel in the workplace. For that reason, we've dedicated an entire chapter to communicating for career success.

PEDAGOGY

Teaching—whether in a textbook, classroom, or online—isn't the same thing as learning. To make sure students can master the concepts in *Essential Communication*, we have created an array of pedagogical resources. These features include:

Learning Objectives   Each chapter opens with a list of objectives that spell out what students need to know. These objectives correspond to the major sections in each chapter, so students always know what's expected of them.

Self-Assessments   Every chapter contains an instrument that lets students see where they stand on key issues like intercultural sensitivity, self-esteem, mindfulness about communication, leadership style, and speech anxiety.

Photo Captions with Questions   Contemporary, engaging, and thought-provoking photos and captions highlight popular movies, television shows, and pop culture references that students can relate to, prompting them to think critically about their own communication.

Marginal Questions   Questions in the margins prompt students to think critically about the essential concepts in each major section.

Marginal Glossary   Key terms are defined in the margins of the main text where they are first bolded, to reinforce key concepts.

Chapter Summaries   End-of-chapter summaries are organized around the learning objectives to ensure that students understand the most important takeaways of the chapter.

Application Check   End-of-chapter questions ask readers to apply each learning objective to their own lives. As a result, every student can see the real-world value of the concepts they have studied.

RESOURCES FOR INSTRUCTORS

We have designed instructional resources in a ready-to-go format for use in a classroom, online, or a mixture of both.

Easily Adaptable Syllabus　A full syllabus template includes assignments, deadlines, a course schedule, assignment descriptions, and handouts.

High-Impact Learning Activities　A variety of experiential learning activities are provided to support every learning objective.

Comprehensive Lesson Plans　Chapter lesson plans include class-preparation checklists, reading quizzes, video links, discussion starters, and more.

Dynamic Audiovisuals　Prezi and PowerPoint presentations for each chapter bring the lesson plans to life.

Annotated Instructor's Edition　The AIE contains marginal notes with useful tips and activities for instructors to use in their classes.

Computerized Test Bank　The comprehensive test bank includes an average of 60 exam questions per chapter in multiple-choice, true/false, matching, and completion formats.

Course cartridges for a variety of e-learning environments　Course cartridges allow instructors to create their own course websites with the interactive material from the ARC and student companion website.

ACKNOWLEDGMENTS

While the authors' names appear on the cover, this book is the product of many people's ideas and efforts.

We are grateful to the many colleagues whose feedback shaped the final product:

Sherry Rhodes
Collin College

James Keller
Lone Star College

Dana Vance Elderkin
Alamance Community College

Dale Guffey
Cleveland Community College

Erin Perry
NHTI–Concord's Community College

Kay B. Barefoot
College of The Albemarle

Meredith Kincaid Ginn
Georgia Highlands College

Diane K. Mason
Fort Hays State University

Nancy J. Willets
Cape Cod Community College

Steve Stuglin
Georgia Highlands College

Herbert Sennett
Palm Beach State College

Frederick Shorter
Bainbridge College

Lillian Zarzar
Ohio University

Tracey Elizabeth Powers
Central Arizona College

Doug Bennett
Pittsburg State University

Paige C. Davis
Lone Star College, Cyfair

Kim G. Smith
Bishop State Community College

Araceli Palomino
Germanna Community College

Laura Beth Daws, PhD
Southern Polytechnic State University

Laurie D. Metcalf, PhD
Blinn College

Therese McGinnis
College of DuPage

Tajsha N. Eaves
Cleveland Community College

Nader H. Chaaban
Montgomery College

We are lucky to have worked with a dream team of professionals at Oxford University Press. Their dedication and talents combine the best practices of traditional publishing with a twenty-first-century sensibility. Our hands-on editor, Mark Haynes, demonstrated a level of caring and involvement that surpasses anything we've experienced in our professional careers. Our unflappable developmental editor, Lisa Sussman, has been consistently insightful, responsive, and diplomatic. Editorial assistants Grace Ross and Paul Longo skillfully and cheerfully kept things moving forward. Intern Allison Collins provided some great pop-culture suggestions. Production manager Lisa Grzan and Senior Production Editor Keith Faivre managed the transition from manuscript to the handsome product you are now reading. We also want to thank our wonderful designer, Michele Laseau, and our Marketing Manager, David Jurman.

On the home front, we thank our spouses for giving us the time and space needed to create this book.

essential

COMMUNICATION

Communication:
What and Why

1.1 Define communication.

1.2 Compare and contrast two models of communication.

1.3 Describe the various types of communication by context.

1.4 Identify characteristics of effective communication and competent communicators.

1.5 Analyze your communication competence with social media.

1.6 Determine how misconceptions about communication can create problems.

COMMUNICATION DEFINED

Communication isn't as simple to define as you might think. The term can refer to everything from messages on T-shirts to presidential speeches, from computer code to chimpanzee behavior. In this book we focus on human communication, and we define **communication** as *the process of creating meaning through symbolic interaction*. But what does this mean? Our definition of communication highlights several important characteristics of communication.

> communication

The process of creating meaning through symbolic interaction.

Communication Is Symbolic

Symbols are used to represent things, processes, ideas, or events in ways that make communication possible. The most significant feature of symbols is their arbitrary nature. For example, there's no logical reason why the letters in the word *book* should stand for the object you're reading now. Speakers of Spanish call it a *libro*, and Lithuanians call it a *knyga*. Even in English, another term would work just as well, as long as everyone agreed to use it in the same way. Effective communication depends on agreement among people about linguistic rules and customs. This is easiest to see when we observe people who don't follow linguistic conventions. For example, think about how unusual the speech of a child or nonnative speaker often sounds.

Symbolic communication allows people to think or talk about the past, explain the present, and speculate about the future. Chapter 4 discusses the nature of symbols in more detail.

> symbol

An arbitrary sign used to represent a thing, person, idea, event, or relationship in a way that makes communication possible.

Communication Is a Process

We often think about communication as if it occurs in discrete, individual acts. But communication is a continuous, ongoing process. Even what appears to be an isolated message is often part of a much larger process. Consider, for example, that your friend tells you you look "fabulous." Your interpretation of those words will depend on a long series of experiences stretching far back in time: What have others said about your appearance in the past? How do you feel about the way you look? Is your friend prone to irony? This simple example shows that it's inaccurate to talk about "acts" of communication as if they occur in isolation. Instead, they unfold like a movie in which the meaning comes from the interrelated series of images.

Q *Have you ever posted a message you wish you could take back?*

Communication Is Irreversible

At certain moments, you have probably wished that you could back up in time, erasing words you've said or actions you've taken and replacing them with better alternatives. But it's no more possible to "unreceive" a message than it is to "unsqueeze" a tube of toothpaste. This principle is especially true online, where a careless message can haunt you virtually forever. For this reason, it's almost always wise to think before you speak, write, message, post, or tweet.

Communication Is Relational, Not Individual

Communication isn't something we do *to* others; rather, it is something we do *with* them. Psychologist Kenneth Gergen captures the relational nature of communication well when he points out how our success depends on interaction with others. As he says, ". . . one cannot be 'attractive' without others who are attracted, a 'leader' without others willing to follow, or a 'loving person' without others to affirm with appreciation."[1] Instead of focusing the blame on just one person for a disappointing interaction, it's usually better to ask, "How did we handle this situation, and what can we do to make it better?"

> Which communication choices enhance your relationships, and which choices damage them?

MODELS OF COMMUNICATION

> **linear communication model**
A characterization of communication as a one-way event in which a message flows from sender to receiver.

> **sender**
The originator of a message.

> **encoding**
The process of putting thoughts into symbols, most commonly words.

> **message**
A sender's planned and unplanned words and nonverbal behaviors.

> **receiver**
One who notices and attends to a message.

> **decoding**
The process in which a receiver attaches meaning to a message.

> **channel**
Medium through which a message passes from sender to receiver.

> **mediated communication**
Messages sent to one person or to many via a medium such as telephone, email, or instant messaging.

> **noise**
External, physiological, and psychological distractions that interfere with the accurate transmission and reception of a message.

One way to explore our definition of communication in more depth is to look at some models that describe what happens when two or more people interact.

A Linear Model

Until about 75 years ago, researchers viewed communication as something that one person "does" to another.[2] In this **linear communication model**, communication is like giving an injection: a **sender encodes** ideas and feelings into some sort of **message** and then conveys them to a **receiver** who **decodes** them (Figure 1-1).

One important element of the linear model is the communication **channel**—the method by which a message is conveyed between people. In addition to the long-used channels of face-to-face contact and writing, **mediated communication** channels include telephone, email, text messaging, voice mail, and videochatting. (The word *mediated* reflects the fact that these messages are conveyed through some sort of communication medium.)

The linear model also introduces the concept of **noise**—a term that describes any force that interferes with effective communication. Three types of noise can disrupt communication—external, physiological, and psychological. *External noise* includes those factors that make hearing difficult, as well as many other kinds of distractions. For instance, an incoming text message might make it hard for you to pay attention in a college

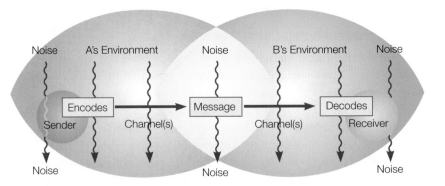

Figure 1-1 Linear Communication Model

lecture. Or, if you are sitting in the back of the room, you might not be able to hear the professor's remarks clearly. External noise can disrupt communication almost anywhere in our model—in the sender, channel, message, or receiver. *Physiological noise* involves biological factors in the receiver or sender that interfere with accurate reception, such as illness and fatigue. *Psychological noise* refers to forces within a communicator that interfere with the ability to express or understand a message accurately. For instance, if you believe that someone dislikes you, you may perceive everything that person says in a negative way.

A linear model shows that communicators often occupy different **environments**—fields of experience that help them understand others' behavior. *Environment* refers not only to a physical location but also to the personal experiences and cultural backgrounds that participants bring to a conversation. It's easy to imagine how your position on economic issues might differ depending on whether you're struggling financially or are well off, and how your thoughts on immigration reform might depend on how long your family has lived in this country.

Notice how the model in Figure 1-1 shows that the environments of A and B overlap. This area represents the background that the communicators have in common. As the shared environment becomes smaller, communication becomes more difficult.

Differing environments make it difficult but not impossible to understand others. Hard work and many of the skills described in this book provide ways to bridge the gap that separates all of us to a greater or lesser degree.

A Transactional Model

The linear model provides a good start to understanding communication, but it oversimplifies the way most communication operates. The transactional communication model in Figure 1-2 presents a more accurate picture in several respects.

Most notably, the **transactional communication model** shows that both sending and receiving are simultaneous. Although some types of

> **environment**
Both the physical setting in which communication occurs and the personal perspectives of the parties involved.

> **transactional communication model**
A characterization of communication as the simultaneous sending and receiving of messages in an ongoing, irreversible process.

New technology like Google Glass allows us to search the Web, take pictures, read emails, and more from a device we wear like eyeglasses. This may simplify life, or it may add to the flood of messages, photos, tweets, pings, and emails that distract us and compete for our attention.

Q *How can you successfully juggle the competing demands of face-to-face conversation and electronic messages?*

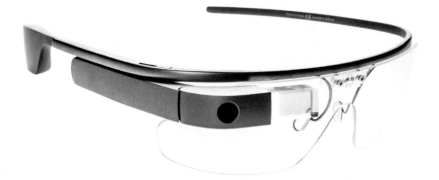

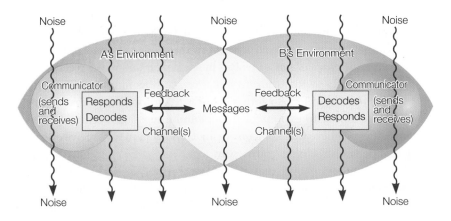

Figure 1-2 Transactional Communication Model

mass communication do flow in a one-way, linear manner, most types of personal communication are two-way exchanges.[3] The roles of sender and receiver that seemed separate in the linear model are now redefined as those of "communicators," reflecting the fact that we are capable of receiving, decoding, and responding to another person's behavior at the same time that he or she receives and responds to ours.

Consider, for instance, what it means when a friend yawns as you complain about your boyfriend or girlfriend, or a new friend blushes at one of your jokes. Nonverbal behaviors like these show that most face-to-face communication is a two-way affair. The discernible response of a receiver to a sender's message is called **feedback**. Not all feedback is nonverbal, of course; sometimes it is oral or written, too. Figure 1-2 makes the importance of feedback clear.

Another weakness of the traditional linear model is the questionable assumption that all communication involves encoding, the conscious process of putting thoughts into a symbolic form such as words or gestures. We certainly choose symbols to convey most verbal messages. But what about the many nonverbal cues that occur: facial expressions, gestures, postures, vocal tones, and so on? Cues like these do offer information about others, although they are often unconscious and thus don't involve encoding. For this reason, the transactional model replaces the term *encodes* with the broader term *responds,* because it describes both intentional and unintentional actions that can be observed and interpreted.[4]

> feedback

The discernible response of a receiver to a sender's message.

CONTEXTS OF COMMUNICATION

There are several types of communication, including intrapersonal, dyadic/interpersonal, small group, organizational, public, and mass communication. Despite some features they all share, each type of communication occurs in a different context and has its own characteristics (Figure 1-3).

In which situations do you feel most comfortable as a communicator? In which do you feel least comfortable?

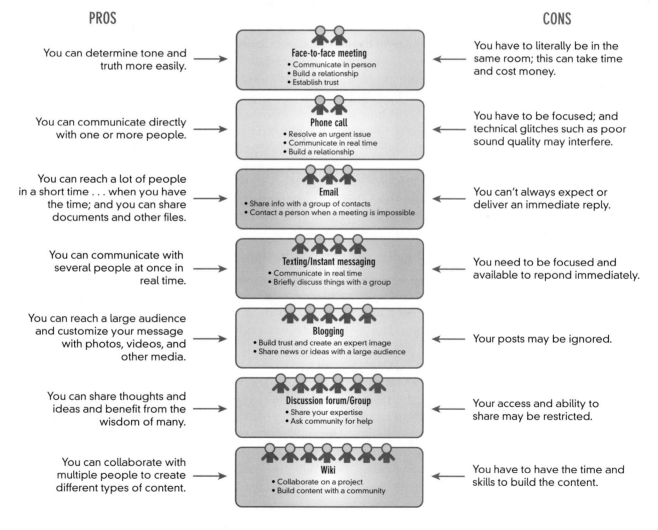

PROS

CONS

You can determine tone and truth more easily.

Face-to-face meeting
• Communicate in person
• Build a relationship
• Establish trust

You have to literally be in the same room; this can take time and cost money.

You can communicate directly with one or more people.

Phone call
• Resolve an urgent issue
• Communicate in real time
• Build a relationship

You have to be focused; and technical glitches such as poor sound quality may interfere.

You can reach a lot of people in a short time . . . when you have the time; and you can share documents and other files.

Email
• Share info with a group of contacts
• Contact a person when a meeting is impossible

You can't always expect or deliver an immediate reply.

You can communicate with several people at once in real time.

Texting/Instant messaging
• Communicate in real time
• Briefly discuss things with a group

You need to be focused and available to repond immediately.

You can reach a large audience and customize your message with photos, videos, and other media.

Blogging
• Build trust and create an expert image
• Share news or ideas with a large audience

Your posts may be ignored.

You can share thoughts and ideas and benefit from the wisdom of many.

Discussion forum/Group
• Share your expertise
• Ask community for help

Your access and ability to share may be restricted.

You can collaborate with multiple people to create different types of content.

Wiki
• Collaborate on a project
• Build content with a community

You have to have the time and skills to build the content.

Figure 1-3 Contexts of Communication

Intrapersonal Communication

By definition, **intrapersonal communication** means "communicating with oneself."[5] One way that each of us communicates internally is by listening to the little voice in our heads. (Before reading on, take a moment to note what your inner voice is saying. Perhaps something like "What little voice? I don't have any little voice!")

Intrapersonal communication affects almost every type of interaction. The way you handle a conversation with a friend, for example, would depend on the intrapersonal communication that precedes or accompanies what you say. Much of Chapter 2 deals with the perception process in everyday situations, and part of Chapter 13 focuses on the intrapersonal communication that can minimize anxiety when you deliver a speech.

Dyadic/Interpersonal Communication

Social scientists call two persons interacting a **dyad**, and they often use the term **dyadic communication** to describe this type of communication. Dyadic communication can occur in person or via mediated channels such as phone, email, text messaging, instant messaging, and social networking sites.

Dyadic is the most common type of personal communication, as evidenced by observing people in a variety of settings ranging from playgrounds to airports and shopping malls.[6] It is sometimes considered identical to **interpersonal communication**, but, as Chapter 7 explains, not all two-person interaction can be considered interpersonal. In fact, you will learn that the qualities that characterize interpersonal communication can also exist in groups of three or more.

Small Group Communication

In **small group communication** every person can participate actively with the other members. Small groups are a common fixture of everyday life. Your family is a group. So are an athletic team; several students working on a class project; and coworkers in Chicago, Singapore, and Mumbai connected online.

Whether small groups meet in person or via mediated channels, they exhibit characteristics that are not present in a dyad. For instance, in a dyad, there is no majority to exert pressure. In a group, however, the majority of members can exert pressure, either consciously or unconsciously, on those in the minority. Majority pressures can also be comforting, leading group members to take risks that they would not dare to take if they were alone or in a dyad. With their greater size, some groups also have the ability to be more creative than dyads, if only because there is a larger base from which to draw ideas. Groups are such an important communication setting that Chapters 9 and 10 focus exclusively on them.

> **intrapersonal communication**
> Communication that occurs within a single person.

> **dyad**
> A two-person unit.

> **dyadic communication**
> Two-person communication.

> **interpersonal communication**
> Communication in which the parties consider one another as unique individuals rather than as objects.

> **small group communication**
> Communication within a group that is small enough for every member to participate actively with all other members.

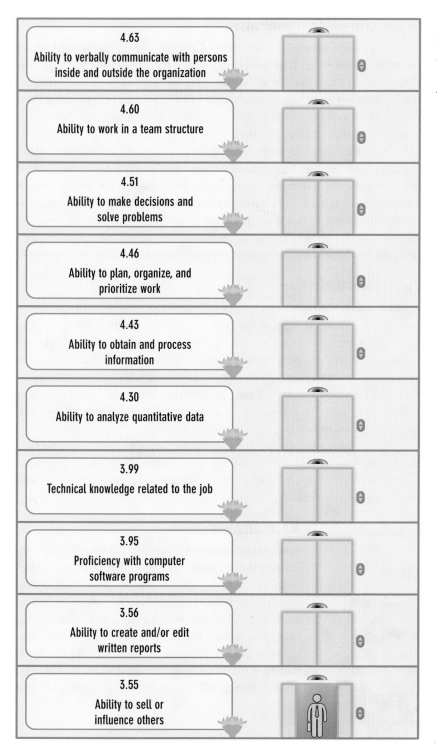

4.63
Ability to verbally communicate with persons inside and outside the organization

4.60
Ability to work in a team structure

4.51
Ability to make decisions and solve problems

4.46
Ability to plan, organize, and prioritize work

4.43
Ability to obtain and process information

4.30
Ability to analyze quantitative data

3.99
Technical knowledge related to the job

3.95
Proficiency with computer software programs

3.56
Ability to create and/or edit written reports

3.55
Ability to sell or influence others

Figure 1-4 Communication skills are consistently rated as a top requirement for career success. How can you use the teamwork skills you learn in classes to become a more appealing candidate for the job you want?

*5-point scale, where 1 = Not at all important; 2 = Not very important; 3 = Somewhat important;
4 = Very important; and 5 = Extremely important

Organizational Communication

> **organizational communication**
Communication that occurs within a structured collection of people in order to meet a need or pursue a goal.

Larger, more permanent collections of people engage in **organizational communication** when they collectively work to achieve goals. Organizations operate for a variety of reasons: business (such as a corporation), nonprofit (such as a charity or religious group), political (a government or political action group), health (a hospital or doctor's office), and even recreational (a YMCA or sports league).

Organizational communication differs from communication in other contexts. Specific roles (sales associate, general manager, corporate trainer) shape what people communicate about and their relationship to one another. Also, culture plays a role in the complicated nature of interaction in organizations. As you'll read in Chapter 3, each organization develops its own culture, and analyzing the traditions and customs of organizations is a useful field of study.

Public Communication

> **public communication**
Communication that occurs when a group becomes too large for all members to contribute. It is characterized by an unequal amount of speaking and by limited verbal feedback.

Public communication occurs when a group becomes too large for all members to contribute. It is generally characterized by an unequal amount of speaking. One or more people are likely to deliver their remarks to the remaining members, who act as an audience. Audience members usually aren't able to engage in two-way conversations with the speaker, although they can give nonverbal feedback. In addition, some audience members may have a chance to ask questions and offer brief comments afterwards, either in person or online.

Public speakers usually have a greater chance to plan and structure their remarks than do communicators in smaller settings. For this reason, several chapters of this book describe the steps you can take to prepare and deliver an effective speech.

> **mass communication**
The transmission of messages to large, usually widespread audiences via broadcast (such as radio and television), print (such as newspapers, magazines, and books), multimedia (such as DVD), online, and other forms of media such as recordings and movies.

Mass Communication

Mass communication consists of messages that are transmitted to large, widespread audiences via electronic and print media: newspapers, magazines, television, radio, blogs, websites, and so on. Mass communication differs from the other communication contexts we've already discussed in several ways.

First, most mass messages are aimed at a large audience without any personal contact between sender and receivers. Books, feature films, and

In less than an hour, Ellen DeGeneres's celebrity-filled Oscar selfie broke the record for the most retweets.

Q *Why do you think the selfie has become a social media phenomenon?*

A tweet becomes mass communication when it is planned by professionals and sent to a large audience. Companies such as JetBlue benefit from the personal quality of social media and often look for job candidates who are skilled in this lucrative area of communication.

 Can you advance your career by capitalizing on your social media savvy?

television programs are all examples, and so are Twitter accounts from celebrities with mass followings.

Second, many of the messages sent via mass communication channels are developed, or at least financed, by large organizations such as advertisers and movie studios. In this sense, mass communication is far less personal and more of a product.

Finally, "old media" outlets, such as newspapers and broadcast television, are mass controlled by many gatekeepers (such as editors, producers, executives, and corporate and government sponsors) who determine what messages will be delivered to consumers, how they will be constructed, and when they will be delivered. It's worth noting that social media like Facebook, Twitter, and YouTube have given ordinary people the chance to bypass gatekeepers and reach enormous audiences. Many home-grown videos posted on YouTube have gone viral, turning formerly anonymous people into minor celebrities.

Identify characteristics of effective communication and competent communicators.

COMMUNICATION COMPETENCE

It's easy to recognize good communicators, and even easier to spot poor ones. But what makes someone an effective communicator? Answering this question has been one of the leading challenges for communication scholars.[7] While they are still working to clarify the nature of **communication competence**, most would agree that effective communication involves achieving one's goals in a manner that, ideally, maintains or enhances the relationship in which it occurs.[8]

> communication competence
Ability to maintain a relationship on terms acceptable to all parties.

Characteristics of Competent Communication

Our definition of communication competence suggests several important characteristics of effective communication. Using a variety of communication styles can be effective, competent behavior varies from one situation to the next and from one relationship to the next, and, perhaps most significantly, competence can be learned.

There Is No "Ideal" Way to Communicate

Some very successful people are serious, whereas others use humor; some are loud, whereas others are quiet; and some are straightforward, whereas others prefer subtlety. Just as there are many kinds of beautiful music and art, there are many kinds of competent communication.

Competence Is Situational

It's a mistake to think that communication competence is a trait that a person either possesses or lacks. It's more accurate to talk about *degrees* or *areas* of competence.[9] You might be quite skillful socializing at a party, but less successful making small talk with professors at office hours. In fact, your competence with one person may vary from one situation to another.

Competence Is Relational

Because communication is transactional, something we do *with* others rather than *to* them, behavior that is competent in one context (e.g., at work) isn't necessarily competent in others (e.g., with friends or family). Researchers have found that no type of behavior is effective or ineffective in every relationship. Findings like these demonstrate that competence arises out of developing ways of interacting that work for you and for the other people involved.[10]

Competence Can Be Learned

Studies of identical and fraternal twins suggest that traits including sociability, anger, and relaxation seem to be partially a function of our genetic makeup.[11] But communication is a set of skills that anyone can learn. Systematic education (such as the class in which you are now enrolled) and a little training can produce dramatic results.[12] Even without systematic training, it's possible to develop communication skills through the processes of trial-and-error and observation. We learn from our own successes and failures, as well as from observing other models—both positive and negative.

Characteristics of Competent Communicators

Although competent communication varies from one situation to another, scholars have identified several common denominators that characterize effective communication in most contexts. Competent communicators can draw on a wide range of behaviors to fit the appropriate setting. They are capable of empathy and of understanding other people's points of view, as well as analyzing the behavior of others. They are able to monitor their own behavior and adjust accordingly. And, perhaps most significantly, competent communicators respect the relationship in which the communication occurs.

Competent Communicators Are Flexible

Many poor communicators are easy to spot by their limited range of responses. Some are chronic jokers. Others always seem to be belligerent.

On a scale of 1 (low) to 10 (high), how would you rate your communication competence? How would someone else rate your competence?

The film *Dallas Buyers Club* chronicles the evolution of real-life Texas cowboy Ron Woodroof (played by Matthew McConaughey) from a homophobic womanizer to a compassionate friend and advocate. After being diagnosed with AIDS, Woodroof's life dramatically changes, as does his communication competence.

Q *How have circumstances in your life affected how empathically and sensitively you communicate with others?*

Still others are quiet in almost every situation. Like a piano player who knows only one tune or a chef who can prepare only a few dishes, these people are forced to rely on a small range of responses again and again, whether or not they are successful. Competent communicators have a wide repertoire from which to draw, and they have the ability to choose the most appropriate behavior for a given situation.

Competent Communicators Are Empathic

You have the best chance of developing an effective message when you understand the other person's point of view. And because others aren't always good at expressing their thoughts and feelings clearly, the ability to *imagine* how an issue might look from someone else's viewpoint is also an important skill. This is why listening is so important. Not only does it help us understand others, it also gives us information to develop strategies about how to best influence them. Because empathy is such an important element of communicative competence, much of Chapter 5 is devoted to this topic.

Competent Communicators Are Cognitively Complex

> cognitive complexity
The ability to construct a variety of frameworks for viewing an issue.

Cognitive complexity is the ability to construct a variety of frameworks for viewing an issue. It allows us to make sense of people using a variety of perspectives. For instance, imagine that your longtime friend seems angry with you. Is your friend offended by something you've done? Or, has something upsetting happened in another part of his or her life? Or perhaps nothing at all is wrong, and you're just being overly sensitive. Researchers have found that the ability to analyze the behavior of others in a variety of ways leads to greater "conversational sensitivity," increasing the chances of acting in ways that will produce satisfying results.[13]

Competent Communicators Self-Monitor

> self-monitoring
The process of paying close attention to one's own behavior and using these observations to shape the way one behaves.

Psychologists use the term **self-monitoring** to describe the process of paying close attention to one's own behavior and using these observations to shape the way one behaves. Chapter 3 explains how too much self-monitoring can be problematic. Still, people who are aware of their behavior and the impression it makes are more skillful communicators than people who are not.[14]

Competent Communicators Are Committed

One feature that distinguishes effective communication in almost any context is commitment. People who seem to care about the relationship communicate better than those who don't.[15] This concern shows up in commitment to the other person and to the message being expressed.

OBJECTIVE 1.5 Analyze your communication competence with social media.

COMMUNICATION COMPETENCE WITH SOCIAL MEDIA

> Web 2.0
A term used to describe how the Internet has evolved from a one-way medium into a combination of mass and interpersonal communication.

> social media
Digital communication channels used primarily for personal reasons, often to reach small groups of receivers.

If you blog, tweet, post photos on a website such as Instagram or Flickr, or maintain a page on Facebook, YouTube, or some other social networking site, you have experience with **Web 2.0**, a term often used to describe how the Internet has evolved from a one-way medium into a combination of mass and interpersonal communication. You're not only a consumer of mediated messages, but a creator of them.

As the name suggests, people use **social media** for personal reasons, often to reach small groups of receivers. You're using social media when you text or message friends or coworkers, exchange emails, or chat, and when you post on social networking websites such as Facebook.

Social media are different from the mass variety in some important ways. Most obvious is the *variable size of the target audience*. Whereas the mass media are aimed at large audiences, the intended audience in social media can vary from a few receivers in a chat room to thousands or more with a blog or tweet.

Unlike traditional forms of mass communication, social media are also distinguished by *user-generated content*. You decide what goes on your Facebook page and what topics are covered on your blog. There generally aren't any market researchers to tell you what the audience wants. No staff writers, editors, designers, or marketers craft your message. It's all you.

Despite these characteristics, the boundary between mass and interpersonal communication isn't as clear as it might first seem. Consider, for example, YouTube and other streaming video websites like Instagram. They provide a way for individuals to publish their own content (your graduation, baby's first birthday party) for a limited number of interested viewers. On the other hand, some videos go "viral," receiving thousands, or even millions, of hits. (The YouTube video "Charlie Bit My Finger" has been viewed more than 500 million times.)

Twitter is another example of the fuzzy boundary between personal and mass media. Many people broadcast updates to a rather small group of interested parties. ("I'm at the concert—Great seats!") On the other hand, millions of fans follow the tweets of favorite celebrities such as Justin Bieber, Lady Gaga, Justin Timberlake, and Taylor Swift. Twitter offers an interesting blend of messages from real friends and celebrities, "strangely intimate and at the same time celebrity-obsessed," as one observer put it.[16] "You glance at your Twitter feed over that first cup of coffee, and in a few seconds you find out that your nephew got into med school and Shaquille O'Neal just finished a cardio workout in Phoenix."

Social media create a need for a set of social agreements that go beyond the general rules of communication competence outlined in this chapter. Here, we offer some guidelines with the caveat that social media etiquette continues to evolve. While these guidelines won't cover every situation involving mediated communication, they can help you avoid some problems and deal more effectively with others that are bound to arise.

Choose the Best Medium

A generation ago, choosing which communication channel to use wasn't very complicated: If a face-to-face conversation wasn't desirable or possible, you either wrote a letter or used the telephone. Today's communicators have many more options.

Sometimes the choice of a medium is a no-brainer. If a friend says "call me while I'm on the road," you know what to do. If your boss or professor only responds to emails, then it would be foolish to use any other approach. But in many other situations, you have a wide array of options. Consider the simple act of sharing a photo. Today, you might post it on Facebook or share it via Snapchat so that it vanishes seconds after the recipient opens it. Or maybe a photo doesn't tell the story you want to share. You can send a video to your friends on Vine.

Choosing the best means of conveying a message can make a real difference in your success. In one survey, managers who were identified as most "media sensitive" were almost twice as likely as their less savvy peers to receive top ratings in performance reviews.[17]

Choosing the right medium is just as important in personal relationships. Anyone who has been dumped via text message knows that it only adds insult to injury. Just because there is an option that allows you to avoid a difficult conversation doesn't mean you should take the easy way out. Many difficult conversations are better when conducted face to face. These types of conversations include, but aren't limited to, sharing really bad news, ending a relationship, and trying to resolve a conflict.

In situations like these, a useful guideline is what's been called the "platinum rule": treating others as *they* would like to be treated. Ask yourself how the recipient of your message would prefer to receive it, and act accordingly.

Be Careful What You Post

Most of us cringe at the sight of old yearbook photos. Older adults can safely assume that most of their questionable, odd, and rebellious behavior is tucked away in those dusty yearbooks, never to be seen by their current friends and coworkers. This isn't true for many of you, however, who may be forever haunted by text and photos you post online.

Consider the case of Jean-Sun Hannah Ahn. A few days after being crowned Miss Seattle in 2012, she tweeted to her friends back in Arizona: "Ew, I'm seriously hating Seattle right now . . . Take me back to az! Ugh can't stand cold rainy Seattle and the annoying people." The message made news in the town where she had just been honored. After she publicly apologized, Ahn vowed that, in the future, "I will call my friends or text them if I'm feeling down or want to complain about something."[18] Her experience is a reminder that, once sent, communication is irreversible.

Be Considerate

The word "etiquette" calls to mind old-fashioned rules. But whatever you call them, mostly unspoken rules of conduct still keep society running smoothly. Most of us don't shove or cut in waiting lines. We return others' greetings, say "please" and "thanks," and (mostly) let others speak without cutting them off. By acting appropriately, we feel good about ourselves, and we're more effective in getting our needs met. Mediated communication calls for its own rules of etiquette. Here are a few.

> Have you ever regretted an email, tweet, or text? How could you have managed the situation better?

Which communication channel would you use?

Consider which communication channel(s) you would use in each situation described here. Be prepared to explain the reasoning behind your choices.

Scenario	Your Communication Choice				
	Face-to-Face	Phone	Email	Text	Social Media (Facebook, Twitter)
1. You have been concerned about a friend. The last time you were together you asked, "Is anything wrong?" Your friend replied, "I'm fine." Now it's been several weeks since you have heard from your friend, and you're worried. Which channel do you think is best for gauging your friend's true emotions?					
2. You're extremely angry and frustrated with a professor and need to deal with this concern before the problem gets worse. Which communication choice offers you the best opportunity to address the problem?					
3. On Thursday your boss tells you it's okay to come in late Monday morning. You're worried he will forget that he gave you permission. What channel(s) can you use to make sure he remembers?					
4. You're applying for a job when a friend says, "You won't believe the photo I took of you at that party last weekend!" How would you like your friend to share the photo with you?					
5. You just had a once-in-a-lifetime encounter with a celebrity and you can't wait to show your friends the pictures. How would you do that most quickly and effectively?					

SCORING Have a classmate read over your list and assign you a grade of either "Channel Expert," "Channel Adequate," or "Channel Challenged." Discuss. ◉

Respect Others' Need for Undivided Attention

If you've been texting and emailing since you could walk, it might be hard to believe that some people are insulted when you divide your attention between them and your phone. As one observer put it, "While a quick log-on may seem, to the user, a harmless break, others in the room receive it as a silent dismissal. It announces: 'I'm not interested.'"[19] Chapter 5 has plenty to say about the challenges of listening effectively when you are

As part of a prank, a Taco Bell employee posted a photo to Facebook that showed him licking a stack of taco shells. Although the shells were never served to the public, the large-scale negative reactions to the photo ultimately led to the employee's termination.

Q *Have you ever posted anything online that might jeopardize your employment?*

> disinhibition

The tendency to transmit messages without considering their consequences.

> flaming

Sending angry and/or insulting emails, text messages, and posts.

multitasking. Even if you think you can do both equally well, it's important to realize that others may perceive you as being rude.

Keep Your Tone Civil

If you've ever posted a snide comment on a blog, shot back a nasty reply to a text or IM, or forwarded an embarrassing email, you know that it's easier to behave badly when the recipient of your message isn't right in front of you.

The tendency to transmit messages without considering their consequences is called **disinhibition**, and research shows it is more likely in mediated channels than in face-to-face contact.[20] Sometimes communicators take disinhibition to the extreme, blasting off angry—even vicious—emails, text messages, and website postings. The common term for these outbursts is **flaming**. Flames are problematic because of their emotional and irreversible nature. Even after you've calmed down, the aggressive message can still cause pain.

Flaming isn't the only type of mediated harassment. Ongoing "cyberbullying" has become a widespread phenomenon, often with dire consequences. More than 4 in 10 teens report being the target of online harassment. Recipients of cyberbullying often feel helpless and scared, to such a degree that one report found they are eight times more likely to carry a weapon to school than other students. There are at least 41 reported cases in which victims of cyberbullying committed suicide in the United States, Canada, Great Britain, and Australia,[21] a sobering statistic in light of reports that 81 percent of cyberbullies admit their only reason for bullying is because "it's funny."[22]

One way to behave better online is to ask yourself a simple question before you send, post, or broadcast: Would you deliver the same message to the recipient in person? If your answer is no, then you might want to reconsider hitting the "enter" key.

Respect Privacy Boundaries

Sooner or later you're bound to run across information about others that you suspect they would find embarrassing. If your relationship is close enough, you might consider mentioning it to them. However, sometimes it can be smart to avoid bringing up what you've discovered.

Be Mindful of Bystanders

If you spend even a little time in most public spaces, you're likely to encounter people who use technology in a way that interferes with others: restaurant patrons talking loudly, pedestrians who are more focused on their smartphone than on avoiding others, or people in line who are trying to pay the cashier and talk on their phone at the same time. If you aren't bothered by this sort of behavior, it can be hard to feel sympathetic with others who are offended by it. Nonetheless, this is another situation in which the "platinum rule" applies: Think empathically and behave toward others the way *they* would like to be treated.

Balance Mediated and Face-to-Face Time

It's easy to make a case that many relationships are better because of social media. But it's worth asking whether there is such a thing as *too much* mediated socializing.

Indeed, there is a link between relying heavily on mediated communication and conditions including depression, loneliness, and social anxiety.[23] People who spend excessive time on the Internet may begin to experience problems at school or work and withdraw further from their offline relationships.[24] Many people who pursue exclusively online social contacts do so because they have social anxiety or low social skills to begin with, and retreating further from offline relationships can make things worse.

Be Safe

As more and more people spend time online, safety has become a major issue. Predators used to be people who burglarized your home or approached you in a dark alley. Now, thieves and con artists don't have to find us, because we find them. Many people fail to realize the hazards of posting certain information in public forums, and other people don't even realize that what they are posting is public. You may post your "on vacation" status in Facebook, assuming that only your friends can see your message. But if a friend uses a public computer or Wi-Fi signal to view your page, unintended recipients might be able to view your information.[25] As a rule, don't use a public-access medium to post or view information that you would not tell a stranger on the street.

Careless use of social media can damage more than your reputation. Talking on a cell phone while driving is just as dangerous as driving under the influence of alcohol or drugs. Cell phone use while driving (handheld or hands-free) lengthens a driver's reaction as much as having a blood alcohol concentration at the legal limit of .08 percent.[26] In the United States alone, drivers distracted by cell phones cause almost 1,000 deaths every year.[27] Texting, of course, poses an even greater hazard on the road than talking, and it is outlawed in many states.

OBJECTIVE 1.6 Determine how misconceptions about communication can create problems.

CORRECTING MISCONCEPTIONS ABOUT COMMUNICATION

Having spent time talking about what communication is, we finish this chapter by reaffirming some things it is not.[28] Correcting misconceptions is important, because following them can get you into trouble. The following section sets the record straight on how communication actually functions.

Communication Does Not Always Require Complete Understanding

Most people operate on the implicit but flawed assumption that the goal of all communication is to maximize understanding between communicators. Although some understanding is necessary for us to understand each other, there are some types of communication in which understanding as we usually conceive it isn't the primary goal.[29] For example, when people in the United States ask social questions such as "How's it going?", they aren't really seeking an exchange of information on how you're doing. And sometimes people want to be purposely ambiguous, as in when they decline unwanted invitations by saying "I can't make it." If their goal was to be perfectly clear, they might say, "I don't really feel like spending time with you."

Sometimes the things we say make things worse rather than better. After Los Angeles Clippers owner Donald Sterling made racist remarks, he appeared on CNN to help repair the damage. Instead, the interview quickly unraveled as Sterling slammed NBA legend Magic Johnson's character, his battle with HIV, and his community outreach efforts.

Q *Have you ever made matters worse by communicating more?*

Communication Will Not Solve All Problems

"If I could just communicate better …" is the sad refrain of many unhappy people who believe that if they could express themselves better, their relationships would improve. Though this is sometimes true, it's an exaggeration to say that communicating—even communicating clearly—is a guaranteed cure-all.

Communication Isn't Always a Good Thing

In truth, communication is neither good nor bad in itself. Rather, its value comes from the way it is used. Communication can be a tool for expressing warm feelings and useful facts, but under different circumstances the same words and actions can cause both physical and emotional pain.

Meanings Don't Rest in Words

There's an axiom that communication scholars like to use: *Meanings are in people, not in words.* By that, they mean that it's a mistake to think that just because you use a word in one way, others will do so, too.[30] Sometimes differing interpretations of symbols are easily caught, as when we might first take the statement "You look sick" to mean that we look ill, when in fact someone means that we look really good. In Chapter 4 you'll read a great deal more about the problems that come from mistakenly assuming that meanings rest in words.

In what sort of situations might less communication be better than more?

Communication Is Not Simple

Most people assume that communication is an aptitude that people develop without the need for training—rather like breathing. After all, we've been swapping ideas with one another since early childhood, and there are lots of people who communicate pretty well without ever having had a class on the subject. This picture of communication as a natural ability is a gross oversimplification.[31]

Many people do learn to communicate skillfully because they have been exposed to models of such behavior by those around them. But communication skills are rather like athletic ability: Even the most inept of us can learn to be more effective with training and practice, and those who are talented can always become better.

More Communication Isn't Always Better

Although it's certainly true that not communicating enough is a mistake, there are also situations when *too much* communication is a problem. Sometimes we "talk a problem to death," going over the same ground again and again without making any headway. And there are times when communicating too much can actually aggravate a problem. We've all had the experience of "talking ourselves into a hole"—making a bad situation worse by pursuing it too far. One key to successful communication, then, is to share an adequate amount of information in a skillful manner. Exploring ways to do that is one of the major goals of this book.

CHECK YOUR UNDERSTANDING

OBJECTIVE 1.1 Define communication.

COMMUNICATION DEFINED

Communication is the process of creating meaning through symbolic interaction.

Use the definition of communication to analyze the success or failure of a recent communication incident.

OBJECTIVE 1.2 Compare and contrast two models of communication.

MODELS OF COMMUNICATION

In the linear model of communication, a sender encodes ideas and feelings into a message and then conveys them to a receiver who decodes them. In the transactional model of communication, sending and receiving occur constantly and simultaneously, representing the process-oriented nature of human interaction.

Apply the transactional model to an incident in which a listener's nonverbal reactions led you to stop talking or to reframe what you were about to say.

OBJECTIVE 1.3 Describe the various types of communication by context.

CONTEXTS OF COMMUNICATION

This chapter introduced several communication contexts that will be covered in more detail in the rest of the book: intrapersonal, dyadic, small group, organizational, public, and mass.

Give an example of how each of the six communication contexts is significant in your own life.

OBJECTIVE 1.4 Identify characteristics of effective communication and competent communicators

COMMUNICATION COMPETENCE

Competent communication varies, and competence is situational, relational, and can be learned. Competent communicators are flexible, empathic, cognitively complex, capable of self-monitoring, and committed to the relationships in which communication occurs.

What are some areas in which your communication can be improved? What are some ways you can increase your competence level?

OBJECTIVE 1.5 Analyze your communication competence with social media.

COMMUNICATION COMPETENCE WITH SOCIAL MEDIA

Web 2.0 is a term used to describe how the Internet has evolved from a one-way medium into a combination of mass and interpersonal communication. Unlike traditional forms of mass communication, social media users create their own content. The audience for social media can vary from a few receivers to thousands or more. When using social media, it's important to choose the best medium, be careful what you post, be considerate, balance mediated and face time, and be safe.

What are some ways you can increase your competence level when using social media?

OBJECTIVE 1.6 Determine how misconceptions about communication can create problems.

CORRECTING MISCONCEPTIONS ABOUT COMMUNICATION

Several misconceptions about communication exist. It's important to understand that communication doesn't always require complete understanding and that it won't solve every problem. In addition, meanings are in people, not in words, and communication is neither simple nor easy.

What misconceptions about communication have caused the greatest problems in your life? How can you approach similar situations more constructively in the future?

KEY TERMS

channel p. 6
cognitive complexity p. 16
communication competence p. 13
communication p. 4
decoding p. 6
disinhibition p. 20
dyad p. 10
dyadic communication p. 10
encoding p. 6
environment p. 7

feedback p. 8
flaming p. 20
interpersonal communication p. 10
intrapersonal communication p. 10
linear communication model p. 6
mass communication p. 12
mediated communication p. 6
message p. 6
noise p. 6
organizational communication p. 12

public communication p. 12
receiver p. 6
self-monitoring p. 16
sender p. 6
small group communication p. 10
social media p. 16
symbol p. 4
transactional communication model
 p. 7
Web 2.0 p. 16

FOR FURTHER EXPLORATION

For more communication resources, see the *Essential Communication* website at www.oup.com/us/ec. There you will find a variety of resources: "Media Room" examples from popular films and television shows to further illustrate important concepts, a list of relevant books and articles, links to descriptions of feature films and television shows at the *Now Playing* website, study aids, and a self-test to check your understanding of the material in this chapter.

The Self, Perception, and Communication

2.1 Describe how the self-concept is formed and its role in communication.

2.2 Recognize tendencies that lead to distorted perceptions of others.

2.3 Explain how perception checking can be used to improve the quality of communication.

2.4 Analyze the nature of identity management in a given situation and, as necessary, suggest more productive alternatives.

Describe how the self-concept is formed and its role in communication.

THE SELF-CONCEPT DEFINED

Nothing is more fundamental to understanding how we communicate than our sense of self. For that reason, this section introduces the notion of self-concept and explains how the way we view ourselves shapes our interaction with others.

The **self-concept** is a set of relatively stable perceptions that each of us holds about ourself. It includes our conception of what is unique about us and what makes us both similar to and different from others. To gain a personal understanding of how this theoretical construct applies to you, answer the question: "Who are you?"

Are you a man or a woman? What is your age? Your religion? Occupation?

There are many ways of identifying yourself. Take a few minutes and list as many traits and characteristics as you can to identify who you are. Try to include all the characteristics that describe you, including:

Physical characteristics (e.g., tall, petite, slim, overweight, dark-skinned, light-skinned, blond hair, brown hair, curly hair, straight hair, etc.)
Social traits (e.g., outgoing, shy, talkative, quiet, funny, serious, generous, selfish, compassionate, callous, etc.)
Social roles (e.g., brother, sister, mother, father, friend, student, teammate, employee, etc.)
Defining interests (e.g., blogger, gamer, musician, actor, athlete, politician, journalist, etc.)
Talents you possess or lack (e.g., intellectual, musical, artistic, dramatic, athletic, etc.)
Your belief systems (e.g., Christian, Jew, Muslim, Mormon, atheist, vegetarian, vegan, etc.)

Even a list of 20 or 30 terms would be only a partial description. To make this written self-portrait complete, your list would have to be hundreds—or even thousands—of words long. Of course, not all items on such a list would be equally important. For example, you might define yourself primarily by your social roles, while someone else might define himself or herself primarily by accomplishments or skills.

Self-Esteem Influences the Self-Concept

An important element of the self-concept is **self-esteem**, our evaluations of self-worth. One person's self-concept might include being athletic or tall.

> self-concept

The relatively stable set of perceptions each individual holds of himself or herself.

> self-esteem

The part of the self-concept that involves evaluations of self-worth.

That person's self-esteem would be shaped by how he or she feels about these qualities: "I'm glad that I am athletic," or "I am embarrassed about being so tall," for example.

Self-esteem has a powerful effect on the way we communicate.[1] People with high self-esteem are typically more willing to communicate, more likely to think highly of others and expect to be accepted by them, and more likely to perform well when others are watching. By contrast, people with low self-esteem are usually less willing to communicate, more likely to be critical of others and expect rejection from them, and more likely to be critical of their own performances and to perform poorly when being watched.

Despite its obvious benefits, self-esteem doesn't guarantee success in personal and professional relationships.[2] People with an exaggerated sense of self-worth may *think* they make better impressions on others, but neither impartial observers nor objective tests verify these beliefs. In fact, people with an inflated sense of self-worth may irritate others by coming across as condescending know-it-alls, especially when their self-worth is challenged.[3]

Significant Others Influence the Self-Concept

Although we inherit some characteristics of our personality from our parents, our identity develops largely from communication with others. The term **reflected appraisal** metaphorically describes how we develop an image

> What messages from others shape your self-esteem? What messages do you send that shape others' self-esteem?

> **reflected appraisal**
The influence of others on one's self-concept.

⸮ How does your self-esteem shape the way you communicate?

	Mostly True	Mostly False
1. People enjoy talking to me.		
2. If someone criticizes my work, I feel horrible.		
3. When I face a difficult communication challenge, I know I can succeed if I work at it.		
4. When people tell me they love me I have a hard time believing it.		
5. I am comfortable admitting when I am wrong.		
6. People would like me more if I were better looking or more successful.		
7. I feel confident making big decisions about my relationships.		
8. I frequently let people down.		
9. It is more important that I am comfortable with myself than that others like me.		
10. I am frequently afraid of saying the wrong thing or looking stupid.		

SCORING Give yourself one point for every odd-numbered question you answered Mostly True and one point for every even-numbered question you answered Mostly False. Add the two together and look for your score on p. 49. Then ask yourself how your self-esteem shapes the way you communicate. ●

Jennifer Hudson's weight loss journey has been as dramatic as her rise to fame, from American Idol contestant to Oscar, Grammy, and Golden Globe winner. Hudson says that people treat her differently now that she has lost 80 pounds. But she maintains that the real victory was learning to value herself when others didn't.

Q *How can you respond to feedback from others in a healthy way?*

> significant other

A person whose opinion is important enough to affect one's self-concept strongly.

of ourselves from the way we think others view us. As we learn to speak and understand language, verbal messages—both positive and negative—contribute to the developing self-concept. These messages continue later in life, especially when they come from what social scientists term **significant others**—people whose opinions we especially value. A teacher from long ago, a coach, a close friend or relative can all leave an imprint on how we view ourselves. How did you arrive at your opinion of yourself as a student, friend, romantic partner, teammate, employee, and so on? In what ways are these self-evaluations influenced by the way others see you?

As we grow older, the influence of significant others is less powerful.[4] However, the evaluations of others still influence our beliefs about ourselves in some areas, such as physical attractiveness and popularity. For instance, if no one responds to your text messages or invites you to parties, this may negatively influence how you view yourself.

Though it's true that some features of the self are immediately apparent, the *significance* we attach to them depends greatly on the social environment. In the United States, young women frequently exposed to media images are more likely than other women to feel they are overweight and to have eating disorders.[5] By contrast, in cultures and societies in which greater weight is considered beautiful (e.g., some Pacific islands, Jamaica, and parts of sub-Saharan Africa), a Western supermodel would be considered unattractive.[6] In the same way, whether you are single or married, solitary or sociable, aggressive or passive takes on meaning depending on the interpretation that others attach to those traits.

Culture Influences the Self-Concept

Cultures affect the self-concept in both obvious and subtle ways. As you'll read in Chapter 3, most non-Western cultures, including Asian ones, are traditionally considered to be collective. In collective cultures, a person gains identity by belonging to a group. If you've ever had to work on a group assignment and been graded based on how well the team as a whole performed rather than on your individual contributions, you have experienced collectivism to some extent. In collectivist cultures, feelings of pride and self-worth are likely to be shaped by the behavior of other members of the community. This linkage to others explains the traditional Asian denial of self-importance—a strong contrast to the self-promotion that is common in more individualistic Western cultures in which individuals gain self-worth and tend to be judged based on their individual contributions.

The Self-Concept Influences Communication with Others

Figure 2-1 illustrates how the self-concept both shapes and is shaped by much of our communication behavior. For example, self-concept has proven to be the single greatest factor in determining whether people who are being teased interpret the teaser's motives as being friendly or hostile,

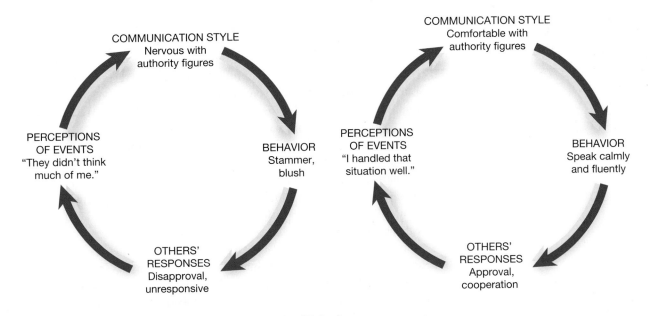

Figure 2-1 The Relationship between the Self-Concept and Behavior

and whether they respond with comfort or defensiveness.[7] Children who have a low opinion of themselves are more likely to see themselves as victims of bullying, both in their classrooms and online.[8]

Suppose, for example, that one element of your self-concept is "nervous with authority figures," such as teachers, former employers, or even police officers. That image may be a result of prior interactions you have had with authority figures, or it may be the result of the evaluations of significant others in the past. If you view yourself as nervous with authority figures, you will probably behave in nervous ways when you encounter them in the future—in a teacher-student conference, a job interview, or a traffic stop. That nervous behavior is likely to influence how others view your personality, which in turn will shape how they respond to you—probably in ways that reinforce the self-concept you brought to the event. Finally, the responses of others will affect the way you anticipate future events: other meetings with professors, job interviews, interactions with police, and so on. This cycle illustrates how the chicken-and-egg nature of the self-concept helps to govern your present behavior and influences the way others view you.

The Self-Concept Influences Future Communication and Behavior

The self-concept is such a powerful force on personality that it not only determines how we communicate in the present but it also can actually influence our behavior and that of others in the future. Such occurrences come about through a phenomenon called the self-fulfilling prophecy.

A **self-fulfilling prophecy** occurs when a person's expectation of an outcome and that person's subsequent behavior make the outcome more likely to occur than would otherwise have been true. Self-fulfilling prophecies occur all the time. For example, if you anticipate having a good (or terrible) time at a party, your expectations might lead you to act in ways that shape the outcome to fit your prediction.

There are two types of self-fulfilling prophecies. The first occurs when your expectations influence your behavior. A second type of self-fulfilling prophecy occurs when another person's expectations govern your actions.[9] This principle was demonstrated in a classic experiment.[10]

Researchers told teachers that 20 percent of the children in a certain elementary school showed unusual potential for intellectual growth. The names of the 20 percent were drawn randomly. Eight months later these unusually "smart" children showed significantly greater gains in IQ than did the remaining children, who had not been singled out for the teachers' attention. The changes in the teachers' behavior toward these randomly selected children led to changes in the children's intellectual performance. Among other things, the teachers gave the "smart" students more time to answer questions and provided more feedback to them. These children did better, not because they were any more intelligent than their classmates and not solely because their teachers believed them to be

> self-fulfilling prophecy

A prediction or expectation of an event that makes the outcome more likely to occur than would otherwise have been the case.

"smarter," but because their teachers—significant others—behaved differently toward them.

The self-fulfilling prophecy is an important force in communication, but it doesn't explain all behavior. Believing you'll do well in a job interview when you're clearly not qualified for the position is unrealistic. Similarly, there will probably be people you don't like and occasions you won't enjoy, no matter what your attitude. In other cases, your expectations will become reality, but not because of the self-fulfilling prophecy. For example, children are not equally well equipped to do well in school, and in such cases it would be wrong to say that a child's good or poor performance was shaped solely by a parent or teacher even if the behavior did match what was expected.

As we keep these qualifications in mind, it's important to recognize the tremendous influence that self-fulfilling prophecies play in our lives. We, and those around us, constantly create our self-concepts.

Breaking through class and gender barriers, Margaret Thatcher became the first and only female British Prime Minister. She was acutely aware of the powerful influence her thoughts had on her behavior and ultimately the outcomes in her life. In the film *The Iron Lady*, Thatcher (portrayed by Meryl Streep, right) warns us about the double-edged nature of self-fulfilling prophecies when she proclaims, "What we think, we become."

Q *What self-fulfilling prophecies (constructive or damaging) have shaped the way you communicate?*

PERCEIVING OTHERS EFFECTIVELY

In the last section, we explored how our self-perceptions affect the way we communicate. In this section, we examine how the ways we perceive others shape our interaction with them.

Correcting Sex and Gender Misconceptions

Social expectations about masculine and feminine behavior have a powerful influence on our identity and how we communicate. For most people, gendered expectations begin the moment we are born—or even before, with the selection of clothing, blankets, toys, and nursery décor. Yet, we don't often question the assumptions that underlie cultural expectations about gender. Following are some realities about sex and gender based on research.

No One Is Exclusively Male or Female

Hormone levels and other factors make biological sex a more complicated formula than you might think. Our feelings and actions are shaped partly by estrogen and testosterone, which influence how the body and mind develop. Because these hormones are present in both men and women in varying degrees, the difference between male and female is more of a continuum than a question of either–or.[11] For example, people who are intersex may have hormonal profiles and physical characteristics of both sexes.

The Terms "Sex" and "Gender" Are Not Identical

In fact, **sex** is a biological category (male, female, and intersex), whereas **gender** is a socially constructed set of expectations about what it means to be "masculine" or "feminine." A statement about a man's long hair looking girlish reveals a particular cultural assumption. In many cultures, long hair is considered masculine. Thus, it is possible—even necessary—for a woman to embody some attributes associated with masculine gender, and vice versa for men. Indeed, there are often advantages to embodying both "masculine" and "feminine" qualities.

Masculine and Feminine Behaviors Are Part of a Continuum

Early theorizing suggested that stereotypical masculine and feminine behaviors are two separate sets of behavior.[12] One alternative to the masculine–feminine dichotomy is the idea of four psychological sex types, including masculine, feminine, **androgynous** (combining masculine and feminine

> sex
A biological category (male, female, and intersex).

> gender
A socially constructed set of expectations about what it means to be "masculine" or "feminine."

> androgynous
Combining masculine and feminine traits.

Lady Gaga, dressed as a man at left and in more feminine attire at right, defies traditional notions about masculinity and femininity.

Q *Have you ever felt stifled by social expectations involving gender roles?*

traits), and undifferentiated (neither masculine nor feminine). These days, we use the term *gender* instead of the phrase "psychological sex type." Thus, whether people are male or female, they might be seen as generally masculine, feminine, androgynous, or undifferentiated, based on society's definitions.[13]

Although the differences between men's and women's behavior are not always as great as many people think, evidence points to some differences at the extremes. For example, masculine males tend to see their interpersonal relationships as opportunities to win something, while feminine females typically see their interpersonal relationships as opportunities to express their feelings and emotions. And, along with androgynous individuals, feminine females tend to give more sympathy to grieving people than do masculine males.[14]

Mistaken Attributions

Some of the biggest problems that interfere with understanding and agreement arise from errors in interpretation, or what psychologists call **attribution**—the process of attaching meaning to behavior. If you assume

> attribution
The process of attaching meaning.

that someone who is standing on a street corner in rumpled clothing is homeless, you're making an attribution. (Someone else might assume the same person is a jogger or a construction worker.) We attribute meaning to both our own actions and the actions of others, but we often use different yardsticks. Research has uncovered several perceptual errors that can lead to inaccurate attributions—and to troublesome communication.[15] By becoming aware of these errors, we can guard against them and avoid unnecessary conflicts.

We Often Judge Ourselves More Charitably Than We Judge Others

In an attempt to convince ourselves and others that the positive face we show to the world is true, we tend to judge ourselves in the most generous terms possible. Social scientists have labeled this tendency the **self-serving bias**.[16] When others suffer, we often blame the problem on their personal qualities. ("She got fired because she didn't work hard enough.") On the other hand, when we suffer, we often find explanations outside ourselves. ("I got fired because my boss is a jerk.") Uncharitable attitudes toward others can, of course, affect communication. Your harsh opinions of others can lead to judgmental messages, and self-serving defenses of your own actions can result in a defensive response when others question your behavior.

We Often Pay More Attention to Negative Impressions Than Positive Ones

Research shows that, when people are aware of both the positive and negative traits of another, they tend to be more influenced by the negative traits. In one study, for example, researchers found that job interviewers were likely to reject candidates who revealed negative information, even when the total amount of information was highly positive.[17] Sometimes it makes sense to focus on details (such as the shaky hands of an otherwise skillful surgeon), but expecting perfection can lead us to reject people on superficial qualities that might not matter very much once we get to know them.

We Tend to Assume That Others Are Similar to Us

People commonly imagine that others possess the same attitudes and motives that they do. For example, research shows that people with low self-esteem imagine that others view them unfavorably, whereas people who like themselves imagine that others do too.[18] It pays to remember, however, that other people don't always think or feel the way we do, and assuming that we are all the same can lead to problems. For example, men are more likely than women to think that flirting indicates an interest in having sex.[19] How can you find out the other person's real position? Sometimes by asking directly, sometimes by checking with others, and sometimes by making an educated guess after you've thought the matter out. All these alternatives are better than simply assuming that everyone would react the way you do.

> self-serving bias
The tendency to interpret and explain information in a way that casts the perceiver in the most favorable manner.

What kind of perceptual errors do you tend to make? What are the consequences?

Explain how perception checking can be used to improve the quality of communication.

OBJECTIVE 2.3

EMPATHY AND PERCEPTION CHALLENGES

By now it's clear that differing perceptions present a major challenge to communicators. One solution is to increase the ability to empathize. **Empathy** is the ability to re-create another person's perspective, to experience the world from the other's point of view.

> empathy
The ability to project oneself into another person's point of view, so as to experience the other's thoughts and feelings.

Dimensions of Empathy

As we'll use the term here, empathy has three dimensions.[20] On one level, empathy involves perspective taking—the ability to take on the viewpoint of another person. This understanding requires us to set aside our own opinions and suspend judgment of the other person. Empathy also has an emotional dimension that allows us to experience the feelings that others have. We know their fear, joy, sadness, and so on. When we combine the perspective-taking and emotional dimensions, we see that empathizing allows us to experience the other's perception—in effect, to become that person temporarily. A third dimension of empathy is a genuine concern for the welfare of the other person that goes beyond just thinking and feeling.

It's easy to confuse empathy with **sympathy**, but the concepts are different in two important ways. Sympathy means you feel compassion for another person's predicament, whereas empathy means you have a personal sense of what that predicament is like. Consider the difference between sympathizing with a homeless person and empathizing with him or her—imagining what it would be like to be in that person's position.

> sympathy
Compassion for another's situation.

Empathy is different from sympathy in a second way. You can empathize with a difficult relative, a rude stranger, or even a criminal without feeling much sympathy for that person. Empathizing allows you to understand another person's motives without requiring you to agree with him or her.

Total empathy is impossible to achieve. Completely understanding another person's point of view is simply too difficult a task for humans with different backgrounds and limited communication skills. Nonetheless, it is possible to get a strong sense of what the world looks like through another person's eyes. You do this through a process called perception checking.

Perception Checking

Perception checking is a communication tool to enhance empathy. To see how it works, consider how others sometimes jump to mistaken conclusions about your thoughts or feelings:

> perception checking
A three-part method for verifying the accuracy of interpretations, including a description of the sense data, two possible interpretations, and a request for confirmation of the interpretations.

How might perception checking have made a difference in your last difficult conversation?

"Why are you mad at me?" (Who said you were?)

"What's the matter with you?" (Who said anything was the matter?)

As you'll learn in Chapter 7, even if one of these interpretations is correct, a dogmatic, mind-reading statement is likely to generate defensiveness. The skill of perception checking provides a better way to handle your interpretations. A complete perception check has three parts: A description of the behavior you noticed, at least two possible interpretations of the behavior, and a request for clarification about how to interpret the behavior.

Perception checks for the preceding examples would look like this:

"Hey, when you slammed the door [behavior]*, I wasn't sure whether you were mad at me* [first interpretation] *or just in a rush* [second interpretation]*. Are we good, or do you want to talk* [request for clarification]*?"*

"You haven't laughed much in the last couple of days [behavior]*. I wonder whether something's bothering you* [first interpretation] *or whether you're just feeling quiet* [second interpretation]*. What's up?* [request for clarification]*"*

Perception checking is a tool for helping to understand others accurately instead of assuming that your first interpretation is correct. Because the goal is mutual understanding, perception checking is a cooperative approach to communication. Besides leading to more accurate perceptions, it minimizes defensiveness. Instead of saying, in effect, "I know what you're thinking . . ." a perception check takes the more respectful approach that states or implies, "I know I'm not qualified to understand your feelings without some help."

Of course, a perception check can succeed only if your nonverbal behavior reflects the open-mindedness of your words. An accusing tone of voice or a hostile glare will contradict the sincerely worded request for clarification, suggesting that you have already made up your mind about the other person's intentions.

In the movie *Freaky Friday*, a mother and her teenage daughter swap bodies for a day, providing insight into how it feels to be the other person in a relationship.

Q *In what ways can you better understand the perspectives of people around you?*

Analyze the nature of identity management in a given situation and, as necessary, suggest more productive alternatives.

OBJECTIVE 2.4

IDENTITY MANAGEMENT

So far we've described how communication shapes the way communicators view themselves and others. In this section, we turn the tables and focus on **identity management**—the communication strategies people use to influence how others view them. You will see that many of our messages are aimed at creating desired impressions.

> **identity management**
> Strategies used by communicators to influence the way others view them.

We Have Public and Private Selves

To understand why identity management exists, we have to discuss the notion of self in more detail. So far we have referred to the "self" as if each of us had only one identity. In truth, each of us possesses several selves, some private and others public. Often these selves are quite different.

The **perceived self** is a reflection of the self-concept. Your perceived self is the person you believe yourself to be in moments of honest self-examination. We can call the perceived self "private" because you are unlikely to reveal all of it to another person. You can verify the private nature of the perceived self by reviewing the self-concept list you developed at the start of the chapter. You'll probably find some elements of yourself there that you would not disclose to many people, and some that you would not share with anyone. You might, for example, be reluctant to share some feelings about your appearance ("I think I'm overweight"), your intelligence ("I'm not as smart as I wish I were"), your goals ("the most important thing to me is becoming rich"), or your motives ("I care more about myself than about others").

> **perceived self**
> The person we believe ourselves to be in moments of candor. It may be identical with or different from the presenting and ideal selves.

In contrast to the perceived self, the **presenting self** is a public image—the way you want to appear to others. In most cases the presenting self we seek to create is a socially approved image: diligent student, loving partner, conscientious worker, loyal friend, and so on. Social norms often create a gap between the perceived and presenting selves.

> **presenting self**
> The image a person presents to others, which may be identical to or different from the perceived and ideal selves.

Sociologist Erving Goffman used the word **face** to describe the presenting self, and he coined the term **facework** to describe the verbal and nonverbal ways we act to maintain our own presenting image and the images of others.[21] He argued that each of us could be viewed as a kind of playwright who creates roles that we want others to believe, as well as the performer who acts out those roles.

> **face**
> The socially approved identity that a communicator tries to present.

> **facework**
> Verbal and nonverbal behavior designed to create and maintain a communicator's face and the face of others.

Facework involves two tasks: managing your own identity and communicating in ways that reinforce the identities that others are trying to present.[22] You can see how these two goals operate by recalling a time when you've used self-deprecating humor to defuse a potentially unpleasant situation. Suppose, for example, that a friend texted you the wrong time for the start of a party, which caused you to be late. "Sorry I'm late," you might have said. "I waited until the last minute and then got stuck in traffic." This sort of mild self-putdown accomplishes two things at once: It preserves the other person's face by implicitly saying, "It's not your fault." At the same time, your mild self-debasement shows that you're a nice person who doesn't find faults in others or make a big issue out of small problems.[23]

We Have Multiple Identities

In the course of even a single day, most of us play a variety of roles: respectful student, joking friend, friendly neighbor, and helpful employee, to suggest just a few. We even play a variety of roles with the same person. With your parents, for instance, perhaps in one context you acted as the responsible adult ("You can trust me with the car!"), and in another context you were the helpless child ("I can't find my shoes!"). At some times—perhaps on birthdays or holidays—you were a dedicated family member, and at other times you may have been antisocial and locked yourself in your room.

The ability to construct multiple identities is one element of communication competence. For example, the style of speaking or even the language itself can reflect a choice about how to construct one's identity. One scholar pointed out that bilingual Latinos in the United States often choose whether to use English or Spanish depending on who they are speaking to and the kind of identity they seek in a given conversation.[24]

Identity Management Is Collaborative

Identity-related communication is a kind of drama in which we perform like actors and collaborate with our "audience"—other actors trying to create their own characters—to improvise scenes in which our characters mesh. You can appreciate the collaborative nature of identity management by thinking about how you might handle a conflict with a friend or family member who has failed to pass along a message that arrived while you were out. Suppose that you decide to raise the issue tactfully in an effort to avoid seeming like a nag (desired role for yourself: "nice person") and

Every day, most of us play a variety of roles.

Q *How many identities do you construct in your dealings with friends, families, classmates, and colleagues?*

also to save the other person from the embarrassment of being confronted (hoping to avoid suggesting that the other person's role is "screw-up"). If your tactful bid is accepted, the dialogue might sound like this:

YOU: "By the way, Jenny told me she came by yesterday. If you wrote a note, I guess I missed seeing it."

OTHER: "Oh . . . sorry. I meant to write a note, but as soon as she left I got a call, and then I had to run off to class."

YOU: *(in friendly tone of voice)* "No worries, but next time a note would be great."

OTHER: "No problem."

In this upbeat conversation, both you and the other person accepted one another's bids for identity as basically thoughtful people. As a result, the conversation ran smoothly. Imagine, though, how different the outcome would be if the other person didn't accept your role as "nice person":

YOU: "By the way, Jenny told me she came by yesterday. If you wrote a note, I guess I missed seeing it."

OTHER: *(defensively)* "Okay, so I forgot. It's not that big a deal. It's not like you're so perfect!"

Your first bid as "nice, face-saving person" was rejected. At this point you have the choice of persisting in trying to play the original role: "Hey, I'm not mad at you, and I know I'm not perfect!" Or, you might switch to the new role of "unjustly accused person," responding with aggravation: "I never said I was perfect. But we're not talking about me here. . . ."

As this example illustrates, *collaboration* doesn't mean the same thing as *agreement*.[25] The small issue of the forgotten message might mushroom into a fight in which you and the other person both adopt the role of combatants. The point here is that virtually all conversations provide an arena in which communicators construct their identities in response to the behavior of others.

Identity Management May Be Conscious or Unconscious

There's no doubt that sometimes we are highly aware of managing our identities. Most job interviews and first dates are clear examples of conscious identity management. But in other cases we unconsciously act in ways that are really small public performances.[26] For example, one study showed that communicators engage in facial mimicry (such as smiling or looking sympathetic in response to another's message) in face-to-face settings more often when their expressions can be seen by the other person. When they are speaking over the phone and their reactions cannot be seen, they tend to not make the same expressions.[27] The people in the experiment probably didn't consciously think, "Since I'm in a face-to-face conversation I'll show I'm sympathetic by mimicking the facial expressions of my conversational partner." Reactions like these are often instantaneous and outside of our conscious awareness.

In the same way, many of our choices about how to act in the array of daily interactions aren't deliberate, strategic decisions. Rather, they rely on "scripts" that we have developed over time. When you find yourself in familiar situations, such as treating customers at work or interacting with friends or family members, you probably slip into these roles quite often. Only when they don't seem quite right do you deliberately construct an approach that reflects how you want the scene to play out.

People Differ in Their Degree of Identity Management

Some people are much more aware of their identity management behavior than others. These high self-monitors have the ability to pay attention to their own behavior and others' reactions, adjusting their communication to create the desired impression. By contrast, low self-monitors express what they are thinking and feeling without much attention to the impression their behavior creates.[28]

There are certainly advantages to being a high self-monitor.[29] People who pay attention to themselves are generally good actors who can act interested when bored, or friendly when they really feel quite the opposite. This allows them to handle social situations smoothly, often putting others at ease. They are also good "people-readers" who can adjust their behavior to get the desired reaction from others. However, the analytical nature of high self-monitors may prevent them from experiencing events completely, because a portion of their attention will always be viewing the situation from a detached position. In addition, it is often difficult to tell how high self-monitors are really feeling. In fact, because they change roles often, they may have a hard time knowing themselves how they really feel.

People who score low on the self-monitoring scale live life quite differently from their more self-conscious counterparts. Low self-monitors are likely to have a narrower repertoire of behaviors, so that they can be expected to act in more or less the same way regardless of the situation. This means that low self-monitors are easy to read. "What you see is what you get" might be their motto. Although this lack of flexibility may make their social interaction less smooth in many situations, low self-monitors can be counted on to be straightforward communicators, and they generally have a simpler and more focused idea of who they are and who they want to be.

By now it should be clear that neither extremely high nor low self-monitoring is the ideal. There are some situations in which paying attention to yourself and adapting your behavior can be useful, but there are other situations in which reacting without considering the effect on others is a better approach. This need for a range of behaviors demonstrates again the notion of communicative competence outlined in Chapter 1: Flexibility is the key to successful communication.

People Manage Identities to Follow Social Rules and Accomplish Goals

Why bother trying to shape others' opinions? Sometimes we create and maintain a front to follow social rules. As children we learn to act polite, even when bored. Likewise, part of growing up consists of developing a set of manners for various occasions: meeting strangers, attending school, going to religious services, and so on. Young children who haven't learned all of the do's and don'ts of polite society often embarrass their parents by behaving inappropriately ("Mommy, why is that man so fat?"), but by the time they enter school, behavior that might have been excusable or even amusing just isn't acceptable. Good manners are often aimed at making others more comfortable. For example, people who are able-bodied often mask their discomfort upon encountering someone who has physical challenges by acting nonchalant or stressing similarities between themselves and the other.[30]

Social rules govern our behavior in a variety of settings. It would be impossible to keep a job, for example, without meeting certain expectations. Salespeople are obliged to treat customers with courtesy. Employees must appear reasonably respectful when talking to the boss. Some forms of clothing would be considered outrageous at work. By agreeing to take on a job, you are signing an unwritten contract that you will present a certain face at work, whether or not that face reflects the way you might be feeling at a particular moment.

Even when social roles don't dictate the proper way to behave, we often manage identities for a second reason: to accomplish personal goals. You might, for example, dress up for a visit to traffic court in the hope that your front (responsible citizen) will convince the judge to treat you sympathetically. You might act sociable to your neighbors so they will agree to your request that they keep their dog off your lawn.

All these examples show that it's difficult—even impossible—not to create impressions. After all, you have to send some sort of message. If you don't act friendly when meeting a stranger, you have to act aloof, indifferent, hostile, or in some other manner. If you don't act businesslike, you have to behave in an alternative way: casual, goofy, or whatever. Often the question isn't whether or not to present a face to others; the question is only which face to present.

People Manage Identities Online

While text messages or posts on social media don't always convey the postures, gestures, or facial expressions of face-to-face communication or the vocal cues of a phone call, communication scholars have begun to recognize that what is missing in mediated communication can actually be an advantage for those who want to manage the impressions they make.

For example, people tend to strategically post photos that make them appear attractive and socially engaged with others.[31] They may edit emails, posts, and tweets until they create just the desired impression.[32] They can

While YouTube catapulted a squeaky-clean Justin Bieber to global megastar status, social media have also played a powerful role in tarnishing his public image.

Q *Have you experienced any challenges managing your identity through social media?*

How closely does your identity on social media match the way you present yourself in person?

choose the desired level of clarity or ambiguity, seriousness or humor, logic or emotion. Unlike face-to-face communication, online correspondence allows a sender to say difficult things without forcing the receiver to respond immediately, and it permits the receiver to ignore a message rather than give an unpleasant response. Options like these show that mediated communication can serve as a tool for impression management at least as well as face-to-face communication.

Managing Your Identity Doesn't Make You Dishonest

After reading this far, you might think that identity management sounds like an academic label for manipulation or phoniness. If the perceived self is the "real" you, it might seem that any behavior that contradicts it would be dishonest.

There certainly are situations in which identity management is dishonest. A manipulative date who pretends to be single, even though he or she is married, is clearly unethical and deceitful. So are job applicants who lie about their academic records to get hired. But managing identities doesn't necessarily make you a liar. In fact, it is almost impossible to imagine how we could communicate effectively without making decisions about which front to present in one situation or another. It would be ludicrous for you to act the same way with strangers as you do with close friends, and nobody would show the same face to a 2-year-old as to an adult. Each of us has a repertoire of faces—a cast of characters—and part of being a competent communicator is choosing the best role for the situation.

CHECK YOUR UNDERSTANDING

OBJECTIVE 2.1 Describe how the self-concept is formed and its role in communication.

THE SELF-CONCEPT DEFINED

The self-concept is a set of relatively stable perceptions that each of us holds about ourself. Perceptions play a key role in how we think about ourselves and others, and, therefore, in how we communicate. Although individuals are born with some innate personality characteristics, the self-concept is shaped dramatically by communication with others. Once established, the self-concept can lead us to create self-fulfilling prophecies that shape how we behave and how others respond to us. Our expectations of others can also shape the way *they* behave.

Describe the most significant messages that have helped shape your self-concept. Identify communication-related self-fulfilling prophecies that you have imposed on yourself, that others have imposed on you, and that you have imposed on others.

OBJECTIVE 2.2 Recognize tendencies that lead to distorted perceptions of others.

PERCEIVING OTHERS EFFECTIVELY

Several perceptual errors can affect the way we view and communicate with others, including misconceptions about sex and gender and errors of attribution. Along with universal psychological influences, cultural factors also affect perceptions.

Describe a case in which the perceptual tendencies described in this chapter have led you to develop distorted perceptions of others.

OBJECTIVE 2.3 Explain how perception checking can be used to improve the quality of communication.

EMPATHY AND PERCEPTION CHALLENGES

Empathizing requires us to set aside our own opinions and suspend judgment. It also enables us to experience the feelings of others and to have genuine concern for their welfare. Perception checking is one tool for increasing the accuracy of perceptions and for increasing empathy. It includes three parts: a description of the behavior you noticed, at least two possible interpretations of the behavior, and a request for clarification about how to interpret the behavior.

Describe a case in which you could use perception checking to clarify your perceptions of others. How would this approach differ from the one you might otherwise have taken?

OBJECTIVE 2.4 Analyze the nature of identity management in a given situation and, as necessary, suggest more productive alternatives.

IDENTITY MANAGEMENT

Identity management consists of strategic communication designed to influence others' perceptions of an individual. Identity management operates when we seek, consciously or unconsciously, to present one or more public faces to others. These faces may be different from the private, spontaneous behavior that occurs outside of others' presence. Some communicators are high self-monitors who are intensely conscious of their own behavior; whereas others are low self-monitors who are less aware of how their words and actions affect others.

Identity management aims to help us follow social rules and conventions and achieve a variety of goals. We engage in creating impressions by managing our manner, appearance, and the settings in which we interact with others. Because we have a variety of faces, choosing which one to present need not be dishonest.

Describe the various identities you attempt to create, the communication strategies you use to do so, and the consequences of your efforts.

KEY TERMS

androgynous p. 36
attribution p. 37
empathy p. 39
face p. 41
facework p. 41
gender p. 36

identity management p. 41
perceived self p. 41
perception checking p. 39
presenting self p. 41
reflected appraisal p. 31
self-concept p. 30

self-esteem p. 30
self-fulfilling prophecy p. 34
self-serving bias p. 38
sex p. 36
significant other p. 32
sympathy p. 39

HOW DOES YOUR SELF-ESTEEM SHAPE THE WAY YOU COMMUNICATE?

SCORES >

8 to 10—You have very high self-esteem.
5 to 7—You have relatively high self-esteem.
3 to 6—You have relatively low self-esteem.
0 to 2—You have very low self-esteem.

FOR FURTHER EXPLORATION

For more communication resources, see the *Essential Communication* website at www.oup.com/us/ec. There you will find a variety of resources: "Media Room" examples from popular films and television shows to further illustrate important concepts, a list of relevant books and articles, links to descriptions of feature films and television shows at the *Now Playing* website, study aids, and a self-test to check your understanding of the material in this chapter.

Communication and Culture

3.1 Define culture, and differentiate between in- and out-groups.

3.2 Identify factors that help shape cocultural identity, and describe how they play a role in communication.

3.3 Explain how cocultural values and norms affect communication within and between cultures.

3.4 Understand the elements of intercultural and cocultural communication competence.

CULTURE DEFINED

> culture

The language, values, beliefs, traditions, and customs people share and learn.

Defining culture isn't an easy task. One early survey of scholarly literature revealed 500 definitions, phrasings, and uses of the concept.[1] For our purposes, here is a clear and comprehensive definition of **culture**: "the language, values, beliefs, traditions, and customs people share and learn."[2] Intercultural communication, then, occurs when people from different cultures encounter one another.

Since its founding, the United States has been a country of immigrants. Today, people come from all over the world to live and work in America, which makes understanding the nuances of different cultures especially significant.

Depending on the situation, cultural differences may seem nearly insurmountable or practically nonexistent. For example, if you're on an

Cultural differences may not be salient when people from different backgrounds are committed to a shared goal. But they may become more significant in other situations.

Q *Can you think of situations in your own life when cultural differences were and were not salient?*

athletic team with members who are Asian American, African American, Latino, and white, cultural differences may mean very little compared to the shared goal of winning the league championship. But away from the games, cultural differences (e.g., expressing emotions or managing conflict) might influence communication. Social scientists use the term **salience** to describe how much weight we attach to cultural characteristics.

We also identify more closely with some people than with others. Social scientists use the label **in-groups** to describe others with whom we identify and are emotionally connected, and **out-groups** to label those we view as different and with whom we have no sense of affiliation.[3]

It's important not to overstate the influence of culture on communication. There are sometimes greater differences within cultures than between them. You might discover more in common with a traveler raised on another continent whom you meet in a Kathmandu hostel than you would with someone from across town. Nonetheless, cultural norms and values can play a powerful role in shaping how we communicate, both within our in-group and with people from different backgrounds.

> salience
How much weight we attach to a particular person or phenomenon.

> in-groups
Groups with which we identify.

> out-groups
Groups of people that we view as different from us.

Why might cultural differences that matter little to a team during a game matter at other times?

Identify factors that help shape cocultural identity, and describe how they play a role in communication.

OBJECTIVE 3.2

COCULTURES AND COMMUNICATION

When you think of cultures, you may think of different nationalities. But *within* a society, differences also exist. Social scientists use the term **coculture** to describe the perception of membership in a group that is part of an encompassing culture. Some of the cocultures in today's society include:

> coculture
The perception of membership in a group that is part of an encompassing culture.

Ethnicity and race (e.g., African American, Asian, Latino)
Region (e.g., Southerner, New Englander)
Sexual orientation and gender identity (e.g., heterosexual, lesbian, gay, bisexual, transgender)
Religion (e.g., Christian, Jewish, Mormon, Muslim)
Physical ability and disability (e.g., wheelchair users, persons who are deaf or blind)
Age and generation (e.g., teen, senior citizen, baby boomer, millennial)
Socioeconomic status (e.g., working class, middle class, upper class)
Language (e.g., native and nonnative speakers)
Activity (e.g., biker, gamer)

Much of how we view ourselves and how we relate to others grows from our cocultural identity—the groups with which we identify within our dominant culture. Here we will look at some—though by no means all—of the factors that help shape our cocultural identity and, therefore, the way we perceive and communicate with others.

Ethnicity and Race

Race is a social construct originally created to explain biological differences among people whose ancestors originated in different regions of the world—Africa, Asia, Europe, and so on. Modern scientists acknowledge that, although there are some genetic differences between people with different heritage, they mostly involve superficial qualities such as hair color and texture, skin color, and the size and shape of facial features. As one analyst puts it:

> There is less to race than meets the eye. . . . The genes influencing skin color have nothing to do with the genes influencing hair form, eye shape, blood type, musical talent, athletic ability or forms of intelligence. Knowing someone's skin color doesn't necessarily tell you anything else about him or her.[4]

There are several reasons why race has little use in explaining individual differences. Most obviously, racial features are often misinterpreted, as when someone from Latin America is mistaken for someone from Italy, Spain, or India. More importantly, there is more genetic variation within races than between them. Even within a physically recognizable population, personal experience plays a far greater role than superficial biological characteristics such as skin color.[5]

Rather than thinking about race, it's more fruitful to think in terms of **ethnicity**, which is a social rather than a biological construct. Ethnicity refers to the degree to which a person identifies with a particular group, usually on the basis of nationality, culture, religion, or some other unifying perspective. For example, people who define themselves as Hispanic embody a wide range of physical characteristics. Despite the differences, the shared social identity is a powerful construct.

But even ethnicity can be problematic, because a single label can't describe a culturally complex background. Consider U.S. President Barack Obama. He is generally recognized as the country's first African American president despite the fact that his mother was white. Obama also experienced a variety of cultures while living in Indonesia, Hawaii, California, New York, Chicago, and Washington, DC, that cannot be easily categorized. Despite its challenges, however, research indicates that multiple group membership can be a bonus and that people who come from culturally rich backgrounds tend to be more comfortable than others about establishing relationships with a diverse array of people, which increases their options for friendships, romantic partners, and professional colleagues.[6]

> **race**
> A social construct originally created to explain biological differences among people whose ancestors originated in different regions of the world.

> **ethnicity**
> A social construct that refers to the degree to which a person identifies with a particular group, usually on the basis of nationality, culture, religion, or some other unifying perspective.

Region

The area that you come from can shape feelings of belonging and how others see you. Accent is a case in point. Speakers of standard ("newscaster") English are typically viewed as more competent and self-confident than others, and the content of their messages gets higher ratings.[7] In one experiment, researchers asked human resource professionals to rate the intelligence, initiative, and personality of job applicants after listening to a brief recording of their voices. The speakers with recognizable regional accents—from the southern United States or New Jersey, for example—were tagged for lower-level jobs, whereas those with less pronounced speech styles were recommended for higher level jobs that involved more public contact.[8]

Even facial expressions have a regional basis. In the United States, unwritten rules about smiling vary from one part of the country to another. People from southern and border states smile the most, and Midwesterners smile more than New Englanders.[9] Given these differences, it's easy to imagine how a first-year college student from North Carolina might view a new roommate from Massachusetts as unfriendly, and how the New Englander might view the Southerner as overly demonstrative.

A fascinating series of studies revealed that climate and geographic latitude were remarkably accurate predictors of communication predispositions.[10] People living in southern latitudes of the United States are less tolerant of ambiguity, higher in self-esteem, more likely to touch others, and more likely to verbalize their thoughts and feelings than people in the North. A Southerner whose relatively talkative, high-touch style seemed completely normal at home might be viewed as pushy and aggressive in New England.

Sexual Orientation and Gender Identity

"NOBODY KNOWS I'M GAY." That witty saying is emblazoned on thousands of T-shirts sold by former comedian Skyler Thomas, a champion of the LGBTQ movement. LGBTQ stands for lesbian, gay, bisexual, transgender, and queer or questioning—a collection of adjectives that describes people with diverse sexual orientations and gender identities.

Not all LGBTQ individuals are gay. Transgender individuals don't feel that their biological sex is a good description of who they are. For example, some people who were born boys identify more with a feminine identity, and vice versa. And people typically describe themselves as queer if they don't feel that other gender adjectives describe them well or if they dislike the idea of gender categorizations in general. The Q, for queer or questioning, underlines the idea that gender is not always a fixed or static construct.[11]

The *"Nobody Knows I'm Gay"* shirts point to a communication dilemma facing many LGBTQ individuals. On the one hand, being open about their gender identity has advantages—including a sense of being authentic with others and belonging to a supportive coculture. On the other hand, the disclosure can be risky, as they may face ridicule, discrimination, and even violence. On average, one in five hate crimes in the United States targets people on the basis of their sexual orientation.[12]

CNN host Anderson Cooper didn't tell the public he was gay for years because he considered it private information, he felt it might put him and

For many people, there is little stigma involved in sharing their sexual orientation. But when Jason Collins became the first openly gay player in the National Basketball League in 2013, many feared that his career would suffer.

Q *Does sharing your cultural or cocultural background have any consequences?*

others in danger, and he thought he could do a better job as a journalist if he "blended in."[13] However, Cooper says his silence sometimes felt disingenuous. "I have given some the mistaken impression that I am trying to hide something," he says. "The fact is, I'm gay, always have been, and I couldn't be more happy, comfortable with myself, and proud."

For people whose "coming out" announcements make headlines, going public happens all at once. However, that is not the case for most LGBTQ individuals. "Coming out is a process that never ends," reflects Jennifer Potter, a physician who is gay. "Every time I meet someone new I must decide if, how, and when I will reveal my sexual orientation."[14] She says it's often easy to "pass" as heterosexual, but then she experiences the awkwardness of people assuming she has a boyfriend or husband, and it saddens her when she cannot openly refer to her partner or invite her to take part in social gatherings.

Although they acknowledge the communication dilemma they face, most individuals don't want the public to see them in tragic terms. Aside from issues of social acceptance, their lives are just as happy and productive as heterosexual people's lives.

Religion

In some cultures, religion is the defining factor in shaping in- and outgroups. Whether you belong to the Shia or Sunni sects is enormously important in many parts of the Islamic world. In some parts of the United States today, religion is a defining characteristic. The first question a newcomer might be asked is "What church do you attend?"

In less extreme but still profound ways, religion shapes how and with whom many people communicate. For example, members of the orthodox Jewish community consider it important to marry within the faith. In one study, some of the young Jewish women interviewed said a man's religious preference is as important, or more important, than his personality.[15] They also described a cultural gap between dating solely to find a suitable spouse and the "American style" of dating, in which couples may spend time together, and even have sex, although they don't plan to marry.

Other research suggests that, in general, teens who believe that only one religion has merit date less frequently than other teens, perhaps because their pool of acceptable partners is smaller.[16] However, religious teens who respect the viewpoints of multiple religions typically date more frequently than their non-religious peers.[17] And the odds are good for interfaith relationships. Studies show that, if they communicate openly and respectfully about matters of faith, interfaith couples are just as likely as other couples to stay together.[18]

Religious beliefs affect family life as well. Members of evangelical churches are likely to view parents as family decision makers and honor children for following their advice without question.[19]

Physical Ability and Disability

Although able-bodied people might view physical challenges as unfortunate, people with disabilities often find that belonging to a community of similar people can be rewarding. Deaf culture is a good example: The shared experiences of deafness can create strong bonds. Most notably, distinct languages build a shared worldview and solidarity. There are Deaf schools, Deaf competitions (e.g., Miss Deaf America), Deaf performing arts (including Deaf comedians), and other organizations that bring people who are Deaf together.

Regardless of the specific physical condition, it's important to treat a disability as one feature, not as the person's defining characteristic. Describing someone as "a person who is blind" is both more accurate and less constricting than calling her a "blind person." This difference might seem subtle—until you imagine which label you would prefer if you lost your sight.

Age and Generation

Imagine how odd it would seem if an 8-year-old or a senior citizen started talking, dressing, or otherwise acting like a 20-year-old. We tend to think of getting older as a purely physical process. But age-related communication reflects culture at least as much as biology. In many ways, we learn how to "do" being various ages—how to dress, how to talk, and what not to say and do—in the same way we learn how to play other roles in our lives.

Relationships between older and younger people are shaped by cultural assumptions that change over time. At some points in history, older adults have been regarded as wise, accomplished, and even magical.[20] At others, they have been treated as "dead weight" and uncomfortable reminders of mortality and decline.[21]

Today, for the most part, Western cultures honor youth, and attitudes about aging tend to be negative. On balance, people over age 40 are twice as likely to be depicted in the media as unattractive, bored, and in declining health when compared with people under age 40.[22] And people over age 60, especially women, are still under-represented in the media. However, the data present a different story. Studies show that, overall, people in their 60s are just as happy as people in their 20s.[23]

People who believe older adults have trouble communicating are less likely to interact with them. Even when these speech styles are well intentioned, they can have harmful effects. Older adults who are treated as less capable than their peers tend to perceive *themselves* as older and less capable.[24] And challenging ageist treatment presents seniors with a dilemma: Speaking up can be taken as a sign of being cranky or bitter, reinforcing negative stereotypes of seniors.[25]

Being young, however, isn't as glamorous as it may seem. Teens and young adults typically experience intense pressure to establish their identity

> Why do people in Western cultures tend to prize youth and exhibit negative attitudes toward aging?

and prove themselves.[26] At the same time, adolescents typically experience what psychologists have called personal fable (the sense that they are different from everybody else) and imaginary audience (a heightened self-consciousness that makes it seem as if people are always observing and judging them), which can lead to some classic communication challenges.[27] Teens often feel that their parents and other people can't understand them because their situations are different and unique, while parents may be baffled that their "extensive experience" and "good advice" are summarily rejected. And young people may wonder why others butt into their affairs with "overly critical judgments" and "irrelevant advice."

Communication challenges also can arise when members of different generations work together. For example, millennials (born between 1980 and 2000) tend to have a much stronger need for affirming feedback than previous generations.[28] They want clear guidance on how to do a job correctly—but do not want to be micromanaged when they do it. After finishing the task, they have an equally strong desire for praise. To a baby boomer manager (born between 1946 and 1960), that type of guidance and feedback may feel more like a nuisance. In the manager's experience, "no news is good news," and not being told that you screwed up should be praise enough. Neither perspective is wrong. But when members of these cocultures have different expectations, communication problems can occur.

Socioeconomic Status

Social class can have a major impact on how people communicate. Research shows that people in the United States typically identify themselves as belonging to the working class, middle class, or upper class, and that they feel a sense of solidarity with people in the same social strata.[29] This is especially true for working class people, who tend to feel that they are united both by hardship and by their commitment to hard, physical work. One working-class college student put it this way:

> I know that when all is said and done, I'm a stronger and better person than they [members of the upper class] are. That's probably a horrible thing to say and it makes me sound very egotistical, but . . . it makes me more glad that I've been through what I've been through, because at the end of the day, I know I had to bust my a** to be where I want, and that makes me feel really good.[30]

The differing communication styles of people from different social classes can have consequences later in life. College professors often find that working-class and first-generation college students who are raised not to challenge authority can have a difficult time speaking up, thinking critically, and arguing persuasively.[31] The effects of social class continue into the workplace, where skills such as assertiveness and persuasiveness are often career enhancers. Individuals who come from working-class families and attain middle- or upper-class careers face special challenges. New speech and language, clothing, and nonverbal patterns often are necessary to gain acceptance.[32]

Even within the same family, educational level can create intercultural challenges. First-generation college (FGC) students feel the intercultural strain of "trying to live simultaneously in two vastly different worlds" of school and home. Communication researchers Mark Orbe and Christopher Groscurth discovered that many FGC students alter their communication patterns dramatically between their two worlds, censoring their speech with classmates and professors to avoid calling attention to their status, and with family members to avoid threatening and alienating them.

At the other end of the socioeconomic spectrum from college students, gangs fit the definition of a coculture. Members have a well-defined identity, both among themselves and according to the outside world. This sense of belonging is often reflected in distinctive language and nonverbal markers such as clothing, tattoos, and hand signals. Gangs provide people who are marginalized by society with a sense of identity and security in an often dangerous and hostile world. But the benefits come at considerable cost. As might be expected, gang members have higher rates of delinquency and drug use. They commit more violent offenses and have higher arrest rates.[33]

OBJECTIVE 3.3   Explain how cocultural values and norms affect communication within and between cultures.

CULTURAL VALUES AND NORMS THAT SHAPE COMMUNICATION

Communication problems don't always occur when people from different backgrounds interact. Those backgrounds must have a significant impact on the exchange before we can say that culture has made a difference. Some cultural influences on communication are obvious. You don't have to be a scholar or researcher to appreciate how different languages can make communication between groups challenging. Along with those obvious differences, however, there are also far less visible values and norms that affect how members of cultures interact.

Individualism and Collectivism

In Chapter 2, we introduced the concepts of individualism and collectivism in terms of how they affect identity. Members of **individualistic cultures**—including the United States, Canada, and Great Britain—tend to view their primary responsibility as helping themselves; whereas

> individualistic culture
A culture in which members focus on the value and welfare of individual members, as opposed to a concern for the group as a whole.

communicators in **collectivistic cultures**—such as China, Korea, and Japan—often feel loyalties and obligations to an in-group (Figure 3-1): one's extended family, community, or even the organization one works for.[34] Individualistic and collectivistic cultures also have very different approaches to communication:

> **> collectivistic culture**
> A culture in which members focus on the welfare of the group as a whole, rather than being concerned mostly about personal success.

Conflict vs Harmony Individualistic cultures are relatively tolerant of conflicts, whereas members of collectivistic cultures place a greater emphasis on harmony.[35] Both orientations have obvious advantages and drawbacks.

Superstar vs Team Player Individualistic societies are far more likely to produce and reward superstars, while collectivistic societies more often produce team players. The best results occur when communicators recognize both and make an effort to address the kinds of communication that do not come naturally.

Personal Accomplishment vs Shared Accomplishment Members of individualistic societies are more likely to tout personal accomplishments that put individuals ahead of the group, whereas members of collectivistic societies are typically less publicly egotistical. This cultural difference can lead to misunderstandings in the classroom and on job interviews. For instance, Americans may mistakenly assume that Asian individuals who are humble lack confidence or achievements.

Independence vs Dependence Individualistic cultures tend to value independence more than collectivistic cultures, and persons raised in individualistic cultures are often less adept at seeing others' points of view. In one study, Chinese and American players were paired together in a game that required them to take the perspective of their partners.[36] By all measures, the collectivist Chinese had greater success in perspective taking than did their American counterparts.

High and Low Context

Social scientists have identified two distinct ways that members of various cultures deliver messages.[37] The first deals with context, the set of circumstances that surround a situation and give it meaning. A **low-context culture**

> **> low-context culture**
> A culture in which people use language primarily to express thoughts, feelings, and ideas as directly as possible.

Individualistic

Collectivist

United States, Canada, and Great Britain

China, Korea, and Japan

Figure 3-1 Individualism and Collectivism

> **high-context culture**
A culture that relies heavily on subtle, often nonverbal cues to maintain social harmony.

uses language primarily to express thoughts, feelings, and ideas as directly as possible. By contrast, a **high-context culture** relies heavily on subtle, often nonverbal cues—such as behavior, history of the relationship, and general social rules—to maintain social harmony.

Research shows that Americans are likely to state their concerns or complaints directly; whereas persons raised in high-context cultures usually hint at them.[38] One Chinese exchange student gave this example:

> Suppose a guy feels bad about his roommate eating his snacks. If he is Chinese, he may try to hide his food secretly or choose a certain time to say, "My snacks run out so fast, I think I need to buy more next time." Before this, he also may think about whether his roommate would hate him if he says something wrong. But Americans may point out directly that someone has been eating their food.[39]

It's easy to see the potential for misunderstanding in situations like this. The roommate from China may feel his displeasure is obvious, based on the situation and his indirect statement. But the American—who may expect his friend to say outright if he is upset—may miss the point entirely.

Mainstream culture in the United States, Canada, northern Europe, and Israel falls toward the low-context end of the scale. Longtime residents generally value straight talk and grow impatient with "beating around the bush." By contrast, people in most Asian and Middle Eastern cultures fit the high-context pattern (Figure 3-2). For them, maintaining harmony is important, so communicators avoid speaking directly if that threatens another person's "face," or dignity.

It's easy to see how the clash between directness and indirectness can present challenges. To members of high-context cultures, communicators with a low-context style can appear overly talkative, redundant, and lacking in subtlety. On the other hand, to people from low-context backgrounds, high-context communicators often seem evasive or even dishonest. As with all cultural influences, however, it's important to remember that members of any culture can and do vary widely in this respect.

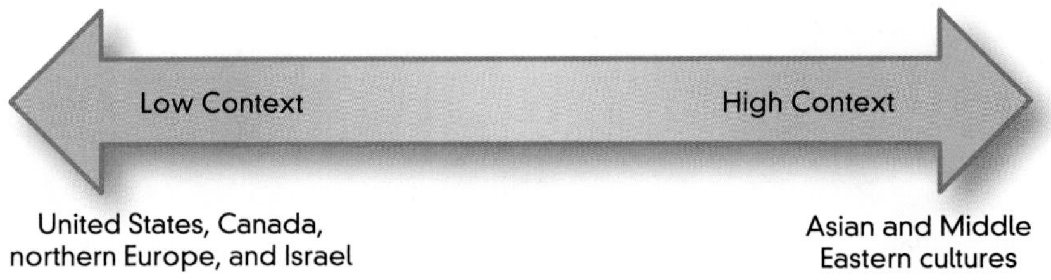

Are you mostly a high- or low-context communicator? How does this influence your conflict management style?

Low Context   High Context

United States, Canada, northern Europe, and Israel

Asian and Middle Eastern cultures

Figure 3-2 Low and High Context

Uncertainty Avoidance

Uncertainty may be universal, but cultures have different ways of coping with an unpredictable future. The term **uncertainty avoidance** is used to reflect the degree to which members of a culture feel threatened by ambiguous situations and how much they try to avoid them.[40] As a group, residents of some countries (including Singapore, Great Britain, Denmark, Sweden, Hong Kong, and the United States) tend to embrace change, while others (such as natives of Belgium, Greece, Japan, and Portugal) tend to find new or ambiguous situations discomforting (Figure 3-3).

A culture's degree of uncertainty avoidance is reflected in the way its members communicate. In countries that avoid uncertainty, people who are different or who express ideas that challenge the status quo are considered dangerous, and intolerance is high. People in these cultures are especially concerned with security, so they have a strong need for clearly defined rules and regulations. It's easy to imagine how most relationships in cultures with a low tolerance for uncertainty—family, work, friendships, and romance—are likely to fit a predictable pattern. By contrast, individuals in a culture that is less threatened by the new and unexpected are more likely to tolerate—or even welcome—those who don't fit the norm.

> uncertainty avoidance
The cultural tendency to seek stability and honor tradition instead of welcoming risk, uncertainty, and change.

Power Distance

Power distance refers to the extent of the gap between social groups who possess power and those who don't. Cultures with low power distance believe in minimizing the difference between various social classes and that one person is as good as another regardless of his or her station in life—rich, poor, educated, or uneducated. Austria, Denmark, Israel, and New Zealand are some of the most egalitarian countries (Figure 3-4). And, anyone familiar with communication in the United States and Canada knows that American and Canadian cultures value equality, even if it's not always perfectly enacted. For example, Americans might call their bosses by their first names or challenge the opinions of people in higher status positions.

> power distance
The degree to which members of a group are willing to accept a difference in power and status.

Avoid Uncertainty   Embrace Uncertainty

Belgium, Greece, Japan, and Portugal

Singapore, Great Britain, Denmark, Sweden, Hong Kong, and the United States

Figure 3-3 Uncertainty Avoidance

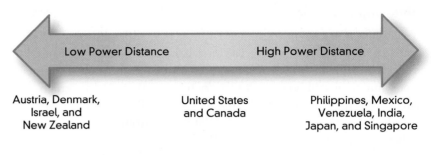

Low Power Distance   High Power Distance

| Austria, Denmark, Israel, and New Zealand | United States and Canada | Philippines, Mexico, Venezuela, India, Japan, and Singapore |

Figure 3-4 Power Distance

At the other end of the spectrum are countries with a high degree of power distance: Philippines, Mexico, Venezuela, India, Japan, and Singapore.[41] In these countries, it may seem rude to treat everyone the same way. In the Japanese workplace, for example, new acquaintances exchange business cards immediately, which helps establish everyone's relative status. The oldest or highest-ranking person receives the deepest bows from others, the best seat, the most deferential treatment, and so on. This treatment isn't regarded as elitist or disrespectful. Indeed, treating a high-status person the same as everyone else would seem rude.

Talk and Silence

Beliefs about the value of talk differ from one culture to another.[42] People in Western cultures tend to view talk as desirable and use it for social purposes as well as to perform tasks. Silence has a negative value in these

A special version of Google is monitored and censored by the Chinese government in an effort to prevent political dissent. The idea that it is wrong to challenge authority is common in high-power-distance cultures.

Q *In what ways do you defer to authority figures? To what extent are you willing to challenge them?*

cultures. It is likely to be interpreted as lack of interest, unwillingness to communicate, hostility, anxiety, shyness, or a sign of interpersonal incompatibility. Westerners are typically uncomfortable with silence, which they find embarrassing and awkward.

On the other hand, for thousands of years, Asian cultures have discouraged the expression of thoughts and feelings (Figure 3-5). Silence is valued, as Taoist sayings indicate: "In much talk there is great weariness" or "One who speaks does not know; one who knows does not speak." Unlike Westerners, who are uncomfortable with silence, Japanese and Chinese people believe that remaining quiet is the proper state when there is nothing to be said. To Asians, a talkative person is often considered a show-off or a fake.

Members of some Native American communities also honor silence. For example, traditional members of western Apache tribes maintain silence when others lose their temper.[43] Apaches also consider that silence has a comforting value. The idea is that words are often unnecessary in periods of grief, and it is comforting to have loved ones present without the pressure to maintain conversations with them.

It's easy to see how these views of speech and silence can lead to communication problems when people from different cultures meet. Both the "talkative" Westerner and the "silent" Asian and Native American are behaving in ways they believe are proper, yet each may view the other with disapproval and mistrust. Only when they recognize the different standards of behavior can they adapt to one another, or at least understand and respect their differences.

Competition and Cooperation

Cultures are a bit like people in that they may be regarded as competitive, cooperative, or somewhere in the middle (Figure 3-6). Competitive (sometimes called masculine) cultures, such as those in Japan, Italy, Nigeria, and Great Britain, embody qualities traditionally associated with masculinity, such as independence, competitiveness, and assertiveness.[44] In those cultures, women are often expected to take care of home and family life, whereas men are expected to shoulder most of the financial responsibilities.

Gender roles are less differentiated in cooperative (sometimes called feminine) cultures—which makes sense when you consider that they

Value Talk   Value Silence

Western cultures   Asian and Native American cultures

Figure 3-5 Talk and Silence

Competitive   Cooperative

Japan, Italy, Nigeria,   Taiwan and the   Iceland, the Netherlands,
and Great Britain   United States   and Norway

Figure 3-6 Competitive and Cooperative

emphasize equality, relationships, cooperation, and consensus building.[45] In Iceland, the Netherlands, and Norway, both men and women tend to consider harmony and cooperation to be more important than competition.

Some countries, such as Taiwan, fall near the midpoint on the scale because natives of those cultures place relatively equal value on cooperative and competitive qualities.[46] The United States has long been considered a moderately competitive culture, but some people feel it's becoming more balanced. In fact, there is speculation that the world is becoming more balanced overall.[47] This is partly because women have entered the workplace in record numbers and partly because technology now exposes people to a world of new ideas, fashions, and outlooks that go beyond traditional gender roles.

OBJECTIVE 3.4

Understand the elements of intercultural and cocultural communication competence.

DEVELOPING INTERCULTURAL COMMUNICATION COMPETENCE

What distinguishes competent and incompetent intercultural communicators? To a great degree, interacting successfully with strangers calls for the same ingredients of general communicative competence outlined in Chapter 1. It's important to be able to draw on a wide range of behaviors and to be skillful at choosing and performing the most appropriate ones in a given situation. A genuine concern for others, cognitive complexity, and the ability to empathize also help. Finally, self-monitoring is important, particularly when dealing with strangers.

But beyond these basic qualities, communication researchers have worked long and hard to identify qualities that are essential ingredients of intercultural communicative competence.[48]

What is your intercultural sensitivity?

Following is a series of statements concerning intercultural communication.[49] There are no right or wrong answers. Imagine yourself interacting with people from a wide variety of cultural groups, not just one or two. Record your first impression to each statement by indicating the degree to which you agree or disagree, using the following scale.

5 = strongly agree   **4** = agree   **3** = uncertain   **2** = disagree   **1** = strongly disagree

_____ **1.** I enjoy interacting with people from different cultures.

_____ **2.** I think people from other cultures are narrow-minded.

_____ **3.** I am sure of myself in interacting with people from different cultures.

_____ **4.** I find it very hard to talk in front of people from different cultures.

_____ **5.** I know what to say when interacting with people from different cultures.

_____ **6.** I get upset easily when interacting with people from different cultures.

For the meaning of your scores, see p. 73. ●

Spend Time with People from Different Backgrounds

More than a half-century of research confirms that, under the right circumstances, spending time with people from different backgrounds leads to a host of positive outcomes: reduced prejudice, greater productivity, and better relationships.[50] The link between exposure and positive attitudes, called the contact hypothesis, has been demonstrated in a wide range of cultural and cocultural contacts.[51]

But exposure isn't enough in itself. In order to make contacts successful, you must have a genuine desire to know and understand others. People who are willing to communicate with others from different backgrounds report a greater number of diverse friends than those who are less willing to reach out.[52] Other conditions—equal status, a low-stress, cooperative climate, and the chance to disconfirm stereotypes—also contribute to positive relationships.

Along with face-to-face contacts, the Internet may enhance contact with people from different backgrounds.[53] Online venues make it relatively easy to connect with people you might never meet in person. Sometimes it's easier to navigate unfamiliar interactions in an online environment, where you have time to gather your thoughts before responding and where you may feel comfortable asking questions about cultural nuances that would seem out of place in person. Online communication also makes status differences less important: Gaps in material wealth or physical appearance may be less apparent.

Develop a Tolerance for Ambiguity

Uncertainty is high when we encounter communicators from different cultures, especially if we are unfamiliar with their language. Pico Iyer captures this feeling well when he describes his growing friendship with Sachiko, a Japanese woman he met in Kyoto:

> Once, when I had to leave her house ten minutes early, she said, "I very sad," and another time, when I simply called her up, she said, "I very happy"—and I began to think her unusually sensitive, or else prone to bold and violent extremes, when really she was reflecting nothing but the paucity of her English vocabulary.[54]

Without a tolerance for ambiguity, the mass of often confusing messages that impact intercultural interactions would be impossible to manage. Some people seem to come equipped with this sort of tolerance, while others have to cultivate it. However, the ability to live with uncertainty is an essential ingredient of intercultural communication competence.

Keep an Open-Minded Attitude

What does it mean to be open-minded? Individuals who are open-minded are willing to listen to and consider new ideas that they may not have considered before. To understand open-mindedness, it's helpful to consider three traits that are incompatible with it: ethnocentrism, prejudice, and stereotyping.

Ethnocentrism is an attitude that one's own culture is superior to that of others. An ethnocentric person thinks—either privately or openly—that anyone who does not belong to his or her in-group is somehow strange, wrong, or even inferior.

Ethnocentrism leads to an attitude of **prejudice**—an unfairly biased and intolerant attitude toward others who belong to an out-group. (Note that the root term in *prejudice* is "pre-judge.") An important element of prejudice is **stereotyping**—exaggerated generalizations about a group. Stereotypical prejudices include the obvious exaggerations that all women are emotional, all men are sex-crazed and insensitive, all older people are out of touch with reality, and all immigrants are welfare parasites.

Two decades of research has revealed that many stereotypes are unconscious and are not motivated by ill will.[55] However, even when unfair stereotypes are automatic, they can be overcome.[56] The answer is not to ignore our differences, but to recognize that each of us reflects such a unique collection of experiences and cultures that generalizations cannot describe us. As Allison Collins, one reviewer of this book, put it:

> The issue I find people voicing today is not "don't hate me because I'm gay" or "don't hate me because I'm black," but more nuanced . . . "Just because I'm gay doesn't mean I hate sports, so accept me both

> ethnocentrism
The attitude that one's own culture is superior to that of others.

> prejudice
An unfairly biased and intolerant attitude toward others who belong to an out-group.

> stereotyping
The perceptual process of applying exaggerated beliefs associated with a categorizing system.

as an individual and as part of a culture," or "I grew up in a black neighborhood and it is a huge part of who I am, so while I may now be a well-paid and highly respected doctor, I still identify with Trayvon Martin."

Simply asking yourself whether you might be succumbing to unfair thinking can be surprisingly effective. Look for ways to appreciate others beyond obvious cues such as race, gender, age, and sexual orientation.

Acquire and Use Culture-Specific Information Appropriately

Attitude alone isn't enough to guarantee success in intercultural encounters. Communicators need to possess enough knowledge of other cultures to know what approaches are appropriate. The rules and customs that work with one group might be quite different from those that succeed with another. The ability to "shift gears" and adapt one's style to the norms of another culture or coculture is an essential ingredient of communication competence.[57]

When has your communication been shaped by unfair stereotyping? How could you be more open-minded?

President Barack Obama raised eyebrows when he kissed Burmese dissident leader Aung San Suu Kyi in public while congratulating her on winning the Nobel Peace Prize. In her culture, public displays of affection are rare.

Q *Have you ever experienced an awkward moment when a behavior that seemed ordinary to you surprised people from different backgrounds?*

How can a communicator acquire the culture-specific information that leads to competence? Scholarship suggests three strategies for moving toward a more mindful, competent style of intercultural communication.[58]

Passive observation involves noticing what behaviors members of a different culture use and applying these insights to communicate in ways that are most effective.

Active strategies include reading, watching films, and asking experts and members of the other culture how to behave, as well as taking academic courses related to intercultural communication and diversity.[59]

Self-disclosure involves volunteering personal information to people from other cultures with whom you want to communicate. One type of self-disclosure is to confess your cultural ignorance: "This is very new to me. What's the right thing to do in this situation?" While some cultures may not value this sort of candor and self-disclosure, most people are pleased when strangers attempt to learn the practices of their culture, and they are usually more than willing to offer information and assistance.

Be Patient and Persistent

Becoming comfortable and competent in a new culture or coculture may be ultimately rewarding, but the process isn't easy. After a "honeymoon" phase, it's typical to feel confused, disenchanted, lonesome, and homesick.[60] To top it off, you may feel disappointed in yourself for not adapting as easily as you expected. This stage—which typically feels like a crisis—has acquired the labels *culture shock* or *adjustment shock*.[61]

You wouldn't be the first person to be blindsided by culture shock. When Lynn Chih-Ning Chang came to the United States from Taiwan for graduate school, she cried every day on the way home from class.[62] All her life, she had been taught that it was respectful and ladylike to sit quietly and listen, so she was shocked that American students spoke aloud without raising their hands, interrupted one another, addressed the teacher by first name, and ate food in the classroom. What's more, Chang's classmates answered so quickly that, by the time she was ready to say something, they were already on a new topic. The same behavior that made her "a smart and patient lady in Taiwan," she says, made her seem like a "slow learner" in the United States.

Communication theorist Young Yum Kim has studied cultural adaptation extensively. She says it's natural to feel a sense of push and pull between the familiar and the novel.[63] Kim encourages those acclimating to a new culture to regard stress as a good sign. It means they have the potential to adapt and grow. With patience, the sense of crisis begins to wane and, and once again, there's energy and enthusiasm to learn more.

Communication can be a challenge while you're learning how to operate in new cultures, but it can also be a solution.[64] Chang, the Taiwanese student adapting to life in America, learned this firsthand. At first, she says, she was reluctant to approach American students, and they were reluctant to approach her. Gradually, she found the courage to initiate conversations, and she discovered that her classmates were friendly and receptive. Eventually, she made friends, began to fit in, and successfully completed her degree.

The transition from culture shock to adaptation and growth is usually successful, but it isn't a smooth, linear process. Instead, people tend to take two steps forward and one step back, and to repeat that pattern many times. Kim calls this a "draw back and leap" pattern.[65] Above all, she says, if people are patient and they keep trying, the rewards are worth it.

CHECK YOUR UNDERSTANDING

OBJECTIVE 3.1 Define culture, and differentiate between in- and out-groups.

CULTURE DEFINED

Culture is the language, values, beliefs, traditions, and customs people share and learn. Social scientists use the label "in-groups" to describe groups with which we identify and are emotionally connected, and they use "out-groups" to label those we view as different and with whom we have no sense of affiliation.

In what situations might you feel like an in- or out-group member? What feelings might arise in each of these circumstances?

OBJECTIVE 3.2 Identify factors that shape cocultural identity, and describe how they play a role in communication.

COCULTURES AND COMMUNICATION

Coculture refers to the perception of membership in a group that is part of an encompassing culture. While cultural characteristics are real and important, they are generalizations that don't apply equally to every member of a group. Furthermore, cultural differences aren't a salient factor in every intergroup encounter. A variety of cocultures exists within our society, defined by factors including ethnicity, regional differences, religion, physical abilities/disabilities, age, and socioeconomic status.

Which of the cocultures described here are most central to your identity? How do they influence the way you communicate with others?

OBJECTIVE 3.3 Explain how cocultural values and norms affect communication within and between cultures.

CULTURAL VALUES AND NORMS THAT SHAPE COMMUNICATION

Many of the values and norms that shape intercultural communication aren't immediately apparent. Members of some cultures value autonomy and individual expression, whereas others are more collectivistic. Some pay close attention to subtle, contextual cues, whereas others pay more attention to the words people use. Cultures differ on other dimensions as well. They include uncertainty avoidance, power distance, and beliefs about talk and silence.

Which of the following feel more comfortable to you: individualistic or collectivistic ideals? high-context or low-context communication? high or low power distance? How does your orientation influence your relationships?

DEVELOPING INTERCULTURAL COMMUNICATION COMPETENCE

There are several dimensions to becoming a more competent communicator in intercultural and cocultural encounters. They include increased exposure, tolerance for ambiguity, open-mindedness, knowledge of differences, skill in conforming to the communication style of others, and patience and perseverance.

List three ways you could communicate more effectively in intercultural and cocultural encounters.

KEY TERMS

coculture p. 53
collectivistic culture p. 61
culture p. 52
ethnicity p. 54
ethnocentrism p. 68
high-context culture p. 62

in-groups p. 53
individualistic culture p. 60
low-context culture p. 61
out-groups p. 53
power distance p. 63
prejudice p. 68

race p. 54
salience p. 53
stereotyping p. 68
uncertainty avoidance p. 63

WHAT IS YOUR INTERCULTURAL SENSITIVITY?

If you agree or strongly agree with the odd-numbered questions, you are probably at ease in intercultural situations. On the other hand, if you agree or strongly agree with the even-numbered questions, there is room for improvement when it comes to intercultural competence. You can do this most effectively by learning all you can about different cultures and seeking out opportunities to engage with a diverse array of people.

FOR FURTHER EXPLORATION

For more communication resources, see the *Essential Communication* website at www.oup.com/us/ec. There you will find a variety of resources: "Media Room" examples from popular films and television shows to further illustrate important concepts, a list of relevant books and articles, links to descriptions of feature films and television shows at the *Now Playing* website, study aids, and a self-test to check your understanding of the material in this chapter.

Language

4.1 Explain how symbols and linguistic rules allow people to achieve shared meaning.

4.2 Identify ways that language shapes our attitudes and reflects how we feel about ourselves and others.

4.3 Recognize and identify ways to remedy vague, confusing, and disruptive language.

4.4 Describe the ways in which male and female speech patterns are typically alike, and how they differ.

Explain how symbols and linguistic rules allow people to achieve shared meaning.

THE NATURE OF LANGUAGE

> language
A collection of symbols, governed by rules and used to convey messages between individuals.

Humans speak about 10,000 dialects.[1] Although most of these sound different from one another, all possess the same characteristics of **language**: a collection of symbols governed by rules and used to convey messages between individuals. A closer look at this definition can explain how language operates and suggest how we can use it more effectively.

Language Is Symbolic

There's nothing natural about calling your loyal four-footed companion a "dog" or the object you're reading right now a "book." These words, like virtually all language, are **symbols**—arbitrary constructions that represent a communicator's thoughts. Not all linguistic symbols are spoken or written words. Sign language, as "spoken" by most people who are deaf, is symbolic in nature and not the pantomime it might seem to non-signers.

> symbols
Arbitrary constructions that represent a communicator's thoughts.

Symbols are more than just labels: They are the way we experience the world. You can prove this by trying a simple experiment.[2] Work up some saliva in your mouth and then spit it into a glass. Take a good look, and then drink it up. Most people find this process mildly disgusting. But ask yourself why this is so. After all, we swallow our own saliva all the time. The answer arises out of the symbolic labels we use. After the saliva is in the glass, we call it *spit* and think of it in a different way. In other words, our reaction is to the name, not the thing.

The naming process operates in virtually every situation. How you react to a stranger will depend on the symbols you use to categorize him or her: gay (or straight), religious (or not), attractive (or unattractive), and so on.

Meanings Are in People, Not in Words

Ask a dozen people what the same symbol means, and you are likely to get 12 different answers. Does an American flag bring up associations of patriots giving their lives for their country? Fourth of July parades? Cultural imperialism? How about a cross: What does it represent? The message of Jesus Christ? Fire-lit rallies of Ku Klux Klansmen? Your childhood Sunday School? The necklace your sister always wears?

As with physical symbols, the place to look for meaning in language isn't in the words themselves but rather in the way people make sense of them. One unfortunate example occurred in Washington, DC, when a city government official used the word *niggardly* to describe an approach to budgeting.[3] Some critics accused him of uttering an unforgivable racial slur. His defenders pointed out that the word, which means "miserly," is derived from Scandinavian languages and that it has no link to the racial slur it resembles. Even though the criticisms eventually died away, they illustrate that, correct or not, the meanings people associate with words have far more significance than do their dictionary definitions.

Problems arise when people mistakenly assume that others use words in the same way they do. It's possible to have an argument about *feminism* without ever realizing that you and the other person are using the word to represent entirely different things. The same goes for *environmentalism*, *Republicans*, *rock music*, and thousands upon thousands of other symbols. Words don't mean; people do—and often in widely different ways.

Despite the potential for linguistic problems, we do communicate with one another reasonably well most of the time. And, with enough effort, we can clear up most misunderstandings. The key to more effective use of language is to avoid assuming that others interpret words the same way we do. In truth, successful communication occurs when we negotiate the meaning of a statement.[4] As one French proverb puts it: The spoken word belongs half to the one who speaks it and half to the one who hears.

Language Is Governed by Rules

Several types of rules govern language: phonological, syntactic, semantic, and pragmatic.

Phonological Rules

The rules that govern how words sound when they are pronounced are called **phonological rules**. For instance, the words *champagne*, *double*, and *occasion* are spelled identically in French and English, but all are pronounced differently. Nonnative speakers learning English are plagued by inconsistent phonological rules, as a few examples illustrate:

> **> phonological rules**
> Linguistic rules governing how sounds are combined to form words.

A farm can produce produce.

The dump was so full it had to refuse refuse.

The present is a good time to present the present.

Syntactic Rules

The rules that govern the structure of language—the way symbols can be arranged—are known as **syntactic rules**. For example, correct English syntax requires that every word contain at least one vowel and prohibits sentences such as "Have you the cookies brought?", which is a perfectly acceptable word order in German. Although most of us aren't able to describe the syntactic rules that govern our language, it's easy to recognize their existence by noting how odd a statement that violates them appears.

> **> syntactic rules**
> Rules that govern the ways in which symbols can be arranged as opposed to the meanings of those symbols.

Technology has spawned versions of English with their own syntactic rules.[5] For example, people have devised a streamlined version of English for instant messages, texts, and tweets that speeds up typing in real-time communication (although it probably makes teachers of composition grind their teeth in anguish):

hey

r u @ home?

ya

k signing off

y

cuz i need to study for finals u can call me tho bye

ttyl

> semantic rules
Rules that govern the meaning of language as opposed to its structure.

Semantic Rules

The rules that deal with the meaning of specific words are called **semantic rules**. They are what make it possible for us to agree that "bikes" are for riding and "books" are for reading. They also help us to know whom we will and won't encounter when we open doors marked "men" or "women." Without semantic rules, communication would be impossible, because each of us would use symbols in unique ways, unintelligible to one another.

Semantic misunderstandings occur when words can be interpreted in more than one way, as the following humorous notices prove:

The peacemaking meeting scheduled for today has been canceled due to a conflict.

For those of you who have children and don't know it, we have a nursery downstairs.

The ladies of the Church have cast off clothing of every kind. They may be seen in the basement on Friday afternoon.

State Representative Lisa Brown was barred from the podium in the Michigan House of Representatives after she used the word *vagina* during a debate about antiabortion legislation. Fellow legislator Mike Callton called her language vile and disgusting. Opinions about the appropriateness of Brown's speech act are grounded in pragmatic rules.

Have others used a set of pragmatic rules different than your own to interpret something you have said?

Pragmatic Rules

The rules that govern how people use and understand language in everyday interactions are known as **pragmatic rules**.[6] Consider the example of a male boss saying, "You look very pretty today," to a female employee. It's easy to imagine how the female employee might be made uncomfortable by a comment that her boss considered an innocent remark. The pragmatic rules people use can differ on many levels. You can understand these levels by imagining how they would operate in our example:

EACH PERSON'S SELF-CONCEPT
Boss: Views himself as a nice guy
Employee: Determined to succeed on her own merits, not on her appearance

> **pragmatic rules**
Rules that govern how people use language in everyday interaction.

PERCEIVED RELATIONSHIP

Boss: Views employees like members of the family

Employee: Depends on boss's goodwill for advancement

CULTURAL BACKGROUND

Boss: Member of generation in which comments about appearance were common

Employee: Member of generation sensitive to sexual harassment

---

OBJECTIVE 4.2

Identify ways in which language shapes our attitudes and reflects how we feel about ourselves and others.

THE POWER OF LANGUAGE

On the most obvious level, language allows us to satisfy basic functions such as describing ideas, making requests, and solving problems. But beyond these functions, the way we use language also influences others and reflects our attitudes in more subtle ways.

Language Shapes Attitudes

Language—sometimes consciously and sometimes not—shapes others' values, attitudes, and beliefs in a variety of ways.

Naming

"What's in a name?" Juliet asked rhetorically. If Romeo had been a social scientist, he would have answered, "A great deal." Research has demonstrated that names are more than just a simple means of identification: They shape the way others think of us, the way we view ourselves, and the way we act.

One study revealed it's often possible to predict who will win an election based on the candidates' surnames.[7] Voters tend to favor names that are simple, easily pronounced, and rhythmic.

Names play a role in shaping and reinforcing a child's personal identity. Naming a baby after a family member (e.g., "Junior" or "Trey") can create a connection between the child and his or her namesake. Name choice can also be a powerful way to make a statement about cultural identity. For example, in recent decades a large percentage of names given to African American babies have been distinctively black (e.g., Marques, LaToya).[8] Researchers suggest that distinctive names such as these are a symbol of pride and solidarity within the African American community.

Status

In the classic musical *My Fair Lady*, Professor Henry Higgins transforms Eliza Doolittle from a lowly flower girl into a high-society woman by

Because our name is closely tied to our identity and connection with others, we often feel embarrassed when we forget someone's name or mispronounce it. John Travolta instantly became the subject of global mockery through social media after introducing singer Idina Menzel as "Adele Dazeem" at the 2014 Oscars.

Q How can you effectively handle a situation in which you have trouble with someone's name?

replacing her cockney accent with an upper-crust speaking style. Decades of research have demonstrated that the power of speech to influence status is a fact.[9]

Several factors combine to create positive or negative impressions: accent, choice of words, speech rate, and even the apparent age of a speaker. In most cases, speakers of standard dialect (without a regional accent) are rated higher than nonstandard speakers in a variety of ways: They are viewed as more competent and more self-confident, and the content of their messages is rated more favorably.

The unwillingness or inability of a communicator to use the standard dialect fluently can have serious consequences. For instance, African

American Vernacular English is a distinctive dialect with its own accent, grammar, syntax, and semantic rules. Unfortunately, research reveals a common misconception—that people who speak the African American vernacular are less intelligent, less professional, less capable, less socially acceptable, and less employable that people who speak standard English.[10] Speakers with other non-standard accents also can be stigmatized.[11]

Sexism and Racism

By now it should be clear that the power of language to shape attitudes goes beyond individual cases and influences how we perceive entire groups of people. For example, Casey Miller and Kate Swift argue that incorrect use of the pronoun *he* to refer to both men and women can have damaging results.

> On the television screen, a teacher of first-graders who has just won a national award describes her way of teaching. "You take each child where you find him," she says. "You watch to see what he's interested in, and then you build on his interests."
>
> A five-year-old looking at the program asks her mother, "Do only boys go to that school?" "No," her mother begins, "she's talking about girls too, but—"
>
> But what? The teacher being interviewed on television is speaking correct English. What can the mother tell her daughter about why a child, in any generalization, is always he rather than she? How does a five-year-old comprehend the generic personal pronoun?[12]

It's not difficult to use nonsexist language. For example, use the terms *humankind, humanity, human beings, human race,* or *people* instead of *mankind;* use *artificial, manufactured,* or *synthetic* in lieu of *man-made;* replace *manpower* with *human power, workers,* or *workforce;* and replace *manhood* with *adulthood.*

The use of labels for racist purposes has a long and ugly past. Names have been used throughout history to stigmatize certain groups.[13] By using derogatory terms to label some people, the out-group is set apart and pictured in an unfavorable light. Diane Mader provides several examples of this:

> We can see the process of stigmatization in Nazi Germany when Jewish people became vermin, in the United States when African Americans became "niggers" and chattel, in the military when the Vietnam-era enemy became "gooks."[14]

Language Reflects Attitudes

Besides shaping the way we view ourselves and others, language reflects our attitudes. Feelings of control, attraction, commitment, responsibility—all these and more are reflected in the way we use language.

How do you balance free speech, on the one hand, and the harmful effects of hateful messages, on the other?

Power

Communication researchers have identified a number of language patterns that add to, or detract from, a speaker's ability to influence others and that reflect how a speaker feels about his or her control over a situation.[15] Let's explore the difference between powerful language and powerless language by comparing the following statements by a student to a professor:

> *"Excuse me, sir, I hate to say this, but I . . . uh . . . I guess I won't be able to turn in the assignment on time. I had a personal emergency and . . . well . . . it was just impossible to finish it by today. I'll have it in your mailbox on Monday, okay?"*

> *"I won't be able to turn in the assignment on time. I had a personal emergency, and it was impossible to finish it by today. I'll have it in your mailbox on Monday."*

The first statement sounds more tentative and not as fluent, which, on the face of it, seems powerless. But in certain circumstances, the first statement may actually have more influence than the second. Perhaps the professor will feel more lenient toward the student who seems to be in greater distress.

In other situations, however, tentative speech may convey the wrong impression entirely. In employment interviews, powerful speech results in more positive attributions of competence and employability than speech perceived to be lacking in confidence or powerless.[16] In general, speakers who communicate with confidence and avoid powerless mannerisms or hedges are typically rated as more competent, dynamic, and attractive than those who hedge and stammer.[17]

Affiliation

Language can also be a way of building and demonstrating solidarity with others. An impressive body of research has demonstrated that communicators who want to show affiliation with one another adapt their speech in a variety of ways. For example, close friends and lovers often develop special terms that serve as a way of signifying their relationship.[18] Using the same vocabulary sets these people apart from others, reminding themselves and the rest of the world of their relationship. The same process works among members of larger groups, ranging from street gangs to military personnel. Communication researchers call this linguistic accommodation **convergence**.

Communicators can experience convergence online as well as in face-to-face interactions. Members of online communities often develop a shared language and conversational style, and their affiliation with each other can be seen in increased uses of the pronoun "we."[19] On a larger scale, when we chat or text, we often create and use shortcuts that we would not use when writing a professional email, letter, or academic paper. However, it can be difficult to keep our more casual abbreviations and language (such as lol) from creeping into everyday conversations.[20]

Abbreviations, emoticons, and other devices can signify affiliation between people of different ages and backgrounds. But when they are misused, the effect can emphasize differences rather than similarities.

Q *Do you think that technology leads to greater or weaker affiliation between people of different ages and backgrounds?*

> convergence

Accommodating one's speaking style to another person, usually a person who is desirable or has higher status.

> **divergence**
A linguistic strategy in which speakers emphasize differences between their communicative style and that of others in order to create distance.

The principle of speech accommodation works in reverse, too. Communicators who want to set themselves apart from others adopt the strategy of **divergence**, speaking in a way that emphasizes their difference from others. For example, non-native English speakers, even though fluent in English, might use their own dialect as a way of showing solidarity with one another—a sort of "us against them" strategy. Divergence also operates in other settings. A physician or attorney, for example, who wants to establish credibility with a client might speak formally and use professional jargon to create a sense of distance. The implicit message here is "I'm different from (and more knowledgeable than) you."

Responsibility

Language can also reveal the speaker's willingness to accept responsibility for a message.

> **"It" vs. "I" Statements** *It's* not finished (less responsible) versus *I* didn't finish it (more responsible).
>
> **"You" vs. "I" Statements** Sometimes *you* make me angry (less responsible) versus Sometimes *I* get angry when you do that (more responsible). "I" statements are more likely to generate positive reactions from others as compared to accusatory ones.[21]
>
> **Questions vs. Statements** Do *you* think we should do that? (less responsible) versus *I* don't think we should do that (more responsible).

OBJECTIVE 4.3 Recognize and identify ways to remedy vague, confusing, and disruptive language.

TROUBLESOME LANGUAGE

Besides being a blessing that enables us to live together, language can be something of a curse. We all have known the frustration of being misunderstood, and most of us have been baffled by another person's overreaction to an innocent comment. In this section, we will look at several kinds of troublesome language, including misunderstandings, disruptive language, and evasive language, with the goal of helping you communicate in a way that makes matters better instead of worse.

Misunderstandings

The most obvious kind of language problems are semantic: We simply don't understand others completely or accurately. Most misunderstandings arise from some common problems that are easily remedied—after you recognize them.

Equivocal Misunderstandings

Equivocal misunderstandings occur when words mean different things to different people. **Equivocal words** have more than one correct dictionary definition. Some equivocal misunderstandings are simple, at least after they are exposed. A nurse once told her patient that he "wouldn't be needing" the materials he requested from home. He interpreted the statement to mean he was near death, whereas the nurse meant he would be going home soon. Some equivocal statements arise from cultural or cocultural differences. In Britain, if someone says, "I'll knock you up in the morning," it generally means "I'll wake you up in the morning." However, in the United States, referring to someone as "knocked up" generally means that she is unmarried and pregnant.

Equivocal misunderstandings can have serious consequences. Equivocation at least partially explains why men may sometimes persist in attempts to become physically intimate when women have expressed unwillingness to do so.[22] Interviews and focus groups with college students revealed that, rather than saying "no" outright to a man's sexual advances, women often used ambiguous phrases such as "I'm not sure that we're ready for this yet." "Are you sure you want to do this?" "Let's be friends," and even "That tickles." Whereas women viewed the indirect statements as meaning "no," men were more likely to interpret them as meaning "maybe." As the researchers put it, "male/female misunderstandings are not so much a matter of males hearing resistance messages as 'go,' but rather their not hearing them as 'stop.'" Under the law, "no" means precisely that, and anyone who argues otherwise can be in for serious legal problems.

> **equivocal words**
> Language with more than one likely interpretation.

Relative Words

Relative words gain their meaning by comparison. Is the school you attend large or small? This depends on what you compare it to: Alongside a campus like Arizona State University, with an enrollment of more than 70,000 students, it may seem small, but compared to a smaller institution, it might seem quite large. In the same way, relative words like *fast* and *slow*, *smart* and *stupid*, *short* and *long* depend on comparisons for their meaning. Using relative words without explaining them can lead to communication problems. For instance, if a new acquaintance says "I'll call you soon," when can you expect to hear from him or her? Have you been disappointed to learn that classes you've heard were "easy" turned out to be hard, that journeys you were told would be "short" were long, that a "hilarious" movie was just OK? The problem in each case came from failing to anchor the relative word used to a more precisely measurable word.

> **relative words**
> Words that gain their meaning by comparison.

Slang and Jargon

Most slang and jargon are related to specialized interests and activities. **Slang** is language used by a group of people whose members belong to a similar coculture or other group. For instance, cyclists who talk about "bonking" are referring to running out of energy. In hip-hop culture, a

> **slang**
> Language used by a group of people whose members belong to a similar coculture or other group.

"ratchet" is a wanna-be diva who lacks class. Other slang consists of *regionalisms*—terms that are understood by people who live in one geographic area but are unknown to outsiders, thus creating a sense of identity and solidarity (Figure 4-1).[23] Residents of the largest U.S. state know that when a fellow Alaskan says, "I'm going outside," he or she is leaving the state. Outsiders are unlikely to interpret that sentence the same way.

Slang can also be age related. Most college students know that if you're "going loko" you are intoxicated from alcohol or drugs, or that if you've been "sexiled" for the night, it means you can't get in to your room because your roommate is having sex.[24]

> **jargon**

The specialized vocabulary that is used as a kind of shorthand by people with common backgrounds and experience.

Almost everyone uses some sort of **jargon**: the specialized vocabulary that functions as a kind of shorthand for people with common backgrounds and experience. Skateboarders have their own language to describe tricks: "ollie," "grind," and "shove it." Some jargon consists of acronyms—initials of terms that are combined to form a word. In finance, P&L (pronounced PNL) translates as "profit and loss," and military people label failure to serve at one's post as being AWOL (absent without leave). The digital age has spawned its own jargon. For instance, "UGC" refers to user-generated content, and "tl;dr" means "too long; didn't read." Likewise, if someone is "checking the bandwidth" it likely means she is checking on the status of something. Some jargon even goes beyond being descriptive and conveys

You Guys (42.53%)

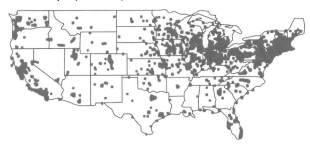

You (24.82%)

Y'all (13.99%)

You All (12.63%)

Figure 4-1 Regionalisms: Most Common Words Used to Address a Group of Two or More People

attitudes. For example, cynics in the high-tech world sometimes refer to being fired from a job as being "uninstalled."[25]

Jargon can be a valuable kind of shorthand for people who understand its use. The trauma team in a hospital emergency room can save time, and possibly lives, by speaking in shorthand, referring to "GSWs" (gunshot wounds), "chem 7" lab tests, and so on, but the same specialized vocabulary that works so well among insiders may mystify and confuse family members of the patient.

Disruptive Language

Not all linguistic problems come from misunderstandings. Sometimes people understand one another perfectly and still end up in conflict. Of course, not all disagreements can, or should be, avoided. But eliminating three bad linguistic habits from your communication repertoire—confusing facts and opinions, confusing facts and inferences, and emotive language—can minimize the kind of clashes that don't need to happen, allowing you to save your energy for the unavoidable and important struggles.

Confusing Facts and Opinions

Factual statements are claims that can be verified as true or false. By contrast, **opinion statements** are based on the speaker's beliefs. Unlike matters of fact, they can never be proved or disproved. Consider a few examples of the difference between factual statements and opinion statements:

> **factual statement**
> A statement that can be verified as being true or false.

> **opinion statement**
> A statement based on the speaker's beliefs.

FACT	OPINION
It rains more in Seattle than in Portland.	The climate in Portland is better than in Seattle.
Kareem Abdul Jabbar is the all-time leading scorer in the National Basketball Association.	Kareem is the greatest basketball player in history.
Per capita income in the United States is higher than in several other countries.	The United States is the best model of economic success in the world.

When factual statements and opinion statements are set side by side, the difference between them is clear. In everyday conversation, however, we often present our opinions as if they are facts, and in doing so we invite an unnecessary argument. For example:

"That was a dumb thing to say!"

"That's a waste of money!"

"You don't have a chance in this country unless you're a white man."

Notice how much less antagonistic each statement would be if it were prefaced by a qualifier like "I think . . . ," or "In my opinion . . . ," or "It seems to me...."

Why do you think we so often present our opinions in ways that make them sound like facts?

> inferential statement
Conclusion arrived at from an interpretation of evidence.

Confusing Facts and Inferences

Difficulties also arise when we confuse factual statements with **inferential statements**—conclusions arrived at from an interpretation of evidence. Consider a few examples:

FACT	INFERENCE
He hit a lamppost while driving down the street.	He was daydreaming when he hit the lamppost.
You interrupted me before I finished what I was saying.	You don't care about what I have to say.
You haven't paid your share of the rent on time for the past three months.	You're trying to weasel out of your responsibilities.

There's nothing wrong with making inferences as long as you identify them as such: "When she stomped out and slammed the door, I thought she was furious." The danger comes when we confuse inferences with facts and make them sound like the absolute truth.

One way to avoid fact–inference confusion is to use the perception-checking skill described in Chapter 2 to test the accuracy of your inferences. Recall that a perception check has three parts: a description of the behavior being discussed, your interpretation of that behavior, and a request for verification. For instance, instead of saying, "Why are you laughing at me?" you could say, "When you laughed at my idea [*description of behavior*], I felt kind of stupid [*interpretation*]. Were you laughing at me [*question*]?"

Emotive Language

Emotive language contains words that sound as if they're describing something when they are really announcing the speaker's attitude toward something. Do you like that old picture frame? If so, you would probably call it "an antique," but if you think it's ugly, you would likely describe it as "a piece of junk."

Emotive words may sound like statements of fact but are always opinions. They convey a subtle (or not so subtle) slant that supports a particular interpretation. For example, a news story might read: "The senator said he was out of the country." This is relatively straightforward, but consider how emotionally loaded the sentence becomes if we simply change the verb:

"The senator explained that he was out of the country."

"The senator claimed that he was out of the country."

Likewise, word choices may convey underlying biases. The same behavior may be described as "assertive" when a man does it, but "bossy" or "bitchy" when a woman does it.

Problems occur when people use emotive words without labeling them as such. You might, for instance, have a long and bitter argument with a friend about whether someone else was being "funny" or

> emotive language
Language that conveys the sender's attitude rather than simply offering an objective description.

"obnoxious," when a more accurate and peaceable way to handle the issue would be to acknowledge that one of you approves of the behavior and the other doesn't.

Along with implicitly judging others, emotive language can be a way of framing our own behavior. For example, men and women use different terms to describe their own levels of alcohol intoxication.[26] Women tend to use terms that describe intoxication levels as moderate, such as "buzzed" and "tipsy." By contrast, men use words suggesting heavy intoxication like "hammered" and "wasted." This sort of difference can shape the amount drinkers consume. "I'm just a little tipsy. I guess I'll have another."

Evasive Language

None of the troublesome language habits we have described so far reflects a deliberate strategy to mislead or antagonize others. Now, however, we'll consider euphemisms and equivocations, two types of language that

Are you a mindful communicator?

Circle the number in each continuum that best represents you.

1. I often pause to think carefully about the words I use. ⟷ I like fast-paced conversations in which I don't have to weigh every word.

         1   2   3   4   5

2. I am precise and factual when I tell a story. ⟷ I tend to exaggerate to get a laugh or make a point.

         1   2   3   4   5

3. I am careful not to offend anyone when I speak. ⟷ I regularly use curse words, and I like to tell an off-color joke now and then.

         1   2   3   4   5

4. When I am upset, I delay talking until I calm down. ⟷ I am upfront about how I feel, even when I'm upset.

         1   2   3   4   5

5. I am careful to use gender-neutral language. ⟷ I see no harm in words such as "policeman" and "salesman."

         1   2   3   4   5

6. I pride myself on speaking proper English. ⟷ I enjoy using up-to-date slang and jargon.

         1   2   3   4   5

7. I'm careful to ask others what they mean rather than assuming I understand their ideas and motives. ⟷ I'm pretty good at understanding what's on others' minds without needing to ask for a lot of clarification.

         1   2   3   4   5

8. In sensitive situations I try to use diplomatic language. ⟷ I am honest, even when it's not what people want to hear.

         1   2   3   4   5

For an interpretation of your responses, see p. 99. ●

speakers use by design to avoid communicating clearly. Although they have some legitimate uses, they also can lead to frustration and confusion.

Euphemisms

A **euphemism** (from the Greek word meaning "to use words of good omen") is a pleasant term substituted for a more direct but potentially less pleasant one. We are using euphemisms when we say "restroom" instead of "toilet" or "full-figured" instead of "overweight." There certainly are cases in which the euphemistic pulling of linguistic punches can be face-saving. It's probably more constructive to ask someone if he or she misspoke rather than to call him or her a liar, for example.

Like many businesses, the airline industry uses euphemisms to avoid upsetting already nervous flyers.[27] For example, rather than saying "turbulence," pilots are more likely to use the term "bumpy air." Likewise, they refer to thunderstorms as "showers," and fog or low visibility as "mist" or "haze."

Equivocation

It's 8:15 P.M., and you are already a half-hour late for your dinner reservation at the fanciest restaurant in town. Your date has finally finished dressing and confronts you with the question "How do I look?" To tell the truth, you hate your date's outfit. You don't want to lie, but on the other hand you don't want to be hurtful. Just as important, you don't want to lose your table by waiting around while he or she changes into something else. You think for a moment and then reply, "What an outfit! Where did you get it?"

Your response in this situation was an **equivocation**—a deliberately vague statement that can be interpreted in more than one way. Earlier in this chapter we talked about how *unintentional* equivocation can lead to misunderstandings, but here we are focused on *intentionally ambiguous speech* that is used to avoid lying on one hand and telling a painful truth on the other. Equivocations have several advantages.[28] They spare the receiver from the embarrassment that might come from a completely truthful answer, and it can be easier for the sender to equivocate than to suffer the discomfort of being honest.

As with euphemisms, high-level abstractions, and many other types of communication, it's impossible to say that equivocation is always helpful or harmful. As you learned in Chapter 1, competent communication behavior is situational. Your success in relating to others will depend on your ability to analyze yourself, the other person, and the situation when deciding whether to be equivocal or direct.

> euphemism
A pleasant-sounding term used in place of a more direct but less pleasant one.

> equivocation
A vague statement that can be interpreted in more than one way.

Describe the ways in which male and female speech patterns are typically alike and how they differ.

OBJECTIVE 4.4

GENDER AND LANGUAGE

So far we have mostly discussed language use as if it were identical for both sexes. Some theorists and researchers, though, have argued that there are significant differences between the way men and women speak, while others have argued that any differences are insignificant.[29] As we explore the research on gender differences in communication, keep in mind that many of the findings describe general characteristics. As an individual, your behavior may not match the findings.

Content

The first research on the influence of gender on conversational topics was conducted more than 70 years ago. Despite the changes in male and female roles since then, some gender-linked patterns remain remarkably similar.[30] For example, both men and women still talk frequently about work, movies, and television. However, women are likely to spend more time discussing relational issues such as family, friends, and emotions, whereas men are more likely to discuss recreational topics such as sports, technology use, and nightlife. The research summarized in Figure 4-2 highlights other differences in the way men and women use language. These differences can lead to frustration when men and women converse with one another. Researchers report that *trivial* is the word often used by both sexes to describe topics discussed by the other sex.

Reasons for Communicating

Research shows that the notion that men and women communicate in dramatically different ways is exaggerated. Both men and women, at least in the dominant cultures of the United States and Canada, use language to build and maintain social relationships.[31] How men and women accomplish these goals is often different, though. Although most communicators try to make their interactions enjoyable, men are more likely than women to emphasize making conversation fun. Their discussions involve a greater amount of joking and good-natured teasing. By contrast, women's conversations focus more frequently on feelings, relationships, and personal problems. In fact, communication researcher Julia Wood flatly states that "for women, talk is the essence of relationships."[32] Nearly 50 percent of the women surveyed said they called friends at least once a week just to talk, whereas less than half as many men did so. In fact, 40 percent of the men surveyed reported that they never called another man just to talk.

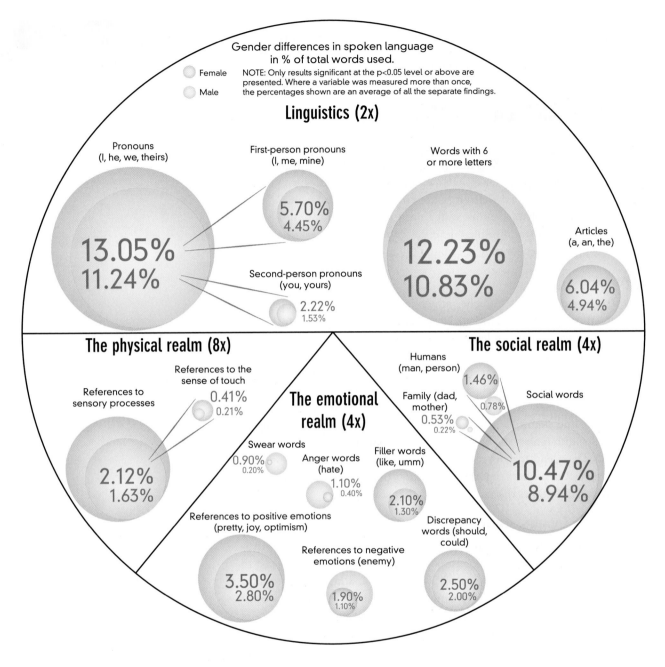

Figure 4-2 Some Gender Differences in Spoken Language

Conversational Style

Some scholarship shows little difference between the ways men and women converse. For example, the popular myth that women are more talkative than men may not be accurate. Researchers found that men and women speak roughly the same number of words per day.[33]

On the other hand, there are ways in which women do behave differently in conversations than do men.[34] For example, women ask more questions in mixed-sex conversations than do men—nearly three times as many, according to one study. Other research has revealed that in mixed-sex conversations, men interrupt women far more than the other way around.

Because women use conversation to pursue social needs, female speech often contains statements that show support for the other person, demonstrate equality, and keep the conversation going. With these goals, it's not surprising that traditionally female speech often contains statements of sympathy and empathy such as "I know what you mean" and "The same thing happened to me!" Women are also inclined to make statements or ask questions that invite the other person to share information, such as "You must have been so mad!" and "What did you do next?" The importance of nurturing a relationship also explains why female speech is often somewhat tentative. Saying, "This is just my opinion …" is less likely to put off a conversational partner than a more definite "Here's what I think.…"

Men's speech is often driven by quite different goals from women's. Men are more likely to use language to accomplish the job at hand than to nourish relationships. This explains why men are less likely than women to disclose their vulnerabilities, which might be considered weaknesses. Because men typically regard talk as a way to solve problems, when someone else is sharing a problem, instead of empathizing, men are prone to offer advice: "That's nothing to worry about …" or "Here's what you need to do.…" Besides taking care of business, men are more likely than women to use conversations to exert control, preserve their independence, and enhance their status. This explains why men more often dominate conversations and one-up their partners. But just because male talk is competitive doesn't mean it's unpleasant. Men often regard talk as a kind of game.[35]

Some gender differences also exist in mediated communication. For example, instant messages written by women tend to be more expressive than ones composed by men.[36] They are more likely to contain laughter ("hehe"), emoticons (smiley faces), emphasis (italics, boldface, repeated letters), and adjectives. However, there are no significant gender differences in a number of other variables—such as questions, words per turn, and hedges.

Given these differences, it's easy to wonder how men and women manage to communicate with one another at all. One reason cross-sex conversations do run smoothly is because women accommodate to the topics men raise. Both men and women regard topics introduced by women as tentative, whereas topics that men introduce are more likely to be pursued. Thus, women seem to grease the wheels of conversation by doing more work than men in maintaining conversations. A complementary difference between men and women also promotes cross-sex conversations: Men are more likely to talk about themselves with women than with other men, and because women are willing to adapt to this topic, conversations are likely to run smoothly, if one-sidedly.

Occupation and Gender Roles

Some of the differences in the ways men and women speak can be attributed to the speaker's occupation and social role. For example, male day-care teachers' speech to their students resembles the language of female teachers more closely than it resembles the language of fathers at home. Overall, doctors interrupt their patients more often than the reverse, although male patients do interrupt female physicians more often than their male counterparts. A close study of trial transcripts showed that the speaker's experience on the witness stand and occupation had more to do with language use than did gender. If women generally use "powerless" language, this may possibly reflect their historical social role in society at large. As the balance of power grows more equal between men and women, we can expect many linguistic differences to shrink.

Another powerful force that influences the way individual men and women speak is their *gender role*—the social orientation that governs behavior—rather than their biological sex. As mentioned in Chapter 2, researchers have identified three gender types: masculine, feminine, and androgynous. These gender types don't always line up neatly with sex. There are "masculine" females, "feminine" males, and androgynous communicators who combine traditionally masculine and feminine characteristics.

Social expectations about the way men and women "should" communicate are presented all around us. Interviewers of *The Amazing Spider-Man* costars asked Andrew Garfield about his experience as an actor, and asked Emma Stone about her hair color and clothing.

Q *Do you ever feel pressured to "behave like a lady" or "act like a man"?*

Research shows that linguistic differences are often a function of gender more than the speaker's biological sex. Masculine communicators—whether male or female—use more dominant language than either feminine or androgynous speakers. Feminine speakers have the most submissive speaking style; and androgynous speakers fall between these extremes.

Biological Factors

Our behavior is driven partly by sex hormones—primarily estrogen and testosterone. Both women and men make the same hormones, but the amounts they produce differ. And within each sex, hormone production varies. For this reason it's more accurate to talk about the link between hormone level and behavior than to make gross generalizations based on biological sex.[37] For example, men with high testosterone levels are more competitive than those with lower levels of the hormone, and they respond more emotionally when faced with setbacks.[38] Research also suggests that men with higher levels of testosterone are less likely than others to engage in emotional, socially connecting language.[39] By contrast, estrogen is associated with heightened emotional experiences and expression of emotion.[40]

Despite these differences, it's overly simplistic to view testosterone as an antisocial substance and estrogen as an emotional one. In some conditions, testosterone can motivate behaviors that are highly altruistic, especially in individuals holding socially protective positions, such as firefighters, police officers, and soldiers.[41] And despite the common belief that women are moody because of cyclic changes in estrogen, only 3 percent to 8 percent of women experience hormonal moods swings beyond the range of everyday emotions.[42] All in all, hormones are one factor, but not usually the most important factor, in how we interact with others.[43]

Social Norms

Along with biology, social norms shape the way men and women communicate. In contemporary society, power and ownership of material things have been widely viewed as measures of success and sources of prestige. In many societies, males have been expected to serve as the providers. By contrast, women have historically had less overt power and occupied more nurturing roles.

Given these facts it's not surprising that men have been associated with the task-focused style of communication described in the previous pages, and that women have historically adopted styles of speech that promote smoothly functioning relationships.

Both styles have obvious advantages. A task-focused style is clear and decisive. Because it is associated with traditionally powerful roles, this approach to speaking is a way to gain and keep control. But along with these advantages, characteristically male speech can be regarded as confrontational and off-putting. And although a no-nonsense approach might be efficient, it isn't ideally suited to keeping personal relationships running smoothly and happily.

The flip side is also true: Speech styles that work well in personal relationships can lead to a lack of recognition and respect in task-oriented environments. Even in personal relationships, being exclusively focused on nurturing can make it hard to stand up to intimidation.

Transcending Gender Boundaries

By now it should be clear that neither stereotypically male nor female styles of speech meet all communication needs. Instead, flexibility is the key to using language effectively. You can improve your linguistic competence by switching and combining styles. If you reflexively take an approach that focuses on the content of others' remarks, consider paying more attention to the unstated relational messages behind their words. If you generally focus on the unexpressed-feelings part of a message, consider being more task oriented. If your first instinct is to be supportive, consider the value of offering advice; and if advice is your reflexive way of responding, think about whether offering support and understanding might sometimes be more helpful.

Research confirms what common sense suggests: A "mixed-gender strategy" that balances the traditionally masculine, task-oriented approach with the characteristically feminine, relationship-oriented approach is rated most highly by both male and female respondents.[44] Choosing the approach that is right for the other communicator and the situation can create satisfaction far greater than that which comes from using a single stereotypical style.

Where does your speech fit on the spectrum from stereotypically masculine to stereotypically feminine?

CHECK YOUR UNDERSTANDING

OBJECTIVE 4.1 Explain how symbols and linguistic rules allow people to achieve shared meaning.

THE NATURE OF LANGUAGE

Any language is a collection of symbols governed by a variety of rules and used to convey messages between people. Because of its symbolic nature, language is not a precise tool: Meanings rest in people, not in words themselves. In order for effective communication to occur, it is necessary to negotiate meanings for ambiguous statements.

Analyze a specific incident in which you used a different linguistic rule than your conversational partner. What was the rule in question? What were the consequences? How might you have managed this situation differently?

OBJECTIVE 4.2 Identify ways that language shapes our attitudes and reflects how we feel about ourselves and others.

THE POWER OF LANGUAGE

Language not only describes people, ideas, processes, and events, it also shapes our perceptions of them in areas including status, credibility, and attitudes about gender and ethnicity. Along with influencing our attitudes, language also reflects our attitudes. The words we use and our manner of speech reflect power, affiliation, and responsibility.

Describe the same person in five different sentences. What do the descriptions suggest about your opinion of this person? How are others likely to view this person based on your word choices?

OBJECTIVE 4.3 Recognize and identify ways to remedy vague, confusing, and disruptive language.

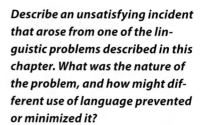

TROUBLESOME LANGUAGE

Many types of language have the potential to create misunderstandings. Other types of language can result in unnecessary conflicts. In still other cases, speech and writing can be evasive to avoid expressing unwelcome messages.

Describe an unsatisfying incident that arose from one of the linguistic problems described in this chapter. What was the nature of the problem, and how might different use of language prevented or minimized it?

Describe the ways in which male and female speech patterns are typically alike and how they differ.

GENDER AND LANGUAGE

The relationship between gender and language is complex. Although there are differences in the ways men and women speak, not all differences in language use can be accounted for by the speaker's gender. Occupation, social philosophy, and orientation toward problem solving also influence the use of language, and gender can be more of an influence than biological sex.

Describe how gender roles influence the way you communicate and what you communicate about. Explain how other factors, such as your major or occupation, influence your communication style. Which factors do you think are most influential?

KEY TERMS

convergence p. 83
divergence p. 84
emotive language p. 88
equivocal words p. 85
equivocation p. 90
euphemism p. 90

factual statement p. 87
inferential statement p. 88
jargon p. 86
language p. 76
opinion statement p. 87
phonological rules p. 77

pragmatic rules p. 79
relative words p. 85
semantic rules p. 78
slang p. 85
symbols p. 76
syntactic rules p. 77

Interpreting Your Responses

If you circled mostly 1s, 2s, and 3s, you tend to be a mindful communicator who regards language as a powerful and precise tool. Low scores on Items 1, 2, and 4 suggest that you typically avoid emotive language and exaggerations. Low scores on Items 3 and 5 indicate that you are cautious about using language that might be considered offensive. A low score on Item 7 shows that you recognize the potential for misunderstandings, even in apparently clear statements. A low score on Item 8 suggests you are tactful, but your language may seem euphemistic or equivocal at times.

If you circled mostly 3s, 4s, and 5s, you tend to use language in artistic and spontaneous ways, but you may sometimes go too far. High scores on Items 1 and 8 suggest that you value open communication and a good debate, but keep in mind that your spontaneity may lead you to risky inferences. High scores on Items 2 and 6 indicate that you value colorful language and are probably an engaging storyteller, but you may confuse people who aren't familiar with your style or vocabulary. If you scored high on Item 4, you probably confront issues head-on, but be careful that your language doesn't become overly emotive, which can escalate an argument. High scores on Items 3 and 5 indicate that you don't take words too seriously, but bear in mind that others may. Your statements may cause offense.

FOR FURTHER EXPLORATION

For more communication resources, see the *Essential Communication* website at www.oup.com/us/ec. There you will find a variety of resources: "Media Room" examples from popular films and television shows to further illustrate important concepts, a list of relevant books and articles, links to descriptions of feature films and television shows at the *Now Playing* website, study aids, and a self-test to check your understanding of the material in this chapter.

5 Listening

learning

learning
Objectives ✳

5.1   Describe the three most common misconceptions about listening.

5.2   Identify faulty listening behaviors and factors that make effective listening difficult.

5.3   Distinguish between the four different types of listening and identify practical strategies for each.

5.4   Explain how efforts at social support are influenced by online communities and gender roles.

CORRECTING MISCONCEPTIONS

We spend more time listening to others than we spend engaged in any other type of communication. In fact, when business executives were asked what skills were most important on the job, they mentioned listening more than any other skill or talent, including technical competence, computer knowledge, administrative talent, and creativity.[1] In spite of its importance, however, listening is misunderstood by most people.

Marlee Matlin, from *Switched at Birth* and many other movies and television programs, is an activist and award-winning actor. As she puts it, she "just happens to be deaf." Many members of the Deaf community say they listen through their eyes and other senses.

Q *In what ways do non-auditory stimuli influence the way you listen?*

Hearing and Listening Are Not the Same

In Chapter 1, we introduced the term *receiving* to describe the process by which a message is decoded. In fact, the process of receiving a message involves multiple stages. **Hearing** is the physiological ability to perceive the presence of sounds in the environment. If we have that ability, hearing occurs automatically when sound waves strike our eardrums and cause vibrations that are transmitted to our brains. By contrast, in a traditional sense, **listening** occurs when the brain reconstructs these electrochemical impulses into a representation of the original sound and then gives them meaning. Unlike hearing, listening has a psychological dimension: It requires conscious effort and skill.

Based on this explanation, you might think that because people who are deaf cannot hear they cannot listen. In fact, many people who are deaf find alternate ways of accomplishing the same objective. The phrase "I listen with my eyes" is common in the Deaf community.[2] It refers not only to sign language but to the ability to gain meaning by using all of the senses. In reality, even those of us who can hear well "listen" with more than our ears.

Many times we hear but do not listen. Sometimes we purposely tune out unwanted signals—everything from a noisy lawn mower or highway traffic to unwanted criticism. A closer look at successful listening shows that it consists of four stages: attending, understanding, responding, and remembering.

1. In **attending**, you pay attention to a signal. What you pay attention to depends on your needs, wants, desires, and interests. For example, you might tune out your roommates' conversation until you hear your name mentioned or notice that they seem to be arguing, in which case you might start paying attention.

2. Through **understanding**, you make sense of a message. Communication researchers use the term **listening fidelity** to describe the degree to which what a listener understands corresponds with the message the sender attempts to communicate.[3] "High fidelity" listening occurs when there is a close match between the sender's thoughts and feelings and the receiver's understanding of them. In "low fidelity" listening, there's a significant mismatch between the two. Understanding often requires that you grasp the syntax of the language being spoken, engage in semantic decoding, and know the pragmatic rules to figure out a speaker's meaning from the context and nonverbal cues surrounding it. In addition to these steps, understanding depends on your ability to organize the information you hear into recognizable form.

3. In **responding** to a message, you give observable feedback to the speaker. Offering feedback serves two important functions: It helps you clarify your understanding of a speaker's message, and it shows that you care about what that speaker is saying. As discussed in Chapter 1,

> **hearing**
The process wherein sound waves strike the eardrum and cause vibrations that are transmitted to the brain.

> **listening**
Process wherein the brain reconstructs electrochemical impulses generated by hearing into representations of the original sound and gives them meaning.

> **attending**
The process of focusing on certain stimuli from the environment.

> **understanding**
The act of interpreting a message by following syntactic, semantic, and pragmatic rules.

> **listening fidelity**
The degree of congruence between what a listener understands and what the message sender was attempting to communicate.

> **responding**
Providing observable feedback to another person's behavior or speech.

> **remembering**
The act of recalling previously introduced information, short-term and long-term.

> **residual message**
The part of a message a receiver can recall after short- and long-term memory loss.

Are you a good listener? How would family members rate your listening skills?

communication is transactional in nature. As listeners we are active participants in a communication transaction. In other words, at the same time that we receive messages we also send them.

4. Through **remembering**, you recall previously introduced information.[4] Research has revealed that people remember only about half of what they hear immediately after hearing it.[5] This goes down to 35 percent eight hours later, and 25 percent in two months. Of course, these amounts vary from person to person and depend on the importance of the information being recalled.[6] Given the amount of information we process every day—from instructors, friends, TV, social media, and other sources—the **residual message** (what we remember) is a small fraction of what we hear.

Listening Is Not a Natural Process

Although it may sometimes appear that listening is like breathing—a natural activity that people do well, the truth is that listening is a skill much like speaking: Everybody does it, though few people do it well.

In the work place, good listeners are typically more influential than their less attentive peers, in large part because they are seen as more agreeable, open, and approachable than people who listen poorly.[7] But perceptions of what makes a good listener vary widely. In one study, 144 managers were asked to rate their listening skills. Astonishingly, not one of the managers described himself or herself as a "poor" or "very poor" listener, whereas 94 percent rated themselves as "good" or "very good."[8] The favorable self-ratings contrasted sharply with the perceptions of the managers' employees, many of whom said their boss's listening skills were weak. The good news is that, although some poor listening is inevitable, it can be improved through instruction and training.[9]

All Listeners Do Not Receive the Same Message

When two or more people are listening to a speaker, we tend to assume that they all hear and understand the same message. In fact, such uniform comprehension isn't the case. In Chapter 3, we pointed out the many factors that cause each of us to perceive an event differently. Physiological factors, social roles, cultural background, personal interests, and needs all shape and distort the raw data we hear into uniquely different messages. For example, your friend might find a joke funny, whereas you consider it silly or even offensive.

Identify faulty listening behaviors and factors that make effective listening difficult.

OBJECTIVE 5.2

CHALLENGES TO EFFECTIVE LISTENING

Given the number of messages to which we're exposed, it's impractical to listen carefully and thoughtfully 100 percent of the time. Social scientists use the term **mindless listening** to describe passive listening in which the receiver absorbs a speaker's ideas passively, rather as a sponge absorbs water.[10] This sort of low-level information processing doesn't involve much give and take. But when the information doesn't require much effort on our part, passive listening offers an advantage: It frees us to focus on messages that require **mindful listening** or more careful, active attention.[11] The physical changes that occur during mindful listening show the effort it takes: Heart rate quickens, respiration increases, and body temperature rises.[12] These changes are similar to the body's reaction to physical effort, and they are often just as taxing.

> **mindless listening**
Passive, low-level information processing.

> **mindful listening**
Active, high-level information processing.

Listening can be a challenge, even when the message is compelling. As Malala Yousafzai talks about her miraculous recovery from a Taliban attack, some members of her audience appear more attentive than others.

How can you listen mindfully in the face of distractions?

Faulty Listening Behaviors

It's okay if you don't listen effectively all of the time, but there is worrisome evidence that we regularly engage in behavior that prevents us from understanding truly important messages.

> pseudolisteners

Receivers who imitate true listening but whose minds are elsewhere.

Pseudolisteners give the appearance of being attentive: They look you in the eye, nod and smile at the right times, and even may answer you occasionally. That appearance of interest, however, is a polite facade to mask thoughts that have nothing to do with what you are saying.

> selective listeners

Receivers who respond only to messages that interest them.

Selective listeners respond only to the parts of a speaker's remarks that interest them. All of us are selective listeners from time to time, as, for instance, when we ignore commercials but pay attention when a weather report comes on. In other cases, selective listening occurs only when the conversation turns to a topic that interests us.

> defensive listeners

Receivers who perceive a speaker's comments as an attack.

Defensive listeners take innocent comments as personal attacks. Teenagers who perceive parents' questions about friends and activities as snooping are defensive listeners, as are insecure breadwinners who explode when their mates mention money and touchy parents who view any questioning by their children as a threat to their authority. Many defensive listeners have low self-esteem and project their insecurities onto others.

In the TV show *Modern Family*, Lily Tucker-Pritchett and sisters Alex and Haley Dunphy experience the usual run-ins of kids and their parents. The older girls, especially, often resist their mom's and dad's advice on the grounds that they are butting into the teens' private affairs. The three are played by Aubrey Anderson-Emmons, Ariel Winter, amd Sarah Hyland (left to right).

Q *When are you a defensive listener?*

Ambushers listen carefully, but only because they are collecting information to attack what you have to say. The cross-examining prosecution attorney is a good example of an ambusher. Using this kind of strategy will justifiably initiate defensiveness on the other's part.

Insulated listeners avoid certain topics. Whenever a subject arises that they'd rather not deal with, insulated listeners simply fail to hear it or, rather, to acknowledge it.

Insensitive listeners are not able to look beyond a speaker's words to understand the real meaning. Instead, they take a speaker's remarks at face value. A classic example of insensitive listening occurs in conversations like this:

A: "How's it going?"

　　　　　B: (With a gloomy expression and a sigh) "Okay, I guess."

A: (Brightly) "Great!"

Stage hogs (sometimes called "conversational narcissists") try to turn the topic of conversations to themselves, often by interrupting, instead of showing interest in the speaker.[13] Stage hogging prevents the listener from learning information and can damage the relationship between the interrupter and the speaker. In fact, applicants who interrupt the questions of an employment interviewer are likely to be rated less favorably than job seekers who wait until the interviewer has finished speaking before they respond.[14]

Reasons for Poor Listening

What causes people to listen poorly? There are several reasons, some of which can be avoided and others that are inescapable facts of life.

Message Overload

The amount of speech most of us encounter every day makes careful listening to everything we hear impossible. Along with the deluge of face-to-face messages, we are bombarded by phone calls, emails, tweets, texts, and chats. This information overload has made the challenge of attending more difficult than at any time in human history.[15] Experts suggest that we may listen better if we don't try to listen every minute. In the interest of focusing on what matters most, they suggest that we turn off communication technology while we work on complex tasks, send clear and brief emails with specific subject lines, and think twice before hitting the "reply to all" button.[16]

Rapid Thought

Although we are capable of understanding speech at rates up to 600 words per minute, the average person speaks between 100 and 140 words per minute.[17] Thus, we have a great deal of mental "spare time" to spend while someone is talking. And the temptation is to use this time in ways that don't relate to the speaker's ideas, such as thinking about personal interests, daydreaming, planning a rebuttal, and so on. To combat these temptations, instead try using spare time to understand the speaker's ideas better. Rephrase the speaker's ideas in your own words. Ask yourself how the ideas might be useful to you. Consider other angles that the speaker might not have mentioned.

Psychological Noise

We are often wrapped up in personal concerns that are of more immediate importance to us than the messages others send. It's hard to pay attention to someone else when you're anticipating an upcoming test or thinking about the wonderful time you had last night. Yet we still feel we have to "listen" politely to others, and so we continue with our charade. It usually takes a conscious effort to set aside your personal concerns if you expect to give others' messages the attention they deserve. Everyone's mind wanders at one time or another, but excessive preoccupation is both a reason for and a sign of poor listening.

Physical Noise

The world in which we live often presents distractions that make it hard to pay attention to others. The sound of traffic, music, others' speech, and the like interfere with our ability to hear well. Also, fatigue or other forms of discomfort (such as excessive heat or cold) can distract us from paying attention to a speaker's remarks. You can often listen better by insulating yourself from outside distractions. This may involve removing the sources of noise: turning off the television, putting away your phone, shutting the book you were reading, closing the window, and so on. In some cases, you and the speaker may need to find a more hospitable place to speak in order to make listening work.

Hearing Problems

Sometimes a hearing problem can affect a person's ability to listen. One survey explored the feelings of adults who have spouses with hearing loss. Nearly two-thirds of the respondents said they feel annoyed when their partner can't hear them clearly. Almost a quarter said that they felt ignored, hurt, or sad. Many of the respondents believed their spouses were in denial about their condition, which made the problem even more frustrating.[18]

Older people aren't the only ones affected. The number of young people with hearing loss is on the rise, in part because of earbuds and similar technology that make it possible to blast our eardrums with dangerously loud noise.[19] Medical experts have found that one in eight children and teens and almost one in five adults have suffered permanent damage to their hearing from excessive exposure to noise.[20] Prevention is the key to preserving hearing. When possible, avoid noisy machines and overly loud music, and use earplugs when you can't as, for example, at a concert.

Which challenges to effective listening affect you the most?

When hearing loss goes undetected, both the person suffering and others can become frustrated and annoyed at the ineffective communication that results. If you suspect that you or someone you know suffers from hearing loss, have a clinician or audiologist perform an examination. Once a hearing problem has been diagnosed, treatment is often possible.

Faulty Assumptions

Sometimes we give others a mental brush-off and assume that their remarks don't have much value. When one business consultant asked some of her clients why they interrupted colleagues, she received the following responses:

> My idea is better than theirs.
> If I don't interrupt them, I'll never get to say my idea.
> I know what they are about to say.[21]

The egotism behind these comments is stunning. Dismissing others' ideas before considering them may be justified occasionally, but consider how you would feel if other people dismissed your comments regularly without hearing you out.

Perceived Advantages of Talking

Whatever the goal—to have a prospective boss hire you, to convince others to vote for the candidate of your choice, or to describe the way you want your hair cut—the key to success *seems* to be the ability to speak well. Speaking also provides the opportunity to gain the admiration, respect, or liking of others—or so you may think. Tell jokes, and everyone may think you're a comedian. Offer advice, and they might be grateful for your help. Tell them all you know, and they could be impressed by your wisdom. Although speaking at the right time can lead people to appreciate you, too much talking often results in stage hogging.

Cultural Differences

The behaviors that define a good listener vary by culture. Americans are most impressed by listeners who ask questions and make supportive statements.[22] By contrast, Iranians, as members of a high-context culture (see Chapter 3), tend to judge people's listening skills based on more subtle nonverbal indicators such as their posture and eye contact.[23] Germans are most likely to think someone a good listener if he or she shows continuous attention to the speaker.[24] In some cultures, people may overlook a quick glance at a phone or TV screen, while in other cultures they may be insulted by such inattentive behavior.

Cocultural differences also shape perceptions of listening. If you grew up texting and tweeting, you may not think that glancing at your phone during a meal is cause for offense. But if you're sharing a meal with a date or a prospective boss, particularly with someone from an older generation, it can be perceived as a lack of attention and respect. It's also worth noting that research shows that multitasking—such as dividing attention between a personal conversation and social media—can cause us to lose focus.[25]

Media Influences

A final challenge to serious listening is the influence of communication media. Figure 5.1 shows how multitasking leads smartphone users to divide their attention between a variety of media. It's hard enough to focus on a person-to-person conversation when you're using even one device. When multiple types of media compete for attention, the difficulty intensifies, especially when it comes to understanding complicated ideas and feelings.

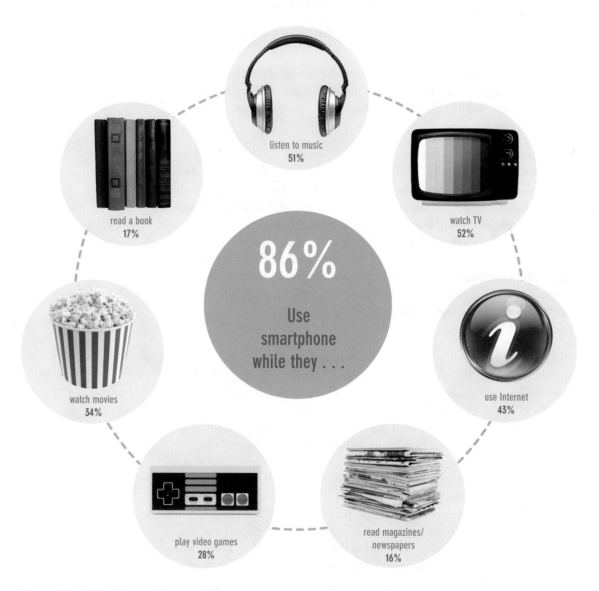

listen to music
51%

watch TV
52%

86%

Use
smartphone
while they . . .

use Internet
43%

read a book
17%

watch movies
34%

play video games
28%

read magazines/
newspapers
16%

Figure 5-1 Multitasking Divides Attention. Eighty-six percent of people surveyed said they used their smartphones while performing other tasks.

Psychologist Sherry Turkle and others propose that an overreliance on social media is eroding our social skills, including our ability to listen well.[26] Given that we are not likely to give up social media any time soon, Turkle offers some tips for listening effectively in this age of electronic distractions:[27]

Don't reach for a device every time you get a free moment. Instead, take stock of what you are seeing, feeling, smelling, and hearing. It will make you more attentive to things and people around you.

Create "device-free zones" such as the dinner table, car, or living room in which you can be alone with your thoughts or converse without distractions.

Share your feelings with someone in person every so often, rather than posting or tweeting them.

Consider actually "being there" for a friend in need rather than just posting or tweeting a message of support.

Distinguish between the four different types of listening and identify practical strategies for each.

TYPES OF LISTENING

By now you can see that listening well isn't easy. However, there are a number of reasons people invest the effort to listen carefully. In this section, we'll distinguish between four different types of listening and discuss some strategies for each type. As you read about the different approaches to listening, you may note that you habitually use some more than others. We can improve our listening by thinking carefully about the goals for an encounter and using a listening style that best suits the situation. When efficiency matters most, use task-oriented listening. When your relationship with the speaker needs attention, adopt a relational approach. When analysis or critical thinking is required, use listening styles best suited to them. You can also boost your effectiveness by assessing the listening preferences of your conversational partners and adapting your style to them.

Task-Oriented Listening

Task-oriented listening is designed to secure information necessary to get a job done. The situations that call for task-oriented listening are endless and varied: following an instructor's comments in class, hearing a description of a new game or app that you're thinking about buying, getting tips from a coach on how to improve your athletic skill, taking directions from your boss—the list goes on and on. When task-oriented listening is appropriate,

> task-oriented listening
A listening style that is primarily concerned with accomplishing the task at hand.

strategies such as extracting key ideas, asking questions, paraphrasing, and taking notes may help you be more effective.

Extract Key Ideas

It's easy to lose patience with long-winded speakers who never seem to get to the point—or have one, for that matter. Nonetheless, most people do have a point. By using your ability to think more quickly than the speaker can talk, you may be able to extract the main point (or what we call a thesis in Chapter 12) from the surrounding mass of words you're hearing.

Ask Questions

When you need additional information to clarify your idea of the sender's message, ask. For instance, if you're meeting friends at a restaurant that you've never been to, you might ask "What's the menu like?" or "Is it casual or upscale?" In more serious situations, questions could include "Why does that bother you so much?" or "You sound upset—is there something wrong?" Questions such as these ask the speaker to elaborate on information already given.

Paraphrase

> paraphrasing

Feedback in which the receiver rewords the speaker's thoughts and feelings to verify understanding, demonstrate empathy, or help others solve their problems.

Sometimes asking questions won't give you the clarification that you seek. Another type of feedback, termed **paraphrasing**, involves restating in your own words the message you thought the speaker sent, without adding anything new.

(To a direction giver) *"You're telling me to drive down to the traffic light by the high school and turn toward the mountains, is that it?"*

(To the boss) *"So you need me both this Saturday* and *next Saturday —right?"*

(To a professor) *"When you said, 'Don't worry about the low grade on the quiz,' did you mean it won't count against my grade?"*

In other cases, a paraphrase will reflect your understanding of the speaker's *feelings*:

"You said you've 'had it with this relationship.' Does this mean you're angry, or that you're breaking up with me?"

"You said you 'have a minute,' but does that mean you're in a rush or you can talk now?"

"You said 'Forget it,' but it sounds like you're mad. Are you?"

Take Notes

Understanding others is crucial, but comprehending their ideas doesn't guarantee that you will remember them. As mentioned previously, listeners usually forget almost two-thirds of what they hear, so it's smart

❓ What is your listening style?

To discover your listening tendencies, fill in the following survey. Use 1 as "strongly disagree" and 7 as "strongly agree." The section(s) in which you mark higher numbers (5, 6, or 7) suggest types of listening that you value.

Task-Oriented Listening							
I am impatient with people who ramble during conversations.	1	2	3	4	5	6	7
I get frustrated when people get off topic during a conversation.	1	2	3	4	5	6	7
I prefer speakers who quickly get to the point.	1	2	3	4	5	6	7
Relational Listening							
I listen to understand the emotions and mood of the speaker.	1	2	3	4	5	6	7
I listen primarily to build and maintain relationships with others.	1	2	3	4	5	6	7
I enjoy listening to others because it allows me to connect with them.	1	2	3	4	5	6	7
Analytical Listening							
I tend to withhold judgment about another's ideas until I have heard everything he or she has to say.	1	2	3	4	5	6	7
When listening to others, I consider all sides of the issue before responding.	1	2	3	4	5	6	7
I fully listen to what a person has to say before forming any opinions.	1	2	3	4	5	6	7
Critical Listening							
I often catch errors in other speakers' logic.	1	2	3	4	5	6	7
I tend to naturally notice errors in what other speakers say.	1	2	3	4	5	6	7
When listening to others, I notice contradictions in what they say.	1	2	3	4	5	6	7

Adapted with the authors' permission from: Bodie, G. D., Worthington, D. L., & Gearhart, C. G. (2013). The Revised Listening Styles Profile (LSP-R): Development and validation. Communication Quarterly, 61, 72–90. *doi: 10.1080/01463373.2012.720343.* ●

to take notes instead of relying on your memory. Sometimes these notes may be simple and brief: a phone number or a list of things to pick up at the store. In other cases—a lecture, for example—your notes need to be much more detailed. Either way, make sure you take notes right away, record only key ideas rather than scrambling to put down every word, and develop a note-taking format that works for you—whether it's an outline or

In the movie *The Help*, Skeeter (Emma Stone) draws upon her journalistic training—including being a good listener and note taker—to chronicle the injustices perpetrated against African American women.

Q *Do you find that taking notes helps you focus more effectively on complex information?*

> relational listening

A listening style that is driven primarily by the goal of building emotional closeness with the speaker.

simply using bolding, underlining, or asterisks to flag especially important information. After you develop a consistent format, your notes will not only help you remember information but also help make that information useful to you.

Relational Listening

The goal of **relational listening** is to emotionally connect with others. Here are some tips for accomplishing that.

Allow Enough Time

Encouraging others to share their thoughts and feelings can take time. If you're in a hurry, it may be best to reschedule a relationally focused conversation for a better time.

Listen for Unexpressed Thoughts and Feelings

People don't always say what's on their minds or in their hearts. There are lots of reasons for this: tact, confusion, lack of awareness, fear of being judged negatively . . . the list is a long one. When relationship building is the goal, it can be valuable to listen for unexpressed messages. Consider a few examples:

STATEMENT	POSSIBLE UNEXPRESSED MESSAGE
"Don't apologize. It's not a big deal."	"I'm angry (or hurt, disappointed) by what you did."
"You're going clubbing tonight? That sounds like fun!	"I'd like to come along."
"Check out this news story. That's my little sister!"	"I'm proud of what she did."
"That was quite a party you [neighbors] had last night. You were still going strong at 3 a.m."	"The noise bothered me."
"You like gaming? I do too!"	"Perhaps we can hang out."

Encourage Further Comments

You can also strengthen relationships simply by encouraging others to say more. Great teachers harness this power regularly. They know that students often learn more when they ask questions and work through problems than when they are given the answers up front.[28]

Even brief interactions may have relational dimensions. Acknowledging the spoken and unexpressed feelings of others can improve the quality of exchanges. To a harassed customer service rep you might sympathetically say, "Busy day, huh?" Or, you might thank an especially patient salesperson by saying, "I really appreciate you taking time to explain this so patiently."

Analytical Listening

Whereas relational listening aims to enhance the relationship, the goal of **analytical listening** is to fully understand the message. Analytical listeners explore ideas or issues from a variety of perspectives in order to understand them as fully as possible. Analytical listening is particularly valuable when issues are complicated, but it can sometimes be time-consuming. Strategies for listening analytically include waiting to evaluate until after you've listened, separating the message from the speaker, and searching for value, even in bad situations.

> analytical listening
Listening in which the primary goal is to fully understand the message, prior to any evaluation.

Listen for Information before Evaluating

The principle of listening for information before evaluating seems almost too obvious to mention. Yet all of us are guilty of judging a speaker's ideas before we completely understand them. The tendency to make premature judgments is especially strong when the ideas we hear conflict with our own beliefs.

Separate the Message from the Speaker

At times you may discount the value of a message because of the person who presents it. Even the most boring instructors, the most idiotic relatives, and the most demanding bosses occasionally make good points. If you write off everything a person says before you consider it, you may be cheating yourself out of some valuable information.

Search for Value

You can find some value in even the worst situations. Consider how you might listen opportunistically when you find yourself locked in a boring conversation with someone whose ideas you believe are worthless. Rather than torture yourself, you could keep yourself amused—and perhaps learn something useful—by listening carefully until you can answer the following (unspoken) questions:

"Is there anything useful in what this person is saying?"

"What led the speaker to come up with ideas like these?"

"What lessons can I learn from this person that will keep me from sounding the same way in other situations?"

Critical Listening

> critical listening

Listening in which the goal is to evaluate the quality or accuracy of the speaker's remarks.

The goal of **critical listening** is to go beyond understanding and analyzing a topic to try to assess its quality. At their best, critical listeners apply the tools of analytical listening to see whether an idea holds up under careful scrutiny. Critical listening can be especially helpful when the goal is to investigate a problem, but some may view critical listeners as nitpickers. When critical listening is appropriate, it's a good idea to examine the speaker's evidence and reasoning, evaluate the speaker's credibility, and assess the speaker's emotional appeals.

Examine the Speaker's Evidence and Reasoning

Speakers usually offer some kind of support to back up their statements. A car dealer who argues that domestic cars are just as reliable as imports might cite frequency-of-repair statistics from *Consumer Reports* or refer you to satisfied customers, for example; and a professor arguing that students don't work as hard as they used to might tell stories about then and now to back up the thesis.

Chapter 12 describes several types of supporting material that can be used to prove a point: definitions, descriptions, analogies, statistics, and so on. Whatever form the support takes, you can ask several questions to determine the quality of a speaker's evidence, such as "Is the evidence recent?" and "Does the evidence come from a reliable source?"

Critical listeners also look at how that evidence is put together to prove a point. Logicians have identified more than 100 logical fallacies—errors in reasoning that can lead to false conclusions.[29] Chapter 14 identifies some of the most common ones.

Evaluate the Speaker's Credibility

The acceptability of an idea often depends on its source. If your longtime family friend, a self-made millionaire, invites you to invest your life savings in jojoba fruit futures, you might be grateful for the tip. If your deadbeat brother-in-law makes the same offer, you would probably laugh off the suggestion. Chapter 14 discusses credibility in detail, but two questions provide a quick guideline for deciding whether or not to accept a speaker as an authority:

Is the speaker competent? Does the speaker have the experience or the expertise to qualify as an authority on this subject? Note that someone who is knowledgeable in one area may not be as well qualified to comment in another area. For instance, your friend who can answer any tech question might be a terrible advisor when the subject turns to the best place to buy shoes.

Is the speaker impartial? Knowledge alone isn't enough to certify a speaker's ideas as acceptable. People who have a personal stake in the outcome of a topic are likely to be biased. The unqualified praise a commission-earning salesperson gives a product may be more suspect than the mixed review you get from a user. This doesn't mean you should disregard any comments you hear from an involved party—only that you should consider the possibility of intentional or unintentional bias.

Assess Emotional Appeals

Sometimes emotion alone may be enough reason to persuade you. You might "lend" your friend $20 even though you don't expect to see the money again soon. In other cases, however, it's a mistake to let yourself be swayed by emotion when the logic of a point isn't sound. The too-good-to-be-true promises in an ad or the lure of low monthly payments probably are not good enough reasons to buy a product you can't afford. Again, the fallacies described in Chapter 14 will help you recognize flaws in emotional appeals.

Which types of listening do you engage in most often?

When they see this ad for Sharpie pens, do you think most people consider international soccer star David Beckham's credentials as an expert on writing utensils, or are they more likely to respond to him on an emotional level?

Q *How might people's feelings about celebrities influence their evaluation of an ad's claims?*

LISTENING AND SOCIAL SUPPORT

As we discussed in the previous section, task-oriented listening is focused on accomplishing something, relational listening can build emotional closeness with the speaker, and analytical and critical listening help us understand a message and evaluate its quality and accuracy. There is, however, another style of listening and responding with a different focus. In **supportive listening**, the primary aim is to help the speaker deal with personal dilemmas. Sometimes the problem is a big one: "I'm not sure this marriage is going to work" or "I can't decide whether to drop out of school." At other times the problem is more modest. A friend might be trying to decide what birthday gift to buy or where to spend a vacation.

> supportive listening

The reception approach to use when others seek help for personal dilemmas.

Social Support Online

In the past, most social support came from personal acquaintances: friends, family, coworkers, and neighbors. More recently, though, there has been an explosion of virtual communities in which strangers share interests and concerns online and seek support from one another on almost every imaginable problem. There are online support groups for addiction, Asperger syndrome, codependency, debt problems, domestic violence, eating disorders, gambling, infertility, miscarriage, sexual abuse, and suicide, to name just a few.[30]

In some aspects, online help is similar to the face-to-face variety. The goals of those who participate or join are to gain information and emotional

In the movie *Her*, Theodore (Joaquin Phoenix) falls in love with Samantha (Scarlett Johansson), the alluring voice of his ultra-sophisticated computer operating system. Although she isn't a real person, Samantha helps Theodore emerge from a prison of self-imposed loneliness.

Q *What qualities would represent your notion of an ideal supportive listener?*

support. In other ways, online support differs from the kind people seek in person.[31] The most obvious difference is *anonymity:* Many members of online communities are strangers who usually have not met in person and may not even know each other's real names. This anonymity may be a benefit that enables people to feel comfortable opening up, but it can also be a drawback, particularly if members are not supportive. For example, the social networking site Reddit has been criticized for encouraging users to post racist, sexist, and homophobic jokes and comments anonymously. Because they cannot be identified, some people may be more likely to say things online that they wouldn't dare say in person.

Other differences between online groups and in-person support include the fact that online groups often focus specifically on a single issue, whereas in a traditional relationship, you're likely to cover a wide range of topics. Another difference involves the rate and amount of self-disclosure. In traditional relationships, people usually reveal personal information slowly and carefully, but with the anonymity of online support groups, they typically open up almost immediately. For millions of people, online support groups provide another valuable tool for getting the help they often desperately need.

Gender and Social Support

Researchers have identified ways that men and women respond differently to others' problems.[32] As a group, women are more likely than men to give supportive responses. They are also usually more skillful at composing supportive messages. By contrast, men tend to respond to others' problems by offering advice or by diverting the topic. In a study of helping styles in sororities and fraternities, researchers found that sorority women frequently responded with emotional support when asked to help. They also rated their sisters as being better than men they knew at listening nonjudgmentally, comforting, and showing concern. Fraternity men, on the other hand, often fit the pattern of offering help by challenging their brothers to evaluate their attitudes and values.

These differences are real, but they aren't as dramatic as they might seem. For example, men are as likely as women to respond supportively when they perceive that the other person is feeling a high degree of emotional stress. Women, on the other hand, are more likely to respond supportively even when others are only moderately stressed.[33]

When and How to Help

Before committing yourself to helping another person—even someone in obvious distress—make sure your support is welcome. In one study, people reported occasions when social support was more harmful than helpful because it made them feel inadequate or incompetent or they received help they didn't feel they needed.[34] Some regarded uninvited help as an intrusion and said it left them feeling more stressed than before.

When help is welcome, there is no single best way to provide it. Depending on the situation and the people involved, any of the styles might work, which is why it is helpful when communicators are comfortable with a wide variety of helping styles. You can boost the odds of choosing the best helping style in each situation by considering three factors.

The situation: Sometimes people need your advice. At other times your encouragement and comfort will be most helpful, and at still other times your analysis or judgment may be truly valuable. There are also times when your prompting and reflecting can help others find their own answers.

The other person: Some people are able to consider advice thoughtfully, whereas others use suggestions to avoid making their own decisions. Many communicators are extremely defensive and aren't capable of receiving analysis or judgments without lashing out. Still others aren't equipped to think through problems clearly.

Your own strengths and weaknesses: You may be best at listening quietly, offering a prompt from time to time. Or perhaps you are especially insightful and can offer a truly useful analysis of the problem. Of course, it's also possible that you may be overly judgmental or too eager to advise, especially when your suggestions aren't invited or productive.

In most cases, the best way to help is to use a combination of responses in a way that meets the needs of the occasion and suits your personal communication style.[35]

How can you use supportive listening to help someone work through a problem?

CHECK YOUR UNDERSTANDING

OBJECTIVE 5.1 Describe the three most common misconceptions about listening.

CORRECTING MISCONCEPTIONS

Even the best message is useless if it goes unreceived or if it is misunderstood. For this reason, listening—the process of giving meaning to an oral message—is a vital part of the communication process. Three myths about listening include that listening and hearing are the same, that listening comes naturally, and that we all receive the same message. Effective listening is a skill that must be developed in order for us to be truly effective in understanding others.

Which of the listening misconceptions described in the chapter characterize your attitudes about listening? What can you do to change your thinking and behavior?

OBJECTIVE 5.2 Identify faulty listening behaviors and factors that make effective listening difficult.

CHALLENGES TO EFFECTIVE LISTENING

There are several faulty listening behaviors that prevent people from understanding truly important messages, including pseudolistening, selective listening, defensive listening, ambushing, insulated listening, insensitive listening, and stage hogging. The reasons why people tend to listen poorly have to do with message overload, rapid thought, psychological and physical noise, hearing problems, faulty assumptions, the perceived advantages of talking, cultural differences, and media influences. Some of these reasons for poor listening can be avoided, while others are inescapable facts of life.

Think of a time when you were not your best as a listener. Did any of the challenges described in this chapter play a role? If so, how? Develop an action plan for managing those factors in the future.

OBJECTIVE 5.3 Distinguish between the four different types of listening and identify practical strategies for each.

TYPES OF LISTENING

There are four main types of listening: task-oriented, relational, analytic, and critical. Effective listeners practice the techniques appropriate to each and are good at choosing listening goals that are appropriate for the circumstances. Task-oriented listening helps people accomplish mutual goals. Relational listening is focused on emotionally connecting with others. Analytic listeners aim to fully understand a speaker's message. Critical listening is appropriate when the goal is to judge the quality of an idea.

Think of specific occasions when you listened to achieve each of the following goals: to accomplish a task, to enhance a relationship, to analyze ideas, and to critically evaluate a message. How effective were you in each type of situation? What could you have done to improve your effectiveness?

OBJECTIVE 5.4 Explain how efforts at social support are influenced by online communities and gender roles.

LISTENING AND SOCIAL SUPPORT

The aim of supportive listening is to help the speaker, not the receiver. Listeners can be most helpful when they use a variety of styles, focus on the emotional dimensions of a message, and avoid being too judgmental. Online communication offers more opportunities for social support than ever before, with the benefit of anonymous and highly focused feedback. In addition, although men and women tend to be equally supportive of people who are in great distress, women typically offer more comfort and concern to moderately stressed friends than men do.

How would people who matter to you most rate your supportive listening skills? What skills and approaches described in this chapter might increase your effectiveness?

KEY TERMS

FOR FURTHER EXPLORATION

For more communication resources, see the _Essential Communication_ website at www.oup.com/us/ec. There you will find a variety of resources: "Media Room" examples from popular films and television shows to further illustrate important concepts, a list of relevant books and articles, links to descriptions of feature films and television shows at the _Now Playing_ website, study aids, and a self-test to check your understanding of the material in this chapter.

Nonverbal Communication

6.1 Explain the characteristics of nonverbal communication.

6.2 Describe the functions served by nonverbal communication.

6.3 Summarize the different types of nonverbal behaviors and assess their possible meanings.

6.4 Identify some ways in which culture and gender affect nonverbal communication.

6.5 Demonstrate an awareness of how to effectively send and receive nonverbal messages.

CHARACTERISTICS OF NONVERBAL COMMUNICATION

There's often a gap between what people say and what they feel. An acquaintance says, "We should do this again sometime" in a way that leaves you suspecting the opposite. A speaker tries to appear confident but acts in a way that almost screams out, "I'm nervous!" You ask a friend what's wrong, and the "nothing" you get in response doesn't ring true. Then, of course, there are times when another's message comes through even though there are no words at all. A look of irritation, a smile, a sigh— signs like these can say more than a torrent of words.

All of these examples share one element in common. They each constitute communication without words, also known as nonverbal communication. This is true even if the communication is vocal (by mouth), as in a laugh or sigh. The opposite is also true: Some communication, such as American Sign Language, is verbal (because it is word-based) although it is not vocal.[1] Table 6-1 further illustrates some of the differences between verbal and nonverbal and vocal and nonvocal communication.

Our working definition of **nonverbal communication** is "messages expressed through nonlinguistic means." This rules out sign languages and written words, but it includes sighs, laughs, and other utterances. Our brief definition only hints at the richness of nonverbal messages. Consider the following characteristics of nonverbal communication.

> nonverbal communication
Messages expressed by other than linguistic means.

Nonverbal Behavior Has Communicative Value

It's virtually impossible to avoid communicating nonverbally.[2] Even if you try, for instance, by closing your eyes or leaving the room, each one of those behaviors still transmits a message. Of course, we don't always intend to

Table 6-1   Types of Communication

	VOCAL COMMUNICATION	NONVOCAL COMMUNICATION
Verbal Communication	Spoken words	Written words
Nonverbal Communication	Tone of voice, sighs, screams, vocal qualities (loudness, pitch, and so on)	Gestures, movement, appearance, facial expression, and so on

Source: Adapted from Stewart, J., & D'Angelo, G. (1980). *Together: Communicating interpersonally* (2nd ed.). Reading, MA: Addison-Wesley, p. 22. Copyright © 1993 by McGraw-Hill. Reprinted/adapted by permission.

Head coach Jim Harbaugh of the San Francisco 49ers shows his emotions during an NFL game.

Q *What are some of the cues that tell you how Harbaugh is feeling?*

send nonverbal messages. Unintentional nonverbal behaviors—such as stammering, blushing, and sweating—differ from intentional ones.[3]

The fact that we all constantly send nonverbal cues is important, because it means that we have a constant source of information available about ourselves and others. If you can tune in to these signals, you will be more aware of how those around you are feeling and thinking, and you will be better able to respond to their behavior.

Nonverbal Behavior Is Primarily Relational

Some nonverbal messages are functional. For example, a police officer uses gestures to direct the flow of traffic, and a conductor leads members of a symphony. But nonverbal communication also serves a far more common (and more interesting) series of social functions.[4] It helps us manage our identities, and it helps us convey emotions that we may be unwilling or unable to express verbally.

Chapter 2 discusses how we strive to create an image of ourselves as we want others to view us. Nonverbal communication plays a role in this process—in many cases a more important role than verbal communication. Consider, for example, what happens when you attend a party at which you are likely to meet strangers whom you would like to get to know better. Instead of projecting your image verbally ("Hi! I'm attractive, friendly, and easygoing"), you behave in ways that will present this identity. You might smile and laugh a lot, and perhaps try to stand in a relaxed pose. It's also likely that you dress carefully—even if the image involves looking as if you haven't given a lot of attention to your appearance.

Nonverbal communication also enables us to convey emotions that we are afraid to express—or ones we may not even be aware of. For example, a professor may notice that you look puzzled even though you were trying to mask your confusion. We call it a "leakage cue" when our nonverbal expressions convey emotions we didn't intend to display to others.

Nonverbal Behavior Is Ambiguous

Nonverbal behavior is often difficult to interpret accurately, and some people are more skillful than others at it.[5] Those who are better senders of nonverbal messages are usually better receivers as well. Decoding ability

> How might you nonverbally communicate that you're bored, nervous, or attracted to someone?

The reunion episodes of *The Real Housewives of Atlanta* have become a master class in the art of "throwing shade," slang for an indirect expression of dislike or disdain.

Q *Do you ever catch yourself rolling your eyes, pursing your lips, or looking down your nose at someone you dislike? How do these cues represent relational communication?*

also increases with age and training, although there are still differences in ability owing to personality. Interestingly, studies have shown that women seem to be better than men at decoding nonverbal messages.[6] Despite these differences, even the best nonverbal decoders do not approach 100 percent accuracy.

When you do try to make sense out of ambiguous nonverbal behavior, you must consider several factors: the context in which they occur (e.g., smiling at a joke suggests a different feeling from what is suggested by smiling at another's misfortune); the history of your relationship with the sender (e.g., friendly, hostile); the other's mood at the time; and your feelings (when you're feeling insecure, almost anything can seem like a threat). Far more importantly, when you become aware of nonverbal messages, you should think of them, not as facts, but rather as clues that need to be checked out.

Nonverbal Communication Is Essential

It's hard to overemphasize the importance of effective nonverbal expression and the ability to read and respond to others' nonverbal behavior. Nonverbal encoding and decoding skills are strong predictors of popularity, attractiveness, and socioemotional well-being.[7] Good nonverbal communicators are more persuasive than people who are less skilled, and they have a greater chance of success in settings ranging from careers to poker to romance. Nonverbal sensitivity is a major part of what some social scientists call "emotional intelligence," and researchers have come to recognize that it is impossible to study spoken language without paying attention to its nonverbal dimensions.[8]

Unlike verbal skills, which are often taught explicitly at home and at school, most people learn about nonverbal skills indirectly, by observing people around them. They judge from people's responses which nonverbal cues are well received and which are not. For example, you might notice that people join in when you yell at a ball game but look shocked and disapproving when you speak above a whisper in church.

For some people, the nuances of nonverbal communication are not readily apparent. Due to a processing deficit in the right hemisphere of the brain, people born with a syndrome called nonverbal learning disorder (NVLD) have trouble making sense of nonverbal cues.[9] They often misinterpret humorous or sarcastic messages and have trouble figuring out how to behave appropriately in new social situations. Likewise, people with autism spectrum disorder may have difficulty recognizing and displaying social cues. For example, they may feel overwhelmed by eye contact and, therefore, avoid looking directly at people. Their behavior may be interpreted as rude or disinterested, but it actually reflects a difference in the way their brains process information.

FUNCTIONS OF NONVERBAL COMMUNICATION

Although verbal and nonverbal messages differ in many ways, the two forms of communication operate together on most occasions. In this section, we explore the many functions of nonverbal communication and the ways that nonverbal messages relate to verbal ones.

Repeating

If someone asks you for directions to the nearest pharmacy, you could say, "North of here about two blocks" and point north with your index finger, thereby repeating your instructions nonverbally. This sort of repetition isn't just decorative: People remember comments accompanied by gestures more than those made with words alone.[10]

Substituting

> emblems

Deliberate nonverbal behaviors with precise meanings, known to virtually all members of a cultural group.

When a friend asks you what's new, you might shrug your shoulders instead of answering in words. Social scientists use the term **emblems** to describe deliberate nonverbal behaviors that have precise meanings known to everyone within a cultural group. For example, most Americans consider that a head nod means "yes," a head shake means "no," and a wave means "hello" or "good-bye." (As discussed in the previous section, these same gestures may mean different things in other cultures, which can cause a great deal of intercultural confusion.) Nonverbal substituting is especially important when people are reluctant to express their feelings in words, but they do so nonverbally without intending to do so, such as raising your eyebrows without thinking when someone makes an off-color comment.

Complementing

Sometimes nonverbal behaviors match the content of a verbal message, reinforcing the sincerity. Consider, for example, a friend apologizing for forgetting an appointment with you. You will be more likely to believe your friend if he uses the right tone of voice and shows an apologetic facial expression. We often recognize the significance of complementary nonverbal behavior when it's missing. If your friend delivers the apology with a shrug, a smirk, and a light tone of voice, you would probably not believe him, regardless of what he says verbally.

Regulating

Nonverbal behaviors can also regulate the flow of verbal communication. For example, parties in a conversation often unconsciously send and receive turn-taking cues.[11] When you are ready to yield the floor, generally the unstated rule is to create a rising vocal intonation pattern and then use a falling intonation pattern, or draw out the final syllable of the clause at the end of your statement before you stop speaking. If you want to maintain your turn when another speaker seems ready to cut you off, you can suppress the attempt by taking an audible breath, by using a sustained intonation pattern (because rising and falling patterns suggest the end of a statement), and by avoiding any pauses in your speech. Other nonverbal cues exist for gaining the floor and for signaling that you do not want to speak. For example, you might raise a finger in the air to show that you have something to say or lower your eyes if you don't wish to speak.

Contradicting

People often simultaneously express different and even contradictory messages in their verbal and nonverbal behaviors. A common example of this sort of mixed message is the experience we've all had of hearing someone with a red face and bulging veins yell, "I'm not angry!"

Even though some of the ways in which people contradict themselves are subtle, mixed messages have a strong impact. Studies suggest that when a receiver perceives an inconsistency between verbal and nonverbal messages, the nonverbal one carries more weight.[12]

Deceiving

Sometimes individuals manage their nonverbal behavior in order to create a false impression. Research shows that women, in particular, become more successful liars as they grow older.[13] People who are highly sensitive to the effects their nonverbal cues have on others are usually better at hiding their deception than communicators who are less self-aware, and raters judge highly expressive liars as more honest than those who are more subdued.[14] Not surprisingly, people whose jobs require them to act differently than they feel—such as actors, lawyers, diplomats, and salespeople—are more successful at deception than the general population.[15]

Decades of research have revealed that there are no sure-fire nonverbal cues that indicate deception.[16] This helps explain why most people have only a 50 percent chance of accurately identifying a liar.[17] We seem to be worse at catching deceivers when we participate actively in conversations than when we observe from the sidelines.[18] It's easiest to catch liars when they haven't had a chance to rehearse, when they feel strongly about the information being hidden, or when they feel anxious or guilty about their lies.[19] Trust (or lack of it) also plays a role in which deceptive messages are successful: People who are suspicious that a speaker may be

Why can it be so difficult to accurately identify someone who is lying?

Table 6-2   **Leakage of Nonverbal Clues to Deception**

DECEPTION CLUES ARE MOST LIKELY WHEN THE DECEIVER	DECEPTION CLUES ARE LEAST LIKELY WHEN THE DECEIVER
Wants to hide emotions being experienced at the moment.	Wants to hide information unrelated to his or her emotions.
Feels strongly about the information being hidden.	Has no strong feelings about the information being hidden.
Feels apprehensive about the deception.	Feels confident about the deception.
Feels guilty about being deceptive.	Experiences little guilt about the deception.
Gets little enjoyment from being deceptive.	Enjoys the deception.
Needs to construct the message carefully while delivering it.	Knows the deceptive message well and has rehearsed it.

Source: Based on material from Ekman, P. (1981). Mistakes when deceiving. In T. A. Sebok & R. Rosenthal (Eds.), *The Clever Hans phenomenon: Communication with horses, whales, apes and people* (pp. 269–278). New York: New York Academy of Sciences.

lying pay closer attention to the speaker's nonverbal behavior (e.g., talking faster than normal, lack of eye contact) than do people who are not suspicious.[20] Table 6-2 lists situations in which deceptive messages are most likely to be obvious.

OBJECTIVE 6.3

Summarize the different types of nonverbal behaviors and assess their possible meanings.

TYPES OF NONVERBAL COMMUNICATION

Now that you understand how nonverbal messages operate as a form of communication, we can look at the various forms of nonverbal behavior. Sometimes nonverbal cues are easy to interpret. Facial expressions reflecting many emotions such as happiness and sadness seem to be recognizable in and among members of almost all cultures.[21] Other expressions may be complex and even contradictory. How well people interpret nonverbal cues depends on how well they know the person, the situation, and the culture, and the nature of the nonverbal cues themselves.[22] In this section, we explain the many types of nonverbal cues present in body movements, voice, appearance, touch, space, environment, and even time.

Body Movements

For many people, the most noticeable elements of nonverbal communication involve visible body movements, or **kinesics**. Our posture, gestures, face, and eyes can all be used to convey meanings.

Posture

If you see a person drag through the door or slump over while sitting in a chair, it's obvious that something significant is going on. But most

> kinesics

The study of body movement, gesture, and posture.

postural cues are more subtle, as when you mimic the posture of another person. One experiment showed that career counselors who used "posture echoes" to copy the postures of clients were rated as more empathic than those who did not reflect the clients' postures.[23] Posture can also communicate a person's degree of vulnerability. One study revealed that rapists sometimes look for postural clues to select victims that they believe will be easy to intimidate.[24]

Gestures

One group of ambiguous gestures consists of what we usually call fidgeting—movements in which one part of the body grooms, massages, rubs, holds, fidgets, pinches, picks, or otherwise manipulates another body part. Social scientists call these behaviors **manipulators**.[25] Research confirms what common sense suggests—that increased use of manipulators is often a sign of discomfort.[26] But not all fidgeting signals uneasiness. People also are likely to use manipulators when they are relaxed. When they let their guard down (either alone or with friends), they will be more likely to fiddle with an earlobe, twirl a strand of hair, or clean their fingernails.

> **manipulators**
Movements in which one part of the body grooms, massages, rubs, holds, fidgets, pinches, picks, or otherwise manipulates another part.

Face

The face is one of the most noticed parts of the body, and its impact can be powerful. Smiling cocktail waitresses earn larger tips than unsmiling ones, and smiling nuns collect larger donations than ones with glum expressions.[27] The influence of facial expressions and eye contact doesn't mean that nonverbal messages are always easy to read. One reason for this is the number of expressions people can produce—as many as five different emotional expressions per second. **Affect blends** are combinations of two or more expressions that show different emotions, such as fearful surprise or angry disgust. In addition, people tend to display different emotions with different parts of the face, sometimes at the same time: happiness and surprise usually show in the eyes and lower face, anger in the lower face and brows and forehead, fear and sadness in the eyes, and disgust in the lower face (Figure 6-1).

> **affect blend**
The combination of two or more expressions, each showing a different emotion.

Eyes

The meaning of eye contact varies by culture. In mainstream Euro-American culture, meeting someone's glance with your eyes is usually a sign of involvement or interest, whereas looking away signals a desire to avoid contact. However, in some cultures—such as traditional Asian, Latin American, and Native American—eye contact may be interpreted as aggressive or disrespectful.[28] It's easy to imagine the misunderstandings that occur when one person's "friendly gesture" feels rude to another, and conversely, how "politely" looking away can feel like a sign of indifference.

Universal facial expression.

According to a 1960's study by psychologist Paul Ekman, all cultures associate these seven facial expressions with the same seven emotions.

Disgust.

R. Clenched nostrils.

S. Pursed lips.

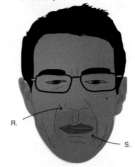

Happy.

T. Primarily, a smile.

Contempt.

U. Primarily, tight lips, raised slightly on one side.

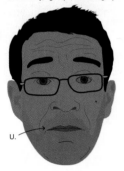

Rest.

Sad.

L. Primarily, a frown (or a furrowed brow).

Anger.

A. Flushed face.

B. An inward and downward brow movement.

C. A hard stare.

D. Flared nostrils.

E. Clenched jaw.

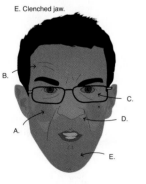

Fear.

M. Widening eyes.

N. Dilated pupils.

O. Risen upper lip.

P. Brows draw together.

Q. Lips stretch horizontally.

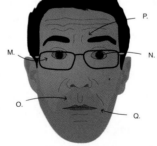

Surprise.

F. Raised and curved eyebrows.

G. Stretched skin below the eyebrows.

H. Horizontal wrinkles across the forehead.

I. Open eyelids.

J. Dropped jaw.

K. Parted lips.

Figure 6-1 Emotions and Faces

In the movie *The Secret Life of Walter Mitty*, Ben Stiller plays a mild-mannered man with an uneventful life. However, viewers attuned to his nonverbal cues may get a glimpse of the exciting adventures he often imagines himself experiencing. Actors are trained to portray subtle and often contradictory emotions.

Q *What nonverbal cues can you identify in this photo? What do they suggest?*

Voice

Social scientists use the term **paralanguage** to describe nonverbal, vocal messages. There are many ways the voice communicates—through tone, speed, pitch, volume, number and length of pauses, and **disfluencies** (such as stammering, use of "uh," "um," "er," and so on). All these factors can do a great deal to reinforce or contradict the message our words convey.

You can begin to understand the power of vocal cues by saying "I love you" twice. The first time, emphasize the word "I." The second time, emphasize "you." It's likely that your first statement will be interpreted differently than the second one, even though the words are the same. This is true in many situations. Listeners tend to judge speakers' attitudes based on *how* they speak.[29] Furthermore, when the words say one thing but vocal cues suggest the opposite, people tend to trust the nonverbal cues.[30]

Sarcasm is one instance in which both emphasis and tone of voice help change a statement's meaning to the opposite of its verbal message. You might say, "No, the holidays weren't stressful" in such a way that suggests that they absolutely were.

Appearance

The way we appear can be just as revealing as the ways we sound and move. For that reason, in this section, we explore the communicative power of physical attractiveness and clothing.

> paralanguage

Nonlinguistic means of vocal expression: rate, pitch, tone, and so on.

> disfluency

A nonlinguistic verbalization such as *um, er, ah.*

Thousands of people became instant fans of Jeremy Meeks after his mug shot appeared on the Facebook page of the Stockton, California, Police Department. His model good looks generated a flurry of tweets and posts, including Photoshopped images of him in designer ads.

Q *While his facial symmetry and piecing blue eyes give him an "objective beauty," what role might other nonverbal cues (e.g., tattoos or the image indicating his arrest) have on his attractiveness level? Have you ever found yourself more attracted to people after learning about their risky behavior?*

Physical Attractiveness

Most people claim that looks aren't the best measure of desirability or character. However, who is most likely to succeed in business? Place your bet on the attractive job applicant. More than 200 managers in one survey admitted that attractive people get preferential treatment both in hiring decisions and on the job.[31] Height is also a factor. Men over 6-foot-2 are typically hired on at higher salaries than shorter men are.[32] And it's probably no surprise that attractiveness is an asset in dating relationships. Although online daters often claim that physical appearance isn't a top priority, they tend to attribute more positive qualities (kindness, confidence, and so on) to people who are physically attractive than those whose aren't.[33]

If you aren't totally gorgeous or handsome, don't despair: Evidence suggests that, as we get to know more about people and like them, we start to regard them as better looking.[34] Moreover, we view others as beautiful or ugly not just on the basis of their "original equipment" but also on how they use that equipment. Posture, gestures, facial expressions, and other behaviors can increase the attractiveness of an otherwise unremarkable person.

Clothing

Besides protecting us from the elements, clothing is a means of nonverbal communication, providing a relatively straightforward (if sometimes expensive) method of impression management. Clothing can be used to convey, for example, economic status, educational level, social status, moral standards, athletic ability and/or interests, belief system (political, philosophical, religious), and level of sophistication. For example, college students in one study judged female peers to be more successful and important when they wore a sweatshirt with an Abercrombie and Fitch logo on it than when they wore a sweatshirt featuring a Kmart logo.[35] But expense isn't the only factor. People with limited budgets and those who wear uniforms to work can make a positive impression by being neat, well groomed, and wearing clothing that fits them properly.[36]

Even the colors we wear may influence how people perceive us. In one study, experimenters asked people to rate the attractiveness of a man and a woman shown in photos. The photos of each person were identical, except that the experimenters digitally changed the color of the models' shirts. Participants consistently rated both models to be more attractive when they were wearing red or black compared to yellow, blue, or green.[37] Before you load your wardrobe with red and black, however, consider that perceptions vary by context. Patients are significantly more willing to share their social, sexual, and psychological problems with doctors wearing white coats or surgical scrubs than those wearing business dress or casual attire.[38]

As we get to know others better, the importance of clothing shrinks.[39] This fact suggests that clothing is especially important in the early stages of a relationship, when making a positive first impression is necessary in order to encourage others to get to know us better. This advice is equally important in personal situations and in employment interviews. In both cases, your style of dress (and personal grooming) can make all the difference between the chance to progress further and outright rejection.

PEOPLE FIRST

"Proper business attire" varies by geography, industry, and organizational culture. At Facebook, the informal tone is set by owner Mark Zuckerberg.

 What is the norm for appropriate dress in your career of choice?

Touch

Physical touch can "speak" volumes. A supportive pat on the back, a high five, or even an inappropriate graze can be more powerful than words, eliciting a strong emotional reaction in the receiver. Social scientists use the term **haptics** when they refer to the study of touch in human behavior.

Romantic partners who frequently touch each other are typically more satisfied with their relationships than other couples are.[40] Even athletes benefit from touch. One study of the National Basketball Association revealed that the touchiest teams had the most successful records, while the lowest scoring teams touched each other the least.[41] Touch can also increase compliance. For example, we are more likely to grant favors to strangers who touch us while they ask.[42] But touch is not always welcome, of course. Whereas it may convey affection or sincerity in some situations, it is downright annoying or frightening in others. In one study, shoppers touched by other shoppers (particularly males) bought less and left the store more quickly than shoppers who were not touched, perhaps because, in that situation, being touched had the unpleasant connotation of being jostled or crowded.[43]

Experts argue that one reason actions speak louder than words is that touch is the first language we learn as infants.[44] Besides being the earliest means we have of making contact with others, touching is essential to healthy development. During the nineteenth and early twentieth centuries many babies who spent a lot of time in orphanages or hospitals died from a disease then called *marasmus*, which, translated from Greek, means "wasting away." Researchers finally realized that this "disease" resulted from a lack of physical contact, not from poor nutrition, medical care, or other factors. The babies hadn't been touched enough, and as a result they died. From this knowledge came the practice of "mothering" children in institutions—picking babies up, carrying them around, and handling them several times each day. At one hospital that began this practice, the death rate for infants fell from between 30 and 35 percent to below 10 percent.[45]

What types of touch do you consider appropriate in professional settings?

Space

There are two ways that space can be used to create nonverbal messages. First, there is the distance we put between ourselves and others, and second, there is the territory we consider to be our own.

Distance

The study of the way people and animals use space has been termed **proxemics**. Preferred spaces are largely a matter of cultural norms. For example, people living in hyperdense Hong Kong manage to live in crowded residential quarters that most North Americans would find intolerable.[46] Anthropologist Edward T. Hall has defined four distances used in mainstream North American culture (Figure 6-2).[47] He says that we choose a

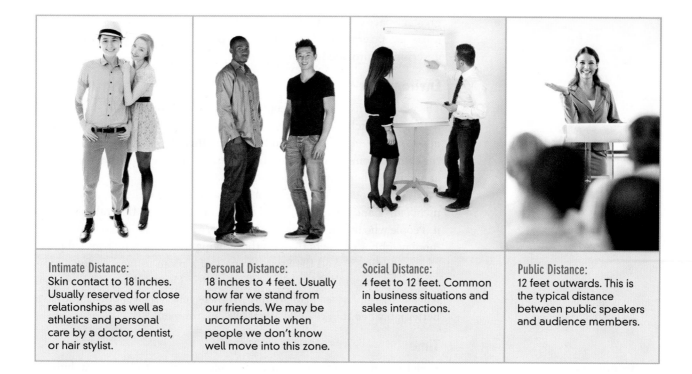

Intimate Distance:
Skin contact to 18 inches. Usually reserved for close relationships as well as athletics and personal care by a doctor, dentist, or hair stylist.

Personal Distance:
18 inches to 4 feet. Usually how far we stand from our friends. We may be uncomfortable when people we don't know well move into this zone.

Social Distance:
4 feet to 12 feet. Common in business situations and sales interactions.

Public Distance:
12 feet outwards. This is the typical distance between public speakers and audience members.

Figure 6-2 Edward Hall's Model of Relationships and Proxemics

particular distance depending on how we feel toward the other person at a given time, the context of the conversation, and our personal goals.

Choosing the optimal distance can have a powerful effect on how we view others and how we respond to them. For example, students are more satisfied with teachers who reduce the distance between themselves and their classes. They also are more satisfied with the course itself, and they are more likely to follow the teacher's instructions.[48] Likewise, medical patients are more satisfied with physicians who don't "keep their distance."[49]

Territory

Whereas personal space is the invisible bubble we carry around as an extension of our physical being, **territory** is fixed space. Any area, such as a room, house, neighborhood, state or country, to which we assume some kind of "rights" is our territory. Not all territory is permanent. We often stake out space for ourselves in the library, at the beach, and so on by using markers such as books, clothing, or other personal possessions.

Generally, we grant people with higher status more personal territory and greater privacy.[50] We knock before entering the boss's office, whereas a boss can usually walk into our work area without hesitating. In traditional schools, professors have offices, dining rooms, and even bathrooms that are private, whereas the students have no such sanctuaries. In the military,

> **territory**
Fixed space that an individual assumes some right to occupy.

greater space and privacy usually come with rank: Privates sleep 40 to a barracks, sergeants have their own private rooms, and generals have government-provided houses.

Environment

The physical environment people create can both reflect and shape interaction. Researchers showed students slides of the interior or exterior of upper-middle-class homes and then asked them to infer the personality of the owners from their impressions.[51] The students were especially accurate at describing homeowners' personalities.

Besides communicating information about the designer, an environment can shape the quantity and quality of interaction that takes place in it. People who live in apartments near stairways and mailboxes have many more neighbor contacts than do those living in less heavily traveled parts of the building.[52] And the attractiveness of a room influences the happiness and energy of the people working in it.[53] The results of this research teach a lesson that isn't surprising: Workers generally feel better and do a better job when they're in an attractive environment.

Time

Social scientists use the term **chronemics** for the study of how human beings use and structure time. The use of time depends greatly on culture.[54] Some cultures (e.g., North American, German, and Swiss) tend to be **monochronic**, emphasizing punctuality, schedules, and completing one task at a time. Other cultures (e.g., South American, Mediterranean,

> chronemics

The study of how humans use and structure time.

> monochronic

The use of time that emphasizes punctuality, schedules, and completing one task at a time.

This work space at Google is furnished in bright colors, with low tables and unconventional chairs that can easily be moved or pushed aside so people can sit on the floor.

Q *How might you interact differently in this environment than in a more traditional office environment?*

and Arab) are more **polychronic**, with flexible schedules in which multiple tasks are pursued at the same time. When a Brazilian-American friend of ours threw a party, she invited her Brazilian friends to show up at 5 pm and her American friends to show up at 7 pm. She anticipated that they would all arrive just after 7 o'clock, and they did. That's not to say the Brazilians were rude. From their perspective, it may have seemed rude to show up at the time specified.

But even within cultures, time is treated differently depending on who is involved. For instance, in the United States, waiting can be an indicator of status. "Important" people (whose time is supposedly more valuable than that of others) may be seen by appointment only, whereas it is acceptable to intrude without notice on those deemed "less important."[55] Likewise, celebrities and prominent politicians often avoid restaurant or airport lines, whereas the presumably less exalted are forced to wait their turn.

> polychronic
The use of time that emphasizes flexible schedules in which multiple tasks are pursued at the same time.

Identify some ways in which culture and gender affect nonverbal communication.

INFLUENCES ON NONVERBAL COMMUNICATION

Much of nonverbal communication is universal. For example, researchers have found at least six facial expressions that all humans everywhere use and understand: happiness, sadness, fear, anger, disgust, and surprise.[56] Even children who have been blind since birth reveal their feelings using these expressions. Despite these similarities, there are crucial differences in the way people use and understand nonverbal behavior.

Culture

The meaning of some gestures varies from one culture to another (Figure 6-3). For example, an American who visits Europe may signal "okay," by joining her thumb and forefinger to form a circle. The gesture is a friendly one back home, but in France and Belgium it is likely to offend. (It means, "You're worth zero" there.)[57] And in Greece and Turkey, the same hand signal is used as a vulgar sexual invitation. Given this sort of cross-cultural ambiguity, it's easy to imagine how an innocent tourist might wind up in serious trouble.

Less obvious cross-cultural differences can damage relationships without the parties ever recognizing exactly what has gone wrong. Edward Hall points out that, whereas Americans are comfortable conducting business at a distance of roughly 4 feet, people from the Middle East stand

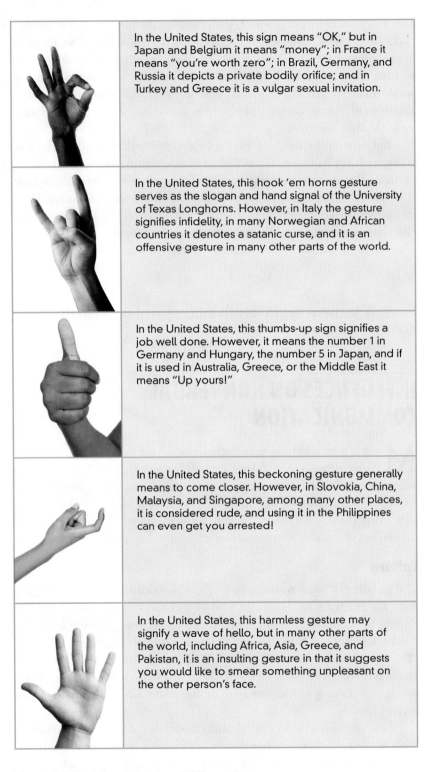

In the United States, this sign means "OK," but in Japan and Belgium it means "money"; in France it means "you're worth zero"; in Brazil, Germany, and Russia it depicts a private bodily orifice; and in Turkey and Greece it is a vulgar sexual invitation.

In the United States, this hook 'em horns gesture serves as the slogan and hand signal of the University of Texas Longhorns. However, in Italy the gesture signifies infidelity, in many Norwegian and African countries it denotes a satanic curse, and it is an offensive gesture in many other parts of the world.

In the United States, this thumbs-up sign signifies a job well done. However, it means the number 1 in Germany and Hungary, the number 5 in Japan, and if it is used in Australia, Greece, or the Middle East it means "Up yours!"

In the United States, this beckoning gesture generally means to come closer. However, in Slovokia, China, Malaysia, and Singapore, among many other places, it is considered rude, and using it in the Philippines can even get you arrested!

In the United States, this harmless gesture may signify a wave of hello, but in many other parts of the world, including Africa, Asia, Greece, and Pakistan, it is an insulting gesture in that it suggests you would like to smear something unpleasant on the other person's face.

Figure 6-3 The Cultural Meaning of Different Gestures

	Rarely	Sometimes	Often	Almost Always
1. I look people in the eye when I talk to them.				
2. I fidget with my hands.				
3. I walk with my shoulders back and my chin level with the ground.				
4. People say they can't tell how I am feeling.				
5. I wear clothing that is neat and clean and that fits me well.				
6. Even when I try to mask my emotions, they show on my face.				
7. When people are speaking to me, I look them in the eye and turn my body to face them.				
8. People ask me to speak up because they can't hear me.				
9. I have a firm handshake.				
10. I am uncomfortable touching others, even to offer a friendly hug or handshake.				

An explanation of your scores appears on p. 149. ●

much closer.[58] It is easy to visualize the awkward advance and retreat pattern that might occur when two diplomats or businesspeople from these cultures meet. The Middle Easterner would probably keep moving forward to close the gap that feels so wide, whereas the American would continually back away. Both would feel uncomfortable, probably without knowing why.

Like distance, patterns of eye contact vary around the world.[59] A direct gaze is considered appropriate for speakers in Latin America, the Arab world, and southern Europe. On the other hand, Asians, Indians, Pakistanis, and northern Europeans tend to gaze at a listener peripherally or not at all. In either case, deviations from the norm are likely to make a listener uncomfortable.

Gender

Although few of us behave like stereotypically masculine or feminine movie characters, there are often recognizable differences in the way men and women look and act. These stem mostly from the way we are raised and the roles men and women have traditionally played.

For example, women are typically more nonverbally expressive than men and better at recognizing others' nonverbal behavior. This may be because they have traditionally been responsible for caring for young children, who communicate mostly through nonverbal cues in their first few years. It may also be because women have historically occupied roles in which they have less power than men. In that context, it pays to understand subtle cues that convey the moods and preferences of the people with greater power.[60] Compared to men, women also tend to smile more, touch others more, stand closer to others, and make more eye contact and gestures. These mostly reflect cultural expectations that women be friendly and supportive of others.[61]

Of course, social roles and expectations are changing. As men assume more childcare responsibilities, they may develop an increased sensitivity to nonverbal cues. Conversely, as women gain higher status in the workplace, they may have less incentive to monitor the nonverbal cues of the people around them. Most people are more keyed into the boss's mood than the other way around. All in all, while social roles and norms certainly have an influence on nonverbal style, they aren't as dramatic as the "men are from Mars, women are from Venus" thesis suggests.

> Based on your own experience, do you find women to be more nonverbally expressive than men?

OBJECTIVE 6.5 Demonstrate an awareness of how to effectively send and receive nonverbal messages.

NONVERBAL COMMUNICATION COMPETENCE

By now you should appreciate the wealth of messages expressed nonverbally. You can use this information to develop your communication skills in two respects—by being more attuned to others, and by becoming more aware of your own nonverbal messages.

Tune Out Words

It's easy to overlook important nonverbal cues when you're only listening to the words being spoken. As you've already read, words sometimes hide, or even contradict, a speaker's true feelings (e.g., "I see your point," spoken with a frown). Even when spoken words accurately reflect the speaker's thoughts, nonverbal cues can reveal important information about feelings and attitudes.

You can develop skill in recognizing nonverbal cues by tuning out the content of a speaker's language. Since it's rude to ignore what a conversational partner is saying, try practicing by watching a movie or TV program in a language you don't understand. That way you can attend to vocal qualities as well as postures, gestures, facial expressions, and other cues. As you get better at recognizing nonverbal cues, you'll find it easier to tune in to them in your everyday conversations.

Use Perception Checking

Since nonverbal behaviors are ambiguous, it's important to consider your interpretations as educated guesses, not absolute translations. The yawn that interrupts a story you're telling may signal boredom, but it might also be a sign that the listener is recovering from a sleepless night. Likewise, the impatient tone that greets your suggestion may be aimed at you, or it could mean that your conversational partner is having a bad day.

Perception checking (Chapter 2) is one way to explore the significance of nonverbal cues. Instead of trying to read the other person's mind, describe the behavior you've noted, share at least two possible interpretations, and ask for clarification about how to interpret the behavior. With practice, perception checks can sound natural and reflect your genuine desire to understand:

> (To a friend) *"Last night you said you were tired and left the party early* [behavior]. *I wasn't sure whether you were bored* [first interpretation] *or whether something else was bothering you* [second interpretation]. *Or maybe you were just tired* [third interpretation]. *What was going on?"*

> (At work) *"I need to ask you about something that happened at the end of yesterday's meeting. When I started to ask about the vacation schedule, you interrupted me and said you had to make an important phone call. I'm wondering whether the phone call was the only reason you cut me off, or whether I said or did something wrong. Can you please clarify?"*

Not every situation is important enough to call for a perception check, and sometimes the meaning of nonverbal cues may seem so clear that you don't need to investigate. But there will certainly be times when exploring alternate interpretations works better than jumping to conclusions.

When is it appropriate to use perception checking to interpret ambiguous nonverbal behaviors?

Pay Attention to Your Own Nonverbal Behavior

Along with attending more carefully to the unspoken messages of others, there's value in monitoring your own nonverbal behavior. You can get an appreciation for this fact by asking someone to take video of you in unguarded moments. If you're like most people, you're likely to be surprised by at least some of what you see. Research suggests that most of us have blind spots when it comes to our own communication.[62] For example, we sometimes overestimate how well we hide our anxiety, boredom,

From twerking in provocative clothing to sliding down a giant replica of her own tongue, Miley Cyrus uses nonverbal communication strategically to distance herself from the Hannah Montana Disney image that made her famous.

Q *How does your behavior as an adult compare to the way you communicated as a child or high school student?*

or eagerness from others. With this in mind, consider the following questions honestly:

> How does your voice sound?
> How closely does your appearance match what you've imagined?
> What messages do your posture, gestures, and face convey?

Once you have a sense of your most notable nonverbal behaviors, you should be better able to monitor them.

CHECK YOUR UNDERSTANDING

OBJECTIVE 6.1 Explain the characteristics of nonverbal communication.

CHARACTERISTICS OF NONVERBAL COMMUNICATION

Nonverbal communication consists of messages expressed by nonlinguistic means, and it is an integral part of virtually all communication. There are several important characteristics of nonverbal communication. First, we all communicate nonverbally; it's impossible not to. Second, nonverbal communication helps us to manage our identity and to convey emotions we may be unwilling or unable to express verbally. Third, nonverbal behavior is ambiguous; there are often many possible interpretations for any behavior, so it's important to verify before jumping to conclusions.

Provide an example of an instance in which you unintentionally communicated a nonverbal message that was ambiguous.

OBJECTIVE 6.2 Describe the functions served by nonverbal communication.

FUNCTIONS OF NONVERBAL COMMUNICATION

Nonverbal communication serves many functions. In some cases, it repeats and complements what we say with words. In other cases, nonverbal cues substitute for words and help us regulate the flow of conversations. Conversely, nonverbal cues can also contradict our verbal behavior.

Give specific examples of times when your nonverbal behavior has served each one of these functions: repeating, substituting, complementing, regulating, and contradicting.

OBJECTIVE 6.3 Summarize the different types of nonverbal behaviors and assess their possible meanings.

TYPES OF NONVERBAL COMMUNICATION

We communicate nonverbally in many ways—through posture, gesture, use of the face and eyes, voice, physical attractiveness and clothing, touch, distance and territory, environment, and time. Without thinking about it, we may mimic the nonverbal behavior of people we like and distance ourselves from people we don't. Many nonverbal cues, such as attractiveness and clothing, influence our first impressions of people but are less persuasive after we get to know them.

Observe two people having a conversation. How many types of nonverbal communication can you identify?

Identify some ways in which culture and gender affect nonverbal communication.

INFLUENCES ON NONVERBAL COMMUNICATION

While there are some universal expressions across cultures, some gestures mean different things. A friendly hand motion in one culture may be an offensive or vulgar gesture in another. Gender also influences nonverbal communication. For the most part, women are more nonverbally expressive and attentive than men, although these differences may arise more from the roles we play than from the genes we inherit.

Identify a situation in which culture or gender influenced the nature of your nonverbal communication.

OBJECTIVE 6.5 Demonstrate an awareness of how to effectively send and receive nonverbal messages.

NONVERBAL COMMUNICATION COMPETENCE

It is difficult to interpret nonverbal cues with certainty. Mindfully focusing on other people's nonverbal behavior, as well as your own, can help, as can practicing. Perception checking may also be used to help verify hunches about your interpretations.

When and how might you appropriately use perception checking to share your interpretation of another person's nonverbal behavior?

KEY TERMS

affect blend p. 133
chronemics p. 140
disfluency p. 135
emblems p. 130
haptics p. 138

kinesics p. 132
manipulators p. 133
monochronic p. 140
nonverbal communication p. 126
paralanguage p. 135

polychronic p. 141
proxemics p. 138
territory p. 139

HOW NONVERBALLY SKILLFUL ARE YOU?

For odd numbered questions, give yourself 3 points for every time you answered *almost always*, 2 points for every time you answered *often*, and 1 point for every *sometimes* answer.

For even numbered questions, give yourself 3 points for every time you answered *rarely*, 2 points for every time you answered *sometimes*, and 1 point for every *often* answer.

20 to 30 points—You are a master at conveying nonverbal cues in the predominant American culture. Your nonverbal displays suggest that you are confident, engaging, and interested in others. Pat yourself on the back! At the same time, remember that the nonverbal behavior that is considered appealing in one culture may seem overly familiar and even aggressive to people from other cultures.

10 to 19 points—By American standards, your nonverbal communication may be sending people mixed messages. In some respects, you come off as self-assured and interested, but at other times, people may assume you are nervous or indifferent. Being mindful about the cues you send to others can help make the difference in how others perceive you.

9 points or fewer—In most North American cultures, eye contact, erect posture, a firm handshake, and tactful expressions of emotion are interpreted as being friendly and confident. Based on those expectations, you are sending people the message that you are not interested in communicating with them. If you don't present these cues, it may hurt your chances of getting the job you want or making friends easily. This is not to say that the cues you exhibit are a hindrance everywhere. In some cultures, the cues that make you seem shy or removed to Americans are regarded as respectful and modest. The trick is to adapt to your communication audience.

FOR FURTHER EXPLORATION

For more communication resources, see the *Essential Communication* website at www.oup.com/us/ec. There you will find a variety of resources: "Media Room" examples from popular films and television shows to further illustrate important concepts, a list of relevant books and articles, links to descriptions of feature films and television shows at the *Now Playing* website, study aids, and a self-test to check your understanding of the material in this chapter.

Communicating in Interpersonal Relationships

7.1 Explain what makes some communication interpersonal.

7.2 Describe two models of self-disclosure, and apply characteristics of effective and appropriate self-disclosure.

7.3 Compare and contrast mediated and face-to-face communication, evaluating the advantages and disadvantages of each.

7.4 Distinguish between confirming and disconfirming messages and behavior, and describe how relational spirals develop.

THE NATURE OF INTERPERSONAL COMMUNICATION

Pause for a moment to consider all the people you encounter in a typical day. Some of them may be close friends and loved ones, while others may be acquaintances, and still others are probably strangers. Now, consider how you communicate with these different people. Are there things you share about yourself with some people but not with others? Which of these people makes you smile or, conversely, frustrates you on a regular basis? In this chapter, we discuss interpersonal communication, first defining what it is and then examining the factors that influence our relational communication climates.

The most obvious way to define *interpersonal communication* is by looking at the number of people involved. In this sense, we could consider

In the TV show *How I Met Your Mother*, some of the characters are friends, a couple are married, and a few of them date on and off.

Q *What constellations of friends, romantic partners, and casual acquaintances are part of your everyday life?*

all dyadic interaction (interaction between two people) as **contextually interpersonal communication**. But consider a routine transaction between a sales clerk and customer or the rushed exchange when you ask a stranger on the street for directions. Those exchanges hardly seem "interpersonal" in any meaningful sense of the word.

The impersonal nature of some two-person exchanges has led some scholars to say that *quality*, not quantity, distinguishes interpersonal communication. **Qualitatively interpersonal communication** occurs when we treat one another as unique individuals, regardless of the context in which the interaction occurs or the number of people involved.[1]

The majority of our communication, even in dyadic contexts, is relatively impersonal. We chat pleasantly but superficially with salespeople or fellow passengers on the train or plane. We discuss the weather or current events with most classmates and neighbors, and we are polite to coworkers. Considering the number of people we communicate with, qualitatively interpersonal interaction is rather scarce—and, therefore, special.

Content and Relational Messages

Virtually every verbal statement—even the most impersonal—contains both a **content message**, which focuses on the subject being discussed, and a **relational message**, which makes a statement about how the parties feel toward one another based on one or more of the following dimensions:[2]

Affinity

The degree to which we like or appreciate others is **affinity**. Sometimes we indicate feelings of affinity explicitly, but more often the clues are nonverbal, such as a pat on the back or a friendly smile.

> **> contextually interpersonal communication**
> Any communication that occurs between two individuals.

> **> qualitatively interpersonal communication**
> Interaction in which people treat one another as unique individuals, regardless of the context in which the interaction occurs or the number of people involved.

> **> content message**
> Communicates information about the subject being discussed.

> **> relational message**
> Conveys the social relationship between two or more individuals.

> **> affinity**
> The degree to which we like or appreciate others.

Long before they became famous comedians, Tina Fey and Amy Poehler became best friends as classmates in an improv class. They clearly have an affinity for one another.

 What common interests unite you and your closest friends?

Respect

> respect
The degree to which we hold others in esteem.

The degree to which we admire others and hold them in esteem is known as **respect**.[3] While respect and affinity might seem similar, they are actually different dimensions of a relationship. For example, you might like a 3-year-old child tremendously without respecting her. Likewise, you could respect a boss or teacher's talents without liking him or her. Respect is a tremendously important and often overlooked ingredient in satisfying relationships. It is a better predictor of relational satisfaction than liking, or even loving.

Immediacy

> immediacy
The degree of interest and attraction we feel toward and communicate to others; usually expressed nonverbally.

Communication scholars use the term **immediacy** to describe the degree of interest and attraction we feel toward and communicate to others. While you can like someone, if you don't communicate or demonstrate that feeling toward the other person, the immediacy will be low.

Control

> control
The social need to influence others.

In every conversation and every relationship there is some distribution of **control**, that is, the amount of influence communicators seek. Control can be distributed evenly among relational partners, or one person can have more and the other(s) less. An uneven distribution of control won't necessarily cause problems in a relationship unless people disagree on how control should be distributed.

You can get a feeling for how relational messages operate in everyday life by imagining two ways of saying, "It's your turn to clear the dishes off the table"—one tone that is demanding and another that is matter-of-fact. The demanding tone says, in effect, "I have a right to tell you what to do around the house," whereas the matter-of-fact one suggests, "I'm just reminding you of something you might have overlooked."

Most of the time we aren't conscious of the relational messages that bombard us every day, particularly when the messages match our belief about the amount of respect, immediacy, control, and affinity that is appropriate. For example, you probably won't be offended if your boss tells you to do a certain job, because it's natural for supervisors to direct employees. However, if your boss delivers the order in a condescending or abusive tone of voice, you probably will be offended. Your complaint wouldn't be with the order itself but rather with the way it was delivered. "I may work for this company," you might think, "but I'm not an idiot. I deserve to be treated like a human being."

As the boss-employee example suggests, relational messages are usually expressed nonverbally. To test this fact for yourself, imagine how you could act while saying, "Can you help me for a minute?" in a way that communicates each of the following attitudes:

superiority	aloofness	friendliness
helplessness	sexual desire	irritation

Remember, however, that although nonverbal behaviors are a good source of relational messages, they are ambiguous. The sharp tone you take as a personal insult might be due to fatigue, and the interruption you take as an attempt to ignore your ideas might be a sign of pressure that has nothing to do with you.

Metacommunication

Social scientists use the term **metacommunication** to describe messages that refer to other messages.[4] In other words, metacommunication is communication about communication. Whenever we discuss a relationship with others, we are metacommunicating: "It sounds like you're mad at me" or "I appreciate how honest you've been." Even "jk" (just kidding) as part of a text or chat is a form of metacommunication.

Tuning in to metacommunication allows us to look below the surface of a message and detect the underlying meanings where the issue often lies. For example, consider a couple arguing because one partner wants to watch TV, while the other wants to talk. Imagine how much better the chances of a positive outcome would be if they used metacommunication: "Look, it's not the TV watching itself that bothers me. It's that I think you're watching because you're mad at me. Am I right?"

Metacommunication isn't just a tool for handling problems. It is also a way to reinforce the good aspects of a relationship: "Thank you for praising my work in front of the boss." Comments such as this let others know that you value their behavior and boost the odds that the other people will continue the behavior in the future.

Bringing relational issues out in the open does have risks. Discussing problems might be interpreted as a sign that the relationship is in trouble—"Our relationship isn't working if we have to keep talking about it." Furthermore, metacommunication does involve a certain degree of analysis ("It seems like you're angry at me"), which can lead to resentment. This doesn't mean verbal metacommunication is a bad idea, but it's a tool that should be used carefully.

> metacommunication
Messages (usually relational) that refer to other messages; communication about communication.

How often do you find yourself engaging in metacommunication within your closest relationships?

Describe two models of self-disclosure, and apply characteristics of effective and appropriate self-disclosure.

OBJECTIVE 7.2

SELF-DISCLOSURE

In some ways, technology makes it easier to share personal information online than in person. We can think carefully before we hit the SEND button, and we may be braver about sharing sensitive information when we aren't looking the other person in the eye. But information shared

> **self-disclosure**
The process of deliberately revealing information about oneself that is significant and that would not normally be known by others.

in person typically involves a richer array of nonverbal cues, which can enhance the meaning we are trying to convey.[5] No matter what the format, **self-disclosure** is the process of deliberately revealing information about oneself that is significant and that would not normally be known by others.

People self-disclose for a variety of reasons. One important factor is how well we know the other person.[6] The most frequent reason people give for volunteering personal information to a friend is that they want to maintain and enhance the relationship. A second important reason is self-clarification—to sort out confusion and to understand ourselves better.

With strangers, reciprocity is the most common reason for disclosing. We offer information about ourselves to strangers to learn more about them, so we can decide whether and how to continue the relationship. The second most common reason is impression formation. We often reveal information about ourselves to strangers to make ourselves look good. This information is usually positive—at least in the early stages of a relationship.

Models of Self-Disclosure

Over several decades, social scientists have created various models to represent and understand how self-disclosure operates in relationships. Two of the best known models are the social penetration model and the Johari window.

Social Penetration Model

> **social penetration model**
A model describing how intimacy can be achieved via the breadth and depth of self-disclosure.

> **breadth**
The range of topics about which an individual discloses.

> **depth**
The level of personal information a person reveals on a particular topic.

Figure 7-1 highlights the **social penetration model**, which shows two ways in which communication can be more or less disclosing.[7] The first dimension of self-disclosure in this model involves the **breadth** of information volunteered—the range of subjects being discussed. For example, as you start to reveal to coworkers information about your personal life—perhaps what you did over the weekend or stories about your family—the breadth of disclosure in your relationship will expand. The second dimension of disclosure is the **depth** of the information being volunteered, the shift from relatively nonrevealing messages ("I went out with friends.") to more personal ones ("I went on this awful blind date set up by my mom's friend….").

What makes the disclosure in some messages deeper than in others? Some revelations are certainly more *significant* than others. Consider the difference between saying, "I love my family" and "I love you." Other statements qualify as deep disclosure because they are *private*. Sharing a secret you've told to only a few close friends is certainly an act of self-disclosure, but it's even more revealing to divulge information that you've never told anyone.

Depending on the breadth and depth of information shared, a relationship can be defined as casual or intimate. The most intimate relationships are those in which disclosure is great in terms of both breadth and

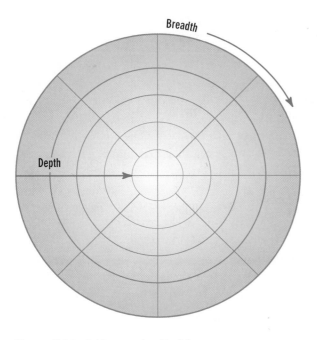

Figure 7-1 **Social Penetration Model**

depth. Each of your personal relationships probably has a different combination of these two factors.

The Johari Window

Another model that helps represent how self-disclosure operates is the **Johari window.**[8] Imagine a frame that contains everything there is to know about you: your likes and dislikes, your goals, your secrets, your needs—everything.

Of course, you aren't aware of everything about yourself. Like most people, you're probably discovering new things about yourself all the time. To represent this, we can divide the frame containing everything about you into two parts: the part you know about (on the left in the diagram) and the part you don't know about (on the right). We can also divide this frame in another way. In this division the first part contains the things about you that others know (the top two quadrants in the diagram), and the second part contains the things about you that you keep to yourself. The bottom quadrant represents this view.

When we put it all together (Figure 7-2) we have a Johari window—*everything about you* divided into four parts. One quadrant represents the information of which both you and the other person are aware. This part is your *open area.* Another represents the *blind area:* information of which you are unaware but that the other person knows. You learn about information in the blind area primarily through feedback. A third represents

> Johari window

A model that describes the relationship between self-disclosure and self-awareness.

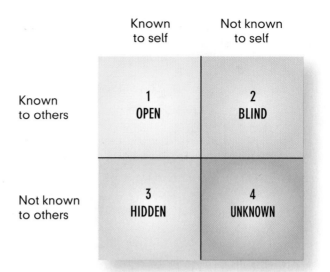

Known
to self

Not known
to self

Known
to others

**1
OPEN**

**2
BLIND**

Not known
to others

**3
HIDDEN**

**4
UNKNOWN**

Figure 7-2 The Johari Window

your *hidden area:* information that you know but aren't willing to reveal to others. Items in this hidden area become public primarily through self-disclosure. And the fourth represents information that is *unknown* to both you and others. It is not unusual to discover, for example, that you have an unrecognized talent, strength, or weakness. Items move from the unknown area into the open area either directly, when you disclose your insight, or through one of the other areas first.

Interpersonal relationships of any depth are virtually impossible if the individuals involved have little open area. Going a step further, you can see that a relationship is limited by the individual who is less open, that is, who possesses the smaller open area. You have probably found yourself in situations in which you felt the frustration of not being able to get to know someone who was too reserved. Perhaps you have blocked another person's attempts to build a relationship with you in the same way. The fact is that self-disclosure on both sides is necessary for the development of any interpersonal relationship.

Questions to Ask Before Self-Disclosing

No single style of self-disclosure is appropriate for every situation. However, there are some questions you can ask to determine when and how self-disclosing may be beneficial for you and others.[9]

Is the Other Person Important to You?

Disclosure may be the path toward developing a more personal relationship with someone. If you value the relationship, sharing more about yourself might bring you closer. However, it can be a mistake to share personal information with people you don't trust or know very well.

Is the Risk of Disclosing Reasonable?

Take a realistic look at the potential risks of self-disclosure. You're asking for trouble when you open up to someone you know is likely to betray your confidences or make fun of you. On the other hand, knowing that your relational partner is trustworthy and supportive makes it more reasonable to speak out.

Keep in mind that revealing personal thoughts and feelings can be especially risky on the job.[10] The politics of the workplace sometimes require that you keep feelings to yourself in order to accomplish both personal and organizational goals. You might, for example, be upset about a recent break-up, but sharing those feelings at the office could be viewed as unprofessional.

Are the Amount and Type of Disclosure Appropriate?

Telling others about yourself isn't an all-or-nothing decision. It's possible to share some facts, opinions, or feelings with one person while reserving riskier ones for others. Before sharing very important information with someone who does matter to you, consider testing reactions by disclosing something less personal.

Kim Kardashian is sometimes criticized for oversharing details about her sex life and posting revealing selfies online.

Q *How do you determine what's appropriate to share with friends and acquaintances or with the whole world online?*

Is the Disclosure Relevant to the Situation at Hand?

A study of classroom communication revealed that sharing all feelings—both positive and negative—and being completely honest resulted in less cohesiveness than having a "relatively" honest climate in which pleasant but superficial relationships were the norm.[11] Even in personal relationships—with close friends, family members—constant disclosure isn't a useful goal. Instead, the level of sharing in successful relationships rises and falls in cycles.

Is the Disclosure Reciprocated?

There's nothing quite like sharing vulnerable information about yourself only to discover that the other person is unwilling to do the same. Unequal self-disclosure creates an unbalanced relationship. One-way disclosure is usually acceptable only in formal, therapeutic relationships in which a client approaches a trained professional with the goal of resolving a problem. For instance, you wouldn't necessarily expect to hear about your physician's personal ailments during a visit to a medical office. Nonetheless, it's interesting to note that one frequently noted characteristic of effective psychotherapists, counselors, and teachers is a willingness to share their feelings with their clients and students.

Will the Effect Be Constructive?

Self-disclosure can be a vicious tool if it's not used carefully. Psychologist George Bach suggests that every person has a psychological "belt line." Below that belt line are areas about which the person is extremely sensitive. Bach says that jabbing "below-the-belt" is a surefire way to disable another person, although usually at great cost to the relationship. It's important to consider the effects of your candor before opening up to others. Comments such as "I've always thought you were stupid" may be devastating—to the listener and to the relationship.

Have you ever jabbed someone "below the belt" with a comment? What impact did this have on the relationship?

Is the Self-Disclosure Clear and Understandable?

When you express yourself to others, it's important that you do so intelligibly by clearly describing the *sources* of your message. For instance, it's far better to describe another's behavior by saying, "When you don't text me back ..." than to complain vaguely, "When you avoid me...." It's also vital to express your *thoughts* and *feelings* explicitly. "I feel like you no longer want to spend time with me" is more understandable than "I don't like the way things have been going."

Compare and contrast mediated and face-to-face communication, evaluating the advantages and disadvantages of each.

OBJECTIVE 7.3

MEDIATED VERSUS FACE-TO-FACE COMMUNICATION

There's no question that mediated relationships can pass the test of being contextually interpersonal. You can stay in touch via social media much more efficiently than in person. But what about the *quality* of mediated interaction? Can it be as personal as face-to-face communication?

Some critics have noted that technology has created an environment in which people are more tuned in to texts and tweets than to humans in the same room. They observe that mobile devices provide a steady stream of information, but that much of it is trivial. For example, even in the middle of an important conversation, the sound of an incoming message may stimulate the urge to check it right away. Having become accustomed to a steady steam of information, it's hard to resist sneaking a peek when something new arrives. All the same, technology doesn't always offer the same depth as face-to-face communication. One survey revealed that people who relied heavily on the Internet to meet their communication needs grew to rely less and less on their face-to-face networks. As a result, they tended to feel more lonely and depressed.[12] Another, more recent, study found that the mere presence of mobile devices can have a negative effect on closeness, connection, and conversation quality during face-to-face discussions of personal topics.[13]

On the other hand, there is evidence that mediated communication can *enhance*, not diminish, the quantity and quality of interpersonal communication under the right conditions. Couples who talk frequently via mobile phone feel more loving, committed, and confident about their relationship than couples who don't.[14] And, people who already feel isolated and lonely in everyday life may use social networking to fill that gap.[15] In addition, online communication can help people stay in touch, even when people have busy schedules and are far away from each other. Almost 60 percent of American teenagers say that the Internet helps them maintain friendships, and almost a third report that it helps them make new friends.[16]

Asynchronous channels, such as email and texts, may also make it easier for people to maintain regular contact with friends in different countries and time zones. The luxury of replying when you are ready to, rather than right away, has other implications. In a study of multimedia use by romantic partners,[17] one woman said she feels more genuine and in control when she has time to think about a message before she sends it.

> How does the quality of your in-person friendships compare with the quality of your online ones?

In online role-playing games, participants who have never met in person can build virtual relationships over time by working together online against opponents.

Q *Have you engaged in online games? If so, do you find it to be more or less appealing than playing games in person? Why?*

As she put it, "you can catch your mistakes or things that might offend the other person" rather than "blurting out" things you don't really mean. But another person interviewed in the same study felt that electronic communication is less genuine than face-to-face conversations because nonverbal cues are lacking and people can be more calculating in their responses. "Arguing over text messages is cheating because you don't have to immediately respond," he said. That person felt that technology can be a "safeguard" that hides people's true feelings.

When it comes to exclusively online relationships, some may develop rapidly, as in the context of online gaming. Particularly when the online game is challenging and requires teamwork, players report that they form close and loyal relationships with each other.[18] These environments create what some scholars have called a "third place" where users can spend time with one another, having fun and sometimes sharing personal information.[19]

You will undoubtedly build and/or maintain relationships with at least some people in your life through technology. In fact, the best of all relationships are those in which people have both in-person and electronic contact with friends. These people are less lonely than their counterparts who have fewer ways of keeping in touch.[20] Findings like these help explain why Steve Jobs, the cofounder of Apple Computer, suggested that personal computers be renamed "*interpersonal* computers."[21]

Distinguish between confirming and disconfirming messages and behavior, and describe how climate spirals develop.

OBJECTIVE 7.4

COMMUNICATION CLIMATES IN INTERPERSONAL RELATIONSHIPS

Personal relationships are a lot like the weather. Some may be fair, warm, and healthy, while others may be stormy, cold, and polluted. Some relationships have stable climates, whereas others change dramatically—calm one moment and turbulent the next. The term **communication climate** refers to the emotional tone of a relationship. A climate doesn't involve specific activities as much as the way people feel about each other as they carry out those activities.

> communication climate

The emotional tone of a relationship as it is expressed in the messages that the partners send and receive.

In the film *The Heat*, an uptight FBI Special Agent (Sandra Bullock) and a loose-cannon Boston cop (Melissa McCarthy) are forced to work a case together, and a negative communication climate immediately develops. After a series of positive exchanges, however, their communication improves, and they form a close bond.

Q Can you identify a turning point in a relationship with a friend or coworker that altered the communication climate for better . . . or worse?

Confirming and Disconfirming Messages

What makes some climates positive and others negative? A short but accurate answer is that the communication climate is determined by the degree to which people see themselves as valued. When we believe others view us as important, we are likely to feel good about our relationship. By contrast, the relational climate suffers when we think others don't appreciate or care about us.

Messages that show you are valued are called **confirming responses**.[22] Whether we post confirming responses publicly online or offer them in person, they say "you exist," "you matter," "you are important." In actuality, however, it's an oversimplification to talk about one type of confirming message. Instead, confirming communication occurs on three increasingly positive levels:[23]

Recognition

The most fundamental act of confirmation is to recognize the other person. Recognition seems easy and obvious, yet there are many times when we do not respond to others on this basic level. Failure to visit a friend is a common example, as is the failure to return a message. Avoiding eye contact with someone you know on the street can also send a negative message. Of course, this lack of recognition may simply be an oversight. You might not notice your friend, or the pressures of work and school might prevent you from staying in touch. Nonetheless, if the other person *perceives* you as avoiding contact, the message has the effect of being disconfirming.

Acknowledgment

Acknowledging the ideas and feelings of others is a stronger form of confirmation. Listening is probably the most common form of acknowledgment. But, counterfeit listening—ambushing, stage hogging, pseudolistening, and so on (Chapter 5)—has the opposite effect of acknowledgment. More active acknowledgment includes asking questions, paraphrasing, and reflecting.

Endorsement

Whereas acknowledgment means you are interested in another's ideas, endorsement means that you agree with him or her. Endorsement is the strongest type of confirming message, because it communicates the highest form of valuing. You need not agree completely in order to endorse a person's message. Even if you disagree with someone, you can probably find something in the message that you endorse. "I can see why you were so angry," you might reply to a friend, even if you don't approve of his or her outburst.

In contrast to confirming communication, messages that deny the value of others have been labeled **disconfirming responses**. These show a lack of regard for the other person by either disputing or ignoring some important part of that person's message.[24] Disagreement can certainly be disconfirming, especially if it attacks the speaker personally. However, disagreement is not the most damaging kind of disconfirmation. It may be tough to hear someone say, "I don't think that's a good idea," but a personal attack such as "You're crazy" or "You're stupid" is even tougher to hear. And maybe the most disconfirming response of all is no response. Ignoring people sends a message that they don't matter enough to even argue with.

Relational Spirals

As soon as two people start to communicate, a relational climate begins to develop. If the messages are confirming, the climate is likely to be a positive one. If they disconfirm one another, the climate is likely to be hostile, cold, or defensive.

Verbal messages certainly contribute to the tone of a relationship, but many climate-shaping messages are nonverbal. The very act of approaching others is confirming, whereas avoiding them can be disconfirming. Smiles or frowns, the presence or absence of eye contact, tone of voice, the use of personal space—all these and other cues send messages about how people feel toward one another (Chapter 6).

After a climate is formed, it can take on a life of its own and give rise to a self-perpetuating **spiral**—a reciprocating communication pattern in which each person's message reinforces the other's.[25] In positive spirals, one person's confirming message leads to a similar response from the other person. This positive reaction leads the first person to be even more reinforcing. Negative spirals are just as powerful, although they leave people feeling worse about themselves and each other. **Escalatory conflict spirals** are the most visible way that disconfirming messages reinforce one another.[26] One attack leads to another until the communication escalates into a full-fledged argument. Although they are less obvious, **avoidance spirals** can also be destructive.[27] Rather than fighting, individuals slowly lessen their dependence on one another, withdraw, and become less invested in the relationship.

Spirals rarely go on indefinitely. Most relationships pass through cycles of progression and regression. If the spiral is negative, partners may switch from negative to positive messages without discussing the matter. In other cases they may engage in metacommunication. "Hold on," one person might say. "We're not getting anywhere." In some cases, however, partners pass the "point of no return," leading to the breakup of a relationship (Chapter 9). However, even the best relationships go through periods of conflict and withdrawal, and some negative communication in relationships is to be expected. The important thing is to achieve balance. People in satisfying relationships tend to maintain at least a 5:1 ratio of positive to negative statements.[28]

> **spiral**
Reciprocal communication pattern in which each person's message reinforces the other's.

> **escalatory conflict spirals**
A pattern in which disconfirming messages reinforce one another, often leading to a full-blown argument.

> **avoidance spiral**
A communication pattern in which the parties slowly reduce their dependence on one another, withdraw, and become less invested in the relationship.

How sunny is your communication climate?

Think of an important person in your life—perhaps a friend, a roommate, a family member, or a romantic partner. Choose the option in each group in the following list that best describes how you communicate with each other, then see what your answers suggest about your relational climate.

1. When I am upset about something, my relational partner is most likely to:
   A. ignore how I feel
   B. say I should have tried harder to fix or avoid the problem
   C. listen to me and provide emotional support

2. When we are planning a weekend activity and I want to do something my partner doesn't want to do, I tend to:
   A. suggest another option we will both enjoy
   B. beg until I get my way
   C. cancel our plans and engage in the activity with someone else

3. When my partner and I disagree about a controversial subject, we usually:
   A. accuse the other person of using poor judgment or ignoring the facts
   B. ask questions and listen to the other person's viewpoint
   C. avoid the subject

4. If I didn't hear from my partner for a while, I would probably:
   A. call or text to make sure everything was okay
   B. not notice
   C. feel angry about being ignored

5. The statement we are most likely to make during a typical conversation sounds something like this:
   A. "Were you saying something?"
   B. "I appreciate the way you . . ."
   C. "You always forget to . . ."

To evaluate your responses, see p. 172.

Defensive and Supportive Behaviors

It's easy to see how disconfirming messages can pollute a communication climate. But what are some alternative ways of communicating that encourage positive relationships? The work of Jack Gibb gives a picture of the kinds of messages that lead to both positive and negative spirals.[29]

After observing groups for several years, Gibb was able to isolate six types of defense-arousing communication and six contrasting behaviors that seemed to reduce the level of threat and defensiveness. The **Gibb categories** are listed in Figure 7-3. Using the supportive types of communication

> Gibb categories

Types of supportive and defensive communication patterns that affect the climate of our relationships.

Defensive Behaviors	Supportive Behaviors
Evaluation: using judgmental statements and "you" language	Description: focusing on the speaker's thoughts and feelings; using "I" language
Control: trying to impose a solution on others	Problem Orientation: seeking a satisfactory arrangement for all parties
Strategy: manipulating others to gain advantage	Spontaneity: being honest about one's goals and motives
Neutrality: acting indifferent to others	Empathy: accepting another's feelings and putting yourself in another's place
Superiority: acting like you are better than someone else	Equality: treating others with respect
Certainty: conveying an unyielding and dogmatic point of view	Provisionalism: being willing to keep an open mind

Figure 7-3 The Gibb Categories of Defensive and Supportive Behaviors

and avoiding the defensive ones will increase the odds of creating and maintaining positive communication climates in your relationships.

Evaluation vs. Description

The first type of defense-provoking behavior Gibb noted is **evaluative communication**. Most people become irritated at judgmental statements, which are likely to be interpreted as indicating a lack of respect. Evaluative language has often been described as "you" language because most such statements contain an accusatory use of that word. For example, "You don't know what you're talking about," "You're not doing your best," or "You drink too much."

On the other hand, **descriptive communication** focuses on the speaker's thoughts and feelings. One form of descriptive communication is "I" language.[30] The descriptive speaker explains the personal effect of the other's action rather than judging the behavior. For instance, instead of saying, "You talk too much," a descriptive communicator would say, "When you don't let me say what's on my mind, I get frustrated." Notice that statements such as this include an account of the other person's behavior plus an explanation of its effect on the speaker and a description of the speaker's feelings.

> **evaluative communication**
Statements interpreted as judgmental; often described as accusatory "you" language, as in, "You are so inconsiderate."

> **descriptive communication**
Messages that focus on the speaker's thoughts and feelings instead of judging the listener.

Control vs. Problem Orientation

A second defense-provoking message involves some attempt to control the other person. **Controlling communication** occurs when a sender seems to be imposing a solution on the receiver with little regard for the receiver's needs or interests. The control can range from relatively small matters (where to eat dinner or what movie to watch) to large ones (whether to remain in a relationship or how to spend a large sum of money).

By contrast, in **problem orientation**, communicators focus on finding solutions that satisfy their own needs *and* those of the others involved. The goal here isn't to "win" at the expense of one's partner but rather to work out some arrangement in which everybody feels like a winner.

Strategy vs. Spontaneity

The third communication behavior that Gibb identified as creating a poor communication climate is **strategy**, or what we'll call *manipulation*. One of the surest ways to make people defensive is to get caught trying to manipulate them. Even well-meant manipulation can cause bad feelings. For example, if your friends drop by unannounced with someone they think you will like, you may feel ambushed and wish that they had asked your permission first.

Spontaneity is the label Gibb used as a contrast to strategy, but a better term might be *honesty*. Honest communication doesn't have to be blurted out as soon as an idea comes to you; it's important to think about what you want to say and express yourself clearly. However, a straightforward message is likely to pay long-run dividends in a positive relational climate. Being spontaneous is the opposite of harboring a hidden agenda. You may accept a friend request on Facebook, only to find that you now receive daily posts about a product your friend wants you to buy. You'd probably feel less manipulated if your friend were upfront about his or her motives from the beginning.

Neutrality vs. Empathy

Gibb used the term **neutrality** or *indifference* to describe a fourth behavior that arouses defensiveness. A neutral attitude communicates a lack of concern for the welfare of another and implies that the other person isn't very important to you. The damaging effects of neutrality become apparent when you consider the hostility that most people have for the large, impersonal organizations with which they have to deal: "I'm just a number to them"; "I feel like I'm dealing with machines rather than people." These two common statements reflect reactions to being handled in an indifferent way.

Empathy means accepting another's feelings and putting yourself in another's place. This doesn't mean you need to agree with that person. Gibb noted the importance of nonverbal messages in communicating empathy. He found that facial and bodily expressions of concern are often more important to the receiver than the words used.

> **controlling communication**
Messages in which the sender tries to impose some sort of outcome on the receiver, usually resulting in a defensive reaction.

> **problem orientation**
A supportive style of communication in which the communicators focus on working together to solve their problems instead of trying to impose their own solutions on one another.

> **strategy**
Gibb's term for manipulative behavior.

> **spontaneity**
Supportive communication behavior in which the sender expresses a message without any attempt to manipulate the receiver.

> **neutrality**
A defense-arousing behavior in which the sender expresses indifference toward a receiver.

> **empathy**
Accepting another's feelings and putting yourself in that person's place, whether or not you agree with him or her.

Superiority vs. Equality

Superiority is a fifth type of communication that creates a defensive climate. When people act as if they think they are better than we are, we are likely to respond defensively.

We often meet people who possess knowledge or talents greater than our own. However, Gibb found ample evidence that many who have superior skills and talents are also capable of conveying an attitude of **equality**. Such people communicate that despite what might be greater talents in certain areas, they still see others as having just as much worth as human beings as they do.

Certainty vs. Provisionalism

Certainty is an unyielding and dogmatic style of communication. Messages that suggest the speaker's mind is already made up are likely to generate defensiveness. Statements such as, "Only an idiot would vote for him" can come off as arrogant and dismissive of other viewpoints.

In contrast to dogmatic communication is **provisionalism**, in which people may have strong opinions but are willing to acknowledge that they don't have a corner on the truth and will change their stand if another position seems more reasonable. You might say, for instance, "My impression is that the candidate has very little experience. What do you know about him?"

There is no guarantee that using Gibb's supportive, confirming approach to communication will build a positive climate, but the chances for a constructive relationship increase when supportive communication is used. Besides boosting the odds of getting a positive response from others, supportive communication can leave you feeling better in a variety of ways: more in control of your relationships, more comfortable, and more positive toward others.

> **superiority**
> A type of communication that suggests one person is better than another.

> **equality**
> Conveyed when communicators show that they believe others have just as much worth as human beings as they do.

> **certainty**
> Messages that dogmatically imply that the speaker's position is correct and that the other person's ideas are not worth considering.

> **provisionalism**
> A supportive style of communication in which the sender expresses a willingness to consider the other person's position.

Which of Gibb's defensive and supportive behaviors do you use most often in your relationships?

CHECK YOUR UNDERSTANDING

OBJECTIVE 7.1 Explain what makes some communication interpersonal.

THE NATURE OF INTERPERSONAL COMMUNICATION

Interpersonal communication is best defined in terms of the quality of interactions, which can be judged on a scale ranging from impersonal to interpersonal. All interpersonal communication consists of both content (literal) messages and relational messages that suggest how we feel about the other person when it comes to dimensions such as affinity, respect, immediacy, and control. Interpersonal exchanges in which the parties talk about the nature of their interaction are called *metacommunication*.

To what extent is communication in your important relationships personal? To what degree is it impersonal? How satisfied are you with that ratio?

OBJECTIVE 7.2 Describe two models of self-disclosure, and apply characteristics of effective and appropriate self-disclosure.

SELF-DISCLOSURE

Self-disclosure is the process of deliberately revealing information about oneself that is significant and that would not normally be known by others. The social penetration model describes how intimacy can be achieved via the breadth and depth of self-disclosure. The Johari window describes the relationship between self-disclosure and self-awareness. While no single style of self-disclosure is appropriate for every situation, you can ask your-self several questions to determine when and how self-disclosing might be beneficial to you and others.

Evaluate the nature of your self-disclosure in an important relationship. How satisfied are you with your findings?

Compare and contrast mediated and face-to-face communication, evaluating the advantages and disadvantages of each.

MEDIATED VERSUS FACE-TO-FACE COMMUNICATION

Mediated channels clearly increase the opportunities to reach a large number of people frequently. There is mixed evidence regarding the way mediated channels shape the quality of interpersonal communication, however. On the one hand, they provide greater opportunities for social interaction by creating low-friction opportunities to interact in both casual and more personal ways. On the other hand, they have the potential to increase social isolation and promote superficial interactions.

How does mediated communication enhance or detract from the quality of your interpersonal relationships?

Distinguish between confirming and disconfirming messages and behavior, and describe how climate spirals develop.

COMMUNICATION CLIMATES IN INTERPERSONAL RELATIONSHIPS

Communication climate refers to the emotional tone of a relationship as it is expressed in the messages being sent and received. Confirming communication occurs on three increasingly positive levels: recognition, acknowledgment, and endorsement. Disconfirming responses, on the other hand, deny the value of others and show a lack of respect. Climate spirals are reciprocating communication patterns that may be either positive or negative. Jack Gibb identified six categories of supportive and defensive behaviors that may affect the communication climate of a relationship.

Identify several disconfirming messages from your own experience and rewrite them as confirming ones, using the Gibb categories of supportive communication.

KEY TERMS

affinity p. 153
avoidance spiral p. 165
breadth p. 156
certainty p. 169
communication climate p. 163
confirming responses p. 164
content message p. 153
contextually interpersonal
     communication p. 153
control p. 154
controlling communication p. 168
depth p. 156

descriptive communication p. 167
disconfirming response p. 164
empathy p. 168
equality p. 169
escalatory conflict spirals p. 165
evaluative communication p. 167
Gibb categories p. 166
immediacy p. 154
Johari window p. 157
metacommunication p. 155
neutrality p. 168
problem orientation p. 168

provisionalism p. 169
qualitatively interpersonal
     communication p. 153
relational message p. 153
respect p. 154
self-disclosure p. 156
social penetration model p. 156
spiral p. 165
spontaneity p. 168
strategy (manipulative behavior)
     p. 168
superiority p. 169

HOW SUNNY IS YOUR COMMUNICATION CLIMATE?

Circle your answers to the self-assessment on page 166 on the grid below.
(Note that they do not appear in alphabetical order.) Then read the fore-
cast on the row where most of your answers appear.

GROUPING 1	GROUPING 2	GROUPING 3	GROUPING 4	GROUPING 5	RELATIONSHIP FORECAST
C	A	B	A	B	Indications are that your relational climate is warm and sunny, with a high probablity of descriptive and supportive communication.
B	B	A	C	C	Your relationship tends to be turbulent, with frequent outbreaks of controlling or defensive behavior. Storm warning: Escalatory conflict spirals can cause serious damage.
A	C	C	B	A	Beware of falling temperatures. It's natural for people to drift apart to some degree, but your relationship shows signs of chilly indifference and neutrality.

For more communication resources, see the *Essential Communication* website at www.oup.com/us/ec. There you will find a variety of resources: "Media Room" examples from popular films and television shows to further illustrate important concepts, a list of relevant books and articles, links to descriptions of feature films and television shows at the *Now Playing* website, study aids, and a self-test to check your understanding of the material in this chapter.

Communicating with Friends and Family

learning
Objectives

8.1 Describe four reasons that adults become friends.

8.2 Identify the dimensions that make friendships different from one another.

8.3 Summarize the communication patterns common in high-quality friendships.

8.4 Explain how patterns of communication differ in some of the most common familial relationships.

8.5 Summarize the optimal communication strategies for building strong family bonds.

HOW WE CHOOSE FRIENDS

Friends matter. Good friends keep us healthy, boost our self-esteem, and make us feel loved and supported.[1] They also help us adjust to new challenges and uncertainty.[2] It's not surprising, then, that people with strong and lasting friendships are happier than those without them.[3]

Friendships are special for a number of reasons. First, unlike a parent-child, teacher-student, or doctor-patient relationship, in which one partner has more authority or higher status than the other, friends typically treat each other as equals.[4] Second, unlike family and romantic relationships that may be limited in number, we can have as many friends as we want or have time for. Finally, we are relatively free to design friendships that suit our needs. We may have close friends we talk to every day and others we see only once in a while.

When researchers asked 4- to 6-year-olds how they made friends at school, the children said they mostly made friends with those who liked the same playground activities and who seemed to like them back.[5] Evidence suggests that adults often become friends for similar reasons, including similarity, complementarity, mutual liking, and rewards.

> In what ways could having too much in common with someone create tension in a friendship?

Similarity

We typically consider people friendship material if they remind us of ourselves. Coworkers in one study were most likely to pursue friendships with colleagues they perceived to be similar to themselves. However, the strength of those friendships ultimately depended on *how* they were alike. Superficial similarities such as appearance did not correlate with lasting friendship, but similarities in terms of ethnicity or working style did.[6]

Complementarity

Differences can strengthen a relationship when they are *complementary*, that is, when each partner's characteristics satisfy the other's needs. For example, when introverts and extroverts pair up as friends, they typically report that the quieter person serves as a steady anchor for the friendship and that the more gregarious partner propels the other to take part in activities he or she might otherwise avoid.[7]

Mutual Liking

We are attracted to people who like us—usually.[8] The power of reciprocal attraction is especially strong in the early stages of a relationship.

Conversely, we will probably not care for people who clearly dislike or seem indifferent toward us.

It's no mystery why reciprocal liking builds affinity. People who approve of us bolster our feelings of self-esteem. This approval is rewarding in its own right, and it can also confirm the part of our self-concept that says, "I'm a likable person." Of course, we aren't drawn toward everyone who seems to like us. If we don't find the other person's attributes attractive, his or her interest can be a turn-off.

Rewards

Some social scientists argue that all relationships—both impersonal and personal—are based on a semi-economic model called **social exchange theory**.[9] This model suggests that we tend to stick with people who can give us rewards that are greater than or equal to the costs we encounter in dealing with them. Rewards may be tangible (sharing a nice apartment, doing favors for us) or intangible (prestige, emotional support, companionship). Costs are undesirable outcomes such as a sense of obligation,

Like the nerdy protagonists in *The Big Bang Theory*, we tend to befriend people who have a lot in common with us. These TV friends are all highly educated scientists with similar lifestyles and quirks. However, they are also different in many ways. One is Indian, one is Jewish, one is from a small Texas town, another is from New Jersey, and so on.

Q *In what ways are your closest friends similar to you? In what ways are they different?*

> social exchange theory
A model that suggests that we stay with people who can give us rewards that are greater than or equal to the costs we encounter in dealing with them.

emotional pain, and so on. According to social exchange theorists, we use this formula (usually unconsciously) to decide whether dealing with another person is a "good deal" or "not worth the effort."

OBJECTIVE 8.2 Identify the dimensions that make friendships different from one another.

TYPES OF FRIENDSHIPS

A quick survey of your social network will confirm that friendships come in many forms. Think of several friends in your life—perhaps a new friend, a long-standing friend, and a colleague at work. Then see how they compare on the dimensions described in this section.

 ## What sorts of friendships do you have?

Think of a friend the same sex as you, a friend of the other sex, a casual acquaintance, and a long-term friend. For each one, respond to the following items:

1. How long have you maintained the friendship? How long do you think it will last?

| Short-term | 1 | 2 | 3 | 4 | 5 | Long-term |

2. Does your friendship primarily revolve around joint activities and hobbies, or do you spend time together just to enjoy each other's company?

| Task-oriented | 1 | 2 | 3 | 4 | 5 | Maintenance-oriented |

3. How much do you tell your friend about yourself? Do you keep your conversations light and superficial, or do you share intimate details of your lives?

| Low disclosure | 1 | 2 | 3 | 4 | 5 | High disclosure |

4. How much would you be willing to do for your friend? How quickly would you respond to a phone call or favor request from your friend?

| Low obligation | 1 | 2 | 3 | 4 | 5 | High obligation |

5. How often do you have contact with your friend?

| Infrequent contact | 1 | 2 | 3 | 4 | 5 | Frequent contact |

What are the similarities and differences between the friendships you assessed? Which of the friendships do you consider most rewarding? Least rewarding? Do you want to change the types of friendships you tend to have? Why or why not? ●

Short-Term vs. Long-Term

Short-term friends tend to change as our lives do. We say goodbye because we move, graduate, switch jobs, or change lifestyles. Perhaps we party less or spend more time off the ball field than we used to. Our social networks are likely to change, too. On the other hand, long-term friends are with us even when they aren't. These friendships tend to survive changes and distance.[10] Particularly today, with so many different ways to stay in touch more easily, people report that—as long as the trust and a sense of connection are there—they feel as close to their long-term friends who live far away as to those who are nearby.[11]

Low Disclosure vs. High Disclosure

The odds are that some of your friends know more about you than others. As you learned in Chapter 7, self-disclosure is associated with greater levels of intimacy such that only a few trusted confidantes are likely to know your deepest secrets. But when it comes to even slightly less personal news, we are experiencing a revolution in terms of self-disclosure.

Today, it is quite common for someone to announce personal news to hundreds of friends and acquaintances with a single post or tweet, leading some researchers to proclaim that self-disclosure has "gone public."[12] This

The friendship between Gayle King and Oprah Winfrey has remained strong for more than 30 years, through multiple career changes and relocations. Because friendships are typically less formal and less ritualized than romantic and family relationships, it's up to us to shape them in unique ways.

Q *What communication practices do you rely on to keep your friendships strong?*

isn't necessarily bad, however, as young adults typically find it comforting when friends are willing to read, respond to, and share online disclosures.

Doing-Oriented vs. Being-Oriented

Companionship comes in many forms. Some friends experience closeness "in the doing." That is, they enjoy performing tasks or attending events together and feel closer because of those shared experiences.[13] In these cases, different friends are likely to be tied to particular interests—a golfing buddy or shopping partner, for example. Other friendships are "being-oriented." For these friends, the main focus is on being together, and they might get together just to talk or hang out.[14]

Low Obligation vs. High Obligation

There are some friends for whom we would do just about anything—no request is too big. For others, we may feel a lower sense of obligation, both in terms of what we would do for them and how quickly we would do it. There is a cultural element at play, as well. For example, friends raised in a low-context culture such as the United States are more likely than those raised in a high-context culture such as China to express their appreciation for a friend out loud (see Chapter 3). The Chinese are more likely to express themselves indirectly—most often by doing favors for friends and by showing gratitude and reciprocity when friends do favors for them.[15] It's easy to imagine the misunderstandings that might occur when one friend puts a high value on words and the other on actions.

Same Sex vs. Other Sex

Friendship varies, to some extent, by sex. Same-sex friendships between men typically involve good-natured competition and a focus on tasks and events, whereas female friends tend to treat each other more as equals and to engage in emotional support and self-disclosure.[16] It can work out well when we bring these expectations to our other-sex friendships. Men often say that they find it validating when female friends encourage them to be more emotionally expressive than usual, and women say they appreciate the opportunity to be concrete and direct with their guy friends.[17] Different expectations can lead to misunderstandings, however.

One question that often comes up is whether it's possible for heterosexual men and women to be *just* friends. The answer depends on whom you ask. Women typically say yes. But men give a decidedly iffy answer. In a study of 88 pairs of college-age male-female friendship partners, most women said the friendship was purely platonic, with no romantic interest on either side.[18] The men were more likely to say that they secretly harbored romantic fantasies about their female friends, and they suspected (often wrongly, it seems) that the feeling was mutual.

Researchers speculate that heterosexual men and women get their wires crossed in part because they communicate differently. Because women usually expect friends to be emotionally supportive and understanding, they engage in self-disclosure and empathy behaviors.[19] From the male perspective, this may feel like the trappings of romance rather than friendship. By contrast, men tend to emphasize independence and friendly competition.[20] Those behaviors may not strike women as particularly romantic.

Sexual orientation is another factor in friendship. Friendships between people who are gay and those who are straight can lead to feelings of belonging and acceptance. Gay men who have close friends that are straight are less likely than their peers to perceive that society judges them harshly for being gay.[21] And there seems to be some truth to the idea that straight women and gay men make great friends. Gay men are nearly twice as likely as lesbian women to have opposite-sex friendships.[22] This may be because gay men and straight women trust each other's advice about love and romance. Both sides say they enjoy getting an opposite-sex perspective without the complications of a hidden sexual agenda.[23]

Why are heterosexual women more likely than heterosexual men to believe that men and women can be "just" friends?

In-Person vs. Mediated

The average person has many more online friends than physical ones—double the amount, according to one report.[24] Quantity isn't the only difference between mediated and offline friendships, however. It turns out that online-only friendships may carry a greater risk that the people involved will be deceptive or hostile toward one another.[25]

Research also suggests that face-to-face friends are typically more interdependent than online friends, especially during the early stages of their relationships. In-person friends are more likely to talk about topics in

In *My Best Friend's Wedding*, Julianne Potter (Julia Roberts) asks her gay friend George Downes (Rupert Everett) to pretend they are engaged to make the man she is in love with jealous.

Q **Why do you think gay men and straight women are so often portrayed as friends in mainstream books, television, and movies?**

depth, and they typically share a deeper level of understanding and commitment than online friends do. And, not surprisingly, in-person friends tend to have more similar social networks. However, as online friendships develop, the difference in quality when compared with in-person friendships tends to diminish.[26] There is also some evidence that online relationships can become even more personal, as time goes on, than the in-person variety.[27]

Online friendships have some other clear advantages. Most obviously, distance isn't a factor: It's just as easy to communcate with someone across the globe as in the same town. Many friendships thrive by making use of both social media and quality in-person time. When busy schedules and distance make face time difficult, the ability to keep up with friends via Twitter, Facebook, Instagram, and many other social media platforms can keep the relationship alive and well.[28] Some relationships that start online graduate to personal contact. Online dating is a good example: More than a third of marriages between 2005 and 2012 began online, and online couples tend to have happier, longer marriages than couples who met in person.[29]

OBJECTIVE 8.3 Summarize the communication patterns common in high-quality friendships.

SUCCESSFUL COMMUNICATION IN FRIENDSHIPS

Experts have identified a number of communication patterns that correspond with high-quality friendships. Some strategies that may lead to more successful communication in friendships include being a good listener, giving advice sparingly, sharing feelings respectfully, being willing to apologize and forgive, validating and appreciating others, staying true through the hard times, being trustworthy and loyal, and showing equal give and take.

Be a Good Listener

Listen not only with your ears, but by paying close attention to your friend's nonverbal cues and by noting what he or she isn't saying. As discussed in Chapter 5, active listening requires putting aside distractions and devoting energy to the speaker. Making this effort is one of the powerful indications of how much you care.

Give Advice Sparingly

A defining feature of friendship is treating each other as equals. Offering advice—especially when it's not requested—suggests that you know better than your friend. And if your friend doesn't take the advice, it may feel awkward for both of you. When a friend is confused or troubled, a better option is to listen attentively and, if appropriate, ask your friend what options he or she imagines and what the pros and cons might be of each.

Share Feelings Respectfully

Friendships benefit when people use the kinds of confirming communication described in Chapter 7. Although it may be tempting to make a snide remark or say "it's nothing" when you feel upset, those strategies are likely to damage friendships.[30] Finding the confidence to speak up without attacking the other person is a good investment in a strong friendship.

Apologize and Forgive

Even the best of friends sometimes slip up, as when they forget an important date or say something that embarrasses the other person. In such cases, admitting the mistake, apologizing sincerely, and promising to do better in the future are usually effective at repairing the damaged friendship.[31] By the same token, knowing that we are likely to slip up ourselves may inspire us to offer forgiveness rather than harbor corrosive grudges.[32]

Be Validating and Appreciative

Friends have a special ability to make us feel good about ourselves. Hugs and validating statements such as "You're the best" and "Thank you" enhance friends' satisfaction, as do favors and small tokens of appreciation.[33] Love isn't limited to romantic relationships, and it's important to show your close friends how much you care.

Stay True through Hard Times

People who believe their friends will be there for them when the going gets rough typically experience less everyday stress and more physical and emotional resilience than other people.[34] This is true even when they don't need friends to do anything in particular for them. Just hearing the words "I'll always be there for you" and backing them up with attentive behaviors makes the difference.

Be Trustworthy and Loyal

A classic study of adolescent friends revealed that the two most dreaded violations of trust are sharing private information with others and saying unkind things about a friend behind his or her back.[35] Conversely, we can be good friends by maintaining confidences and standing up for our friends, even when they aren't around.

Give and Take Equally

It may seem that the best kind of friend is one who does a lot for us. However, we are actually happiest when there is equal give and take. In fact, one benefit of a great friendship is the sense that we make a difference in someone's life, not just that someone makes a difference in ours.[36]

Why do we so often feel the need to give our friends advice when they haven't asked for it?

Even though they aren't the most conventional friends, in the classic film *The Wizard of Oz*, Dorothy, the Scarecrow, the Tin Man, and the Lion provide valuable lessons about friendship—accept your friends for who they are, recognize when they might need your help, and remember that good friends can provide tremendous support through life's journey.

Q *What do you find most rewarding about your friendships?*

Explain how patterns of communication differ in some of the most common familial relationships.

TYPES OF FAMILY RELATIONSHIPS

We have been talking about what makes a great friendship. Now we turn to a different type of relationship—one that probably began when we were born and will continue throughout our lives.

In today's world, it's not easy to define what makes a family. Theorist Martha Minnow proposes a solution: She suggests that people who share affection and resources as a family and who think of themselves and present themselves as a family *are* a **family**. [37] Your own experiences probably tell you that this concept of a family might encompass (or exclude) bloodline relatives, adopted family members, stepparents, honorary aunts and uncles, blended families in which the siblings were born to different parents, and others. This makes it easy to understand why people can be hurt by questions such as "Is he your natural son?" and "Is she your real mother?" Calling some family members "real" implies that others are fake or that they don't belong. [38]

Here we examine some of the most common familial relationships: children and parents, siblings, and grandparents and grandchildren.

Parents and Children

It's probably no surprise that we learn how to behave from our parents, but at a more subtle level, we also learn from them how to think about the world around us and how to manage our emotions. Consider which of the following communication patterns and parenting styles remind you most of your family.

Communication Patterns

Power and influence play a major role in any relationship, but especially in the dynamic between parents and children. For example, imagine the issue of a curfew for a teenage member of the family. If the family communication pattern emphasizes **conversation**, the teen and his or her parents probably negotiate the curfew by talking openly about it and listening to each other. However, if the emphasis is on **conformity**, the teen will be expected to follow mom and dad's rules, beliefs, and values without challenging them. [39]

> **family**
People who share affection and resources as a family and who think of themselves and present themselves as a family, regardless of their genetic commonality.

> **conversation**
A family communication pattern in which members are encouraged to communicate openly about rules and expectations.

> **conformity**
A family communication pattern in which members are expected to adhere to an established set of rules, beliefs, and values.

The film *The Kids Are Alright* illustrates the changing nature of families in today's society. A same-sex couple raises two children conceived by artificial insemination, who bring their father into their family life.

Q *What forms of families have you witnessed? To what extent does their composition affect the kinds of communication you have observed?*

Most evidence suggests that children who grow up with the conversation approach are better at expressing their emotions confidently and effectively as they grow older.[40,41] As you might imagine, children who don't engage in much give-and-take communication with their parents are usually less comfortable using that style with other people as well.

Among children who grow up with a confirmatory pattern, the advantage goes to those who perceive that their parents are motivated by love and concern. They tend to grow up to be more emotionally resilient than children who believe their parents control their behavior for selfish reasons.[42]

Parenting Styles

Now let's focus on specific parenting styles.[43] **Authoritarian** parents are strict and demanding, and they expect unquestioning obedience. We might characterize this as a "do it because I said so" style. **Authoritative** parents are also firm, clear, and strict, but they encourage children to communicate openly with them. These parents have high expectations, but they are willing to discuss them and to listen to children's input and even negotiate the rules when it seems merited. Finally, **permissive** parents are open to dialogue, and they do not require children to follow many rules.

Of these styles, most evidence favors the authoritative style in terms of fostering children's happiness and their adaptability throughout life.[44] As researchers Jordan Hamon and Paul Schrodt put it, authoritative parents provide the dual benefits of structure and compassion—they are "warm, responsive, assertive without being overly intrusive or restrictive."

Siblings

Sibling relationships involve an interwoven, and often paradoxical, collection of emotions. Children are likely to feel both intense loyalty and fierce competition with their brothers and sisters and to be both loving and antagonistic toward them. In the midst of this complexity—what some theorists call the "playing and arguing, joking and bickering, caring and fighting"[45] of sibling life—children learn a great deal about themselves and how to relate to others.[46]

Here, we focus on six types of sibling relationships people usually settle into as they become adults, as reflected in the work of Robert Stewart and colleagues.[47]

Supportive

Siblings classified as supportive talk regularly and consider themselves to be accessible and emotionally close to one other. Supportive relationships are most common among siblings who are of similar ages, particularly if they come from large families.[48]

Longing

Siblings in the longing category typically admire and respect one other. However, they interact less frequently and with less depth than they would like.

> authoritarian
An approach in which parents are strict and demanding and expect unquestioning obedience.

> authoritative
An approach in which parents are firm, clear, and strict, but encourage children to communicate openly with them.

> permissive
An approach in which parents are open to dialogue but do not require children to follow many rules.

Competitive

Sibling rivalry usually diminishes as brothers and sisters emerge from adolescence into adulthood.[49] However, some siblings remain competitive in their adult years, most often if they perceive that their parents continue to play favorites.[50]

Apathetic

Siblings classified as apathetic only communicate with one another on special occasions, such as holidays or weddings, or rarely at all.

Hostile

Siblings who report being hostile toward each other usually say they have given up on communication all together.[51] Unlike apathetic siblings, who may drift apart without hard feelings, hostile siblings usually feel a lingering sense of jealousy, resentment, and anger.

Grandparents and Grandchildren

Less than 100 years ago, adults seldom lived long enough to know their grandchildren. Now children more often reach adulthood knowing their grandparents and even their great-grandparents. Longer life spans have made grandparent relationships possible, but other factors play a role as well.

For one, it is now common for both parents to work outside the home and for single parents to raise children. In many cases, grandparents have pitched in to help fill the gaps—providing child care, after-school activities, and sometimes even a place to live. One in 10 American children will live with a grandparent at some time in his or her life, making intergenerational communication more important than ever before.[52]

Another factor involves communication technology. The number of people age 65 and older who use social media tripled between 2009 and 2013, and the trend shows no sign of slowing.[53] Older adults active on Facebook and other social media avenues typically have stronger ties with multi-generational family members as a result.[54]

The trick for grandparents, say many theorists, is to manage the balance between "being there" and "interfering."[55] When grandparents help with the children, it may be difficult to know

At the center of the animated film *Frozen* are two disconnected sisters who eventually reconcile and discover the power of family.

Q *If you have a sibling, what role has conflict played in your relationship? If you don't have a sibling, how do you think that has affected your communication with others?*

In the TV show *Last Man Standing*, Mike (Tim Allen) and Vanessa Baxter (Nancy Travis) share a home with their three daughters and a grandson. The result is a collection of supportive communication and, sometimes, unwelcome parenting advice.

Q *What role have grandparents (either biological or honorary) played in your life?*

Why is it sometimes so challenging for grandparents to balance their role in the family?

when or whether they should serve as disciplinarians or parenting advisors. It's a touchy subject. Bruce Feiler, who researches and writes about family dynamics, and his wife Linda encourage the grandparents in their daughters' lives to indulge the girls, befriend them, listen to them, and spend time with them. But Feiler says he hopes they will "grandparent" them rather than "parent" them:

> You may think you're merely commenting on our children. But you're really commenting on our marriage. As parents, we often disagree on these matters, and suddenly we find you in the middle of our relationship. No matter how much we love you, we certainly don't want you there.[56]

Feiler and his family have drafted a set of written rules that serve the girls' interests as well as those of the grandparents. For example, one rule is: *Our house our rules, your house your rules*. He says that communicating about expectations openly has strengthened family ties.

The bonuses of grandparent–grandchild relationships usually outweigh the potential pitfalls. Grandparents often have the time and inclination to spend time with younger members of the family. They can provide loving attention and fun without having to scold or punish. It's a positive dynamic both sides can appreciate.[57]

Children frequently report that their grandparents are caring and supportive listeners who are always there for them. And sharing time together when the kids are young pays off down the line. Children who interact frequently with their grandparents are more likely than others to remain in close contact with them later in life.[58]

OBJECTIVE 8.5

Summarize the optimal communication strategies for building strong family bonds.

SUCCESSFUL COMMUNICATION IN FAMILY RELATIONSHIPS

Communicating with family members can be a challenge, but it's also an opportunity to build our skills. Following are some strategies for successful communication based on experts' advice.

Share Family Stories

One of the greatest predictors of children's emotional resilience is how well they know their families' stories.[59] This is particularly true when the stories involve rich details about family members' struggles and accomplishments.

In *August: Osage County*, Meryl Streep plays Violet, the verbally abusive family matriarch who targets much of her anger toward her family and their relationships.

Q *How influential are your family's beliefs when you choose a romantic partner? What factors might influence whether you introduce a love interest to your family?*

Family stories contribute to a shared sense of identity, they convey that adversity and triumph are natural parts of life, and they suggest strategies people can use when they encounter hurdles of their own.[60]

Listen to Each Other

It's a lesson that has popped up several times in this chapter: People who are involved in reflection and conversation learn how to manage and express their feelings better than people who don't. And, they tend to have better relationships as a result.[61,62] Listening to each other is good for our relationships and healthy for us personally.

Negotiate Privacy Rules

When family members feel their privacy has been violated, they often experience that something uniquely theirs has been stolen.[63] At the same time, too much privacy can mean that families overlook dangerous behavior and avoid distressing but important topics. Experts suggest that families talk about privacy expectations and "co-own" the rules they agree upon. These might involve whether children "friend" their parents on Facebook, how much the children are allowed to know about their parents' health and financial status, when a secret shouldn't be kept secret, and so on.

In what ways does your family communicate the values most dear to you?

In the movie *Rocky Balboa*, a son's struggle with identity triggers a conversation about dealing with rejection and failure and the power that comes with believing in yourself.

Q *Why do supportive messages from our families tend to carry so much weight?*

Coach Conflict Management

Many parents assume that children should manage their own squabbles or they will never learn how. The evidence suggests otherwise.[64] In reality, effective conflict management doesn't just happen. It is a sophisticated process that often goes against our fight-or-flight instincts. For better or worse, most of us develop our conflict management strategies at home. Families can help by creating safe environments in which members can talk about how they feel and strive for mutually agreeable solutions. Parents who coach their children through this process are usually more effective than those who take a hands-off approach to conflict with their children.

Go Heavy on Confirming Messages

Supportive messages by family members can give us the confidence to believe in ourselves. Compliments such as "you are a very thoughtful person," and "I know you will do a great job" tend to be self-fulfilling. For example, teens whose parents frequently compliment and encourage them are less likely than others to drop out of high school.[65]

Have Fun

Happy families make it a point to minimize distractions and spend time together on a regular basis. They establish togetherness rituals that suit their busy lives, such as sharing dessert before bedtime when sitting down for dinner is out of the question,[66] and they engage in adventures together, both large and small.

CHECK YOUR UNDERSTANDING

OBJECTIVE 8.1 Describe four reasons that adults become friends.

HOW WE CHOOSE FRIENDS

We typically choose people as friends who have a good deal in common with us, have characteristics that complement our own, who like us back, and who offer rewards that are worth the costs.

Think of your closest friend. Are you mostly similar to each other, or are your characteristics complementary? What is most rewarding about the friendship?

OBJECTIVE 8.2 Identify the dimensions that make friendships different from one another.

TYPES OF FRIENDSHIPS

Friendships come in different forms. They may vary in terms of how long they last, how much we share with each other, what we do together, and how obligated we feel toward one another. Friendships can also vary depending on the sex and sexual orientation of the people involved.

If you could design the ideal friendship, would it involve high or low amounts of self-disclosure? Would you mostly spend time just being together or engaging in shared activities? Would your ideal friend be male or female? Explain your answers.

OBJECTIVE 8.3 Summarize the communication patterns common in high-quality friendships.

SUCCESSFUL COMMUNICATION IN FRIENDSHIPS

We can nurture our friendships by being good listeners, giving advice sparingly, sharing our feelings respectfully, apologizing and forgiving, being validating and appreciative, being there through hard times, remaining loyal, and by giving as much as we receive.

Think of an important friendship in your life. How would you rate your own communication in terms of each of the following: listening, sharing feelings, apologizing and forgiving, and giving as much as you receive? How would you rate your friend in each of these categories?

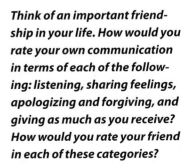

OBJECTIVE 8.4 Explain how patterns of communication differ in some of the most common familial relationships.

TYPES OF FAMILY RELATIONSHIPS

Families are better defined in terms of affection, collective resources, and shared identity than by biology. Family communication patterns usually embody an ideal of either conversation or conformity, and parents' approach to rule following may be authoritarian, authoritative, or permissive. Sibling relationships often involve complex and contradictory feelings, but by adulthood most of them are either supportive, longing, competitive, apathetic, or hostile. The involvement of grandparents in our lives is a relatively recent phenomenon. While it can be challenging to define the parameters, grandparents and grandchildren often share a special bond.

Were the authority figures in your family more likely to emphasize conversation about the rules or conformity to them? Does that affect the way you communicate with others today?

OBJECTIVE 8.5 Summarize the optimal communication strategies for building strong family bonds.

SUCCESSFUL COMMUNICATION IN FAMILY RELATIONSHIPS

Experts have identified strategies for strengthening family relationships. People in happy families usually share stories, listen to and support each other, respect each other's privacy, engage in effective conflict management, give each other compliments, and have fun together.

Evaluate the current communication practices used in your own family. What alternatives might improve the satisfaction of all members?

KEY TERMS

authoritarian p. 186
authoritative p. 186
conformity p. 185

conversation p. 185
family p. 185
permissive p. 186

social exchange theory p. 177

FOR FURTHER EXPLORATION

For more communication resources, see the *Essential Communication* website at www.oup.com/us/ec. There you will find a variety of resources: "Media Room" examples from popular films and television shows to further illustrate important concepts, a list of relevant books and articles, links to descriptions of feature films and television shows at the *Now Playing* website, study aids, and a self-test to check your understanding of the material in this chapter.

Communicating with Romantic Partners

9.1 Define intimacy and describe a range of options for conveying intimate messages.

9.2 Analyze the themes of a close relationship using both Knapp's model of relationship development and the dialectical model.

9.3 Identify the functions served by altruistic lies, evasions, and self-serving lies.

9.4 Distinguish between constructive and destructive styles and methods of dealing with interpersonal conflict.

THE NATURE OF INTIMACY

Romantic love is the stuff of songs, fairy tales, and happy endings. So it might surprise you that the butterflies-in-your-belly sense of romantic bliss isn't a great predictor of happiness. A much better predictor is the effort that couples put into their communication. Factors such as trust, agreeableness, and emotional expressiveness are primarily responsible for long-term relationship success.[1,2] In this chapter, we explore the role of communication in forming and sustaining romantic relationships.

By definition, romantic **intimacy** requires that we express ourselves personally through physical contact, shared experiences, intellectual sharing, and emotional disclosures.[3] Being open with another person in this manner involves vulnerability. But intimacy also yields some of life's

> intimacy

A state of closeness between people that can be manifested physically, intellectually, emotionally, and via shared activities.

Pauletta and Denzel Washington say they have stayed happily married for 30 years because their relationship is rewarding on multiple levels.

Q *Which aspects of intimacy characterize your closest relationships?*

greatest rewards, including a sense of being understood, accepted, and supported.[4] As you will see, romantic intimacy may mean different things to different people, and communication can be a tool for both enhancing and diminishing it.

Male and Female Intimacy Styles

Until recently, most social scientists believed that women were better at developing and maintaining intimate relationships than men. This belief grew from the assumption that the most important ingredients of intimacy are sharing personal information and showing emotions. Most research does show that women (taken as a group, of course) *are* more willing than men to share their thoughts and feelings.[5] However, male-female differences aren't as great as they seem,[6] and emotional expression isn't the *only* way to develop close relationships.

Whereas women typically value personal talk, men often demonstrate caring by doing things for their partners and spending time with them. It's easy to imagine the misunderstandings that result from this. Indeed, women's most frequent complaint is that men don't stop to focus on "the relationship" enough.[7] Men, however, are more likely to complain about what women do or don't do in an instrumental sense. For example, they may consider it highly significant if a woman doesn't call when she says she will.

Men and women may view sex differently as well. Whereas many women think of sex as a way to express intimacy that has already developed, men are more likely to see it as a way to *create* that intimacy.[8] In this sense, the man who encourages sex early in a relationship or after a fight may view the shared activity as a way to build closeness. By contrast, the woman who views personal talk as the pathway to intimacy may resist the idea of physical closeness before the emotional side of the relationship has been discussed.

What happens when both partners are of the same sex? Research is limited so far, but much of it suggests that, on average, same-sex couples are more satisfied with their relationships than are heterosexual couples. Same-sex couples typically report greater harmony, less emotional distance, and more shared activities than male-female romantic partners.[9] Researchers speculate that this may be because same-sex couples have been socialized to communicate in similar ways and to have similar expectations. And, because they are likely to treat each other as equals, same-sex couples tend to seek common ground when faced with decisions and conflict.[10]

Love Languages

Some intimacy styles have less to do with sex or gender than with personal preferences. Relationship counselor Gary Chapman[11] observes that people typically orient to one of five love languages. The odds are that you value

In the film *Friends with Benefits*, friends Dylan (Justin Timberlake) and Jamie (Mila Kunis) are reluctant to begin a romantic relationship. So they attempt a casual alternative in which they remain friends but share physical intimacy without emotional entanglements.

Q *What kinds of intimacy mean the most to you? How can you communicate better in order to get the closeness you seek?*

all of these love languages to some degree, but you probably give some greater weight than others. Good intentions lead you astray, however, if you assume that your partner feels the same way you do. The golden rule—that we should do unto others as we would have them do unto us—can lead to misunderstandings when our partner's primary love language differs from ours.[12]

Affirming Words

This language includes compliments, thanks, and statements that express love and commitment. Even when you know someone loves and values you, it's often nice to hear it in words. The happiest couples continue to flirt with each other, even after they have been together for many years.[13]

Quality Time

Some people show love by completing tasks together, talking, or engaging in some other mutually enjoyable activity. The good news is that, even when people can't be together physically, talking about quality time can be an important means of expressing love. For example, partners separated

What is your love language?

Answer these questions to learn more about the love languages you prefer:

1. You have had a stressful time working on a team project. The best thing your romantic partner can do for you is:
   a. Set aside distractions to spend some time with you
   b. Do your chores so you can relax
   c. Give you a big hug
   d. Pamper you with a dessert you love
   e. Tell you the team is lucky to have someone as talented as you

2. What is your favorite way to show that you care?
   a. Go somewhere special together
   b. Do a favor without being asked
   c. Hold hands and sit close together
   d. Surprise your romantic partner with a little treat
   e. Tell your loved one how you feel in writing

3. With which of the following do you most agree?
   a. The most lovable thing someone can do is give you his or her undivided attention
   b. Actions speak louder than words
   c. A loving touch says more than words can express
   d. Your dearest possessions are things your loved one has given you
   e. People don't say "I love you" nearly enough

4. Your anniversary is coming up. Which of the following appeals to you most?
   a. An afternoon together, just the two of you
   b. A romantic, home-cooked dinner (you don't have to lift a finger)
   c. A relaxing massage by candlelight
   d. A photo album of good times you have shared
   e. A homemade card that lists the qualities your romantic partner loves about you

For the meaning of your scores, see pg. 223. ●

by military deployments often say they feel closer to each other just talking about everyday activities and future plans.[14]

Acts of Service
People may show love by performing favors such as caring for each other when they are sick, doing the dishes, making meals, and so on. Committed couples report that sharing daily tasks is the most frequent way they show their love and commitment.[15] Although each person need not contribute

Beyoncé and Jay-Z were recently named one of the celebrity couples most prone to public displays of affection in social media.

Q *How important is physical affection in your romantic relationships?*

Which love languages do you prefer? Why?

in exactly the same ways, an overall sense that they are putting forth equal effort is essential to long-term happiness.[16]

Gifts

It's no coincidence that we buy gifts for loved ones on Valentine's Day and other occasions such as birthdays and anniversaries. For some people, receiving a gift—even an inexpensive or free one such as a flower from the garden or a hand-made card—adds to their sense of being loved and valued.[17]

Physical Touch

Loving touch may involve a hug, a kiss, a pat on the back, or having sex. For some people, touch is such a powerful indicator of intimacy that even an incidental touch can spur interest. In one study, a woman asked men in a bar for assistance adding a key to her key ring.[18] She lightly touched some of the men but not others. Afterwards, the men who had been touched were more romantically interested in the woman than the other men were. Touch is potent even in long-term relationships. Researchers in one study asked couples to increase the number of times they kissed each other. Six weeks later, the couples' stress levels and relational satisfaction, and even their cholesterol levels, had significantly improved.[19]

Analyze the themes of a close relationship using both Knapp's model of relationship development and the dialectical model.

OBJECTIVE 9.2

COMMUNICATING IN ROMANTIC RELATIONSHIPS

Some romances ignite quickly, whereas others grow gradually. Either way, couples are likely to progress through a series of stages as they define what they mean to each other and what they should expect in terms of shared activities, exclusivity, commitment, and their public identity. All the while, they are involved in a balancing act as they negotiate between autonomy and togetherness, openness and privacy, and other factors.

A Developmental Perspective

One of the best-known explanations of how communication operates in different phases of a relationship was developed by communication scholar Mark Knapp. His **developmental model** depicts five stages of intimacy development (coming together) and five stages in which people distance themselves from each other (coming apart).[20] Other researchers have suggested that the middle phases of the model can also be understood in terms of keeping stable relationships operating smoothly and satisfactorily (**relational maintenance**).[21] Figure 9-1 shows how Knapp's 10 stages fit into this three-part view of communication in relationships. As you read on,

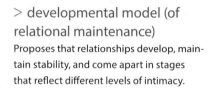

> developmental model (of relational maintenance)
Proposes that relationships develop, maintain stability, and come apart in stages that reflect different levels of intimacy.

> relational maintenance
The process of keeping stable relationships operating smoothly and satisfactorily.

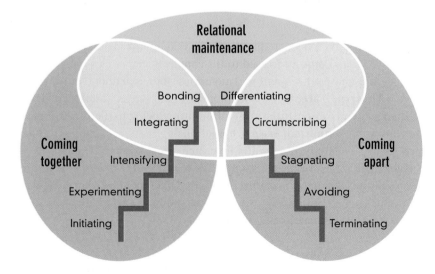

Figure 9-1 **Knapp's Stages of Relational Development**

consider how well these stages reflect communication in the close relationships you have experienced.

Initiating

The initiating stage occurs when people first encounter one another. Knapp restricts this stage to conversation openers, such as "It's nice to meet you" and "How's it going?" During this stage, people form first impressions and have the opportunity to present themselves in an appealing manner.

Experimenting

People enter the experimental stage when they begin to get acquainted through "small talk." They may ask, "Where are you from?" and "What do you do?" or "Do you know Josephine Mandoza? She lives in San Francisco, too." Comments during this stage are generally pleasant and uncritical, and commitment is minimal. Though small talk might seem meaningless, Knapp points out that it presents a valuable opportunity: Small talk allows us to interact with a wide range of people to determine who is worth getting to know better.

Intensifying

In this stage, truly interpersonal relationships develop as people begin to express how they feel about each other. It's often a time of strong emotions and optimism that may lead either to a higher level of intimacy or to the end of the relationship, if, for example, one partner feels pressured and the other rejected. Dating couples often navigate this uncertainty by flirting, hinting around, asking hypothetical questions, giving compliments, and being more affectionate than before. They become bolder and more direct only if their partners seem receptive to these gestures.[22] At this point, couples begin to see themselves as "we" instead of as separate individuals.

Integrating

In the integration stage, couples begin to take on an identity as a social unit. Invitations come addressed to the couple. Social circles merge. Couples begin to share possessions and memories—our apartment, our car, our song.[23] The term "Facebook official" applies to this stage. Couples are likely to change their relationship status online, announcing to their friends that they are in a committed, exclusive relationship.[24] As it becomes a given that they will share resources and help each other, partners become comfortable making relatively straightforward requests of each other. Gone are the elaborate explanations, inducements, and apologies. In short, partners in an integrated relationship expect more from one another than they do in less intimate associations.

Bonding

The bonding stage is likely to involve a wedding, a commitment ceremony, or some other public means of communicating to the world that this is a

Thirty-three gay and straight couples married at the 2014 Grammys during Macklemore and Lewis's performance of "Same Love." While some believe that marriage should be reserved exclusively for heterosexual partners, increasing acceptance of same-sex marriages is viewed by others as an important step toward a more tolerant society.

Q *In what ways are your romantic relationships supported by others? In what ways, if any, do people express disapproval?*

relationship meant to last. Bonding generates social support for the relationship and demonstrates a strong sense of commitment and exclusivity.

Differentiating

Not all relationships last forever. Even when the bonds between partners are strong and enduring, it is sometimes desirable to create some distance. In the differentiating stage, the emphasis shifts from "how we are alike" to "how we are different." For example, a couple who moves in together may find that they have different expectations about doing chores, sleeping late, what to watch on TV, and so on. This doesn't necessarily mean the relationship is doomed. Differences remind partners that they are distinct individuals. To maintain this balance, couples in this stage may demonstrate verbally and nonverbally that they wish to have space. They may claim different areas of the home for their private use and reduce their use of nicknames, gestures, and words that distinguish the relationship as intimate and unique.[25]

Circumscribing

In the circumscribing stage, communication decreases significantly in quantity and quality. Rather than discuss a disagreement, which requires some degree of energy on both parts, partners may withdraw mentally by using silence, daydreaming, or fantasizing. They may also withdraw physically by spending less time together. Circumscribing entails a shrinking of interest and commitment.

Stagnating

If circumscribing continues, the relationship begins to stagnate. Partners behave toward each other in old, familiar ways without much feeling. Like workers who have lost interest in their jobs yet continue to go through the motions, sadly, some couples unenthusiastically repeat the same conversations, see the same people, and follow the same routines without any sense of joy or novelty.

Avoiding

When stagnation becomes too unpleasant, partners distance themselves in more overt ways. They might use excuses, such as "I've been busy lately," or direct requests, such as "Please don't call. I don't want to see you now." In either case, the writing about the relationship's future is clearly on the wall.

Terminating

Characteristics of this final stage include summary dialogues about where the relationship has gone and the desire to break up. The relationship may end with a cordial dinner, a note left on the kitchen table, a phone call, or a legal document stating the dissolution. Depending on each person's feelings, this stage can be quite short, or it may be drawn out over time.

One key difference between couples who get together again after a break-up and those who go their separate ways is how well they communicate about their dissatisfaction and negotiate for a mutually appealing fresh start. Unsuccessful couples deal with their problems by avoidance, indirectness, and reduced involvement with one another. By contrast, couples who repair their relationships more often air their concerns and spend time and effort negotiating solutions to their problems.

A number of practical lessons emerge from the developmental perspective:

Each stage requires different types of communication. Partners may find that talking about highly personal issues deepens their bond in the intensifying stage but is overwhelming sooner than that. Likewise, the polite behavior of the first two stages may seem cool and distant as intimacy increases.

Relational development involves risk and vulnerability. At any stage—even those associated with coming together—the relationship may falter. Intimacy only evolves if people are willing to take a chance of becoming gradually more self-disclosive.[26]

Partners can shape relational trajectories. The direction a relationship takes isn't inevitable. Partners may recognize the early signs of "coming apart" in time to reverse the trend. For example, partners who realize they are differentiating or stagnating can refresh their relationship by focusing energy on the intimacy-enhancing communication of experimenting, intensifying, and integrating. As Knapp puts it, movement is always to a new place.[27]

A Dialectical Perspective

The dialectical perspective is similar to the developmental model in that both of them focus on communication as a means of creating relational closeness and distance. However, while the development model focuses on communication in particular phases, the dialectic perspective addresses how partners use communication to negotiate meaning throughout their relationships.

Communication may change across relational stages, but some themes remain the same throughout a relationship. Couples grapple with the same kinds of challenges, whether their relationships are brand new or have lasted for decades. The **dialectical model** suggests that relational partners continually must struggle to satisfy opposing or incompatible forces, both within themselves and with one another.[28] The way we manage these challenges defines the nature of relationships and our communication within them.

Partners face three main types of dialectical tensions throughout the life of their relationship. As you read about each set of opposing needs, consider how they operate in your life.

> **dialectical model (of relational maintenance)**
>
> A model claiming that, throughout their lifetime, people in virtually all interpersonal relationships must deal with equally important, simultaneous, and opposing forces such as connection and autonomy, predictability and novelty, and openness versus privacy.

Connection Versus Autonomy

The conflicting desires for connection and independence are embodied in the connection–autonomy dialectic. One of the most common reasons for breaking up is that one partner doesn't satisfy the other's need for connection.[29]

"We barely spent any time together."

"She/he wasn't committed to the relationship."

"We had different needs."

But couples split up for the opposite reason as well.[30]

"I felt trapped."

"I needed freedom."

Even within ourselves, we are faced with the same sort of contradiction. On one hand we desire intimacy, but we often feel the need to maintain some distance as well.

Managing dialectic tensions is tricky, because our needs change over time. Author Desmond Morris suggests that each of us repeatedly goes through three stages: "Hold me tight," "Put me down," and "Leave me alone."[31] In marriages, for example, the "Hold me tight" bonds of the first year are often followed by a desire for independence. This need for autonomy can manifest itself in a number of ways, such as the desire to make friends or engage in activities that don't include the spouse, or making a career move that might disrupt the relationship. Movement toward autonomy may lead to a breakup, but it can also be part of a cycle that redefines the relationship in ways that allow partners to recapture or even surpass the closeness that existed previously. For example, you might find that spending some time apart makes you miss and appreciate your partner more than ever.

Openness Versus Privacy

As explained in Chapter 8, disclosure is one characteristic of interpersonal relationships. Yet, along with the need for intimacy, your experience probably shows an equally important need for you to maintain some space between yourself and others. These sometimes-conflicting drives create the openness–privacy dialectic.

Even the strongest interpersonal relationships require some distance. Lovers may go through periods of sharing and times of relative withdrawal. Likewise, they may experience periods of passion and then periods of little physical contact.

Figure 9-2 illustrates variable patterns of openness uncovered in a study of college students' communication patterns.[32] The students reported the degree of openness in one of their important relationships—a friendship, romantic relationship, or marriage—over a range of 30 conversations. The graphs show moderate fluctuations between disclosure and privacy in growing and stable relationships, but an erratic series of ups and downs in relationships that were deteriorating.

Predictability Versus Novelty

Stability is an important need in relationships, but too much predictability can lead to feelings of staleness and boredom. People differ in their desire for stability and surprises—even from one time to another. The classic example is becoming engaged just before graduation or military deployment, when life may seem particularly novel and uncertain. Commitment may balance some of the uncertainty people feel in that situation. However, it may feel too predictable once life settles into a routine. There are a number of strategies people can use to manage contradictory drives such as these.

Strategies for Managing Dialectical Tensions

Dialectical tensions are a fact of life in intimate relationships. But there are a number of ways partners can deal with these. Some of these strategies are more productive than others.[33] As you read about them, consider which ones you use and how well they meet your relational needs.

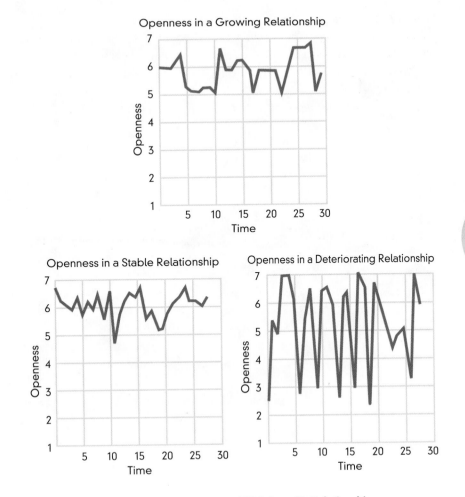

Figure 9-2 **Cyclical Phases of Openness and Withdrawal in Relationships**

How would you graph the fluctuations in openness and privacy in one of your important relationships?

Denial

One of the least functional responses to dialectical tensions is to deny that they exist. People in denial insist that "everything is fine." For example, some couples refuse to deal with conflict, ignoring any problems or pretending that they agree about everything.

Disorientation

When communicators feel so overwhelmed and helpless that they are unable to confront their problems they are said to be disoriented. In the face of dialectical tensions they might fight, freeze, or even leave the relationship. A couple who discovers soon after the honeymoon that living a "happily ever after" conflict-free life is impossible might view their marriage as a mistake and seek a divorce.

He's gentle and noncommittal, she's hotheaded and selfish. But after four decades, Kermit the Frog and Miss Piggy maintain a loving relationship.

Q **Why do you think it is so challenging for people in real-life relationships to manage dialectical tensions successfully?**

Selection

When partners employ the strategy of selection, they respond to one end of the dialectical spectrum and ignore the other. For example, a couple caught between the conflicting desires for stability and novelty may decide that predictability is the "right" or "responsible" choice and put aside their longing for excitement.

Alternation

Communicators sometimes alternate between one end of the dialectical spectrum and the other. For example, partners may spend time apart during the week, but reserve weekends for couple time.

Polarization

In some cases, couples find a balance of sorts by each staking a claim at opposite ends of a dialectic continuum. For example, one partner might give up nearly all personal interests in the name of togetherness, while the other maintains an equally extreme commitment to being independent. In the classic demand-withdraw pattern,[34] the more one partner insists on closeness the more the other feels suffocated and craves distance.

Segmentation

In segmentation, couples compartmentalize different areas of the relationship. For example, a couple might manage the openness–privacy dialectic by sharing almost all their feelings about mutual friends with one another but keeping certain parts of their past romantic histories private.

Moderation

The moderation strategy is characterized by **compromises** in which couples back off from expressing either end of the dialectical spectrum. A couple might decide that taking separate vacations is too extreme for them, but they will make room for some alone time while they are traveling together.

> compromise
An approach to conflict resolution in which both parties attain at least part of what they seek through self-sacrifice.

Reframing

Communicators can also respond to dialectical challenges by reframing them in terms that redefine the situation so that the apparent contradiction disappears. Consider partners who regard the inevitable challenges of managing dialectical tensions as exciting opportunities to grow instead of as relational problems.

Reaffirmation

A final strategy for handling dialectical tensions is reaffirmation— acknowledging that dialectical tensions will never disappear and accepting or even embracing the challenges they present. Communicators who use reaffirmation view dialectical tensions as part of the ride of life.

Couples who understand the dialectical perspective can better appreciate several facets of relationship maintenance:

> **Relationships involve continual change and negotiation.** Couples who understand dialectical tensions can give up the unrealistic notion that they will always be in sync or that negotiating relationship options should be effortless.
> **Partners can be in sync in some ways, but not in others.** Recognizing different dialectic tensions may help couples identify the critical issue when things feel out of balance between them.
> **Some approaches are more conducive to relational satisfaction than others.** It may be tempting to deny opposing tensions, to polarize, or to exit the relationship altogether. However, other options are usually more effective in satisfying each individual's needs and strengthening the relationship.

What means of negotiating dialectical tensions do you use most often, and how well do they work?

Identify the functions served by altruistic lies, evasions, and self-serving lies.

DECEPTION IN ROMANTIC RELATIONSHIPS

Partners are likely to experience deceit, even in their closest, most intimate relationships. In fact, people lie more than they realize. Research shows that most people lie, on average, once or twice per day[35] and even more when they meet someone new. Upon first meeting, the average is about three lies in the first 10 minutes, especially when romantic attraction is a factor.[36]

Not all lies are equally devastating. The greatest damage occurs when the relationship is most intense, when the importance of the subject is high, and when there have been previous doubts about the deceiver's honesty. Of these three factors, the one most likely to cause a relational crisis is the sense that one's partner lied about something important.[37]

Experts suggest that, if you are considering a deception, you consider how others would respond if they knew about it.[38] Would they accept your reasons for being untruthful, or would they be hurt by them? In light of that, we explore three types of lies here: altruistic lies, evasions, and self-serving lies.

Altruistic Lies

Altruistic lies are defined, at least by the people who tell them, as being harmless, or even helpful, to the person to whom they are told.[39] For example, you might tell the host of a dinner party that the food was delicious even if it wasn't. Or you might compliment your boyfriend or girlfriend's new haircut to avoid hurting his or her feelings. For the most part, white lies such as these fall in the category of being polite, and effective communicators know how and when to use them without causing offense.

Evasions

Evasions aren't outright mistruths. Rather, they evade full disclosure by being deliberately vague. Often motivated by good intentions, gray lies are based on the belief that less clarity can be beneficial for the sender, the receiver, or sometimes both.[40]

One type of gray lie is **equivocation**—deliberately ambiguous statements with two or more equally plausible meanings.[41] As you read in Chapter 4, people sometimes send equivocal messages without meaning to, resulting in confusion. But other times we are deliberately vague. For instance, when your partner asks what you think of an awful outfit, you could say, "It's really unusual—one of a kind!"

Hinting is a second type of evasion. People hint around to bring about a desired response without asking for it directly. Some hints are designed

> **altruistic lie**
Deception intended to be nonmalicious, or even helpful, to the person to whom it is told.

> **equivocation**
Language with more than one likely interpretation.

> **hinting**
Saying something to bring about a desired response without asking for it directly.

to save the *receiver* from embarrassment. For example, a face-saving guest might hint to her host by saying, "It's getting late," rather than, "I'm bored and want to leave now." Other hints are strategies for saving the *sender* from embarrassment, as when someone says, "I'm pretty sure smoking isn't allowed here" instead of the blunter "Your smoking bothers me." Clearly, hints only work if people pick up on them.

Equivocations and hints are generally offered in a spirit meant to avoid hurting people's feelings. If your friend hits on you and you are not romantically interested, you might be evasive with an equivocal statement such as, "Your friendship means a lot to me, and I wouldn't want anything to ruin that."

Self-Serving Lies

Self-serving lies are attempts to manipulate the listener into believing something that is untrue—not primarily to protect the listener, but to advance the deceiver's agenda. For example, people might lie on their income tax returns or deny that they have been drinking if a cop pulls them over.

Self-serving lies involve an **omission** or a **fabrication**—withholding information that another person deserves to know or deliberately misleading another person for one's own benefit. For example, a romantic partner may keep a love affair secret or claim to be somewhere that she or he wasn't.

It's no surprise that such lies can destroy trust. For one thing, they lead the deceived person to wonder if anything the other person says is true and what else might be a lie. However, some couples rebound from serious deceptions, particularly if the lie involves an isolated incident and the wrongdoer's apology seems sincere.[42] The most reliable predictor of what will happen after a deception is whether romantic partners communicate openly about it or not. Those who avoid the issue typically lose the chance to work through it, even if they want to.[43]

Have you ever been caught telling a self-serving lie to a loved one? How did it affect your relationship?

> **omission**

A type of deception in which one person withholds information that another person deserves to know.

> **fabrication**

A message in which the speaker deliberately misleads another person in a mean-spirited or manipulative way.

Characters in the film *American Hustle* lie shamelessly in order to achieve their romantic goals with one another.

Q *To what extent do you bend the truth to get what you want from others?*

Distinguish between constructive and destructive styles and methods of dealing with interpersonal conflict.

MANAGING INTERPERSONAL CONFLICT

Regardless of what we may wish for or dream about, a conflict-free relationship just doesn't exist. For many people, the inevitability of conflict is depressing. However, effective communicators realize that, although it's impossible to *eliminate* conflict, there are ways to *manage* it effectively. The first step in managing conflicts is to understand the wide range of communication options.

Styles of Expressing Conflict

There are various approaches to resolving conflicts, and some are more productive than others. As you read on, ask yourself which styles you use most often, and how these styles affect the quality of your close relationships.

Nonassertion

> nonassertion
The inability or unwillingness to express one's thoughts or feelings.

The inability or unwillingness to express thoughts or feelings in a conflict is known as **nonassertion**. A partner may insist that "nothing is wrong" even when it is. Sometimes nonassertion comes from a lack of confidence. At other times, people lack the awareness or skill to use a more direct means of expression.

Nonassertion can take a variety of forms. One is *avoidance*—either steering clear of the other person or avoiding the topic. People who avoid conflicts usually believe it's easier to put up with the status quo than to face the problem head-on and try to solve it. *Accommodation* is another type of nonassertive response. Accommodators deal with conflict by giving in, putting the other's needs ahead of their own.

While nonassertion won't solve a difficult or long-term problem, there are situations in which accommodating or avoiding is a sensible approach. Avoidance may be the best course if a conflict is minor and short-lived. For example, you might forgive your partner for being grumpy if he or she has had a particularly difficult day. For important or long-standing issues, though, nonassertion rarely helps.

Direct Aggression

> directly aggressive message
An expression of the sender's thoughts or feelings, or both, that attacks the position and dignity of the receiver.

Whereas nonasserters avoid conflicts, communicators who use direct aggression embrace confrontation. A **directly aggressive message** confronts the other person in a way that attacks his or her position, or even dignity. Many directly aggressive responses are easy to spot:

"You don't know what you're talking about."

"That was a stupid thing to do."

"What's the matter with you?"

Other forms of direct aggression come more from nonverbal messages. It's easy to imagine a hostile way of expressing statements such as

"What's wrong now?"

"I need some peace and quiet."

Aggressive messages between romantic partners are most common when one partner feels that he or she is contributing more than the other.[44] If you are generally tempted to make aggressive statements, see what happens if you bring up an issue in a calm manner instead. Verbal aggressiveness may get you what you want in the short run, but it generally makes a relationship even worse over the long term.[45]

Passive Aggression

Passive aggression is far more subtle and sometimes even more damaging than direct aggression. **Passive aggression** occurs when a communicator expresses hostility in an ambiguous way. For example, someone may pretend to agree ("I'll be on time from now on.") but not comply with a request for change. Using guilt is another way to express aggression indirectly

> **passive aggression**
An indirect expression of aggression, delivered in a way that allows the sender to maintain a facade of kindness.

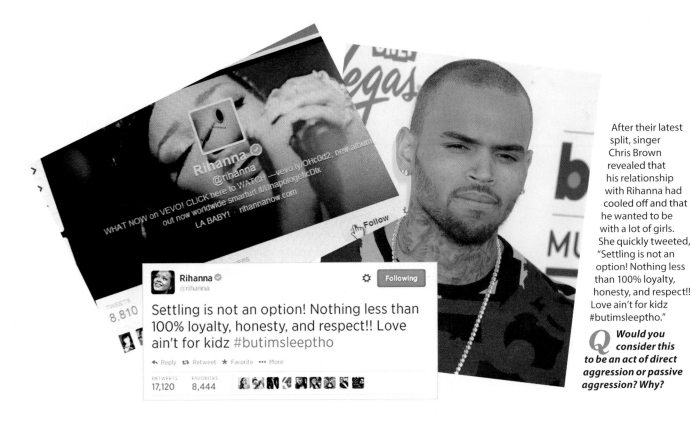

After their latest split, singer Chris Brown revealed that his relationship with Rihanna had cooled off and that he wanted to be with a lot of girls. She quickly tweeted, "Settling is not an option! Nothing less than 100% loyalty, honesty, and respect!! Love ain't for kidz #butimsleeptho."

Q *Would you consider this to be an act of direct aggression or passive aggression? Why?*

("I really should be studying, but I'll give you a ride."). Using humor as a weapon is another form of passive aggression ("Where's your sense of humor?"). Trivial tyrannies can also be used as weapons. For example, you might do small things such as "forgetting" to clean the kitchen or teasing about a sensitive issue to annoy a partner instead of directly expressing a complaint. Another indirect way to punish someone is to withhold courtesy, affection, or humor. It's easy to understand the destructive effects of passive aggression.

Indirect Communication

Indirect communication conveys a message in a roundabout manner. Although indirect communication lacks the clarity of an aggressive or assertive message, it has none of the hostility of passive-aggressiveness. The goal is to get what you want without arousing the hostility of the other person.

Hinting, as described earlier in this chapter, is the most common form of indirect communication. It is a way for partners to make their point without threatening or challenging the other person. In addition, hints can also protect the initiator from expressing uncomfortable feelings or thoughts.

The risk of an indirect message, of course, is that the other party will misunderstand you or fail to get the message at all. There are also times when the importance of an idea is so great that hinting lacks the necessary punch.

Assertion

When clarity and directness are your goals, an assertive approach is in order. **Assertive communication** means directly expressing your needs, thoughts, or feelings in a way that does not attack the other person's dignity. Assertive partners make it clear that the problem at hand is theirs by using the kinds of "I" language described in Chapter 4. They describe their concern without judging others or dictating to them. For example, a partner who has noticed that arguments erupt early in the week might approach the issue by saying:

> I've noticed that we're often impatient with each other on Monday mornings. I think I'm especially tense because I dread the weekly staff meeting. I'd like to spend some time every Sunday preparing for that meeting. I think that will make me less stressed, and maybe that will help us start the week together on a positive note. Is there something we can to do make Monday mornings less stressful for you?

As this scenario suggests, being respectfully assertive usually means talking about an issue when you both have cool heads rather than in the heat of the moment. It also means abstaining from accusations and assumptions.

> **indirect communication**
> Hinting at a message instead of expressing thoughts and feelings directly.

> **assertive communication**
> A style that directly expresses the sender's needs, thoughts, or feelings, delivered in a way that does not attack the receiver's dignity.

The extra effort is usually worth it. Couples who approach conflict in a patient and loving way often feel closer to each other as a result.[46]

Abusive Relationships

The maxim "We always hurt the one we love" reflects the unfortunate fact that abuse—physical and psychological—occurs in intimate relationships. Abusers don't fit a predictable profile. People of all ages, races, and backgrounds may be abusive in private, even if they seem charming to outside observers.

Psychologically Abusive Relationships

After four decades of studying how couples communicate, psychologist John Gottman can predict with a rate of accuracy approaching 90 percent whether or not a married couple is headed toward divorce.[47] He has identified four types of abusive communication, which he terms the "Four Horsemen of the Apocalypse" because their continued presence signals that a relationship faces decline and doom.[48] While these styles don't cause physical harm, they can damage a person's self-esteem and the relationship in which the communication occurs.

Criticism In contrast to complaints, which may focus on the other person, **criticism** is personal, all-encompassing, and accusatory ("You're lazy." or "The only person you think about is yourself.").

> **criticism**
> Personal, all-encompassing, and accusatory messages.

Contempt While criticism focuses on the other person, **contempt** reflects the attitude of the critic ("You disgust me."). Expressions of contempt may be explicit, but more commonly they're expressed nonverbally: by facial nonverbal cues such as sneering, eye rolling, and a condescending or mocking tone of voice. Gottman flatly states that the single best single predictor of divorce is contempt.[49]

> **contempt**
> Reflects the speaker's negative attitude or opinion toward another person.

Defensiveness When faced with criticism and contempt, it's not surprising that partners react with **defensiveness**—protecting their self-worth by counterattacking ("You're calling *me* a careless driver? *You're* the one who got a speeding ticket last month."). Once a pattern of attack-and-defend develops, communication turns into the kind of escalatory and avoidance spirals described in Chapter 7.

> **defensiveness**
> Striking back when one feels attacked by another.

Stonewalling Arguably one of the more harmful disconfirming messages is **stonewalling**—a form of avoidance in which one person refuses to engage with the other. Giving one's partner the silent treatment conveys the message "you aren't even worth my attention." Disengagement may seem like a better alternative than arguing, but taken to extremes, it creates distance between partners and can convey that the stonewaller doesn't value the other partner or the relationship.

> **stonewalling**
> A form of avoidance in which one person refuses to engage with the other.

Arguments routinely fueled with name-calling, disdain, and blame, like the ones between Gary (Vince Vaughn) and Brooke (Jennifer Aniston) in *The Breakup*, indicate a relationship that does not have a strong chance of survival.

Q *Can you identify any of the Four Horsemen in a difficult conversation you've had with a partner? Were you able to replace them with more positive communication patterns?*

Physically Abusive Relationships

Why do people stay in damaging relationships? Some abused partners believe that a bad relationship is better than no relationship at all. They may be afraid of what will happen if the relationship ends, or they may have trouble imagining better alternatives.[50] Once they decide to stay, self-deception and rationalization can set in. One study found that people in abusive dating relationships underestimate how unhappy they really are and overestimate how unhappy they would be if the relationship were to end.[51]

Some people believe that, by communicating or behaving in certain ways, they can prevent abusive partners from engaging in these behaviors. The reality is that people who abuse others make the choice to be abusive. No one forces them to behave in that manner, and no one can prevent someone from being abusive once that person makes the choice to engage in that behavior.[52] There are no magic communication formulas to prevent or stop abuse, but there are steps you can take to protect yourself and get help if you find yourself in an abusive relationship:[53,54]

Don't keep abuse a secret. One tactic abusers use is to isolate their partners from friends and loved ones and to keep them from telling other people.[55] That's because it's easier to control you if you don't have a strong network of people who know what's going on. Avoid this trap by keeping close contact and open communication with people you trust. Tell a trusted friend or family member what's happening to you—and then ask that person to assist you in getting help. **Watch for patterns.** Abuse often happens in cycles. If you're in the upside of a cycle and all is calm, it can be easy to ignore or overlook previous violations. But if someone has been abusive before, it probably won't be the last time.

Develop strategies. Let trusted people know where to find you. Program emergency numbers into your phone. Agree on code words you can use with people you trust to signify that you feel uneasy and need help. If possible, don't share passwords that will allow the abuser to access your communication with others or find other ways to threaten or harm you.

Don't blame yourself. Recipients of abuse often believe they are at fault for what is happening to them, and that somehow they deserve it or "had it coming." Remember—*no one deserves abuse.*

If professional help is necessary for breaking free from an abusive relationship, many sources are available. One source of information and assistance is *www.healthyplace.com/abuse.*

Applying Win-Win Problem Solving

Presuming you are with a partner who is not abusive and who has proven to be trustworthy, it is often possible to move into the realm of productive conflict management. Some conflicts result in one partner winning and one losing ("either we live in Italy or we move to Chicago") or both of them losing ("If you don't care about my career, let's break it off.") Still others are solved by compromises in which both people get at least some of what they want, but both give up something as well ("we'll spend part of our time in Italy and part of it in Chicago"). Of these options, compromise often seems the most satisfying. Indeed, it can be an efficient way to solve interpersonal problems, but compromise often results in less-than-satisfying solutions for both partners. If the goal of living in Italy or Chicago is to launch a career there, shuttling back and forth between the two might make it difficult for either person to succeed.

A fourth option—win-win problem solving—is typically the most satisfying and relationship-friendly. In **win–win problem solving**, the goal is to find a solution that satisfies both people's needs. Neither tries to win at the other's expense. Instead, both parties believe that, by working together, it is possible to find a solution that reaches all of their goals. Finding a win-win situation usually involves looking below the surface at what both parties are trying to achieve.

Suppose you want a quiet evening at home tonight and your partner wants to go to a party. On the surface, only one of you can win. However, by listening carefully to each other, you realize you can both get your way. You don't feel like getting dressed up and talking to a room full of people. Your partner isn't crazy about that part of it either, but would like to connect with two old friends who are going to be at the party. Once you understand the underlying goals, a solution presents itself: Invite those two friends over for a casual dinner at your place before they head off to the party. In this way, neither you nor your partner compromises on what you want to achieve. Indeed, the evening may be more fun than either of you expected.

> **win-win problem solving**
A means of resolving conflict in which the goal is a solution that satisfies both people's needs.

Even when they aren't fighting zombies in order to survive, Glenn and Maggie (Stephen Yeun and Lauren Cohan) in the TV series *The Walking Dead* have formed a close relationship by solving problems that meet both of their needs.

Q *Have you ever experienced a conflict that was transformed when you focused on a win-win solution?*

Win-win problem solving doesn't happen by accident. It is a highly structured activity. However, after you have practiced the approach a number of times, this style of managing conflict will become more comfortable. You'll then be able to approach your conflicts without the need to follow the step-by-step approach.

Step 1: Identify Your Problem and Unmet Needs

Before you speak out, it's important to realize that the problem that is causing conflict is *yours*. For example, perhaps you are bothered by your partner's tendency to yell at other drivers. Because *you* are the person who is dissatisfied, the problem is yours. Realizing this will make a big difference when the time comes to approach your partner. Instead of feeling and acting in an evaluative way, you'll be more likely to share your problem in a descriptive way, which will not only be more accurate but also will reduce the chance of a defensive reaction.

The next step is to identify the factors that leave you feeling dissatisfied. Perhaps you're afraid your partner will offend someone you know. Maybe you're worried that excess emotion will lead to unsafe driving. Or it might be that you would love to use the car ride as an opportunity for conversation.

The ability to identify your real needs plays a key role in solving interpersonal problems. For now, the point to remember is that, before you voice your problem to your partner, you ought to be clear about which of your needs aren't being met.

Step 2: Make a Date

Unconstructive fights often start because the initiator confronts a partner who isn't ready. Sometimes a person isn't in the right frame of mind to face a conflict: perhaps owing to fatigue, being busy with something else, or not feeling well. At times like these, it's unfair to "jump" on a person without notice and expect to get his or her full attention.

After you have a clear idea of the problem, approach your partner with a request to try to solve it. For example: "Something's been bothering me. Can we talk about it?" If the answer is "yes," then you're ready to go further. If it isn't the right time to confront your partner, find a time that's agreeable to both of you.

Step 3: Describe Your Problem and Needs

Your partner can't possibly meet your needs without knowing why you're upset and what you want. Therefore, it's up to you to describe your problem as specifically as possible. When you do so, it's important to use terms that aren't overly vague or abstract. You might say,

"I look forward to riding home from work together because I like the chance to hear about your day and make plans for later [need/desire]. I know you get frustrated with city traffic [empathy], but it bothers me when you yell at other drivers instead of talking with me [problem]."

Step 4: Check Your Partner's Understanding

After you've shared your problem and described what you need, it's important to make sure that your partner has understood what you have said. As you may remember from the discussion of listening in Chapter 5, there's a good chance—especially in a stressful conflict situation—of your words being misinterpreted.

Step 5: Solicit Your Partner's Needs

After you've made your position clear, it's time to find out what your partner needs in order to feel satisfied about this issue. There are two reasons why it's important to discover your partner's needs. First, it's fair. After all, the other person has just as much right as you to feel satisfied, and if you expect help in meeting your needs, then it's reasonable that you behave in the same way. Second, just as an unhappy partner will make it hard for you to become satisfied, a happy one will be more likely to cooperate in letting you reach your goals. Thus, it is in your own self-interest to discover and meet your partner's needs.

You can learn about your partner's needs simply by asking: "Now that you know what I want and why, tell me what you need from me." After your partner begins to talk, your job is to use the listening skills discussed in Chapter 5 to make sure you understand.

Step 6: Check Your Understanding of Your Partner's Needs

Paraphrase or ask questions about your partner's needs until you are certain you understand them. The surest way to accomplish this is to use the paraphrasing skills you learned in Chapter 5. Perhaps the conversation reveals that your partner is frustrated because of work, or because he or she does all the driving, or because he or she is hungry.

Step 7: Negotiate a Solution

Now that you and your partner understand each other's needs, the goal becomes finding a way to meet them. This is done by first trying to develop as many potential solutions as possible. The key word here is *quantity*. Write down every thought that comes up, no matter how unworkable it seems at first.

Next, evaluate the alternative solutions. This is the time to talk about which solutions will work and which won't. If a solution is going to work, you both have to support it.

Then, after looking at all the alternatives, pick the one that looks best to both of you. Your decision doesn't have to be final, but it should look potentially successful. It's important to be sure you both understand the solution and are willing to try it out.

To go back to our driving example, perhaps you decide to meet for dinner and then drive home once the rush-hour traffic has subsided. Or, perhaps you decide to alternate who drives home each night. The point is that the solution should meet both of your needs.

Step 8: Follow Up on the Solution

You can't be sure the solution will work until you try it out. After you've tested it for a while, it's a good idea to set aside some time to talk over how things are going. You may find that you need to make some changes or even rethink the whole problem. The idea is to keep on top of the problem and to keep using creativity to solve it.

All of this being said, win-win solutions aren't always possible. There will be times when even the best-intentioned people simply won't be able to find a way of meeting all their needs. When that happens, compromising may be the most sensible approach. You will encounter instances when pushing for your own solution is reasonable, and times when it makes sense to willingly accept the loser's role. But even when that happens, the steps we've discussed haven't been wasted. The genuine desire to learn what the other person wants and to try to satisfy those desires will build a climate of goodwill that can help you find the best solution to the present problem and also improve your relationship in the future.

> How often do you pause to consider your partner's needs and feelings?

CHECK YOUR UNDERSTANDING

OBJECTIVE 9.1 Define intimacy and describe a range of options for conveying intimate messages.

THE NATURE OF INTIMACY

Intimacy can be created and expressed in a variety of ways: physically, emotionally, intellectually, and through shared activities. The notion of intimacy varies somewhat by gender and personal preference. Toward this end, recognizing which of the "love languages" (affirming words, quality time, acts of service, gifts, or physical touch) are most meaningful to you and significant others is an important step.

Describe the ways of expressing intimacy that characterize your ideal romantic relationship. Which of the love languages described in this chapter resonate most strongly for you? How could you ensure that you demonstrate your feelings best by communicating in the love language of a romantic partner?

OBJECTIVE 9.2 Analyze the themes of a close relationship using both Knapp's model of relationship development and the dialectical model.

COMMUNICATING IN ROMANTIC RELATIONSHIPS

Some communication theorists suggest that intimate relationships pass through a series of stages, each characterized by a unique mode of communication. These stages fall into the broad phases of coming together (initiating, experimenting, intensifying), sustaining the relationship (integrating, bonding, differentiating, and circumscribing), and coming apart (stagnating, avoiding, and terminating). Other theorists take a dialectical view, arguing that a series of opposing desires operates throughout the entire span of a relationship. These dialectical drives include autonomy versus connection, openness versus privacy, and predictability versus novelty.

Describe the dialectical tensions you have experienced in a close relationship and the strategies you have used to manage them. How successful were those strategies? Would others have been more effective?

Identify the functions served by altruistic lies, evasions, and self-serving lies.

DECEPTION IN ROMANTIC RELATIONSHIPS

People are likely to experience deceit even in their closest and most intimate relationships. Not all lies are equally devastating, however. Altruistic lies fall in the category of being polite, and effective communicators know how to use them without causing offense. Evasions are deliberately vague and include equivocation and hinting. They are generally offered in a spirit meant to avoid hurting people's feelings. Self-serving lies are attempts to manipulate the listener into believing something that is untrue. They involve omission or fabrication.

Conduct an audit of the frequency and importance of the altruistic lies, evasions, and self-serving lies you have communicated in a close relationship. Describe the long-term consequences of these practices. Would there have been better ways of managing the truth? If so, what could you have done differently?

Distinguish between constructive and destructive styles and methods of dealing with interpersonal conflict.

MANAGING INTERPERSONAL CONFLICT

Conflict is a fact of life in every relationship, and the way we handle conflicts plays a major role in the quality of our relationships. There are five ways people can behave when faced with a conflict: nonassertive, directly aggressive, passive-aggressive, indirect, and assertive.

Abuse—both psychological and physical—can damage both the relationship and the individual parties. If an abusive relationship can't be changed, it is essential for someone who is being abused to take protective measures.

In a healthy relationship, win-win conflict resolution is often possible if both parties have the proper attitudes and skills. The process involves identifying your problem, setting up a time to discuss the problem, describing your problem and needs, checking your partner's understanding, soliciting your partner's needs, checking your understanding of your partner's needs, negotiating a solution, and following up on the solution.

Describe the communication styles that you and your partner used in a significant, representative conflict. How successful was the communication you identified in meeting the needs of each partner and in managing your relationship? What forms of communication might have been more effective?

KEY TERMS

altruistic lie p. 210
assertive communication p. 214
contempt p. 215
compromise p. 209
criticism p. 215
defensiveness p. 215
developmental model (of relational maintenance) p. 201

dialectical model (of relational maintenance) p. 205
directly aggressive message p. 212
equivocation p. 210
fabrication p. 211
indirect communication p. 214
hinting p. 210
intimacy p. 196

nonassertion p. 212
omission p. 211
passive aggression p. 213
relational maintenance p. 201
stonewalling p. 215
win-win problem solving p. 217

For insight about your primary love languages, see which of the following best describes your answers.

Quality Time

If you answered "a" to one or more questions, you probably feel loved when people set aside life's distractions to spend time with you. Keep in mind that everyone defines quality time a bit differently. It may mean a thoughtful phone call during a busy day, a picnic in the park, or a few minutes every evening to share news about the day. Consider what "quality time" means to you and to the special people in your life.

Acts of Service

Answering "b" means you feel loved when people do thoughtful things for you such as washing your car, helping you with a repair job, bringing you breakfast in bed, or bathing the children so you can put your feet up. Even small gestures say "I love you" to people whose love language involves acts of service.

Physical Touch

Options labeled "c" are associated with the comfort and pleasure we get from physical affection. If your sweetheart texts to say, "Wish we were snuggled up together!" he or she is speaking the love language of touch.

Gifts

If you chose "d," chances are you treasure thoughtful gifts from loved ones. Your prized possessions are likely to include items that look inconsequential to others but have sentimental value to you because of who gave them to you.

Words of Affirmation

Options labeled "e" refer to words that make us feel loved and valued. These may be conveyed in a note, a homemade card or poem, a romantic letter, a song, or an unexpected text that simply says, "I love you." To people who speak this love language, hearing that they are loved (and why) is the sweetest message imaginable.

FOR FURTHER EXPLORATION

For more communication resources, see the *Essential Communication* website at www.oup.com/us/ec. There you will find a variety of resources: "Media Room" examples from popular films and television shows to further illustrate important concepts, a list of relevant books and articles, links to descriptions of feature films and television shows at the *Now Playing* website, study aids, and a self-test to check your understanding of the material in this chapter.

Communicating for Career Success

10.1 Describe communication behaviors conducive to finding a job that matches your skills.

10.2 Identify application and interviewing strategies that are likely to lead to employment.

10.3 Explain and practice skills for communicating with followers, leaders, and peers in a professional manner on the job.

10.4 Choose and effectively use the most situationally appropriate and effective approaches to leading and following at work.

STRATEGIES FOR FINDING A JOB

Whatever your ideal or chosen career, communication consistently ranks in the top tier of skills that employers seek—higher even than technical knowledge related to the position.[1,2] And, once you are hired, communication skills can make the difference between success and disappointment. One survey of corporate recruiters revealed that good communication skills and the ability to work with others are the main factors contributing to job success. In fact, technical workers who have good communication skills earn more than those who don't, and those who are weak communicators suffer across the board.[3] This chapter introduces you to a set of communication skills that will serve you well in your professional relationships. However, it all starts with cultivating personal networks and presenting your best self during interviews.

Cultivating Personal Networks

In today's competitive workplace, good jobs go to proactive communicators who locate the jobs they want and work hard to get them. One of the most proven ways to do this is through **networking**—the strategic process of meeting people and maintaining relationships that yield information and advice relevant to career success. If you doubt the value of this approach, consider the numbers: A whopping three out of four people in the workplace obtained their jobs with the help of personal networking.[4]

A little reflection explains why networking is such a valuable approach. If you're looking for a job, personal contacts can tell you about positions that may not even be public yet. After you've identified a position you want and you are competing with others to land an interview or offer, people you know can put in a good word for you with potential employers, and they can give you tips on how to pursue the position you're seeking.

Networking will only work, however, if you are the kind of person others recognize as being worth endorsing. If you are willing to work hard and you have the necessary skills to do a job (or are willing to learn those skills), there are several steps you can take to create and benefit from a personal network.

View Everyone as a Networking Prospect

Besides the people in your immediate everyday networks, you have access to a wealth of other contacts. These include former coworkers, schoolmates, alumni from your alma mater, teammates, people you've met at

> networking

The strategic process of deliberately meeting people and maintaining contacts.

In the film *The Social Network*, Napster founder Sean Parker (Justin Timberlake) and Mark Zuckerberg (Jesse Eisenberg) use personal networking to transform a college project called "The Facebook" into the world's most popular social networking site.

Q *Why is it so important to view everyone as a networking prospect?*

social and community events, professional people whose services you have used … the list can be quite long and diverse.

Seek Referrals

Each contact in your immediate network has connections to people you don't already know who might be able to help you. Social scientists have verified that the "six degrees of separation" hypothesis is true. The average number of links separating any two people in the world is indeed only half a dozen.[5] You can take advantage of this by only seeking people removed from your personal network by just one degree: If you ask 10 people for referrals, and each of them knows 10 others who might be able to help, you have the potential of support from 100 people.

Show Appreciation

The best way to repay people who help you is by expressing gratitude for their help. Beyond a sincere thank you, take the time to maintain relationships and let your contacts know when their help has made a difference in your career advancement. Besides being the right thing to do, your thoughtfulness will distinguish you as the kind of person worth hiring or helping again in the future.

Engage in Online Networking

Numerous websites offer professional networking opportunities. A few of the most popular are LinkedIn, SunZu, Xing, and Plaxo. It may be useful to join at least a few of these and set up a personal profile. Most offer basic memberships for free. Posting information about yourself online can allow you to showcase a worthy project, volunteer work, awards, accomplishments, and interests. But do consider how your profile information will look to all viewers. You may be proud of your membership in the National Rifle Association or Planned Parenthood, but a prospective employer might not find your affiliations so admirable. Political philosophy, religious affiliations, and even your musical preferences may all be better kept private, or at least behind a secure firewall where only the people you know and trust will see them.

Monitor Your Online Identity

Even information you think is private may be accessible online. According to the *New York Times*, 70 percent of U.S. recruiters have rejected job candidates because of personal information online.[6] To see if you are at risk, Google yourself and see what comes up. Then expand your search to include other search engines such as Yahoo!, MSN Search, MetaCrawler, Dogpile, and Ask.com because no individual search index will find everything on the Internet. Also double-check the privacy settings on your social media accounts.

You might find that unfavorable information pops up about someone with the same name as you. One job seeker Googled herself out of curiosity, only to find that the first hit was the Facebook page of a person with the same name whose personal profile was loaded with immature comments. To minimize the chances of mistaken identity, consider distinguishing yourself by including your middle name or middle initial on your résumé and all other information you post where online seekers might find it.

If you discover incorrect, unfair, and potentially damaging information about yourself online, and you are unable to remove it yourself, consider seeking professional help to set the record straight. For example, reputationdefender.com will monitor your online identity and ask the managers of offending websites to remove unflattering information. Of course, a far less expensive and burdensome approach is to minimize the chances of reputation damage by being on your best public behavior.

Conducting Informational Interviews

Sooner or later your networking and personal research are likely to point you toward people whose knowledge, experience, and contacts could shape your career. These may be people you already know—such as friends or

> How can you manage your online identity to protect and enhance your professional image?

neighbors, or people you casually meet, perhaps at a social or alumni event—or even a total stranger. Talking to these people may give you a perspective that could transform your career.

Regardless of the source, with a little initiative and planning, you can approach these contacts and request an **informational interview**, that is to say, a structured meeting in which you seek answers from a source whose knowledge can help enhance your success. A good informational interview will help you achieve the following three goals:

> **Conduct research** that helps you understand a job, organization, or field.
>
> **Be remembered favorably** by the person you are interviewing (so he or she may mention you to others who can also advance your career).
>
> **Gain referrals** to other people who might also be willing to help you.

> informational interview
A structured meeting in which you seek answers from a source whose knowledge can help enhance your success.

Make Your First Contact in Writing

Unless you know a prospective interviewee well, the best approach is usually to make your first contact in writing. While a phone call might be easier, you may miss the person and be forced to leave a voice mail message that can either be too short to explain yourself or too long to hold your recipient's attention. And, even if the potential interviewee answers your call, you may have caught him or her at a bad time. With an email, or even a printed letter through the mail, you can carefully edit your introduction until it's just right, and assume that the recipient will read it whenever he or she is ready.

In your written message, you should:

> **Introduce yourself.**
>
> **Explain your reason for the interview**; be sure to emphasize that you're seeking information, not asking for a job.
>
> **Identify the amount of time your questions are likely to take**; the shorter amount of time you request, the better are your odds of being seen.
>
> **State a range of dates when you are available to meet or speak**; be as flexible as possible.

Prepare Questions Ahead of Time

More than any other factor, the questions you ask and the way you ask them will determine the success or failure of an interview. Good questions rarely come spontaneously, even to the best of interviewers. They take time and thought.

The first thing to realize is that a career-related informational interview is ultimately about *you*, and not the person you're talking with. Fascinating as it might be, dwelling on the life story of the person you're interviewing isn't likely to help advance your career. Instead, probe your interviewee for information that will help you succeed, such as "What are the three fastest-growing companies in this field?" and "What do you think about the risks of working for a start-up company?"

Most of the time, the best way to get information is to ask a direct question. But there are times when a straightforward reply would be embarrassing or risky. For instance, you probably wouldn't want to ask a question such as, "What's your salary?" At times like these, it's wise to seek information by using indirect questions, such as, "What kind of salary might I expect if I ever held a position like yours?"

Sometimes you'll need to ask only an initial, primary question. Other times, it will help to follow your first question with secondary ones. While a primary question might be, "In your opinion, who are the best people to ask about careers in the financial planning field?," a secondary follow-up question might be, "What do you think is the best way for me to go about meeting them?" While it can be smart to develop a list of secondary questions to each primary one, in many cases the best follow-ups will occur to you naturally during the interview.

Be Sure to Follow Up

Good manners call for sending a note of thanks to the interviewer who has taken time to give you advice and information. Such a note can also be strategically savvy: It serves as a tangible reminder of you, and it provides a written record of your name and contact information. It can be smart to keep your contact alive by sending follow-up messages letting your interviewee know how you have put his or her advice to good use. If the interviewee has referred you to other people, be sure to let him or her know the results of your conversations with those people.

OBJECTIVE 10.2 Identify application and interviewing strategies that are likely to lead to employment.

STRATEGIES FOR GETTING HIRED

Once you have done the research into various positions, consider whether you are right for the job and vice versa. If it doesn't seem like the relationship will be mutually beneficial, it's wise to keep looking. But if it seems like a good match, it's time to move to the next phase—establishing yourself as an interested and qualified candidate for the position.

Applying for a Job

It's impossible to include everything there is to know about applying for a job here. Entire books are written about the subject, and industries differ.

However, what follows are general guidelines and strategies that should serve you well when applying for most entry-level jobs.

Create a Polished Résumé

No matter how extensive and supportive your network, you will need a polished résumé to provide a snapshot of your professional strengths and achievements. For guidelines on the various types of résumés, type "create résumé" into your favorite search engine. A flawed résumé can do more harm than good (Figure 10-1). Many employers immediately put resumes that include typos or grammatical errors in the "no" stack. So be sure to proofread. It's also smart to have a staff member at your school's career center critique your résumé. The final document should be clear, honest, succinct, and free of typos and other errors, and ideally it should fit on one page.

Create a Cover Letter

When submitting your résumé for a specific position, include a cover letter that creates a positive first impression. This letter gives you a chance to make the case for why you would be a good hire. As one expert put it, a cover letter is "an introduction, a sales pitch, and a proposal for further action all in one."[7]

If at all possible, cover letters should be directed to a specific individual. If you don't know the appropriate person, call the company and ask for the individual's name. Be certain that you get the spelling and title correct. A good cover letter should:

Identify the position you are applying for, how you know of the position, and any connection you have to the company. If you are responding to an advertisement, mention the job title, number, and publication. If you are writing at the suggestion of a mutual acquaintance or as a result of your research, say so.

Introduce yourself or reintroduce yourself if the reader may not know or remember who you are.

Briefly describe your most impressive accomplishments that are relevant to the job at hand. Remember: Don't just say you can help the organization. Offer some specific evidence that backs up your claim.

Demonstrate your knowledge of the company to show your interest in the job and your initiative.

State the next step you hope to take—usually a request for an interview. If you must, mention any pertinent information about limits on your availability, but keep these to an absolute minimum.

Express appreciation to the reader for considering you.

Follow Application Instructions

You may need to upload your résumé and cover letter to an employer's website when applying for a position. You may also benefit from posting your

Worst Résumé Blunders Ever

It's tough out there. You don't need a bad résumé making things worse.
Here's a look at some actual résumé blunders seen by top recruiters.

Don't make these mistakes yourself!

Links to Inappropriate Content

Recruiters will check your online profiles so clean up that Facebook page!

Mobile Uploads
Howie's Night Out
Like Comment Share

Howard "Bada Bing" Hollis
1234 West 67th Street, Carlisle, MA 01741,
hotdude61@yourmail.com • 617-555-5555 • facebook.com/h.badabing

Unprofessional Title & Email Address

"Bada Bing" and "hotdude61" do not exactly scream, "I am a professional." Get yourself a proper email address.

OBJECTIVE
Accomplished and dynamic *Accounting Professional* with proven cost cutting, productivity improvement, and analytical skills seeking Accounting position with progressive organization offering opportunities for growth.

Objective Statement

Objectives are obsolete. They tend to focus too much on what you WANT rather than what you can OFFER.

PERSONAL PROFILE
With a 25-year background in accounting and finance, I possess strong experience in creating and working with P&L/financial statements, management reports, general ledger, and complex billing processes. I also have experience in diverse areas of business operations including staff training and direction, inventory variances allocation, and job costing. I have worked with top firms in a variety of industries, managing their high net worth financial accounts. I possess a high attention to detail and have no patience for sloppy work. While eager to interview, please note that I am currently on trial for embezzlement and my availability at the moment is limited.

Don't Get Personal

There is no "I" in "résumé." Avoid using pronouns and instead, use more action verbs.

PROFESSIONAL EXPERIENCE

Jackson & Solomon, Boston, MA   1998- present
Accountant & Pubic Financial Analyst
- Duties include full-cycle accounts payable, weekly check processing and GL coding to account reconciliation to allocation weekly check processing and GL coding to account reconciliation to allocation.
- Strategically develop innovative order processes and procedures that have been adopted by company and remain in use to date
- Apply sharp organization, analytical, and multitasking abilities toward managing accounts payable and multiple account reconciliations, as well as forecasting financial models using public accounting data

Proofread & Proofread Again

"Pubic" Financial Analyst? Really? Remember to proofread to avoid embarrassing slipups.

Too Much Information

What you exclude from your résumé is just as important as what you include.

Western Enterprise, Newton, MA   1992-1998
Ass. Accountant
- Efficiently manage payables and receivables including reconciliations, payroll, and general ledger accounts
- Compiled and prepared detailed financial statements, management reports, and balance sheets

Improper Abbreviations

Better to spell out words in full than potentially conveying the wrong message.

EDUCATION
Fisher College of Business, Dayton, Ohio
Bachelorette of Science – **Accounting**   1988-1992
Concentration in Financial Accounting & Management Science
Hunter High School, Cleveland, Ohio   1984-1988

Why List High School?

If you have some college education, there is no need to list your high school.

Don't Rely on Spell Check

Spell Check is not always your friend. Have a fresh set of eyes read your résumé as well.

SKILLS & AWARDS
- Lotus 1-2-3
- Microsoft Office Suite
- Quickbooks
- Visual Basic
- SQL Plus
- UNIX Operating System
- Mac & PC proficient
- Typing: 40 wpm

Awards
- 1996 Accounting Association Award for Innovation in Accounting Design
- 2005 Jameson Society Award for Oustanding Accounting Literature Award
- 2008 National Record Holder for most eggs eaten in 2 minutes (45 eggs)

Stay Grounded…on Planet Earth

Make sure items on your résumé are relevant to the position.

SOURCE: LiveCareer.com

Figure 10-1 Résumé Blunders to Avoid

résumé to online job banks (sometimes called job boards) such as Simply-Hired, Indeed, CareerBuilder, Dice, Monster, Computer Jobs, and US.jobs.

When posting your résumé and cover letter online or emailing them, ensure that you follow all application instructions exactly. While there are always stories of someone who does something so drastically different that it catches a hiring manager's attention, in the majority of cases, if you don't follow instructions you will be summarily rejected. If the posting asks you to submit your materials in PDF format, then don't send them in Word. If the posting says "no phone calls please," then don't call. As one high-level recruiter puts it: "If you can't follow clear, simple directions, how can I trust that you will be able to give great attention to the details of your job?"[8] Finally, be sure that you supply a professional email address for correspondence that includes your name. If you don't have one, then create a new one.

Keep Organized Records of Your Communications

If you are applying to several organizations, keeping a record of messages you've sent and received can save you from embarrassment. Even if your search is focused on one organization, sooner or later you'll need to refer to your previous contacts. Record *who* you've communicated with, *when* the message was sent or received, and *what* the exchange was about.

Preparing for the Selection Interview

For many people the short time spent facing a potential employer is the most important interview of a lifetime. A **selection interview** may occur when you are being considered for employment, but it may also occur when you are being evaluated for promotion or reassignment. In an academic setting, selection interviews are often part of the process of being chosen for an award, a scholarship, or admission to a graduate program. Being chosen for the position you seek depends on making a good impression on the person or people who can hire you, and your interviewing skills can make the difference in whether or not you receive a job offer. There are several steps you can take to boost your chances for success.

Do Your Research

Displaying your knowledge of an organization in an interview is a terrific way to show potential employers that you are a motivated and savvy person. In some organizations, failure to demonstrate familiarity with the organization or job is an automatic disqualifier.

Along with what you've learned from informational interviews, diligent Web browsing can reveal a wealth of information about a prospective employer and the field in which you want to work. Beyond an organization's own website, you can almost certainly find what others have published about these places. In your search engine, type the name of the organization and/or key people who work there. Use your research to prepare some good questions to ask during and at the end of the interview.

> selection interview

A formal meeting (in person or via communication technology) to exchange information that may occur when you are being considered for employment or being evaluated for promotion or reassignment.

Prepare for Likely Questions

Regardless of the organization and job, most interviewers have similar concerns, which they explore with similar questions. Table 10-1 provides some of the most common ones, with commentary on how you can prepare to answer them. It has also become more common for some employers, particularly tech companies, to ask non-traditional questions to see how well candidates think on their feet, how they handle problems, and how creative they are.[9] Some examples of non-traditional questions include: "If you could have any superpower, what would it be?," "Name five uses for a stapler with no staples in it," and "If you were a sweater, what kind would you be?" If asked one of these questions, it's important to maintain your composure and to use your answers to demonstrate the qualities that the employer seems to be seeking. For example, one possible response to the

Table 10-1 Common Interview Questions

QUESTION	WHAT THEY'RE ASKING FOR	TIPS
Tell me something about yourself.	This broad, opening question gives you a chance to describe what qualities you possess that can help the employer (e.g., enthusiastic, motivated, entrepreneurial).	Be sure to keep your answer focused on the job for which you're applying. This isn't a time to talk about your hobbies, family, or pet peeves.
What makes you think you're qualified to work for this company?	This question may sound like an attack, but it really is another way of asking, "How can you help us?" It gives you another chance to show how your skills and interests fit with the company's goals.	Prepare for a question like this by making a table with three columns: one listing your main qualifications, one listing specific examples of each qualification, and one explaining how these qualifications would benefit your prospective employer.
What accomplishments have given you the most satisfaction?	Your accomplishments might demonstrate creativity, perseverance in the face of obstacles, self-control, or dependability.	The accomplishments you choose needn't be directly related to former employment, but they should demonstrate qualities that would help you be successful in the job for which you're interviewing.
Why do you want to work for us?	This question offers you the chance to demonstrate your knowledge of the employer's organization and to show how your talents fit with its goals.	Employers are impressed by candidates who have done their homework about the organization.
What college subjects did you like most and least?	Whatever your answer, show how your preferences about schoolwork relate to the job for which you are applying.	Sometimes you will need to show how seemingly unrelated subjects illustrate your readiness for a job. For example, you might say, "I really enjoyed cultural anthropology courses because they showed me the importance of understanding different cultures. I think that those courses would help me a lot in relating to your overseas customers and suppliers."

QUESTION	WHAT THEY'RE ASKING FOR	TIPS
Where do you see yourself in five years?	This familiar question is really asking: "How ambitious are you?" "How well do your plans fit with this company's goals?" "How realistic are you?"	If you have studied the industry and the company, your answer will reflect an understanding of the workplace realities and a sense of personal planning that should impress an employer.
What major problems have you faced, and how have you dealt with them?	What (admirable) qualities did you demonstrate as you grappled with the problems you have chosen to describe? Perseverance? Calmness? Creativity?	The specific problems aren't as important as the way you responded to them. You may even choose to describe a problem you didn't handle well, to show what you learned from the experience that can help you in the future.
What are your greatest strengths?	The "strength" question offers another chance to sell yourself.	As you choose an answer, identify qualities that apply to employment. "I'm a pretty good athlete" isn't a persuasive answer, unless you can show how your athletic skill is job related. For instance, you might talk about being a team player, having competitive drive, or having the ability to work hard and not quit in the face of adversity.
What are your greatest weaknesses?	Whatever answer you give to the "weakness" question, try to show how your awareness of your flaws makes you a desirable person to hire.	There are four ways to respond to this question: (1) Discuss a weakness that can also be viewed as a strength: "When I'm involved in a big project I tend to work too hard, and I can wear myself out." (2) Discuss a weakness that is not related to the job at hand, and end your answer with a strength that is related to the job: "I'm not very interested in accounting. I'd much rather work with people selling a product I believe in." (3) Discuss a weakness the interviewer already knows about from your résumé, application, or the interview: "I don't have a lot of experience in multimedia design at this early stage of my career. But my experience in other kinds of computer programming and my internship in graphic arts have convinced me that I can learn quickly." (4) Discuss a weakness you have been working to remedy: "I know being bilingual is important for this job. That's why I've enrolled in a Spanish course."
What are your salary requirements?	Give your answer naming a salary range and backing up your numbers.	Your answer should be based on knowledge of the prevailing compensation rates in the industry and geography in question. Shooting too high can knock you out of consideration, whereas shooting too low can cost you dearly.

sweater question might be, "I would be stylish and classy, but not flashy, so I would have enduring value as trends change. I would give great value for the price ... not too cheap, but not too expensive. I would be flexible, so I could be used in many different situations." Notice that the attributes of the sweater are also the qualities that would make the candidate a good person to hire.

Dress for Success

First impressions can make or break an interview. Research shows that many interviewers form their opinions about applicants within the first four minutes of conversation.[10] Physical attractiveness is a major influence on how applicants are rated, so it makes sense to do everything possible to look your best. The basic rules apply, no matter what the job or company: Be well groomed and neatly dressed, and don't overdo it with too much makeup or flashy clothes.

The proper style of clothing can vary from one type of job or organization to another. But when in doubt, it's best to dress formally and conservatively. It's unlikely that an employer will think less of you for being overdressed, but looking too casual can be taken as a sign that you don't take the job or the interview seriously.

Take Copies of Your Résumé and Portfolio

Arrive at the interview with materials that will help the employer learn more about why you are ready, willing, and able to do the job. Take extra copies of your résumé. If appropriate, take copies of your past work: reports you've helped prepare, performance reviews by former employers, drawings or designs you have created for work or school, letters of commendation, and so on. Besides showcasing your qualifications, items like these demonstrate that you know how to sell yourself. Take along the names, addresses, and phone numbers of any references you haven't listed in your résumé.

Know When and Where to Go

Don't risk sabotaging the interview before it begins by showing up late. Be sure you're clear about the time and location of the meeting. Research parking or public transportation to be sure you aren't held up by delays. There's virtually no good excuse for showing up late. Even if the interviewer is forgiving, a bad start is likely to shake your confidence and impair your performance.

Reframe Your Anxiety as Enthusiasm

Feeling anxious about an employment interview is natural. After all, the stakes are high—especially if you really want the job. Managing your feelings during an interview calls for many of the same strategies that you'll want to take when managing your apprehension while giving a speech (see Chapter 13). Realize that a certain amount of anxiety is understandable. If

In the film *The Butler*, Cecil Gaines (Forest Whitaker) interviews with the condescending head butler (Colman Domingo), who coldly informs him that "we have no tolerance for politics in the White House." (The two are shown here in a more cordial moment.)

Q *How can you best prepare to handle a challenging interviewer?*

you can reframe those feelings as *excitement* about the prospect of holding a great job, the feelings can even work to your advantage.

During the Interview

Once the time comes for your interview, it's your chance to shine. You've done the preparation, and now it's time to present yourself in a positive and confident light. Make sure you follow proper business etiquette, keep your answers succinct and specfic, and ask good questions of your own.

Mind Your Manners

It's essential to demonstrate proper business etiquette from the moment you arrive for an interview. "You may be riding on the elevator with the head of your interview team," advises one business etiquette expert.[11] Turn off your phone before you enter the building, smile at people, put your shoulders back and head up, and don't fiddle with your clothing, hair, or belongings. In short, behave at all times as the sort of engaged, professional, and attentive coworker everyone wants on their team. When you meet people, look them in the eye, shake hands firmly, and demonstrate an attentive listening posture—shoulders parallel to the speaker's, eyes focused on the speaker, and facial expressions that show you are paying attention. If multiple people are present, be sure to shake hands with all of them and include all of them in your comments and eye contact throughout the interview.

Follow the Interviewer's Lead

Let the interviewer set the tone of the session. Along with topics and verbal style, pay attention to the kinds of nonverbal cues described in Chapter 6: the interviewer's posture, gestures, vocal qualities, and so on. If he or she is informal, you can loosen up and be yourself, but if he or she is formal and proper, you should act the same way.

Keep Your Answers Succinct and Specific

It's easy to ramble in an interview, either out of enthusiasm, a desire to show off your knowledge, or nervousness, but in most cases long answers are not a good idea. Generally, it's a good idea to keep your responses concise, but to be sure to provide specific examples to support your statements.

Describe Relevant Challenges, Actions, and Results

Most sophisticated employers realize that past performance can be the best predictor of future behavior. For that reason, there is an increasing trend toward **behavioral interviews**—sessions that explore specifics of the applicant's past performance as it relates to the job at hand. Typical behavioral questions include the following:

Describe a time you needed to work as part of a team.

Tell me about a time when you had to think on your feet to handle a challenging situation.

Describe a time when you were faced with an ethical dilemma, and discuss how you handled it.

When faced with behavioral questions, answer in a way that shows the prospective employer how your past performance demonstrates your ability to handle the job you are now seeking. Figure 10-2 offers some strategies for constructing such answers.

Ask Good Questions of Your Own

Besides answering the employer's questions, the selection interview is also a chance for you to learn whether the job and organization are right for you. In this sense, the potential boss and the prospective employee are interviewing each other.

Near the end of the interview, you'll probably be asked if you have any questions. You might feel as if you already know all the important facts about the job, but asking questions based on your knowledge of the industry, the company, and the position can produce some useful information, as well as show the interviewer that you have done your research and that you are realistically assessing the fit between yourself and the organization. In

> behavioral interview

A formal meeting (in person or via communication technology) to exchange information about an applicant's past performance as it relates to the job at hand.

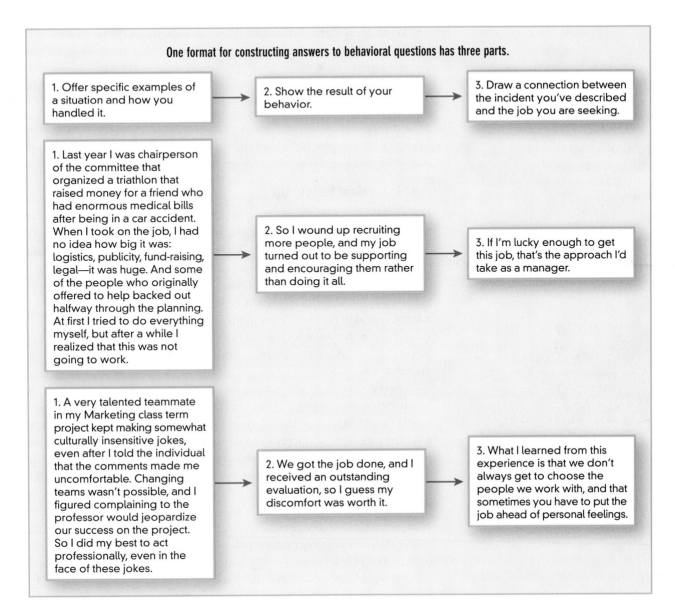

One format for constructing answers to behavioral questions has three parts.

1. Offer specific examples of a situation and how you handled it. → 2. Show the result of your behavior. → 3. Draw a connection between the incident you've described and the job you are seeking.

1. Last year I was chairperson of the committee that organized a triathlon that raised money for a friend who had enormous medical bills after being in a car accident. When I took on the job, I had no idea how big it was: logistics, publicity, fund-raising, legal—it was huge. And some of the people who originally offered to help backed out halfway through the planning. At first I tried to do everything myself, but after a while I realized that this was not going to work. → 2. So I wound up recruiting more people, and my job turned out to be supporting and encouraging them rather than doing it all. → 3. If I'm lucky enough to get this job, that's the approach I'd take as a manager.

1. A very talented teammate in my Marketing class term project kept making somewhat culturally insensitive jokes, even after I told the individual that the comments made me uncomfortable. Changing teams wasn't possible, and I figured complaining to the professor would jeopardize our success on the project. So I did my best to act professionally, even in the face of these jokes. → 2. We got the job done, and I received an outstanding evaluation, so I guess my discomfort was worth it. → 3. What I learned from this experience is that we don't always get to choose the people we work with, and that sometimes you have to put the job ahead of personal feelings.

Figure 10-2 Strategies for Responding to Behavioral Questions

addition to generating questions specific to the company or organization, the following list offers examples of some good questions to ask:

- Why is this position open now? How often has it been filled in the past five years? What have been the primary reasons people have left it in the past?
- What is the biggest problem facing your staff now? How have past and current employees dealt with this problem?

What strategies might you use to distinguish yourself from other candidates during an interview?

- What are the primary results you would like to see me produce?
- How would you describe the management style I could expect from my supervisors?
- Where could a person go who is successful in this position? Within what time frame?

Important note: Never ask about salary or benefits during a selection interview unless you have been offered the position, as many employers may view this as presumptuous or arrogant.

Post-Interview Follow-Up

Follow up your interview with a prompt, sincere, and personalized note of thanks to the interviewer. A thoughtful and well-written thank-you note can set you apart from other candidates. And failing to send a thank-you note within a day of your interview can eliminate you from the running.

A good thank-you should express your appreciation for the chance to get acquainted with the company or organization. It should explain why you see a good fit between you and the job, highlighting your demonstrated skills. Finally, it should let the interviewer know that the conversation left you excited about the chance of becoming associated with the company or organization.

Most employment advisors agree that this is one situation in which a handwritten message can be appropriate. Whether your thank-you message is handwritten or emailed, reread it carefully several times, and have a skilled proofreader review it, as a mistake here can damage your prospects. One job seeker ruined her chances of employment by mentioning the "report" (instead of "rapport") that she felt with the interviewer.

Phone and Video Interviews

In an age when budgets are tight, communication technology is pervasive, and work teams are geographically distributed, it's no surprise that a growing number of interviews are conducted via phone and video conference. All of the guidelines discussed previously apply to mediated interviews. In addition, several tips can help you succeed when you're communicating by phone or video chat.

Create a Professional Identity

Use a screen name that won't embarrass you. As one expert colorfully put it, "If I'm talking to somebody for a business interview and their Skype address is 'motherofalldrugaddicts' or something, I certainly think that would be problematic."[12]

Consider How You Look and Sound

Minimize background noise: A barking dog or noisy roommates will likely jeopardize your prospects of impressing a potential employer. Likewise, pay attention to what you wear if it's a video conference. You might hang out with friends or family in your workout gear, but that would be a

In the comedy *The Internship*, Owen Wilson and Vince Vaughn are wristwatch salesmen who interview for an internship at Google after their company folds. They take part in the interview from a public computer and shout at the top of their lungs, among other videoconference faux pas, exuding obvious technical incompetence.

Q *What do you think are the greatest challenges when interviewing via phone or video?*

mistake in an interview. In addition, think about the background of the room in which you will be conducting the interview. A neutral backdrop without distractions is ideal.

Check Every Detail in Advance

Technology problems can end a distance interview before it begins. Make sure you have a solid Internet connection with enough speed to handle the conversation. Double-check your camera, microphone, and speakers to confirm that they function properly. Make sure the lighting works so the interviewer at the other end can see you clearly. If you're using a phone or tablet, set it up on a tripod or other stable device to avoid distracting jiggles. If you're using a laptop, make sure the camera captures you head-on rather than at an unflattering angle.

Ensure You Have the Right Time for the Interview

There is nothing worse than being an hour late. Confirm the time in advance, especially when different time zones are involved (if you're not sure, search the web for "world clock"). For example, "I'm looking forward to speaking with you next Tuesday at 8 a.m. Pacific/11 a.m. Eastern."

Look at the Camera, Not the Screen

Looking at your monitor may feel natural. However, it creates the impression you're not making eye contact with the interviewer. Instead, look directly at the camera on the device you're using for the interview.

Conduct a Dress Rehearsal

Practicing is the best way to ensure you are prepared. Recruit a trusted friend (or, even better, someone at your school's career center) to play the role of interviewer. Be sure to practice under the actual circumstances of the interview—remotely and with the same equipment and services you'll use for the real thing. Besides ironing out potential glitches, rehearsals should leave you feeling more confident.

Interviewing and the Law

Most laws governing what topics can and can't be covered in job interviews boil down to two simple principles: First, questions may not be aimed at discriminating on the basis of race, color, religion, gender, sexual orientation, disabilities, national origin, or age. Second, questions must be related to what the U.S. government's Equal Employment Opportunity Commission (EEOC) calls *bona fide occupational qualifications.* In other words, prospective employers may only ask about topics that are related to the job at hand. Examples of illegal questions include those that ask about where you were born, any unrelated physical impairments you may have, whether you have children, your religion, or your political affiliation.

Despite the law, there is a good chance that interviewers will ask illegal questions. This will probably have more to do with being uninformed than malicious. Still, when faced with a question that's not legal, you will need to know how to respond tactfully. There are several options:

> **Answer without objecting.** Answer the question, even though you know it is probably unlawful: "No, I'm not married. But I'm engaged." Recognize, though, that this could open the door for other illegal questions—and perhaps even discrimination in hiring decisions.
>
> **Seek explanation.** Ask the interviewer firmly and respectfully to explain why this question is related to the job: "I'm having a hard time seeing how my marital status relates to my ability to do this job. Can you explain?"
>
> **Redirect.** Shift the focus of the interview away from a question that isn't job related and toward the requirements of the position itself: "What you've said so far suggests that age is not as important for this position as knowledge of accounting. Can you tell me more about the kinds of accounting that are part of this job?"
>
> **Refuse.** Explain politely but firmly that you will not provide the information requested: "I'd rather not talk about my religion. That's a very private and personal matter for me."
>
> **Withdraw.** End the interview immediately and leave, stating your reasons firmly but professionally: "I'm very uncomfortable with these questions about my personal life, and I don't see a good fit between me and this organization. Thank you for your time."

There's no absolutely correct way to handle illegal questions. The option you choose will depend on several factors: the likely intent of the interviewer, the nature of the questions, your desire for the job—and finally, your "gut level" of comfort with the whole situation.

Explain and practice skills for communicating with followers, leaders, and peers in a professional manner on the job.

OBJECTIVE 10.3

STRATEGIES FOR COMMUNICATING ON THE JOB

Once you are offered a job, pat yourself on the back. However, note that getting hired is only the beginning. In this section, we offer communication strategies that can help you succeed on the job. Again, keep in mind that every company or organization is different and may have varying rules and norms.

Communicating with Followers, Leaders, and Peers

Throughout your career, you will most likely work with three types of people: leaders (supervisors or those in management positions), followers (employees or those who may work for you), and peers (colleagues with whom you work). Successful communication in each of these relationships presents its own challenges and calls for different skills.

Communicating with Followers

Downward communication occurs when supervisors initiate messages to the people they supervise. Downward communication can take the form of goals or objectives, instructions, procedures, policies, and performance appraisals, for example.[13] In the early stages of your career you're most likely to be on the receiving end of downward messages, but in today's fast-paced professional world, this may quickly change.

> **downward communication**
> Messages from supervisors to the people they supervise.

With downward communication, it's essential to be clear and respectful and to make sure employees understand expectations and that they have the resources needed to do their jobs. A study at General Electric revealed that "clear communication between boss and worker" was the most important factor in job satisfaction for most people.[14] Despite its importance, downward communication often is lacking. One of employees' most frequent complaints is that they don't know where they stand with their supervisors.[15]

Many companies are starting to take a more enlightened approach to feedback. Ed Carlson, former president of United Airlines, is generally credited with turning the company from a loser into a winner during his tenure. Part of his success was due to keeping United's employees—all of them—aware of how the company was doing. "Nothing is worse for morale than a lack of information down in the ranks," he said. "I call it NETMA—Nobody Ever Tells Me Anything—and I have tried hard to minimize that problem."[16]

Communicating with Leaders

> **upward communication**
Messages from team members to supervisors.

Messages from team members to supervisors are labeled **upward communication.** This may include communication about problems, progress reports, grievances, financial information, or suggestions for improvement.[17] Businesses that are open to upward communication can profit from the ideas of employees.[18] Sam Walton, founder of Wal-Mart, the largest retailer in the United States, once claimed that "our best ideas come from clerks and stockboys."[19]

Supervisors can use a number of tools to enhance upward messages: an open-door policy, grievance procedures, periodic interviews, group meetings, and a suggestion box, to name a few. While most of the responsibility for improving upward communication rests with managers, there are also strategies you can use as a team member to gain recognition for your ideas—and yourself:[20]

Present proposals to your boss. Don't wait for your boss to recognize your value or choose you for a prime assignment. Develop a specific plan that demonstrates your understanding of the company's needs and offer to present your ideas for meeting those needs.

Volunteer for assignments. Create opportunities to expand your working relationships. After completing assignments, submit concise summaries to your boss.

Circulate your ideas. Contribute quality writing to company publications, association or professional journals, and blogs. Share copies with your boss.

Use thoughtful gestures to raise your profile. Devote a few minutes every day to raising your visibility by thanking people who worked with you on projects. Be sure to cc or otherwise share your words of praise with their supervisors (with a blind copy to the one whose help you received) and feed your gratitude into the grapevine.

Share your accomplishments. Without bragging, be prepared to weave your accomplishments into an interesting story you can tell whenever the opportunity arises.

Communicating with Peers

> **horizontal communication**
Messages between members of an organization with equal power.

A third type of organizational interaction is **horizontal communication**. It consists of messages between members of an organization with equal power.[21] The most obvious type of horizontal communication is between members of the same division of an organization: office workers in the same department or coworkers on a construction project. In other cases, lateral communication occurs between people from different areas: the accounting staff calls the maintenance department to get a machine repaired, or a clerk in hospital admissions calls intensive care to reserve a bed.

Despite the importance of good horizontal communication, several forces work to discourage communication between peers.[22] These include rivalry (people who feel threatened by one another, perhaps because of competition for a promotion or raise, are not likely to be cooperative); specialization (sometimes it can be difficult for people with different technical backgrounds to understand one another); information overload (we are inundated with messages every day, which may discourage employees from reaching out to others in different areas); lack of motivation (sometimes people simply are unwilling to spend the time or effort that reaching out to others in an organization entails); and physical barriers (having offices scattered throughout different buildings, for example, can interfere with horizontal connections). One of the best strategies for combatting these challenges and others is to ensure that you communicate in a professional way.

Communicating in a Professional Manner

Technical competence by itself is necessary, but it isn't sufficient for career success. Surviving and thriving in the workplace depends as much on your personal communication skills. Social scientists have labeled this skill **social intelligence**—the capacity to effectively negotiate complex social relationships and environments.[23] Like technical competence, emotional intelligence can be learned and sharpened. Following are some guidelines for communicating in a professional manner.

> social intelligence
The capacity to effectively negotiate complex social relationships and environments.

Be Sensitive to Cultural and Cocultural Differences
In an increasingly diverse workforce, it's essential to navigate differences in what's considered appropriate behavior. Chapter 2 introduced many dimensions of intercultural and cocultural communication. It's worth reviewing them as you think about succeeding in your career.

Remember that cultural differences involve more than nationality. For example, consider generational preferences in work styles. Members of the millennial generation, born between 1982 and 2004, are typically comfortable working from remote sites and multitasking—mixing communication via portable devices with face-to-face conversations. Older bosses tend to feel differently. Nearly half of them feel that millennials are lazy and distracted on the job, partly because, even when they are present, they seem more tuned in to their phones or tablets than to the people around them.[24]

Don't Overshare
It may seem important to "be yourself," but there are times when disclosing information about your personal life can damage your chances for professional success—or just flat out annoy people.[25] The "don't overshare" rule applies to online communication, too. Photos of your wild vacation aren't like to impress the boss or potential employers. When information about you might be used as the basis for discrimination, the best rule is to disclose cautiously, especially if the topic is a sensitive one such as dealing with religion, sexual relationships, or health.[26] A trusted colleague may be able to offer advice about how much to share.

While the nature of today's workplace has changed considerably from the shocking behavior in the film *9 to 5* and the show *Mad Men*, employees continue to violate many rules and norms.

Q *How would you handle a coworker acting inappropriately?*

"Friendly formality" is especially appropriate when you interact with people from other cultures.[27] Many Americans display what researchers call "instant intimacy."[28] They often address even new acquaintances, elders, and authority figures by first name. They engage in a great deal of eye contact, touch their conversational partners, and ask personal questions. To people from different backgrounds, the same behavior can seem disrespectful. An Australian exchange student in the United States reflected on her experience: "There seemed to be a disproportionate amount of really probing conversations. Things I normally wouldn't chat about on a first conversation."[29]

Communicate in a Principled Manner

Communicating with integrity isn't always easy. The culture in some organizations favors gossiping, bad-mouthing, competing, and even breaking laws to make more money.[30] Nevertheless, principled communication means following your own set of ethics rather than relying on the approval of others. It may be helpful to know if someone was promoted, reprimanded, or fired, and why—but malicious gossip can mark you as untrustworthy and damage the spirit of teamwork on which your success depends.[31] One executive proposed this test: Before you start talking, stop and ask yourself, "Is it kind?"[32]

Exceed Expectations

You may have heard the phrase *don't sweat the small stuff*. In fact, making a good impression requires paying attention to every detail. Show up for work well groomed and professionally dressed. Avoid using language that might offend others. Another method for standing out is to do more than is required.[33] For example, you might finish a job ahead of schedule, do a better job than other people anticipated, volunteer to serve on a committee, work on a weekend or after hours (if it's allowed), offer to deliver a presentation, or tackle a project that keeps getting delayed. The time that jobs like this take will be well worth the reputation they earn you.

Keep Your Cool

Losing control under pressure can jeopardize your career. Consider the extreme case of a Jet Blue flight attendant who was fired after he became frustrated with a passenger, grabbed two beers, and jumped off the (parked) plane via an evacuation chute.[34] Even less dramatic freak-outs—raising your voice or dashing off an angry email or text message—can damage your reputation and even land you among the unemployed.

You can employ a variety of techniques to stay collected when you feel yourself getting agitated. Take a few deep breaths or a break, stop to listen and ask questions before responding, and vent your emotions to trusted associates while off the clock.[35] While losing your composure may be acceptable in personal relationships in which people love and understand you, you don't have the same luxury at work.

Be E-Savvy

You may have to rush to keep up with the demands of correspondence; but if you are careless, SEND can be your worst enemy. Here are a few rules to keep your online communication professional:

> **Use correct grammar, spelling, and punctuation.** Messages such as "i gotta go now" or "OMG," may be fine among friends, but they risk causing coworkers and managers to doubt your professionalism and your literacy skills.
>
> **Beware of overly curt messages.** While it can be tempting to reply quickly and briefly, remember that brevity can sometimes be misunderstood. It's ok to get to the point, but do so in a courteous manner.
>
> **Don't convey sensitive information electronically.** If you need to deliver bad news, criticism, or private information, remember that any message you send electronically may end up in the wrong inbox. If you wouldn't be comfortable having your words become public knowledge, don't send them electronically.[36]

Acknowledge Gaffes and Move On

What if you accidentally say "I love you" while ending a call with your boss? Or your eyes fill with tears during a stressful business meeting? Minor lapses in professionalism are bound to occur, even among seasoned professionals. You can usually recover your dignity and your reputation by following these four steps: don't panic, acknowledge the gaffe, apologize, and return to life as usual.[37] For example, you might say, "I'm in the habit of saying 'I love you' when I talk to my family. I didn't mean to end our call that way. I'm sorry for the slip-up! I'll be more careful in the future." It's okay to laugh if the other

Have you ever lost your composure in a professional situation? What strategies did you use to recover?

person does, but don't dwell on the mistake. You want your reputation to be centered on your impressive performance instead of your goof.

Working with a Difficult Boss

Good bosses can make the most challenging work more satisfying.[38] The converse is also true: A bad boss can make even the most glamorous, high-paying work unpleasant, and downright unhealthy.[39] Perhaps as bad, a poor manager can reduce productivity and damage the careers of his or her employees.[40]

Unless you're self-employed or extremely lucky, sooner or later you are likely to encounter a difficult boss. She or he may be a micromanager, or perhaps so hands-off that you might as well be on your own. Your difficult boss may be unreasonably demanding, shower you with verbal abuse, or engage in passive-aggressive behavior—perhaps being nice enough to you in person but sabotaging you behind your back. Or your difficult boss may simply be incompetent. What should you do if you encounter such a manager? While every job and situation is different, if you can't avoid a difficult boss, here are a few strategies that may help you manage the relationship:[41]

Adapt to Your Boss
Meeting your boss's expectations can make your life easier. If your boss is a micromanager, invite her or his input. If your boss is a stickler for detail, invest extra effort providing more information than you would otherwise do. If your manager values hard work, try to show up before he or she does

In the movie *Horrible Bosses*, Dr. Julia Harris (Jennifer Aniston) and Dave Harken (Kevin Spacey) terrorize and harass their employees.

Q *Have you ever had to deal with a challenging manager? What strategies did you employ to maintain your composure?*

and/or leave afterwards. The extra effort may show your boss that you care and take the job seriously.

Filling in for your boss's weaknesses is another way to manage an imperfect situation. If she's forgetful, diplomatically remind her of important details. If he's disorganized, provide the necessary information before he even asks. As one consultant points out, "Making yourself indispensable and someone your boss can rely on to help him do his job is a valuable asset when you start to look to 'what's next?'"[42]

Seek Advice from Others

Gratuitous complaining about your boss is a bad idea. But if other people in your organization have encountered the same problems, you might discover useful information by seeking their advice.

Try to Clarify and Improve the Situation

If your best efforts don't solve the problem, consider requesting a meeting to discuss the situation. It's essential that you communicate in a professional manner using the strategies we have outlined throughout this book. Rather than blaming, use "I" language. Solicit your boss's point of view, and listen nondefensively to what he or she has to say. Paraphrase and use perception checking as necessary to clarify your understanding. As much as possible, seek a win-win outcome. After all, having a boss who approves of you will make your work life much more satisfying.

Manage Your Expectations

You may not be able to change your boss's behavior, but you can control your attitude about the situation. Sometimes accepting that there are things over which you have little control may help you to adjust your attitude and expectations.

Keep a Professional Demeanor

Even if your boss has awful interpersonal skills, you will gain nothing by sinking to the same level. It's best to take the high road, practicing the professional communication skills described elsewhere in this chapter.

Prepare to Move On

A well-known maxim makes the point concisely: "People join companies, but they leave managers." If you can't fix an intolerable situation, the smartest approach may be to look for more rewarding employment. Even though you may be tempted to have a "take this job and shove it" moment, it's far wiser to use the job-seeking tips discussed earlier in this chapter to plan a strategic move.

Exiting Graciously

The most important thing you do on the job might be the last thing you do. At some point, everyone who is employed will leave a job either voluntarily (for instance to change jobs, go back to school, or embark on some other personal endeavor) or involuntarily (for instance if you are laid off or fired).

Many professionals make the mistake of burning bridges when they leave a company. To assure that a bad reference doesn't haunt you in the future, follow these steps if you choose to leave voluntarily:[43]

Write a brief, gracious resignation letter. Include the date you will leave (allow at least two weeks for the transition), a diplomatic explanation for why you are leaving (". . . new opportunities for growth"), and a statement of appreciation for what you have learned on the job.

Deliver the letter in person to your boss. Make sure to tell your boss that you're leaving before he or she hears the news from someone else. Be professional and calm in the meeting, even if you are leaving under less-than-ideal conditions.

Unless instructed otherwise, let your coworkers know. When you deliver the news, don't engage in criticism or complaints.

Help during the transition. You may be asked to finish key projects, create to-do lists and guides, or train new staff members, and you should do these things graciously and to the best of your ability as time allows.

Don't complain about your former employer. Badmouthing your old boss or the company you used to work for won't improve anything, and it is likely to make new colleagues wonder if you might criticize them in the future.

OBJECTIVE 10.4 Choose and effectively use the most situationally appropriate and effective approaches to leading and following at work.

LEADERSHIP, FOLLOWERSHIP, AND POWER

When you ask most people to visualize a leader, you're likely to hear descriptions of charismatic figures using the force of their personalities to stir masses of followers. The real story is far less dramatic, but more encouraging for aspiring leaders. Harvard Business School professor Quinn Mills explains: "Most leading in a corporation is done in small meetings and it's done at a distance, through written and video communications. It's not done in big groups."[44] In other words, leaders of the world's largest organizations rely on the same communication principles that you will use in the groups to which you belong.

Another misconception is that leaders must be outgoing and have powerful personalities. The reality is often just the opposite. Management guru Peter Drucker described the defining communication style of effective leaders he observed in a decades-long career: They had little or no "charisma," he stated flatly.[45] A quick look at some famous leaders bears out this description. Leaders as diverse as corporate titans Bill Gates and

Marissa Mayer started making headlines when she became Yahoo's youngest CEO at age 37. While she has earned high marks for improving the company's products and generating excitement through acquisitions, she has also been criticized for ending the company's work-from-home privileges and for prohibiting napping on the job.

Q *Why do you think Mayer's leadership has been so closely scrutinized and reported?*

Mark Zuckerberg or civil rights heroes Rosa Parks and Nelson Mandela won hearts and minds through their revolutionary ideas and actions, not their commanding personalities.

Approaches to Leadership

The question of effective leadership has occupied philosophers, rulers, and, more recently, social scientists, for centuries. The lessons learned by those who came before us can help prepare us to be more effective today.

More than 2,000 years ago, Aristotle proclaimed, "From the hour of their birth some are marked out for subjugation, and others for command."[46] This is a radical expression of **trait theories of leadership**, sometimes labeled as the "great man" or "great woman" approach. Conventional wisdom suggests that people who are strong willed and demanding are "natural born" leaders, but that isn't usually true. The most effective leaders are self-aware, considerate of others, and inclined to partner with others rather than order them around.[47] The lesson is that, far from finishing last, nice guys (and gals) are likely to lead the way.[48] (See Figure 10-3 for more characteristics of effective leaders.)

> **trait theories of leadership**
> The belief that it is possible to identify leaders by personal traits, such as intelligence, appearance, or sociability.

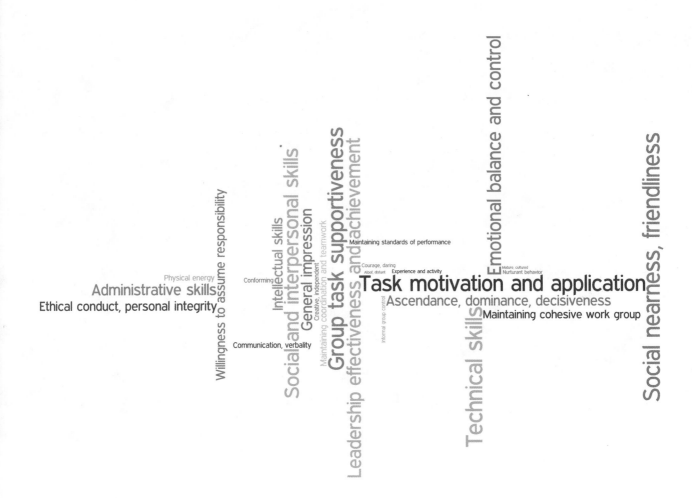

Figure 10-3 Some Traits Associated with Leaders

Despite these general findings, trait theories have limited practical value. Many other factors are important in determining leader success, and not everyone who possesses these traits becomes a leader. Moreover, some qualities that many people associate with leadership aren't actually very important.

Most contemporary scholars are convinced that the best style of leadership varies from one set of circumstances to another.[49] The principle of **situational leadership** holds that a leader's style should change with the circumstances.[50] A task-oriented approach works best when conditions are either highly favorable (good leader-member relations, strong leader power, and clear task structure) or highly unfavorable (poor leader-member relations, weak leader power, and an ambiguous task), whereas a more relationship-oriented approach is appropriate in moderately favorable or moderately unfavorable conditions.

> situational leadership

A theory that argues that the most effective leadership style varies according to leader-member relations, the leader's power, and the task structure.

¿? What is your leadership style?

Check the item in each of the following groupings that *best* characterizes your beliefs as a leader:

1. I believe a leader's most important job is to:

____ a. make sure people stay focused on the task at hand.

✓ b. help team members build strong relationships.

____ c. make sure the work place is an enjoyable environment.

2. When it comes to team members, I believe:

✓ a. people have a natural inclination to work hard and do good work.

____ b. people work best when there are clear expectations and oversight.

____ c. people are most productive when they are happy and enjoying themselves.

3. When a problem arises, I am mostly likely to:

____ a. solve it myself or smooth things over.

✓ b. ask team members' input on how to solve it.

____ c. implement a new policy or procedure to avoid the same problem in the future.

4. If team members had to describe me in a few words, I would like them to be:

____ a. competent and in control.

____ b. pleasant and friendly.

____ c. attentive and trustworthy.

5. When I see team members talking and laughing in the hallway, I am most likely to:

____ a. feel frustrated that they are goofing off.

____ b. share my latest joke with them.

____ c. feel encouraged that they get along so well.

Evaluating Your Responses

Circle your answers on the grid below. Note that they do not appear in alphabetical order.

Grouping 1	Grouping 2	Grouping 3	Grouping 4	Grouping 5
b	a	b	c	c
a	b	c	a	a
c	c	a	b	b

For an explanation of your responses, see pg. 259. ●

More recently, some social scientists have suggested that a leader's focus on task or relational issues should vary according to the readiness of the group being led.[51] Readiness involves the members' level of motivation, willingness to take responsibility, and the amount of knowledge and experience they have in a given situation. For example, a new, inexperienced group needs more task-related direction, whereas a more experienced group might require more social support and less instruction about how to do the job. A highly experienced group could probably handle the job well without much supervision at all. This approach suggests that, because an employee's readiness changes from one job to another, the best way to lead should vary as well.

> Do you think traits or leadership style most important to leadership success? Why?

Becoming a Leader

Even in groups that begin with no official leader, members can take on that role. Committees elect chairpersons, teams choose captains, and negotiating groups elect spokespeople. The subject of leadership emergence has been studied extensively.[52]

Emergent leaders gain influence without being appointed by higher-ups. A group of unhappy employees might urge one person to approach the boss and ask for a change. A team of students working on a class project might agree that one person is best suited to take the lead in organizing and presenting their work. Whether or not the role comes with a title, emergent leaders can gain influence in a variety of ways.[53] One method is through a process of elimination in which potential candidates are gradually rejected for one reason or another until only one remains.[54] Once clearly unsuitable members have been eliminated, certain behaviors will boost the odds of someone emerging as the formal or informal leader:

> **Stay engaged** Getting involved won't guarantee that you'll be recognized as a leader, but failing to speak up will almost certainly knock you out of the running.

> **Demonstrate competence** Make sure your comments identify you as someone who can help the team succeed. Talking for its own sake will only antagonize other members.

> **Be assertive, not aggressive** It's fine to be assertive, but don't try to overpower other members. Treat other members' contributions respectfully, even when they differ from yours.

> **Support other members** The endorsement of other members (some researchers have called them "*lieutenants*") increases your credibility and influence.

> **Provide a solution in a time of crisis** How can the team get the necessary resources? Resolve a disagreement? Meet a deadline? Members who find answers to problems like these are likely to rise to a position of authority.

The Importance of Followers

"What are you, a leader or a follower?" we're asked, and we know which position is generally considered the better one. One reason is a fundamental misunderstanding about what it means to be a follower. Despite the common belief that leaders are the most important group members, good followers are indispensable.

Effective followers share many of the same qualities as effective leaders, including honesty, competence, intelligence, and character.[55] Good followers are loyal, dependable, and cooperative, but they aren't blindly obedient. Management consultant Robert Kelley observes that effective followers "think for themselves, are very active, and have very positive energy,"[56, 57] Overall, the lesson seems to be that followership involves a sophisticated array of skills, a good measure of self-confidence, and a

> emergent leader

A member who assumes leadership roles without being appointed by higher-ups.

strong commitment to excellence, even if that means questioning the status quo.

All followers don't communicate or contribute equally, however. Barbara Kellerman, a theorist who writes about both leaders and followers, observes that followers fall into five categories.[58] *Isolates* are indifferent to the overall goals of the organization and communicate very little with people outside their immediate environment. *Bystanders* are engaged, but they hang back and watch rather than play an active role. (You may find yourself in a bystander role occasionally, especially when you are in a new situation.) *Participants* attempt to have a constructive impact. Some support leaders' efforts, whereas others contribute differing perspectives. *Activists* are energetically and passionately engaged—either in accordance with, or in opposition to, leaders' efforts. *Diehards* may sacrifice themselves for the cause. Their commitment is unrivaled, but sometimes it's difficult to contain their enthusiasm, even when it runs counter to other people's goals.

Power in the Workplace

People often assume that leaders have all the power, but followers have more than you might think. Instead of talking about someone as "powerful" or "powerless," it's more accurate to talk about how much influence he or she exerts. **Power** is the ability to influence others. It comes in a variety of forms.[59, 60]

Legitimate Power

Sometimes called position power, **legitimate power** arises from the title one holds, such as supervisor, professor, or coach. People with legitimate power are said to be **nominal leaders**, which means they have been officially designated as being in charge of a group. To gain legitimate power, become an authority figure; speak up without dominating others; demonstrate competence on the subject; follow group norms and show that you respect the group's customs; and gain the visible support of influential members.

> **power**
The ability to influence others' thoughts and/or actions.

> **legitimate power**
The ability to influence a group owing to one's position in a group.

> **nominal leaders**
People who have been officially designated as being in charge of a group.

Sometimes called "the other Steve" in relation to his famous partner, Steve Wozniak (shown here in 1987) was content to work mostly behind the scenes at Apple and let the more extroverted Steve Jobs take the limelight.

Q *How can you be a quiet yet important contributor to groups?*

Expert Power

> **expert power**

The ability to influence others by virtue of one's perceived expertise on the subject in question.

Expert power comes from what team members know or can do. If you're lost in the woods, it makes sense to follow the advice of a group member who has wilderness experience. If your computer crashes at a critical time, you turn to the team member with IT expertise. In groups, it isn't sufficient to be an expert: The other members have to view you as one. To gain expert power make sure members are aware of your qualifications, be certain the information is accurate, and don't act superior.

Connection Power

> **connection power**

Influence granted by virtue of a member's ability to develop relationships that help the group reach its goal.

As its name implies, **connection power** comes from a member's ability to develop relationships that help the group reach its goal. For instance, a team seeking guest speakers at a seminar might rely on a well-connected member to line up candidates. To gain connection power seek out opportunities to meet new people, nurture relationships through open and regular communication, and don't allow petty grievances to destroy valued relationships.

Reward and Coercive Power

> **reward power**

The ability to influence others by the granting or promising of desirable consequences.

Reward power exists when others are influenced by the granting or promise of desirable consequences. Rewards come in a variety of forms. The goodwill of other members can sometimes be even more valuable than accolades from the official leader of a group. For example, in a presentation to your class, having your fellow students applaud you and give you a standing ovation might be a more powerful reward than the grade you receive from the instructor.

> **coercive power**

The power to influence others by the threat or imposition of unpleasant consequences.

Coercive power comes from the threat or actual imposition of unpleasant consequences. Nominal leaders certainly can coerce members via compensation, assignments, and even termination from the group. But members also possess coercive power. Working with an unhappy, unmotivated teammate can be punishing. For this reason, it's important to keep members feeling satisfied ... as long as it doesn't compromise the team's goals. To use reward and coercive power effectively try to use rewards as a first resort and punishment as a last resort, make rewards and punishments clear in advance, and be generous with praise.

Referent Power

> **referent power**

The ability to influence others by virtue of the degree to which one is liked or respected.

Referent power comes from the respect, liking, and trust others have for a member. If you have high referent power, you may be able to persuade others to follow your lead because they believe in you or because they are willing to do you a favor. Members acquire referent power by behaving in ways others in the group admire and by being genuinely likable. To gain referent power: listen to others' ideas and honor their contributions; do what you can to gain the liking and respect of other members without compromising your principles; and present your ideas clearly and effectively in order to boost your credibility.

CHECK YOUR UNDERSTANDING

OBJECTIVE 10.1 Describe communication behaviors conducive to finding a job that matches your skills.

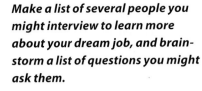

STRATEGIES FOR FINDING A JOB

The chances of landing a great job and succeeding at it are bolstered by good communication skills. It pays to establish strong networks and to participate in informational interviews in order to find out more about the job market and how to prepare for the career you want.

Make a list of several people you might interview to learn more about your dream job, and brainstorm a list of questions you might ask them.

OBJECTIVE 10.2 Identify application and interviewing strategies that are likely to lead to employment.

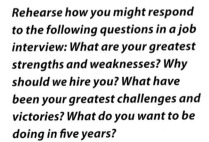

STRATEGIES FOR GETTING HIRED

Begin your job search with a strong résumé. Adapt your cover letter to each position, and follow the application instructions precisely. Prepare in advance for each interview by researching the company and the industry, considering how you will answer key questions, and what questions you might ask. Whether you are interviewed in person, on the phone, or via video conference, display professional etiquette and answer questions succinctly but specifically to showcase your qualifications. Don't forget to send a personal note of thanks afterwards.

Rehearse how you might respond to the following questions in a job interview: What are your greatest strengths and weaknesses? Why should we hire you? What have been your greatest challenges and victories? What do you want to be doing in five years?

OBJECTIVE 10.3 Explain and practice skills for communicating with followers, leaders, and peers in a professional manner on the job.

STRATEGIES FOR COMMUNICATING ON THE JOB

Communicating effectively as a professional involves an array of skills, whether you are interacting with leaders, followers, or peers. The most successful professionals make their accomplishments known while supporting others, honor diversity, behave appropriately and ethically, go the extra mile to do a great job, stay calm under pressure, and exhibit technological savvy. When they leave an organization, they do so graciously and considerately.

Imagine yourself working in a fast-paced environment that requires you to juggle online and in-person communication. What are some strategies you might employ to show that you have what it takes to succeed and to move into a leadership position?

Choose and effectively use the most situationally appropriate and effective approaches to leading and following at work.

LEADERSHIP, FOLLOWERSHIP, AND POWER

Leaders who focus on the objectives and the situation accomplish more than those who are primarily motivated by the desire to achieve personal glory or maintain harmony. Leaders often emerge naturally, as the ones who are most engaged and capable when needs arise. Followers' contributions are often undervalued, but the contributions of people who actively participate can be substantial. Both leaders and followers embody many types of power that arise from being respected as experts, being good relationship-builders, having the ability to reward or coerce others, or simply because people like and admire them.

Think of a group you have been part of. What type of leader or follower are or were you? What types of power can or did you use most effectively?

KEY TERMS

behavioral interview p. 238
coercive power p. 256
connection power p. 256
downward communication p. 243
emergent leader p. 254
expert power p. 256
horizontal communication p. 244

informational interview p. 229
legitimate power p. 255
networking p. 226
nominal leaders p. 255
power p. 255
referent power p. 256
reward power p. 256

selection interview p. 233
situational leadership p. 252
social intelligence p. 245
trait theories of leadership p. 251
upward communication p. 244

WHAT IS YOUR LEADERSHIP STYLE?

Relationship Orientation

If the majority of your answers appear in the yellow row, you are a relationship-oriented leader. You are likely to show team members a great deal of respect and attention, which often brings out the best in people. Most people consider this to be the ideal leadership style as long as your focus on relationships does not mean that you neglect task concerns.

Task Orientation

If your answers appear mostly in the green row, you are a task-oriented leader. You tend to emphasize productivity and may be frustrated by inefficiency. The danger is that you will overlook relationships in your zeal to get the job done, which can be counterproductive in the long run.

Country Club Orientation

If most of your answers are in the blue row, your focus on strong relationships and a pleasant work environment is likely to be appreciated by team members. However, you have a tendency to take that too far. A more moderate focus, in which you emphasize both relationships and tasks, may ultimately be more rewarding for everyone involved.

Mixed Orientation

If your answers are mostly spread all over the grid, you don't show a clear priority for either relationship or task goals. Perhaps you focus on both of them equally, or you may neglect both of them. It's important to consider that both relationships and tasks are highly important.

FOR FURTHER EXPLORATION

For more communication resources, see the *Essential Communication* website at www.oup.com/us/ec. There you will find a variety of resources: "Media Room" examples from popular films and television shows to further illustrate important concepts, a list of relevant books and articles, links to descriptions of feature films and television shows at the *Now Playing* website, study aids, and a self-test to check your understanding of the material in this chapter.

Communicating in Groups and Teams

learning
Objectives

11.1 Identify the characteristics that distinguish groups and teams from other collections of people.

11.2 Understand how groups are affected by rules, norms, patterns of interaction, and roles.

11.3 Determine the ideal conditions for group problem solving, and outline the stages of problem solving most groups encounter.

11.4 Describe the optimal problem-solving formats and decision-making methods for arriving at effective solutions.

11.5 Summarize strategies for communicating effectively during group discussions.

Identify the characteristics that distinguish groups and teams from other collections of people.

THE NATURE OF GROUPS AND TEAMS

Groups probably play a bigger role in your life than you realize. Some groups are informal, such as friends and family. Others are part of work and school. Project groups, sports teams, and study groups are common types, and you can probably think of more examples that illustrate how central groups are in your life. However, that doesn't mean that all groups are equally important or that every group experience is a good one.

Group work can be immensely gratifying, but it can also be unrewarding or even downright miserable. In some cases, it's easy to see why a group succeeds or fails, but in others, the reasons aren't immediately clear.[1] In many cases, the differences between success and failure, between satisfaction and frustration, involve communication.

What a Group Is

> group

A small collection of people whose members interact with one another, usually face-to-face, over time in order to reach goals.

What do we mean when we use the word *group?* For our purposes a **group** consists of a small collection of people who interact with one another, usually face-to-face, over time in order to reach goals.

Interaction

Without interaction, a collection of people isn't a group. Students who passively listen to a lecture don't technically constitute a group until they begin to exchange messages verbally and nonverbally with one another and their instructor. This explains, in part, why some students feel isolated even though they spend so much time on a crowded campus.

Interdependence

In groups, members don't just interact: Group members are interdependent.[2] The behavior of one person affects all the others in a ripple effect.[3] When one member behaves poorly, his or her actions shape the way the entire group functions, and likewise positive actions may have ripple effects, too.

Time

A collection of people who interact for a few minutes doesn't qualify as a group. True groups work together long enough to develop a sense of identity and history that shapes their ongoing effectiveness.

Size

Our definition of groups includes the word *small*. Most experts in the field set the lower limit at three members.[4] There is less agreement about the maximum number of people.[5] As a rule of thumb, an effective group is

A "minion" is a powerless subordinate. However, in the *Despicable Me* movies, the so-called Minions save the world by working together.

Q *In what ways are you more effective as a member of a team than you might be working alone?*

small enough for members to know and react to every other member, and no larger than necessary to perform the task at hand effectively.[6] Small groups usually have between 3 and 20 members.

Group and Individual Goals

Two underlying motives drive group communication. The first involves **group goals**—the outcomes members collectively seek by joining together. A group goal might be to win a contest, create a product, or provide a service. Some group goals are social, such as meeting other people and having fun.

Another set of forces that drive groups are **individual goals**, the personal motives of each member. Sometimes individual goals can help the larger group. For example, a student seeking a top grade on a team project will probably help the team excel. However, problems arise when individual motives conflict with the group's goal. Consider a group member whose primary goal is to be the center of attention so she or he monopolizes the discussion, or a team member who engages in **social loafing**—lazy behavior that some members use to avoid doing their share of the work.

How a Group Becomes a Team

A **team** shares the same qualities as a group, but it takes collective action to a higher level. You probably know a team when you see it: Members are proud of their identity. They trust and value one another and cooperate. They seek, and often achieve, excellence.

> group goals
Goals that a group collectively seeks to accomplish.

> individual goals
Individual motives for joining a group.

> social loafing
Lazy behavior that some members use to avoid doing their share of the work.

> team
A group that has clear and inspiring shared goals, a results-driven structure, competent team members, unified commitment, a collaborative climate, external support and recognition, and principled leadership.

Teamwork has brought us computers, cars, space travel, the Internet, and many other innovations. Employees typically say that effective teamwork makes them feel more powerful and empowered than before, more appreciated, more successful, closer to their colleagues, and more confident that team members will support and encourage them in the future.[7]

When it comes to getting a job, employers are looking for team players. In a nationwide survey, employers rated the ability to work effectively in teams as the top quality they seek when hiring.[8] Teamwork is essential in virtually every scientific discipline,[9] and it has also been identified as the top nontechnical job skill.[10]

Teamwork doesn't come from *what* the group is doing, but *how* they do it. No matter what they are trying to achieve—climbing a mountain, completing a class project, winning a championship game—high-achieving teams share several important characteristics:[11]

Clear and Inspiring Shared Goals Members of a winning team know why their group exists, and they believe that purpose is important and worthwhile.

Results-Driven Structure Members of winning teams focus on getting the job done in the most effective manner. They do whatever is necessary to accomplish the task.

Competent Team Members Members of winning teams have the skills necessary to accomplish their goals.

Unified Commitment People in successful teams put the group's goals above their personal interests.

Collaborative Climate Another word for collaboration is *teamwork*. People in successful groups trust and support one another.

Standards of Excellence Doing outstanding work is an important norm in winning teams. Each member is expected to do his or her personal best.

External Support and Recognition Successful teams need an appreciative audience that recognizes their effort and provides the resources necessary to get the job done.

Principled Leadership Winning teams usually have leaders who can create a vision of the group's purpose, unleash the talent of group members, and challenge members to get the job done.

Based on what you've experienced or seen, how do high-functioning teams distinguish themselves from less capable groups?

Despite these virtues, not all groups need to function as teams, particularly if the goal is fairly simple, routine, or quickly accomplished. But when the job requires a great deal of thought, collaboration, and creativity, nothing beats teamwork. This is because we literally have greater brainpower when we work together and because most people feel more confident tackling complex issues when they share the challenge as a team.[12]

Understand how groups are affected by rules, norms, patterns of interaction, and roles.

OBJECTIVE 11.2

CHARACTERISTICS OF GROUPS

Whether or not a group is a team, there are certain characteristics that groups and teams share. Understanding these characteristics—which include rules and norms, patterns of interaction, and roles—is the first step to behaving more effectively in your own groups and teams.

Rules and Norms

Whether or not members know it, groups and teams have guidelines that govern members' behavior. You can appreciate this fact by comparing the ways you act in class or at work with the way you behave with your friends. The differences show that guidelines about how to communicate do exist.

Rules are official guidelines that govern what the group is supposed to do and how the members should behave. They are usually stated outright. In a classroom, rules include how absences will be treated, the firmness of deadlines, and so on.

Alongside the official rules is an equally powerful set of unspoken standards called **norms**. **Social norms** govern how we interact with one another (e.g., what kinds of humor are/aren't appropriate, how much socializing is acceptable on the job). **Procedural norms** guide operations and decision making (e.g., "We always start on time" or "When there's a disagreement, we try to reach consensus before forcing a vote"). **Task norms** govern how members get the job done (e.g., "Does the job have to be done perfectly, or is an adequate, if imperfect, solution good enough?"). On the one hand, following group norms helps us fit in. On the other hand, it can be helpful to point out norms that interfere with the group's success.

It is important to realize two things about norms. First, our norms don't always match ideals. Consider punctuality, for example. A cultural norm in our society is that meetings should begin at the scheduled time, yet the norm in some groups is to delay talking about real business until 10 or so minutes into the meeting. Second, group norms don't emerge immediately or automatically. Groups typically experience a stage of coming together and then a period of conflict before they enter a phase in which they find a comfortable rhythm together, and ideally, progress to a phase in which they function cohesively.[13]

Patterns of Interaction

In interpersonal and public speaking settings, two-way information exchange is relatively uncomplicated. But in a group, the possibilities of

> **rule**
> An explicit, officially stated guideline that governs group functions and member behavior.

> **norms**
> Shared values, beliefs, behaviors, and procedures that govern a group's operation.

> **social norms**
> Group norms that govern the way members relate to one another.

> **procedural norms**
> Norms that describe rules for the group's operation.

> **task norms**
> Group norms that govern the way members handle the job at hand.

Communication norms among the inmates in *Orange Is the New Black* would be considered outrageous by most people.

Q *What norms govern the groups to which you belong?*

> all-channel network

A communication network pattern in which group members are always together and share all information with one another.

> chain network

A communication network in which information passes sequentially from one member to another.

> wheel network

A communication network in which a gatekeeper regulates the flow of information from all other members.

complications increase exponentially. If there are five members in a group, there are 10 possible combinations for two-person conversations and 75 combinations involving more than two people. Besides the sheer quantity of information exchanged, the more complex structure of groups affects the flow of information in other ways, too. Figure 11-1 illustrates three common networks in small groups.

In an **all-channel network** group members share the same information with everyone on the team. Emails are a handy way to accomplish this. But while it's nice to be in the loop, too much sharing can lead to information overload.

Another option is a **chain network**, in which information moves sequentially from one member to another. This is an efficient way to deliver simple messages, but it's not very reliable for lengthy or complex verbal messages because the content can change as information passes from one person to another.

Another communication pattern is the **wheel network**, in which one person acts as a clearinghouse, receiving and relaying messages to all other members. Groups sometimes use wheel networks when relationships are

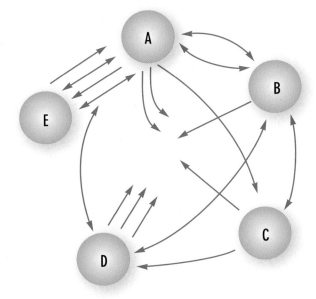

Figure 11-1 Patterns of Interaction in a 5-person Group

strained between two or more members. Success depends heavily on the skill of the **gatekeeper**, the person through whom information flows. If the gatekeeper intentionally or unintentionally distorts messages, the group is likely to suffer.

Roles

Roles define patterns of behavior expected of members. Just like norms, some roles are officially recognized. **Formal roles** are explicitly assigned by an organization or group. They usually come with a label, such as assistant coach, treasurer, or customer service representative. By contrast, **informal roles** (sometimes called "functional roles") are rarely acknowledged by the group in words.[14]

Informal group roles fall into two categories: task and maintenance. **Task roles** help the group accomplish its goals. These roles include information seeker, opinion giver, energizer, and critic. **Social roles** (also called "maintenance roles") help the relationships among the members run smoothly. These may include encourager, harmonizer, tension-reliever, and so on. Not all informal roles are constructive. For example, people may serve as attackers, withdrawers, or unrelenting jokesters. Dysfunctional roles like these prevent a group from working effectively. As you might expect, research suggests that groups are most effective when people fulfill positive social roles and no one fulfills the dysfunctional ones.[15]

Roles members take may powerfully influence the success of a team. Experts, therefore, offer the following advice.

> **gatekeepers**
Producers of mass messages who determine what messages will be delivered to consumers, how those messages will be constructed, and when they will be delivered.

> **roles**
The patterns of behavior expected of group members.

> **formal role**
A role assigned to a person by group members or an organization, usually to establish order.

> **informal roles**
Roles usually not explicitly recognized by a group that describe functions of group members, rather than their positions. These are sometimes called "functional roles."

> **task roles**
Roles group members take on in order to help solve a problem.

> **social roles**
Emotional roles concerned with maintaining smooth personal relationships among group members. Also termed *"maintenance functions."*

When might a social role become a dysfunctional one?

Seek the Optimal Ratio of Task and Social Roles

For the most part, the ideal ratio between task and social functions is 2:1.[16] This ratio allows the group to get its work done and take care of the personal needs and concerns of the members.

Look for Unfilled Roles

Review the roles in Figure 11-2 and consider which of them your team members play. For instance, there may be no information giver to provide vital knowledge or no harmonizer to smooth things over when members disagree. After you have identified unfilled task and social roles, you may be able to help the group by filling them yourself. If key facts are missing, take the role of information seeker and try to dig them out. Even if you are not suited by skill or temperament to a job, you can often encourage others to fill it.

Avoid Duplicating Roles

In some situations, too many people try to fill the same roles. It's probably helpful to have one critic and direction-giver, but too many members playing roles like these can be problematic. One remedy is to point out

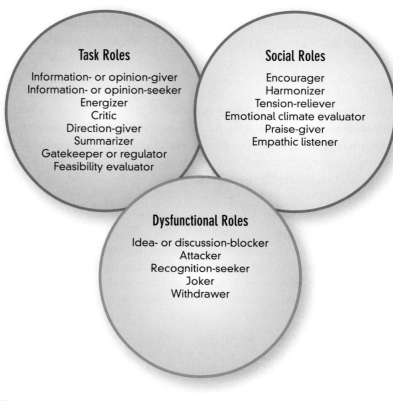

Task Roles

Information- or opinion-giver
Information- or opinion-seeker
Energizer
Critic
Direction-giver
Summarizer
Gatekeeper or regulator
Feasibility evaluator

Social Roles

Encourager
Harmonizer
Tension-reliever
Emotional climate evaluator
Praise-giver
Empathic listener

Dysfunctional Roles

Idea- or discussion-blocker
Attacker
Recognition-seeker
Joker
Withdrawer

Figure 11-2 Roles That Team Members Play

other ways those members can contribute: "Now that we've looked at the potential problems, where can we get the information to overcome them?"

Avoid Role Fixation

Don't fall into familiar roles if they aren't needed. You may be a world-class coordinator or critic, but these talents will only annoy others if you use them when they aren't needed.

Avoid Dysfunctional Roles

It may be gratifying to clown around or intimidate people, especially when you are frustrated with a group, but playing these roles typically does nothing to help the group succeed, and it can damage your reputation as a team player.

Determine the ideal conditions for group problem solving, and outline the stages of problem solving most groups encounter.

PROBLEM SOLVING IN GROUPS

Perhaps because most people aren't aware of the problem-solving techniques available to them, groups sometimes get a bad name. *Solving problems*, as we define it here, doesn't refer only to situations in which something is wrong. Several friends planning a surprise party or a family deciding where to go for its vacation might better be considered *challenges*, but the same principles of problem solving can be applied.

In *American Horror Story: Coven*, modern-day witches come together at a school in New Orleans to protect themselves from the persecution of the outside world. Each member has special skills, and they must work together to succeed.

Q *What factors can help you decide when a problem needs to be solved by a group rather than alone?*

Advantages of Group Problem Solving

Years of research show that, in most cases, groups can produce more solutions to a problem than individuals working alone, and the solutions will be of higher quality. There are several reasons why groups are effective.[17]

Resources

For many tasks, groups have access to a greater collection of resources than individuals do. For example, three or four people can put up a tent or dig a ditch better than a lone person. And think about times when you have studied with other students for a test and learned material you might have overlooked if not for the group.

Accuracy

Another benefit of group work is the increased likelihood of catching errors. At one time or another, we all make stupid mistakes, like the man who built a boat in his basement and then wasn't able to get it out the door. Working in a group increases the chance that foolish errors like this won't slip by.

Commitment

Besides coming up with superior solutions, groups also generate a higher commitment to carrying them out. Members are most likely to accept solutions they have helped create, and they will work harder to carry out those solutions.

Diversity

Although we tend to think in terms of "lone geniuses" who make discoveries and solve the world's problems, most breakthroughs are actually the result of collective creativity—people working together to create options no one would have thought of alone.[18] Although diversity is a benefit of teamwork, it requires special effort, especially when members come from different cultural backgrounds.

When to Use Groups for Problem Solving

Despite their advantages, groups aren't always the best way to solve a problem. Answering the following questions will help you decide when to solve a problem using a group and when to tackle it alone:[19]

> **Is the job beyond the capacity of one person?** Some jobs call for more time or information than a single person possesses.
>
> **Are individuals' tasks interdependent?** Remember that a group is more than a collection of individuals working side-by-side. The best tasks for groups are ones in which the individuals can help one another in some way.
>
> **Is there more than one decision or solution?** Groups are best suited to tackling problems that have no single, cut-and-dried answer.

Gaining the perspectives of every member boosts the odds of finding high-quality solutions, and so a problem with only one solution won't take full advantage of a group's talents.

Is there potential for disagreement? Tackling a problem as a group is essential if you need the support of everyone involved and the issue is likely to be contentious.

Developmental Stages in Group Problem Solving

Successful groups often follow a four-stage process when arriving at a decision: orientation, conflict, emergence, and reinforcement.[20] Knowing these phases can help curb your impatience and help you feel less threatened when the inevitable and necessary conflicts take place. Don't be

> What sort of accomplishments can be achieved by individuals acting alone, and what sort of accomplishments call for teamwork?

How effective is your team?

Think of a team you belong to (or were part of in the past) with the goal of solving a problem or making the most of an opportunity. Select the number on each row that best describes your response.

	Disagree				Agree
1. Team members know and like one another.	1	2	3	4	5
2. We tend to shy away from issues about which we don't agree.	1	2	3	4	5
3. We enjoy tackling challenging situations together.	1	2	3	4	5
4. We enjoy one another's company so much that we often lose focus on what we are trying to achieve.	1	2	3	4	5
5. We trust one another to be responsible and respectful.	1	2	3	4	5
6. Members spend more energy competing with one another than cooperating with one another.	1	2	3	4	5
7. We encourage everyone on the team to have input.	1	2	3	4	5
8. We tend to spend more time complaining about issues than solving them.	1	2	3	4	5
9. We approach challenges in a systematic and creative manner.	1	2	3	4	5
10. Members aren't highly committed to the group or its purpose.	1	2	3	4	5

ANALYZING YOUR RESULTS Add up the scores you indicated on the odd-numbered questions. Then reverse the scores on the even-numbered questions (5 = 1, 4 = 2, 3 = 3, 2 = 4, 1 = 5). Add both totals together and see how you did on pg. 286. ●

surprised if your team moves through this four-stage process with each new issue, such that their interaction takes on a cyclic pattern. Groups may also skip steps, such as leapfrogging over the preliminary phases to focus on the solution.

Orientation Stage

In the **orientation stage**, members approach the problem and one another tentatively. Rather than state their own positions clearly and unambiguously, they test out possible ideas cautiously and rather politely. This cautiousness doesn't mean that members agree with one another. Rather, they are sizing up the situation before asserting themselves. There is little outward disagreement at this stage.

Conflict Stage

After members understand the problem and become acquainted, a successful group enters the **conflict stage**. Members take strong positions and defend them against those who oppose their viewpoints. Coalitions are likely to form, and the discussion may become polarized. The conflict needn't be personal, however, and it should preserve the members' respect for one another. Even when the climate does grow contentious, conflict seems to be a necessary stage in group development. The give and take of discussion tests the quality of ideas, and weaker ones may be justly eliminated.[21]

Emergence Stage

After a period of conflict, effective groups move to an **emergence stage**. One idea might emerge as the best one, or the group might combine the best parts of several plans into a new solution. As they approach consensus, members back off from their dogmatic positions. Statements become more tentative again: "That seems like a pretty good idea," "I can see why you think that way."

Reinforcement Stage

Finally, an effective group reaches the **reinforcement stage**. At this point not only do members accept the group's decision, they also endorse it. Even if members disagree with the outcome, they do not voice their concerns at this stage.

> orientation stage

A stage in problem-solving groups when members become familiar with one another's position and tentatively volunteer their own.

> conflict stage

A stage in problem-solving groups when members openly defend their positions and question those of others.

> emergence stage

A stage in problem-solving groups when members back off from their dogmatic positions.

> reinforcement stage

A stage in problem-solving groups when members endorse the decision they have made.

Describe the optimal problem-solving formats and decision-making methods for arriving at effective solutions.

OBJECTIVE 11.4

GROUP PROBLEM-SOLVING STRATEGIES AND FORMATS

There are several formats and approaches to group problem-solving. The summary we provide here is not meant to be exhaustive, but it should give you a sense of how a group's structure can shape its ability to come up with high-quality solutions.

Problem-Solving Formats

There are many options for structuring idea sessions. Some of the most popular are breakout groups, problem-census groups, focus groups, panel discussions, symposia, forums, and dialogues.

Competing chefs on *Hell's Kitchen* are presented with challenges such as ingredient preparation, meal preparation, and taste tests. Although each task is defined for them, the solution relies on their creativity and skill, and often on how well they work with their teammates.

Q *When you are faced with a daunting challenge, how do you get started? What process do you follow?*

> breakout groups

A strategy used when the number of members is too large for effective discussion. Subgroups simultaneously address an issue and then report back to the group at large.

> problem census

A technique used to equalize participation in groups when the goal is to identify important issues or problems. Members first put ideas on cards, which are then compiled by a leader to generate a comprehensive statement of the issue or problem.

> focus group

A procedure used in market research by sponsoring organizations to survey potential users or the public at large regarding a new product or idea.

> panel discussion

A discussion format in which participants consider a topic more or less conversationally, without formal procedural rules. Panel discussions may be facilitated by a moderator.

> symposium

A discussion format in which participants divide the topic in a manner that allows each member to deliver in-depth information without interruption.

> forum

A discussion format in which audience members are invited to add their comments to those of the official discussants.

Breakout Groups

When the number of members is too large for effective discussion, **breakout groups** can maximize effective participation. In this approach, subgroups (usually consisting of five to seven members) simultaneously address an issue and then report back to the group at large. The best ideas of each breakout group are then assembled to form a high-quality decision.

Problem-Census Groups

Problem census works especially well when some members are more vocal than others, because it equalizes participation. Members use a separate card to list each of their ideas. The leader collects all cards and reads them to the group one-by-one, posting each on a board visible to everyone. Because the name of the person who contributed each item isn't listed, issues are separated from personalities. As similar items are read, the leader posts and arranges them in clusters. After all items are read and posted, the leader and members consolidate similar items into a number of ideas that the group needs to address.

Focus Groups

Focus groups are used as a market research tool to enable sponsoring organizations to learn how potential users or the public at large view a new product or idea. Unlike some of the other groups discussed here, focus groups don't include decision makers or other members who claim any expertise on a subject. Instead, the comments of focus group participants are used by decision makers to figure out how people in the wider world might react to ideas.

Panel Discussions

In a **panel discussion**, participants talk over the topic informally, much as they would in an ordinary conversation. A leader or moderator helps the discussion along by encouraging the comments of some members, cutting off overly talkative ones, and seeking consensus when the time comes to make a decision.

Symposia

In a **symposium**, participants divide the topic in a manner that allows each member to deliver in-depth information without interruption. Although this format lends itself to good explanations of each person's decision, the one-person-at-a-time nature of a symposium won't lead to a group decision. The contributions of the members are followed by the give-and-take of an open discussion.

Forums

A **forum** allows nonmembers to add their opinions to the group's deliberations before the group makes a decision. This approach is commonly used by public agencies to encourage the participation of citizens in the decisions that affect them.

Dialogues

Dialogue is a process in which people let go of the notion that their ideas are superior to those of others and instead try to understand the issue from many perspectives.[22] In a genuine dialogue, members acknowledge that everything they "know" and believe is an assumption based on their own, unavoidably limited experiences. People engage in curious and open-minded discussion about that assumption and guard against either-or thinking. The goal is to understand one another better, not to reach a decision or debate an issue.

Solving Problems in Virtual Groups

The explosion of communication technologies has led to the growth of **virtual groups**—teams that interact with one another through mediated channels, without meeting in person. With the right technology, members of a virtual group can swap ideas as easily as if they were in the same room.[23] And virtual communication has clear advantages. Most obviously, getting together is fast and easy, even if the members are widely separated.

However, where problem solving is concerned, virtual interaction presents some unique challenges. For one, geographically distant members may feel left out and disconnected.[24] For another, if members can't see one another clearly, it may be difficult to convey and to understand one another's emotions and attitudes. Third, it may take virtual teams longer to reach decisions than those who meet face-to-face.[25] Fourth, the string of separate messages that may be generated as part or as a result of the meeting can be hard to track, sort out, and synthesize in a meaningful way. Finally, people may feel less committed to the group and less accountable for their actions if they don't know their teammates well. For example, students who are part of group work in online classes sometimes find that team members are more likely than usual to shirk their responsibilities and avoid communication attempts.[26] Experts offer the following communication tips to make the most of virtual interactions:[27]

> **Encourage socializing and self-disclosure.** Building relationships is especially important when members don't have the chance to socialize in person. Make time for members to get acquainted and enjoy one another's company.
> **Strive for face time.** If possible, create opportunities for members to meet in one place, especially when the group is first formed.
> **Allow and encourage side channels.** As in face-to-face groups, members need a chance to work one-to-one. Phone calls, emails, and messaging can be an efficient way to speed up the group's work.
> **Show enthusiasm.** Don't assume that your interest in the group's mission and tasks is obvious. Express your enthusiasm.
> **Demonstrate attentiveness.** Pay particular attention to your nonverbal communication while you are on camera. Although it is tempting

> **dialogue**
> A process in which people let go of the notion that their ideas are more correct or superior to those of others and instead seek to understand an issue from many different perspectives.

> **virtual groups**
> People who interact with one another via mediated channels, without meeting face-to-face.

What sorts of problems or challenges might be best resolved by virtual groups?

to leaf through papers on your desk, it may send the signal that you are disinterested.

Make expectations clear. Are deadlines firm or negotiable? How much detail should a job contain? What does excellent work look like? Setting clear expectations will help members know what is acceptable and what isn't.

Provide training as necessary. Not everybody joins a group with the same level of technological savvy. Make it easy for members to master the communication tools they need to make the team function effectively.

A Structured Problem-Solving Approach

As early as 1910, John Dewey introduced his famous "reflective thinking" method as a systematic approach to solving problems.[28] Since then, other experts have suggested modifications of Dewey's approach. Although no single approach is best for all situations, a structured procedure produces better results than "no pattern" discussions.[29]

The problem-solving model included in this section contains the elements common to most structured approaches developed in the last century: identify the problem, analyze the problem, develop creative solutions, evaluate the solutions, implement the plan, and follow up on the plan. Although these steps provide a useful outline for solving problems, they are most valuable as a general set of guidelines and not as a precise formula that every group should follow. Certain parts of the model may need emphasis depending on the nature of the specific problem (see Figure 11-3), but the general approach will give virtually any group a useful way to consider and solve a problem.

Identify the problem

Sometimes a group's problem is easy to identify. There are many times, however, when the problems facing a group aren't so clear. In a work group with a low-performing member, it may be helpful to ask why that person is underperforming. It may be because he or she has personal problems, feels unappreciated by members, or hasn't been challenged. The best way to understand a group's problem is to look below the surface and identify the concerns of each member.

Analyze the problem

After you have identified the general nature of the problem, you are ready to look at the problem in more detail.

Word the problem as a broad, open question. If you find that an underperforming group member feels excluded and unappreciated, it's probably better to ask, "What can we do as group members to make sure everyone feels included?" than to pose a yes-or-no question, such as "Would you like us to cc you on emails?" Open-ended questions encourage members to contribute input and work cooperatively.

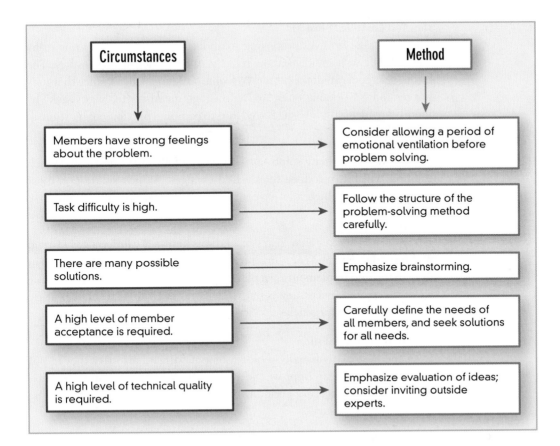

Circumstances	Method
Members have strong feelings about the problem.	Consider allowing a period of emotional ventilation before problem solving.
Task difficulty is high.	Follow the structure of the problem-solving method carefully.
There are many possible solutions.	Emphasize brainstorming.
A high level of member acceptance is required.	Carefully define the needs of all members, and seek solutions for all needs.
A high level of technical quality is required.	Emphasize evaluation of ideas; consider inviting outside experts.

Figure 11-3 **Adopting Problem-Solving Methods.**

Identify criteria for success. Knowing what members want puts a group on the road to achieving its goal. If some group members feel excluded because they are new to the team, you might make relationship-building a priority.

Gather relevant information. It's foolish to choose a solution before you know all the options and factors at play. For example, don't assume that underperforming team members are simply lazy. They may lack the resources or authority to do a good job, even though they are highly motivated.

Identify supporting and restraining forces. After members understand their goals, one useful tool for identifying forces that stand in the way is the **force field analysis:** a list of the forces that help and hinder the group.[30] Perhaps it's easy for some group members to interact because they work near each other, while distance excludes others from everyday conversations. You might decide to schedule daily web chats with all members.

> force field analysis
A method of problem analysis that identifies the forces contributing to resolution of the problem and the forces that inhibit its resolution.

Develop Creative Solutions

The next stage involves proposing solutions through brainstorming or by contributing written ideas anonymously. Avoid criticism at this stage. The more ideas generated, the better. Welcome outlandish ideas, since they may trigger more workable ones, and encourage members to "piggyback" by modifying ideas already suggested and to combine previous suggestions.

Evaluate the Solutions

A good way to evaluate solutions is to ask the following questions: Which solution will best produce the desired changes? Which solution is most achievable? and Which solution contains the fewest serious disadvantages?

Implement the Plan

Everyone who makes New Year's resolutions knows the difference between making a decision and carrying it out. There are several important steps in developing and implementing a plan of action. You should identify specific tasks, determine necessary resources, define individual responsibilities, and provide for emergencies.

Follow Up on the Solution

Even the best plans usually require some modifications after they're put into practice. You can improve the group's effectiveness and minimize disappointment by meeting periodically to evaluate progress and revise the approach as necessary.

Decision-Making Methods

There are several approaches a group can use to make decisions: consensus, majority control, expert opinion, minority control, and authority rule. We'll look at each of them now, examining their advantages and disadvantages.

Consensus

Consensus occurs when all members of a group support a decision. Full participation can increase the quality of the decision as well as the commitment of the members to support it. However, consensus can take a great deal of time, which makes it unsuitable for emergencies, and it is often frustrating. Emotions and impatience can run high on important matters. Because of these factors, consensus calls for more communication skill than do other decision-making approaches. As with many things in life, consensus has high rewards, which come at a proportionately high cost.

Majority Control

Many people naively believe that the democratic method of majority rule is always superior. It has advantages when the support of all members isn't necessary, but in more important matters it is risky. Even if a 51 percent majority of the members favors a plan, 49 percent might still oppose it—hardly

The approach judges take for advancing or eliminating contestants differs on *American Idol* (majority control) and *The Voice* (expert opinion).

Q *Do you think one approach is more effective than the other? Why?*

sweeping support for any decision that needs the support of all members in order to work. Besides producing unhappy members, decisions made under majority rule are often inferior to decisions hashed out by a group until the members reach consensus.[31]

Expert Opinion

Sometimes one group member will be defined as an expert and, as such, will be given the power to make decisions. This method can work well when that person's judgment is truly superior. However, a member may think he or she is the best qualified to make a decision even when that is not the case.

Minority Control

Sometimes a few members of a group decide matters. This approach works well with noncritical questions that would waste the whole group's time. But when an issue is so important that it needs more support, it's best at least to have a group report its findings for the approval of all members.

Authority Rule

Though it sounds dictatorial, there are times when this approach has advantages. There are cases when there simply isn't time for a group to decide what to do. The approach is also acceptable with routine matters that don't require discussion in order to gain approval. When overused, however, this approach causes problems. Much of the time, group decisions are of higher quality and gain more support from members than those made by an individual. Thus, failure to consult with members can lead to a decrease of effectiveness, even when the leader's decision is a reasonable one.

MAKING THE MOST OF GROUP DISCUSSION

Even groups with the best of intentions often find themselves unable to reach satisfying decisions. At other times, they make decisions that later prove to be wrong. Though there's no foolproof method of guaranteeing high-quality group work, several changes can be avoided by utilizing the following approaches.

Build Cohesiveness

> cohesiveness
The totality of forces that causes members to feel themselves part of a group and makes them want to remain in that group.

Cohesiveness is the degree to which members feel connected with and committed to their group. In highly cohesive groups, members spend more time interacting and express more positive feelings for one another than in groups that lack cohesion. They also report more satisfaction and loyalty. However, beyond a certain point, the mutual attraction members feel for one another can interfere with the group's efficient functioning. To achieve a good balance:

Focus on shared and compatible goals. People draw closer when they share a similar aim or when their goals can be mutually satisfied.

Celebrate progress toward goals. While a group is making progress, members feel highly cohesive; when progress stops, cohesiveness decreases. Observe accomplishments along the way to reaching your final goal.

Establish shared expectations. Although successful groups tolerate and even thrive on some differences in members' attitudes and behavior, wide variation will reduce cohesiveness. Work together to establish what is desirable and acceptable in terms of humor, finance, degree of candor, and proportion of time allotted to work and play.

Minimize competition between members. Sometimes competition arises within groups, and as a result members feel threatened. Sometimes there is a struggle over who will be the leader or decision maker. Whether the threat is real or imagined, the group must neutralize it or face the consequences of reduced cohesiveness.

Establish interdependence. Groups become cohesive when their needs can be satisfied only with the help of other members.

Recognize threats from outside the group. When members perceive a threat to the group's existence or image, they grow closer together. It is unproductive to fixate too much on a "common enemy," but recognizing external threats can enhance internal cohesiveness.

Build relationships. Groups often become close because the members like one another. Devote time and energy to building camaraderie and friendship within the group.

Share group experiences. When members have been through some unusual or trying experience, they draw together. Use shared experiences as a way of creating a common identity and group closeness.

Encourage Equal Participation

The key to effective participation is balance. Domination by a few vocal or high-status members can reduce a group's ability to solve a problem effectively. You can encourage the useful contributions of quiet members in a variety of ways:

Keep the group small. In groups with three or four members, participation is roughly equal, but after the size increases to between five and eight, there is a dramatic gap between the contributions of members.[32]

Solicit and recognize the opinions of quiet members. It isn't necessary to go overboard by gushing about a quiet person's brilliant remark, but a word of thanks and an acknowledgment of the value of an idea increase the odds that the contributor will speak up again in the future.

Assign specific tasks to normally quiet members. The need to report on these tasks guarantees that they will speak up.

Ask to hear from other members. Particularly if one member is talking too much, politely express a desire to hear from others.

Question the relevance of remarks that are off topic. If nothing else works, you might say something such as, "I'm confused about what last Saturday's party has to do with the job we have to do today. Am I missing something?"

Avoid Information Underload and Overload

Make sure team members know the information and nuances that bear on a problem. At the same time, recognize that too much information makes it hard to sort out what is essential from what isn't. In such cases, experts suggest parceling out areas of responsibility instead of expecting each member to explore every angle of the topic, taking a quick look at each piece of information to see whether it has real value for your task, and limiting your search.[33]

Avoid Pressure to Conform

There's a strong tendency for group members to go along with the crowd, which often results in bad decisions. The term **groupthink** describes the tendency of some groups to support ideas without challenging them or providing alternatives.[34] The motivation might be to avoid a conflict or to seem like supportive "team players." Or, group members may engage in groupthink because they overestimate the group's good judgment or its privileged status, because they fear retribution if they speak up, or because people just want to get the discussion over with.[35]

> groupthink
A group's collective striving for unanimity that discourages realistic appraisals of alternatives to its chosen decision.

What makes groupthink so appealing to even smart, capable people?

One prominent example of groupthink was the Pennsylvania State University sex abuse scandal. It came to light in 2011 that for over 14 years, numerous individuals had known that a former assistant football coach, Jerry Sandusky, had been sexually abusing underage boys. They had not reported the abuse, however, because they feared they would lose their jobs or damage the institution's reputation if they went public with the information.[36] Groups can avoid the harmful and sometimes tragic effects of groupthink by adopting the following practices:[37]

Recognize the signs of groupthink as they begin to manifest. If agreement comes quickly and easily, the group may be avoiding the tough but necessary search for alternatives.

Groupthink contributed to the 1986 explosion of the space shuttle *Challenger*, which killed seven U.S. astronauts. In an effort to meet deadlines, administrators ignored engineers who warned that the spacecraft was not designed to be launched in cold weather.

Q *Have you ever gone along with a group decision despite having misgivings about it?*

Minimize status differences. If the group has a leader, he or she must be careful not to use the various types of power that come with the position to intimidate members.

Develop a group norm that legitimizes disagreement. After members recognize that questioning one another's positions doesn't signal personal animosity or disloyalty, a constructive exchange of ideas can lead to top-quality solutions. If people at Penn State had felt safe blowing the whistle when they became aware that Sandusky was abusing children, they might have prevented a great deal of harm and preserved the university's reputation.

Designate a person or subgroup as a "devil's advocate." It's this person's job to remind the others about the dangers of groupthink and challenge the trend toward consensus.

Make the Most of Diversity

Working in diverse groups adds an additional layer of complexity. Here are experts' tips for maximizing the benefits and minimizing the pitfalls of multicultural teams:

Allow more time than usual for group development and discussions. When members have different backgrounds and perspectives, it can take extra time and effort to understand and appreciate where each person is coming from.

Agree on clear guidelines for discussions, participation, and decision making. If members come to the group with different expectations, it may be necessary to negotiate mutually acceptable ground rules.

Use a variety of communication formats. Based on cultural preferences, people may be more or less comfortable speaking to the entire group, putting their thoughts in writing, speaking one on one, and so on.

If possible, achieve an even distribution of people from various cultures. Research shows that being a "minority member" is especially challenging and not conducive to open communication.[38]

Educate team members about the cultures represented. We are less likely to make unwarranted assumptions (that a person is lazy, disinterested, overbearing, or so on) if we understand the cultural patterns at play.

Open your mind to new possibilities. Assumptions and too-quick solutions short-circuit the advantage of diverse perspectives.

CHECK YOUR UNDERSTANDING

OBJECTIVE 11.1 Identify the characteristics that distinguish groups and teams from other collections of people.

THE NATURE OF GROUPS AND TEAMS

Groups are distinguishable from other communication contexts in that they involve interaction and interdependence over time among a small number of participants with the purpose of achieving one or more goals. Some groups achieve the status of teams. That is, they embody a high level of shared goals and identity, commitment to a common cause, and high ideals. Groups have their own goals, as do individual members. Sometimes individual and group goals are compatible, and sometimes they conflict.

Think of the most effective and least effective groups to which you have belonged. Which of the factors described in this chapter distinguish one group from the other?

OBJECTIVE 11.2 Understand how groups are affected by rules, norms, patterns of interaction, and roles.

CHARACTERISTICS OF GROUPS

Groups of all types share certain characteristics, including the existence of official rules, group norms (the unofficial guidelines), patterns of interaction that are shaped by the group's structure, and individual roles for members, including formal and informal ones.

Think of some groups to which you belong. What official rules and norms govern your interactions in those groups? Are group norms more influential than official rules in any instances? If so, why do you think that is? If not, why not?

OBJECTIVE 11.3 Determine the ideal conditions for group problem solving, and outline the stages of problem solving most groups encounter.

PROBLEM SOLVING IN GROUPS

Groups have their shortcomings, but they are an effective way to handle many tasks. They command greater resources than do individuals or collections of people working in isolation, their work can result in more effective solutions, and participation typically leads to greater commitment from members. However, groups aren't always the best forum for solving

Identify one problem you have experienced that was handled by a group. How well did that problem fit the criteria covered in this section? How might cohesiveness have been further enhanced?

problems. They should be used when the problem is beyond the capacity of one person to solve, when tasks are interdependent, when there is more than one desired solution or decision, and when the agreement of all members is essential. Groups are most effective when members recognize that it is normal to move through several stages as they solve a problem: orientation, conflict, emergence, and reinforcement.

OBJECTIVE 11.4 Describe the optimal problem-solving formats and decision-making methods for arriving at effective solutions.

GROUP PROBLEM-SOLVING STRATEGIES AND FORMATS

Groups use a wide variety of discussion formats when solving problems. The best format depends on the nature of the problem and the characteristics of the group. Because face-to-face meetings can be time-consuming and difficult to arrange, virtual groups can be a good alternative for some group tasks. No matter what the format, groups stand the best chance of developing effective solutions to problems if they begin their work by identifying the problem and recognizing the hidden needs of individual members, then analyzing the problem, developing possible solutions, identifying the best one, implementing it, and monitoring the situation carefully and making any necessary changes.

Imagine that you're part of a group of students tasked with identifying ways to reduce the college dropout rate at your institution. What decision-making format would be optimal for this group and task? How can you apply the systematic problem-solving steps discussed in this section to your task?

OBJECTIVE 11.5 Summarize strategies for communicating effectively during group discussions.

MAKING THE MOST OF GROUP DISCUSSION

Smart group members avoid common dangers that threaten a group's effectiveness. They build cohesiveness by focusing on shared goals and productive relationships. They make sure that participation is equal by encouraging the contributions of quiet members and by keeping more talkative people on track. They make sure to get the information they need, without succumbing to overload. They guard against groupthink by minimizing pressure on members to conform for the sake of harmony or approval, and they learn about and respect diversity.

Recall a group you've encountered with an underperforming member. (That member may have been you.) What strategies discussed in this section could have enhanced that member's contributions?

all-channel network p. 266
breakout groups p. 274
chain network p. 266
cohesiveness p. 280
conflict stage p. 272
dialogue p. 275
emergence stage p. 272
focus group p. 274
force field analysis p. 277
formal role p. 267
forum p. 274
gatekeepers p. 267

group p. 262
groupthink p. 281
group goals p. 263
individual goals p. 263
informal roles p. 267
norms p. 265
orientation stage p. 272
panel discussion p. 274
problem census p. 274
procedural norms p. 265
reinforcement stage p. 272
roles p. 267

rule p. 265
social loafing p. 263
social norms p. 265
social roles p. 267
symposium p. 274
task norms p. 265
task roles p. 267
team p. 263
virtual groups p. 275
wheel network p. 266

HOW EFFECTIVE IS YOUR TEAM?

40–50 points

Congratulations! You have created a team that is cohesive and goal oriented. Although there are likely to be ups and downs, if you maintain your focus on great results and effective teamwork, you are likely to be highly successful together.

30–39 points

You have potential, but this team isn't ready for the big leagues yet. The problem may be that you haven't taken the time to build strong relationships or that not everyone is inspired by the challenge before you. Teams who have high trust and high motivation are typically eager to focus on the issue, and they welcome diverse ideas.

Less than 30 points

Either your team is very new or you are stuck in an unproductive groove. Over time, the less you accomplish, the less excited and confident members become, which means that commitment and cohesion suffer. Consider how you might turn things around. Perhaps you can host a dialogue session about the group process itself. When you better understand what is holding members back, you may be able to take positive steps to build a more cohesive and productive team.

For more communication resources, see the *Essential Communication* website at www.oup.com/us/ec. There you will find a variety of resources: "Media Room" examples from popular films and television shows to further illustrate important concepts, a list of relevant books and articles, links to descriptions of feature films and television shows at the *Now Playing* website, study aids, and a self-test to check your understanding of the material in this chapter.

Preparing Speeches

12.1 Analyze both the audience and the occasion in any speaking situation.

12.2 Understand the steps involved with planning a successful speech.

12.3 Create an effective and well-organized speech structure and outline.

12.4 Develop an effective introduction and conclusion, and integrate smooth transitions.

12.5 Choose supporting material that makes your ideas clear, memorable, and convincing.

Analyze both the audience and the occasion in any speaking situation.

ANALYZING YOUR SPEAKING SITUATION

E ven if you never took a course in which you had to give a speech, you will almost certainly face the challenge of giving a speech at some point. It might be a job-related presentation or something more personal, such as a wedding toast or a eulogy for a lost friend. For many people, the thought of giving a speech creates anxiety. In fact, when people are asked to list their common fears, public speaking comes up more often than do insects, heights, accidents, and even death.[1]

While there's no guarantee that we can make you learn to love giving speeches, we do promise to give you the tools you need to design and deliver remarks that are clear, interesting, and effective. One of the first steps in the process is to analyze the speaking situation: the audience and the occasion. Every choice you make—such as your purpose, topic, and materials— must be appropriate to both of these components.

The Audience

The purpose of **audience analysis** is to develop remarks that are appropriate to the characteristics and goals of your listeners. Just as you have a purpose for speaking, audience members have a reason for gathering. While it may sometimes be difficult to discern an audience's motives, observing audience demographics may help.

Demographics are characteristics of your audience that can be categorized, such as age, gender, cultural background, educational level, and economic status. In a college class, demographics such as hometown, year in school, and major subject might also be important. Analyzing the demographics of audience members will help you make an educated guess about their attitudes, beliefs, and values—in essence, what they think.[2] In turn, this will help you develop a speech that speaks *to* and not *at* them.

Attitudes, beliefs, and values reside in human consciousness, like the layers of an onion (see Figure 12-1). **Attitudes** lie closest to the surface and reflect a predisposition to view you or your topic in a favorable or unfavorable way. **Beliefs** lie a little deeper and deal with a person's underlying conviction about the truth of an idea. **Values** are deeply rooted feelings about a concept's inherent worth or worthiness.

While attitudes, beliefs, and values are all important, experts in audience analysis, such as professional speechwriters, often try to concentrate on values. As one team of researchers pointed out, "Values have the advantage of being comparatively small in number, and owing to their abstract

> **audience analysis**
> A consideration of characteristics including the type, goals, demographics, beliefs, attitudes, and values of listeners.

> **demographics**
> Audience characteristics that can be analyzed statistically, such as age, gender, education, and group membership.

> **attitude**
> Predisposition to respond to an idea, person, or thing favorably or unfavorably.

> **belief**
> An underlying conviction about the truth of an idea, often based on cultural training.

> **value**
> A deeply rooted belief about a concept's inherent worth.

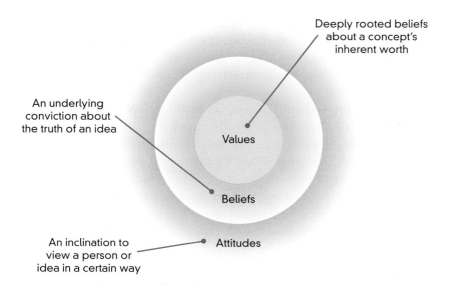

Deeply rooted beliefs about a concept's inherent worth

An underlying conviction about the truth of an idea

Values

Beliefs

An inclination to view a person or idea in a certain way

Attitudes

Figure 12-1 Structure of Attitudes, Beliefs, and Values

nature, are more likely to be shared by large numbers of people."[3] Stable American values include the ideas of good citizenship, work ethic, tolerance of political views, individualism, and justice for all.

Michael Kelley, a student at Kansas State University, appealed to the values of his audience of college students and professors when he wanted to make the point that unemployment discrimination was unfair:

> Jobless discrimination occurs when a company or business refuses to employ an individual unless they are already employed elsewhere. This should alarm us for several reasons. The Bureau of Labor Statistics, as of April 6, 2012, points out that there are 5.3 million Americans who have been unemployed for seven months or more because of the recession. It's not fair to discriminate against them. . . . We need to make jobless discrimination just as illegal as refusing to hire someone because of their sex, race or religion.[4]

Kelly's analysis had suggested that the value of fairness would be important to his audience, and so he pointed out that discriminating against unemployed people was basically unfair. You can often make an inference about audience members' attitudes by recognizing the beliefs and values they are likely to hold.

The Occasion

The second phase in analyzing a speaking situation should focus on the occasion. The occasion of a speech is determined by the circumstances surrounding it, such as time, place, and audience expectations. Keep in mind that every occasion is unique.

In which speaking instances might using humor be appropriate? In which might it be inappropriate?

The length of time for your speech, as well as the time of day that you are speaking, will affect your audience's energy and hunger levels. Your physical surroundings, such as the size of the room, temperature, and noise level, might also be significant to your speech topic or affect your audience's comfort level.

Of equal importance, however, are audience expectations. A speech presented in a college class is usually expected to reflect a higher level of thought and intelligence than if you were discussing the same subject with a group of friends over coffee. But this doesn't mean that your speech should be boring or humorless. In fact, wit and humor are indicative of intelligence and may also help you develop a connection with your audience. One way to fulfill expectations in a college class is to gather interesting and effective information that will help you build a successful speech.

On HBO's comedy *Veep*, Julia Louis-Dreyfus plays Vice President Selina Meyer. She often fails miserably at her attempts to adapt her messages for different audiences, or completely loses interest in what others have to say.

Q *Have you ever listened to a speech you considered off-base or irrelevant to your interests as an audience member?*

PLANNING YOUR SPEECH

Having analyzed your audience and occasion, it's now time to plan your speech. You must choose a topic, define your purpose, write a purpose statement, state your thesis, and gather information to support your purpose and thesis.

Choose Your Topic

The first question many student speakers face is "What should I talk about?" Try to pick a topic that interests you, one that your audience will care about, and one that is right for the situation.

Define Your Purpose

No one gives a speech or expresses *any* kind of message without having a reason to do so. Formulate a clear and precise statement of that reason.

Write a Purpose Statement

Your **purpose statement** should be expressed in the form of a complete sentence that describes your **specific purpose**—exactly what you want your speech to accomplish. It should stem from your **general purpose**, which might be to inform, persuade, or entertain. Beyond that, though, there are three criteria for an effective purpose statement:

> **A purpose statement should be result-oriented.** Having a result orientation means that your purpose is focused on the outcome you want to accomplish with your audience members.
> **A purpose statement should be specific.** To be effective, a purpose statement should have enough details so that you will be able to measure or test your audience, after your speech, to see if you have achieved your purpose.
> **A purpose statement should be realistic.** It's fine to be ambitious, but you should design a purpose that has a reasonable chance of success. If your purpose is to "convince your audience to make federal budget deficits illegal," unless audience members happen to be a joint session of Congress, they won't have the power to do this. A better purpose statement might be something like this: *After listening to my speech, my audience members will be able to list four simple steps to lower their college expenses.*

> **purpose statement**
A complete sentence that describes precisely what a speaker wants to accomplish.

> **specific purpose**
The precise effect that the speaker wants to have on an audience. Expressed in the form of a purpose statement.

> **general purpose**
One of three basic ways a speaker seeks to affect an audience: to entertain, inform, or persuade.

It's not generally necessary to include your purpose statement word for word in your actual speech. Rather, a purpose statement usually is a tool to keep you focused on your goal as you plan your speech.

State Your Thesis

After you have defined the purpose, you are ready to start planning what is arguably the most important sentence in your entire speech. The **thesis statement** tells your listeners the central idea of your speech and is the one idea that you want your audience to remember after it has forgotten everything else you had to say.

> **> thesis statement**
> A complete sentence describing the central idea of a speech.

Unlike your purpose statement, your thesis statement is almost always delivered directly to your audience. The thesis statement for a speech about winning in small claims court might be worded like this: *Arguing a case on your own in small claims court is a simple, five-step process that can give you the same results you would achieve with a lawyer.*

Gather Information

It takes time, interest, and knowledge to develop a topic well. Setting aside a block of time to reflect on your own ideas is essential. However, you will also need to gather information from outside sources.

Your first instinct may be to do an online search, and it is a good place to start. However, you will need to carefully consider the credibility, objectivity, and the currency of the information you find through these searches (see Figure 12-2).

How can you make your thesis statement more memorable for your audience?

---

1. **Credibility: Is the information trustworthy?**
   - ❏ Who created the site? Anonymous sources should not be used.
   - ❏ If the sources *are* listed, are their credentials listed?
   - ❏ What institution sponsors the site? What is their purpose?
   - ❏ Are there obvious proofreading errors/grammatical mistakes?

   Remember that a sleek site design doesn't guarantee high-quality information, but misspellings and grammatical mistakes are good signs of low quality.

2. **Objectivity: Is the information unbiased?**
   - ❏ What is the domain name of the site? The domain names .edu, .gov, and .org, are generally more reliable than .coms
   - ❏ What opinions (if any) are expressed by the author?
   - ❏ If a topic is controversial, are opposing sides equally represented/covered?
   - ❏ Does the site have advertising? If so, how much, and what types?

3. **Currency: Is the information up-to-date?**
   - ❏ When was the site created?
   - ❏ When was the site last updated?
   - ❏ How up-to-date are any links? If any of the links are dead, that is a sign that the information might not be current.

Figure 12-2 Evaluating Credibility, Objectivity, and Currency for Online Research

In the movie *The Great Debaters*, Professor Melvin Tolson (Denzel Washington) inspires students at Wiley College in Texas to form the school's first debate team. Under Tolson's guidance, students learn the importance of extensive preparation.

Q *What steps can you take during the planning stages to ensure the effectiveness of your speech?*

While you might be tempted to go to Wikipedia as a starting point, keep in mind that many professors forbid its use as a primary source because anyone can edit the information.

However you use the Web, remember that it is a good addition to, but *not* a substitute for, library research. Most libraries have catalogs, reference works, periodicals, nonprint materials, and even databases that are not available to outside users without hefty subscription fees. In addition, library experts can help you make sense of and determine the validity of the information you find.

Another method for gathering information is to conduct a survey of your audience members beforehand to determine their attitudes about a topic. Finally, you might want to interview an expert for facts and perspectives to use in your speech.

Create an effective and well-organized speech structure and outline.

OBJECTIVE 12.3

STRUCTURING YOUR SPEECH

Having a clear purpose and thesis as well as interesting and credible information to speak about is important. But if the material is not well organized, your audience will not understand your message. In addition to making your message clear to your audience, structuring a message effectively is essential to helping you refine your ideas and construct more persuasive messages.

> **basic speech structure**
The division of a speech into introduction, body, and conclusion.

> **working outline**
Constantly changing organizational aid used in planning a speech.

> **formal outline**
A consistent format and set of symbols used to identify the structure of ideas.

How can you pick an organizational pattern that best develops your thesis?

> **time pattern**
Organizing plan for a speech based on chronology.

> **space pattern**
Organizing plan for a speech that arranges points according to their physical location.

Every speech outline should follow the **basic speech structure** that includes an introduction, body, and conclusion. This structure demonstrates the old aphorism for speakers: "Tell what you're going to say, say it, and then tell what you said." The finer points of your speech structure will be shown in your outlines.

Outlines

Outlines come in all shapes and sizes. Your **working outline** is for your eyes only, and you'll probably create several drafts of it as you refine your ideas. On the other hand, a **formal outline** uses a consistent format and set of symbols to identify the structure of ideas. Another person should be able to understand the basic ideas included in your speech by reading the formal outline. In fact, that's one test of the effectiveness of your outline. Figure 12-3 provides an annotated outline for a sample speech (included in the appendix), which a student presented at a national college event.

Speaking Notes

Like your working outline, your speaking notes are for your use only, so the format is up to you. Many teachers suggest that speaking notes should be in the form of a brief keyword outline, with just enough information listed to jog your memory but not enough to get lost in.

Many teachers also suggest that you fit your notes on one side of one 3-by-5-inch note card. Others recommend having your introduction and conclusion or longer quotations on note cards. Notes for a speech about the impact of suicide on family members might look like the ones in Figure 12-4.

Organizational Patterns

An outline should reflect a logical order for your points and one that best develops your thesis. You might arrange them from newest to oldest, largest to smallest, best to worst, or in a number of other ways, including by time, space, topic, problem-solution, cause-effect, and Monroe's Motivated Sequence.

Time

Arrangement according to **time patterns**, or chronology, is one of the most common patterns of organization. The period of time could be anything from centuries to seconds. In a speech on airline food, a time pattern might look like this:

   I. Early airline food: a gourmet treat
  II. The middle period: institutional food at thirty thousand feet
III. Today's airline food: the passenger starves

Space

Space patterns are organized according to area. The area could be stated in terms of continents or centimeters or anything in between. If you were

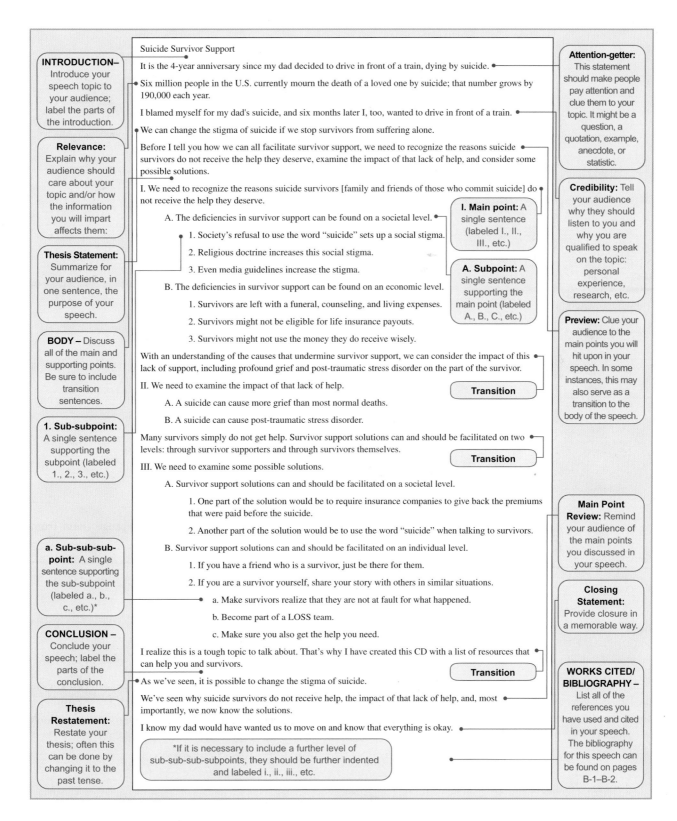

Figure 12-3 **Formal Outline**

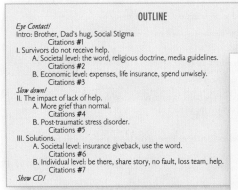

OUTLINE

Eye Contact!
Intro: Brother, Dad's hug, Social Stigma
   Citations #1
I. Survivors do not receive help.
 A. Societal level: the word, religious doctrine, media guidelines.
   Citations #2
 B. Economic level: expenses, life insurance, spend unwisely.
   Citations #3
Slow down!
II. The impact of lack of help.
 A. More grief than normal.
   Citations #4
 B. Post-traumatic stress disorder.
   Citations #5
III. Solutions.
 A. Societal level: insurance giveback, use the word.
   Citations #6
 B. Individual level: be there, share story, no fault, loss team, help.
   Citations #7
Show CD!

CITATIONS #1

A. Jill Pantania of the American Association of Suicidology: "there are 6 million people in the US that currently mourn the death of a loved one by suicide. And that number grows by 190,000 each year."

B. *Harvard Mental Health* newsletter of November 2009 " . . . the death of a loved one because of suicide leads to a higher risk for several types of psychiatric disorders."

C. *Hampton Roads Survivors of Suicide* website: "Survivors are 5 times more likely to commit suicide themselves."

CITATIONS #2

A. The website *Suicide.org* says we make excuses, but we don't use the word "suicide."

B. "Religion and Suicide," *Journal of Religion and Health*, 2009.

C. *American Foundation for Suicide Prevention*: guidelines.

D. KHAS-TV, April 14, 2011, did not cover student's death.

Figure 12-4 Speaking Notes

discussing the Great Lakes, for example, you could arrange them from west to east:

 I. Superior
 II. Michigan
 III. Huron
 IV. Erie
 V. Ontario

Topic

A topical arrangement or **topic pattern** is based on types or categories. These categories could be either well known or original. For example, a division of college students according to well-known categories might look like this:

 I. Freshmen
 II. Sophomores
 III. Juniors
 IV. Seniors

> topic pattern

Organizing plan for a speech that arranges points according to logical types or categories.

How well can you organize ideas?

To get an idea of your ability to organize ideas according to an outline, set the "stopwatch" function on your phone and see how long it takes you to fit the following concepts for a speech titled "The College Application Process" into outline form:

CONCEPTS	RECOMMENDED OUTLINE FORM
Participation in extracurricular activities	I.
Visit and evaluate college websites	A.
Prepare application materials	B.
Career ambitions	II.
Choose desired college	A.
Letters of recommendation	B.
Write personal statement	C.
Visit and evaluate college campuses	III.
Choose interesting topic	A.
Test scores	B.
Include important personal details	1.
Volunteer work	2.
Transcripts	3.

Find our suggested organization for these points on p. 315. ●

Well-known categories are advantageous because audiences quickly understand them. But familiarity also has its disadvantages. One disadvantage is the "Oh, this again" syndrome. If the members of an audience feel they have nothing new to learn, they may not bother listening to you. To avoid this, you could invent original categories like this:

I. Grinds: Students who go to every class and read every assignment before it is due.
II. Renaissance students: Students who find a satisfying balance of scholarly and social pursuits.
III. Burnouts: Students who have a difficult time finding the classroom, let alone doing the work.

Problem-Solution

The **problem-solution pattern** describes what's wrong and proposes a way to make things better. It is usually (but not always) divisible into two distinct parts, as in this example:

I. The Problem: Addiction (which could then be broken down into addiction to cigarettes, alcohol, prescribed drugs, and street drugs)

> **problem-solution pattern**
> Organizing pattern for a speech that describes an unsatisfactory state of affairs and then proposes a plan to remedy the problem.

II. The Solution: A national addiction institute (which would study the root causes of addiction in the same way that the National Cancer Institute studies the root causes of cancer)

Cause-Effect

Cause-effect patterns are similarly two-part patterns: First you discuss something that happened, and then you discuss its effects.

A variation of this pattern reverses the order and presents the effects first and then the causes. Persuasive speeches often have effect-cause or cause-effect as the first two main points. Elizabeth Hallum, a student at Arizona State University, organized the first two points of a speech on "workplace revenge"[5] like this:

I. The effects of the problem
    A. Lost productivity
    B. Costs of sabotage
II. The causes of the problem
    A. Employees feeling alienated
    B. Employers' light treatment of incidents of revenge

The third main point in this type of persuasive speech is often "solutions," and the fourth main point is often "the desired audience behavior." Elizabeth's final points were:

III. Solutions: Support the National Employee Rights Institute
IV. Desired Audience Response: Log on to www.disgruntled.com.

Monroe's Motivated Sequence

The **Motivated Sequence** was proposed by a scholar named Alan Monroe in the 1930s.[6] In this persuasive pattern, the problem is broken down into an attention step and a need step, and the solution is broken down into a satisfaction step, a visualization step, and an action step. In a speech on "Random Acts of Kindness,"[7] the motivated sequence might break down like this:

I. The attention step draws attention to your subject.
    "Just the other day Ron saved George's life with a small, random, unimportant act of kindness."

II. The need step establishes the problem.
    "Millions of Americans suffer from depression, a life-threatening disease."

III. The satisfaction step proposes a solution.
    "One random act of kindness can lift a person from depression."

IV. The visualization step describes the results of the solution.
    "Imagine yourself having that kind of effect on another person."

V. The action step is a direct appeal for the audience to do something.
    "Try a random act of kindness today!"

> cause-effect pattern

Organizing plan for a speech that demonstrates how one or more events result in another event or events.

> motivated sequence

A five-step organizational pattern for persuasive speeches.

In one of the most watched TED talks in history, neuroanatomist Jill Bolte takes a complex and technical topic—the science of the brain—and transforms it into a highly engaging and moving speech.

Q *How might you creatively bring attention to subjects or issues in your speech?*

Develop an effective introduction and conclusion, and integrate smooth transitions.

OBJECTIVE 12.4

USING INTRODUCTIONS, CONCLUSIONS, AND TRANSITIONS

The introduction and conclusion of a speech are vitally important, although they usually will occupy less than 20 percent of your speaking time. Listeners form their impression of a speaker early, and they remember what they hear last. It is, therefore, essential to make those few moments at the beginning and end of your speech work to your advantage.

<blockquote>
> introduction (of a speech)
The first structural unit of a speech, in which the speaker captures the audience's attention and previews the main points to be covered.
</blockquote>

The Introduction

There are five functions of the speech **introduction**. It serves to capture the audience's attention, preview the main points, set the mood and tone of the speech, demonstrate the importance of the topic, and establish credibility.

Capture Attention

There are several ways to capture an audience's attention. The checklist in Figure 12-5 shows how some of these ways might be used in a speech titled "Communication between Plants and Humans."

Preview the Main Points

After you capture the attention of the audience, an effective introduction will almost always state the speaker's thesis and give the listeners an idea of the upcoming main points. Katherine Graham, the former publisher of

Television personality, actor, and comedian Steve Harvey dispenses advice on the *Steve Harvey Radio Show* by gaining audience attention with amusing anecdotes.

Q *How can you capture the attention of your audience in a way that prepares them for the message that follows?*

Figure 12-5 Capturing Audience Attention

the *Washington Post*, addressed a group of businessmen in a male-only club this way:

> I am delighted to be here. It is a privilege to address you. And I am especially glad the rules have been bent for tonight, allowing so many of you to bring along your husbands. I think it's nice for them to get out once in a while and see how the other half lives. Gentlemen, we welcome you.
>
> Actually, I have other reasons for appreciating this chance to talk with you tonight. It gives me an opportunity to address some current questions about the press and its responsibilities, whom we are responsible to, what we are responsible for, and generally how responsible our performance has been.[8]

Thus, Graham previewed her main points:

1. To explain whom the press is responsible to
2. To explain what the press is responsible for
3. To explain how responsible the press has been

Sometimes your preview of main points will be even more straightforward:

"I have three points to discuss: They are _____, _____ , and _____ .

Sometimes you will not want to refer directly to your main points in your introduction. Perhaps you want to create suspense or a humorous effect, or perhaps you are stalling for time to win over a hostile audience. In that case, you might preview only your thesis:

"I am going to say a few words about _____ ."

"Did you ever wonder about _____ ?"

"_____ is one of the most important issues facing us today."

Set the Mood and Tone of Your Speech

Notice, in the previous example, how Katherine Graham began her speech by joking with her audience. She was a powerful woman speaking before an all-male organization; the only women in the audience were the members' wives. That is why Ms. Graham felt it necessary to put her audience members at ease by joking with them about women's traditional role in society. By beginning in this manner, she assured the men that she would not berate them for the sexist bylaws of their organization. She also showed them that she was going to approach her topic with wit and intelligence. Thus, she set the mood and tone for her entire speech. Imagine how different that mood and tone would have been if she had begun this way:

Before I start today, I would just like to say that I would never have accepted your invitation to speak here had I known that your organization does not accept women as members. Just where do you get off, excluding more than half the human race from your little club?

Demonstrate the Importance of Your Topic to Your Audience

Your audience members will listen to you more carefully if your speech relates to them as individuals. Based on your audience analysis, you should state directly *why* your topic is of importance to your audience members. For example, Stephanie Hamilton, a student at North Dakota State University, presented a speech about loopholes in the justice system when crimes of violence occur on cruise ships. After telling the story of a rape aboard ship, she established the importance of her topic this way:

Each year, millions of people take to the seas on cruises. Many of us have taken cruises of our own or plan to take one someday, and practically everyone knows at least someone who has taken a cruise. Even if we will never take a cruise, we are a part of society and a possible target for crime. If someone were found guilty of a crime, would we want them free? That is exactly what is happening without laws of recourse in place for our protection. We don't need to let our family, friends, neighbors or ourselves be taken advantage of and never given justice.[9]

Establish Credibility

One final consideration for your introduction is to establish your credibility to speak on your topic. One way to do this is to be well prepared. Another is to appear confident as soon as you face your audience. A third technique is to tell your audience about your personal experience with the topic, in order to establish why it is important to you.

The Conclusion

The **conclusion**, like the introduction, is an especially important part of your speech. The conclusion has three essential functions: to restate the thesis, to review your main points, and to provide a memorable final remark.

You can review your thesis either by repeating it or by paraphrasing it. Or, you might devise a striking summary statement for your conclusion to help your audience remember your thesis. Grant Anderson, a student at Minnesota State University, gave a speech against the policy of rejecting blood donations from gays and lesbians. He ended his conclusion with this statement: "The gay community still has a whole host of issues to contend with, but together all of us can all take a step forward by recognizing this unjust and discriminatory measure. So stand up and raise whatever arm they poke you in to draw blood and say 'Blood is Blood' no matter who you are."[10] Grant's statement was concise but memorable.

Your main points can also be reviewed artistically. For example, first look back at that example of an introduction by Katherine Graham, then read her conclusion to that speech:

> So instead of seeking flat and absolute answers to the kinds of problems I have discussed tonight, what we should be trying to foster is respect for one another's conception of where duty lies, and understanding of the real worlds in which we try to do our best. And we should be hoping for the energy and sense to keep on arguing and questioning, because there is no better sign that our society is healthy and strong.

Table 12-1 takes a closer look at how and why this conclusion was effective. Ms. Graham posed three questions in her introduction. She dealt with those questions in her speech and reminded her audience, in her conclusion, that she had answered the questions.

> Why is it important to establish speaker credibility early in the speech?

> **conclusion (of a speech)**
The final structural unit of a speech, in which the main points are reviewed and final remarks are made to motivate the audience to act or help listeners remember key ideas.

Table 12-1   An Artistic Review of Main Points in the Conclusion

PREVIEW (FROM SPEECH INTRODUCTION)	REVIEW (FROM CONCLUSION)
1. To whom is the press responsible?	1. To its own conception of where its duty lies
2. What is the press responsible for?	2. For doing its best in the "real world"
3. How responsible has the press been?	3. It has done its best

> transition

Phrase that connects ideas in a speech by showing how one relates to the other.

Transitions

Transitions are phrases that connect ideas in your speech by showing how each idea relates to the other. They keep your message moving forward by referring to previous and upcoming points and showing how they relate to one another and to the thesis. Transitions usually sound something like this:

> "Like [previous point], another important consideration in [topic] is [upcoming point]."

> "But _____ isn't the only thing we have to worry about. _____ is even more potentially dangerous."

> "Yes, the problem is obvious. But what are the solutions? Well, one possible solution is. . . ."

Sometimes a transition includes an internal review (a restatement of preceding points), an internal preview (a look ahead to upcoming points), or both:

> "So far we've discussed _____, _____, and _____. Our next points are _____, _____, and _____.

OBJECTIVE 12.5   Choose supporting material that makes your ideas clear, memorable, and convincing.

USING SUPPORTING MATERIAL

It is important to organize ideas clearly and logically. But clarity and logic by themselves won't guarantee that you'll amuse, enlighten, or persuade others; these results call for the use of supporting materials. The facts and information that back up and prove your ideas and opinions are the flesh that fills out the skeleton of your speech.

Types of Support

Supporting material clarifies your ideas, proves your points, and generally makes your speech more interesting and memorable. Supporting material can take the form of definitions, examples, statistics, analogies/comparison-contrast, anecdotes, and quotations/testimonies.

Definitions

It's a good idea to give your audience members definitions of your key terms, especially if those terms are unfamiliar to them or are being used in an unusual way. A good definition is simple and concise. When Elizabeth Hobbs, a student at Truman State University in Missouri, gave a speech on U.S. torture policy, she needed to define a key term, "extraordinary rendition":

> "Extraordinary rendition" is the phrase used by the CIA to describe the U.S. practice of secretly sending terrorist suspects to countries where torture is routine.[11]

Examples

An **example** is a specific case that is used to demonstrate a general idea. Examples can be either factual or hypothetical, personal or borrowed. In Elizabeth Hobbs's speech on U.S. torture policy, she used the following example:

> He was kidnapped while making a business trip to Macedonia. To be transported to a secret prison in Afghanistan, he was beaten, his underwear was forcibly removed and he was put into a diaper, and chained spread eagle inside the plane. In Afghanistan he was beaten, interrogated and put into solitary confinement. To get out, he started a hunger strike, but after 37 days without food, a feeding tube was forced through his nose and into his stomach. Nearly five months later he was released, with no explanation of his imprisonment.
>
> Does this sound like Chile under the Pinochet regime? Prisoner abuse in Uzbekistan? A Russian gulag? It wasn't. This is a story of a victim of America's War on Terror.[12]

> **example**
> A specific case that is used to demonstrate a general idea.

Hypothetical examples can often be more powerful than factual examples, because hypothetical examples ask audience members to imagine something, thus causing them to become active participants in the thought. Stephanie Wideman of the University of West Florida used a hypothetical example to start off her speech on oil prices:

> The year is 2020. One day you are asked not to come into work, not because of a holiday, but instead because there is not enough energy available to power your office. You see, it is not that the power is out, but that they are out of power.[13]

> **hypothetical example**
> Example that asks an audience to imagine an object or event.

In HBO's *Game of Thrones*, Daenerys Targaryen (Emilia Clarke) raises a loyal army with an inspiring speech to a group of slaves that asks them to imagine a different life for themselves.

Have you ever been moved to take action by a powerful speech that used hypothetical examples?

> statistics

The arrangement or organization of numbers to show how a fact or principle is true for a large percentage of cases.

Statistics

Statistics are numbers that are arranged or organized to show that a fact or principle is true for a large percentage of cases. Statistics are actually collections of examples, which is why they are often more effective as proof than are isolated examples. Here's the way a newspaper columnist used statistics to prove a point about gun violence:

> I had coffee the other day with Marian Wright Edelman, president of the Children's Defense Fund, and she mentioned that since the murders of Robert Kennedy and the Rev. Martin Luther King Jr. in 1968, well over a million Americans have been killed by firearms in the United States. That's more than the combined U.S. combat deaths in all the wars in all of American history. "We're losing eight children and teenagers a day to gun violence," she said. "As far as young people are concerned, we lose the equivalent of the massacre at Virginia Tech about every four days."[14]

Because statistics can be powerful proof, you should make sure that they make sense and that they come from a credible source. You should also cite the source of the statistic when you use it. And to achieve maximum effect, you should reduce the statistic to a concrete image if possible. For example, $1 billion in $100 bills would be about the same height as a sixty-story building. Using concrete images such as this will make your statistics more than "just numbers" when you use them. One observer expressed the idea of Bill Gates's wealth by combining statistics with a memorable analogy:

> Examine Bill Gates' wealth compared to yours: Consider the average American of reasonable but modest wealth. Perhaps he has a net worth of $100,000. Mr. Gates' worth is 400,000 times larger. Which means that if something costs $100,000 to him, to Bill it's as though it costs 25 cents. So for example, you might think a new Lamborghini Diablo would cost $250,000, but in Bill Gates dollars that's 63 cents.[15]

Analogies/Comparison-Contrast

We use **analogies**, or comparisons, all the time, often in the form of figures of speech, such as similes and metaphors. A simile is a direct comparison that usually uses *like* or *as*, whereas a metaphor is an implied comparison that does not use *like* or *as*. So if you said that the rush of refugees from a war-torn country was "like a tidal wave," you would be using a simile. If you used the expression "a tidal wave of refugees," you would be using a metaphor.

Analogies are extended metaphors. They can be used to compare or contrast an unknown concept with a known one. For example, here's how one writer made her point against separate Academy Awards for men and women:

> Many hours into the 82nd Academy Awards ceremony this Sunday, the Oscar for best actor will go to Morgan Freeman, Jeff Bridges, George Clooney, Colin Firth, or Jeremy Renner. Suppose, however, that the Academy of Motion Picture Arts and Sciences presented separate honors for best white actor and best non-white actor, and that Mr. Freeman was prohibited from competing against the likes of Mr. Clooney and Mr. Bridges. Surely, the Academy would be derided as intolerant and out of touch; public outcry would swiftly ensure that Oscar nominations never again fell along racial lines. Why, then, is it considered acceptable to segregate nominations by sex, offering different Oscars for best actor and best actress?[16]

Anecdotes

An **anecdote** is a brief story with a point, often (but not always) based on personal experience. The word *anecdote* comes from the Greek, meaning "unpublished item." Aaron Sorkin, the acclaimed film and television producer, used an anecdote to make an important point in a commencement address at Syracuse University:

> analogy
Extended comparison that can be used as supporting material in a speech.

> anecdote
A brief personal story used to illustrate or support a point in a speech.

I've made some bad decisions. I lost a decade of my life to cocaine addiction. You know how I got addicted to cocaine? I tried it. The problem with drugs is that they work, right up until the moment that they decimate your life. Try cocaine, and you'll become addicted to it. Become addicted to cocaine, and you will either be dead, or you will wish you were dead, but it will only be one or the other.

My big fear was that I wasn't going to be able to write without it. There was no way I was going to be able to write without it. Last year I celebrated my 11-year anniversary of not using coke. (applause) Thank you. In that 11 years, I've written three television series, three movies, a Broadway play, won the Academy Award and taught my daughter all the lyrics to "Pirates of Penzance." I have good friends.[17]

Quotation/Testimony

Using a familiar, artistically stated saying will enable you to take advantage of someone else's memorable wording. For example, if you were giving a speech on personal integrity, you might quote Mark Twain, who said, "Always do right. This will gratify some people, and astonish the rest." A quotation like that fits Alexander Pope's definition of "true wit": "What was often thought, but ne'er so well expressed."

You can also use quotations as **testimony**, to prove a point by using the support of someone who is more authoritative or experienced on the subject than you are. When Rajiv Khanna, a student at Newman University in Kansas, wanted to prove that the distortion of history was a serious problem, he used testimony this way:

 testimony

Supporting material that proves or illustrates a point by citing an authoritative source.

Award-winning screenwriter, producer, and playwright Aaron Sorkin delivered a stirring commencement address at Syracuse University using stories about his own life.

Q *What personal experiences could you use to make a speech more clear, memorable, and convincing?*

Eugene Genovese, Professor Emeritus of History at Emory University, states in the July 11 issue of the *Chronicle of Higher Education*, "The distortion of history remains a serious problem to the academic community and the country at large." He continues, "As individuals who are history-making animals, we remain rooted in the past, and we are shaped by our society's version of its history."[18]

Sometimes testimony can be paraphrased. For example, when one business executive was talking on the subject of diversity, he used a conversation he'd had with Jesse Jackson Sr., an African American leader, as testimony:

> At one point in our conversation, Jesse talked about the stages of advancement toward a society where diversity is fully valued. He said the first stage was emancipation—the end of slavery. The second stage was the right to vote and the third stage was the political power to actively participate in government—to be part of city hall, the Governor's office and Capitol Hill. Jesse was clearly focused, though, on the fourth stage which he described as the ability to participate fully in the prosperity that this nation enjoys. In other words, economic power.[19]

Styles of Support

Most of the forms of support discussed in the preceding section could be presented in either of two ways: through narration or through citation. **Narration** involves telling a story with your information. You put it in the form of a small drama, with a beginning, middle, and end. For example, Evan McCarley of the University of Mississippi narrated the following example in his speech on the importance of drug courts:

> Oakland contractor Josef Corbin has a lot to be proud of. Last year his firm, Corbin Building Inc., posted revenue of over 3 million dollars after funding dozens of urban restoration projects. His company was ranked as one of the 800 fastest-growing companies in the country, all due to what his friends call his motivation for success. Unfortunately, until 1996 Corbin used this motivation to rob and steal on the streets of San Francisco to support a heroin and cocaine habit. But when he was charged with possession in 1996, Josef was given the option to participate in a state drug court, a program targeted at those recently charged with drug use, possession, or distribution. The drug court offers offenders free drug treatment, therapy, employment, education, and weekly meetings with a judge, parole officer and other accused drug offenders.[20]

Citation, unlike narration, is a simple statement of the facts. Citation is shorter and more precise than narration, in the sense that the source is carefully stated. Citation will include such phrases as "According to the

> **narration**
> Presentation of speech-supporting material as a story with a beginning, middle, and end.

> Which style of support would you find to be most compelling when using examples or analogies?

> **citation**
> Brief statement of supporting material in a speech.

July 25, 2010, edition of *Time* magazine," or "As Mr. Smith made clear in an interview last April 24." Evan McCarley cited statistics later in his speech on drug courts:

> Fortunately, Corbin's story, as reported in the May 30th *San Francisco Chronicle*, is not unique, since there are currently over 300 drug courts operating in 21 states, turning first-time and repeat offenders into successful citizens with a 70% success rate.[21]

Some forms of support, such as anecdotes, are inherently more likely to be expressed as narration. Statistics, on the other hand, are nearly always cited rather than narrated. However, when you are using examples, quotation/testimony, definitions, and analogies, you often have a choice.

CHECK YOUR UNDERSTANDING

OBJECTIVE 12.1 Analyze both the audience and the occasion in any speaking situation.

ANALYZING YOUR SPEAKING SITUATION

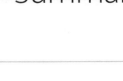

Your first task is to analyze the speaking situation, including the audience and the occasion. When analyzing your audience, you should consider the audience purpose, demographics, attitudes, beliefs, and values. When analyzing the occasion, you should consider the time (and date) your speech will take place, the location, and audience expectations.

Analyze both the audience and the occasion for your chosen speech. Describe how your analysis can shape your approach in a way that maximizes your chances of success.

OBJECTIVE 12.2 Understand the steps involved with planning a successful speech.

PLANNING YOUR SPEECH

Once you have analyzed your audience and occasion, your next tasks will be to choose and develop a topic, understand your purpose so that you can stick to it as you prepare your speech, and formulate a thesis statement, which identifies the central idea of your speech. You will also need to gather information in support of your purpose and thesis statement.

Choose a topic, formulate a purpose statement, and write a thesis statement for a speech that you plan to deliver.

OBJECTIVE 12.3 Create an effective and well-organized speech structure and outline.

STRUCTURING YOUR SPEECH

Speech structure begins with the formulation of a working outline, which can be developed into a formal outline or reduced to speaking notes. Organization follows a pattern, such as time, space, topic, problem-solution, cause-effect, or motivated sequence arrangements.

Produce a formal outline for a speech you will present.

OBJECTIVE 12.4 Develop an effective introduction and conclusion, and integrate smooth transitions.

USING INTRODUCTIONS, CONCLUSIONS, AND TRANSITIONS

A speech introduction will gain your audience's attention, preview the main points, set the mood and tone of the speech, demonstrate the importance of your topic to the audience, and establish credibility. The conclusion will review your thesis and/or main points and supply the audience with a memory aid. Transitions will connect the ideas of your speech and keep your message moving forward.

Produce a sample introduction, conclusion, and at least one transition for a speech you will present.

OBJECTIVE 12.5 Choose supporting material that makes your ideas clear, memorable, and convincing.

USING SUPPORTING MATERIAL

Supporting materials are the facts and information you use to back up what you say. Types of support include definitions of key terms; examples, which can be real or hypothetical; statistics, which show that a fact or principle is true for a large percentage of cases; analogies, which compare or contrast an unknown or unfamiliar concept with a known or familiar one; anecdotes, which add a lively, personal touch; and quotations and testimony, which are used for memorable wording as well as ideas from a well-known or authoritative source. Support may be narrated (told in story form) or cited (stated briefly).

Which forms of support will be most effective for the speech you are preparing? Why?

KEY TERMS

HOW WELL CAN YOU ORGANIZE IDEAS?

Suggested organization of main points and subpoints from pg. 299.

I. Choose desired college
    A. Visit and evaluate college websites
    B. Visit and evaluate college campuses
II. Prepare application materials
    A. Transcripts
    B. Test scores
    C. Letters of recommendation
III. Write personal statement
    A. Choose interesting topic

    B. Include important personal details
      1. Participation in extracurricular activities
      2. Volunteer work
      3. Career ambitions

You can score yourself as follows:

30 seconds or less: Congratulations, organization comes naturally to you.
31 to 60 seconds: You have typical skills in this area.
61 to 90 seconds: Give yourself extra time while building your speech outline.

FOR FURTHER EXPLORATION

For more resources, see the *Essential Communication* website at www .oup.com/us/EC. There you will find a variety of free resources: "Media Room" clips from popular films and television shows to further illustrate important concepts, a list of books and articles, links to descriptions of feature films and television shows at the *Now Playing* website, study aids, and a self-test to check your understanding of the material in this chapter.

Presenting Speeches

13.1 Understand the sources and remedies of stage fright.

13.2 Distinguish among four different types of speech delivery.

13.3 Use visual aids effectively.

13.4 Become familiar with strategies for effectively practicing a speech.

iPhone
Apple reinvents the phone

MANAGING SPEECH ANXIETY

The terror that strikes many beginning speakers at the mere thought of giving a speech is commonly known as stage fright, and it is called speech anxiety by communication scholars.[1] Whatever term you choose, it's important to realize that this fear about speaking in front of others can be managed.

Helpful and Unhelpful Speech Anxiety

The first step in feeling less apprehensive about speaking is to realize that a certain amount of nervousness is not only natural but also helpful. Just as totally relaxed actors or musicians aren't likely to perform at the top of their potential, speakers think more rapidly and express themselves more energetically when they experience **helpful speech anxiety**.

It is only when the level of anxiety is very intense that it becomes unhelpful. Intense fear causes trouble in two ways. First, the strong emotion keeps you from thinking clearly.[2] This has been shown to be a problem even in the preparation process: Students who are highly anxious about giving a speech will find the preliminary steps, including research and organization, to be more difficult.[3] Second, intense fear leads to an urge to do something, anything, to make the problem go away. This urge to escape often causes a speaker to speed up delivery, which in turn leads to mistakes, which only add to the speaker's anxiety.

Sources of Unhelpful Speech Anxiety

Before learning to manage **unhelpful speech anxiety**, it's useful to understand the reasons why people are afflicted with the problem in the first place.[4] There are two main reasons for this type of anxiety: previous negative experiences and irrational thinking.

Previous Negative Experience

Many of us are uncomfortable doing *anything* in public, especially if we know others are going to be evaluating our talents and abilities. An unpleasant experience in one type of performance can cause you to expect that a future similar situation will also be unpleasant.[5] You might come to expect paralyzing mental blocks, for example, or rude audience members. These expectations can become reality through the self-fulfilling prophecies discussed in Chapter 3.

A traumatic failure at an earlier speech and low self-esteem from critical parents during childhood are common examples of experiences that

> **helpful speech anxiety**
> A moderate level of apprehension about speaking before an audience that helps improve the speaker's performance.

> **unhelpful speech anxiety**
> Intense level of apprehension about speaking before an audience, resulting in poor performance.

can cause later speech anxiety. But not everyone who has bungled a speech or had critical parents is debilitated in the future. To understand why some people are affected more strongly than others by past experiences, we need to consider another cause of speech anxiety.

Irrational Thinking

Cognitive psychologists argue that it is not events that cause people to feel nervous but rather the beliefs they have about those events. Certain irrational beliefs leave people feeling unnecessarily apprehensive. Psychologist Albert Ellis lists several such beliefs, or examples of **irrational thinking**, which we call "fallacies" because of their illogical nature.[6]

People who succumb to the **fallacy of catastrophic failure** operate on the assumption that, if something bad can happen, it probably will. One way to escape the fallacy of catastrophic failure is to take a more realistic look at the situation. Will your audience members really boo you off the stage? Will they really think your ideas are stupid? Even if you do forget your remarks for a moment, will that make your entire speech a disaster? It helps to remember that nervousness is more apparent to the speaker than to the audience.[7] Beginning public speakers, when congratulated for their poise during a speech, are apt to say, "Are you kidding? I was dying up there."

Speakers who succumb to the **fallacy of perfection** expect to deliver a flawless presentation. While such a standard of perfection might serve as a target and a source of inspiration, it is not realistic to believe you will write and deliver a perfect speech, especially as a beginner. And, remember, audiences don't expect you to be perfect either.

The **fallacy of approval** is based on the idea that it is vital to gain the approval of everyone in the audience. It is rare that even the best speakers please everyone, especially on topics that are at all controversial. To paraphrase Abraham Lincoln, you can't please all the people all the time; and it is irrational to expect you will.

The **fallacy of overgeneralization** might also be labeled the fallacy of exaggeration, because it occurs when a person blows one poor experience out of proportion, or when a speaker treats occasional lapses as if they were the rule rather than the exception. This sort of mistake usually involves extreme labels, such as "always" or "never."

"I always forget what I want to say."

"I can never come up with a good topic."

"I can't do anything right."

How to Overcome Unhelpful Speech Anxiety

While irrational thinking or bad past experiences may make you apprehensive about speaking, there are several steps you can take to manage and oftentimes minimize speech anxiety:

How can you use a previous negative experience to your advantage in your next speaking opportunity?

> **irrational thinking**
Beliefs that have no basis in reality or logic; one source of unhelpful speech anxiety.

> **fallacy of catastrophic failure**
The irrational belief that the worst possible outcome will probably occur.

> **fallacy of perfection**
The irrational belief that a worthwhile communicator should be able to handle every situation with complete confidence and skill.

> **fallacy of approval**
The irrational belief that it is vital to win the approval of virtually every person a communicator deals with.

> **fallacy of overgeneralization**
Irrational beliefs in which (1) conclusions (usually negative) are based on limited evidence or (2) communicators exaggerate their shortcomings.

A surprising number of well-known celebrities battle communication anxiety. In a *Rolling Stone* interview, Adele admitted, "I'm scared of audiences.... One show in Amsterdam, I was so nervous I escaped out the fire exit.... I have anxiety attacks a lot." Despite her speech anxiety, Adele is a consummate performer.

Q *What can you do to better manage your speech anxiety?*

Use nervousness to your advantage. A little nervousness can actually help you deliver a successful speech. Being completely calm can take away the passion that is one element of a good speech. It's important to control your anxiety but not to eliminate it completely.

Understand the difference between rational and irrational fears. Fears based on irrational thinking aren't constructive. It's not realistic to expect that you'll deliver a perfect speech, and it's not productive or rational to indulge in catastrophic fantasies about what might go wrong. If you haven't prepared for a speech, however, that is a legitimate and rational fear.

Maintain a receiver orientation. Paying too much attention to your own feelings even when you're feeling good about yourself will take energy away from communicating with your listeners. Concentrate on your audience members rather than on yourself. Focus your energy on keeping them interested and on making sure they understand you.

Keep a positive attitude. Build and maintain a positive attitude toward your audience, your speech, and yourself as a speaker. Some

Do you suffer from speech anxiety?

1. What is your overall level of anxiety about speech making?

   A. Nonexistent   B. Moderate   C. Severe

2. Are you in control of your speech anxiety, or is your speech anxiety in control of you?

   A. I'm in control   B. Half and half   C. Anxiety is in control

What level of the following do you experience while speaking?

3. Sweating/sweaty palms

   A. Nonexistent   B. Moderate   C. Severe

4. Rapid breathing

   A. Nonexistent   B. Moderate   C. Severe

5. Restless energy

   A. Nonexistent   B. Moderate   C. Severe

6. Forgetting what you wanted to say

   A. Nonexistent   B. Moderate   C. Severe

Give yourself one point for every A, two points for every B, and three points for every C. For an explanation of your results, see p. 339. ●

---

communication consultants suggest that public speakers should concentrate on three statements immediately before speaking:

I'm glad I have the chance to talk about this topic.

I know what I'm talking about.

I care about my audience.

Repeating these statements (until you believe them) can help you maintain a positive attitude.

Another technique for building a positive attitude is known as **visualization**.[8] This technique has been used successfully with athletes. It requires you to use your imagination to visualize the successful completion of your speech. Visualization can help make the self-fulfilling prophecy discussed in Chapter 3 work in your favor.

Be prepared! Preparation is the most important key to controlling speech anxiety. You can feel confident if you know from practice that your remarks are well organized and supported and your delivery is smooth.

> visualization

A technique for behavioral rehearsal (e.g., for a speech) that involves imagining the successful completion of the task.

Researchers have determined that the highest level of anxiety occurs just before speaking, the second highest level at the time the assignment is announced and explained, and the lowest level during the time you spend preparing your speech.[9] You should take advantage of this relatively low-stress time to work through the problems that would tend to make you nervous during the actual speech. For example, if your anxiety is based on a fear of forgetting what you are going to say, make sure that your note cards are complete and effective and that you have practiced your speech thoroughly. If, on the other hand, your great fear is "sounding stupid," then get started early with lots of research.

OBJECTIVE 13.2   Distinguish among four different types of speech delivery.

CHOOSING A TYPE OF DELIVERY

One of your first considerations in being prepared is selecting the right way to deliver your speech. There are four basic types of delivery: extemporaneous, impromptu, manuscript, and memorized. Each type creates a different impression and is appropriate under different conditions. Any speech may incorporate more than one of these types of delivery.

Extemporaneous

> **extemporaneous speech**
A speech that is planned in advance but presented in a direct, conversational manner.

An **extemporaneous speech** is planned in advance but presented in a direct, spontaneous manner. Extemporaneous speeches are conversational in tone, which means that they give the audience members the impression that you are talking to them, directly and honestly. Extemporaneous speaking is the most common type of delivery in the "outside" world, and for most instructors, it is the *only* type of delivery allowed in the classroom.

Impromptu

> **impromptu speech**
A speech given "off the top of one's head," without preparation.

An **impromptu speech** is given off the top of one's head, without preparation. This type of speech is spontaneous by definition, but it is a delivery style that is necessary for informal talks, group discussions, and comments on others' speeches. It is also a highly effective training aid that teaches you to think on your feet and to organize your thoughts quickly.

Manuscript

> **manuscript speech**
A speech that is read word for word from a prepared text.

Manuscript speeches are read word for word from a prepared text. They are necessary when you are speaking for the record, as when speaking at legal proceedings or when presenting scientific findings. The greatest disadvantage of a manuscript speech is the lack of spontaneity that may result.

Glee's Chris Colfer, winner of a 2011 Golden Globe award, proclaimed: "To all the amazing kids that watch our show and the kids that our show celebrates—who are constantly told 'NO' by the people in their environments, by bullies at school that they can't be who they are or have what they want because of who they are. Well, screw that, kids!"

12 Years a Slave's Lupita Nyong'o, winner of a 2013 Academy Award, confided: "It doesn't escape me for one moment that so much joy in my life is thanks to so much pain in someone else's."

When both Nyong'o and Colfer won awards for their work, they spoke extemporaneously from the heart, and their words were memorable.

Q *Why do you think extemporaneous speeches are often so much more effective than other types?*

Memorized

Memorized speeches are those learned by heart. Like manuscript speeches, they may be necessary on special occasions. They are often used in oratory contests and also as training devices for memory. Of all the delivery types, memorized speeches are the most difficult. And, because of their excessive formality, they may often be the least effective.

> memorized speech
A speech learned and delivered by rote without a written text.

Which type (or types) of delivery would be most appropriate to use for a toast at your best friend's wedding?

USING VISUAL AIDS

No matter which type of delivery you decide to use, another integral part of the preparation process is to decide whether or not to use visual aids. **Visual aids** are graphic devices that may be used in any type of speech to illustrate and support ideas. They can be extremely useful when you want to show how things look (photos of your trek to Nepal or the effects of malnutrition) or how things work (a demonstration of a new ski binding, a diagram of how seawater is made drinkable). Visual aids can also show how things relate to one another (a graph showing the relationships among gender, education, and income).

> **> visual aids**
> Graphic devices used in a speech to illustrate or support ideas.

> Which type of visual aid would be most appropriate for showing the increase in social media use by different groups over the past ten years?

Types of Visual Aids

There is a wide variety of types of visual aids. The most common types include objects and models, diagrams, word and number charts, pie charts, bar and column charts, and line charts.

Objects and Models

Sometimes the most effective visual aid is the actual thing you are talking about. This is true when the thing you are talking about is portable enough to carry and simple enough to use during a demonstration before an audience: a piece of sports equipment such as a lacrosse racket or a small piece

Legendary Apple CEO Steve Jobs never used a single bullet point. Even during product demos, his slides were remarkably simple, relying on powerful images and carefully selected words.

Q *Why do you think plain language and vivid imagery can make more of an impact than text-heavy slides?*

of weight-training equipment. A **model** is a scaled representation of the object you are discussing and is used when that object is too large (the new campus arts complex) or too small (a DNA molecule) or simply doesn't exist anymore (a *Tyrannosaurus rex*).

Diagrams

A **diagram** is any kind of line drawing that shows the most important properties of an object. Diagrams show just those parts that the audience most needs to be aware of and understand. Blueprints and architectural plans are common types of diagrams, as are maps and organizational charts. A diagram is most appropriate when you need to simplify a complex object or phenomenon and make it more understandable to the audience.

Figure 13-1 shows a depiction of "the true size of Africa." By superimposing the United States, China, India, Japan and most of Europe over an outline of Africa, it demonstrates that that continent is larger than all of

> **model (in speeches and presentations)**
Replica of an object being discussed. Usually used when it would be difficult or impossible to use the actual object.

> **diagram**
A line drawing that shows the most important components of an object.

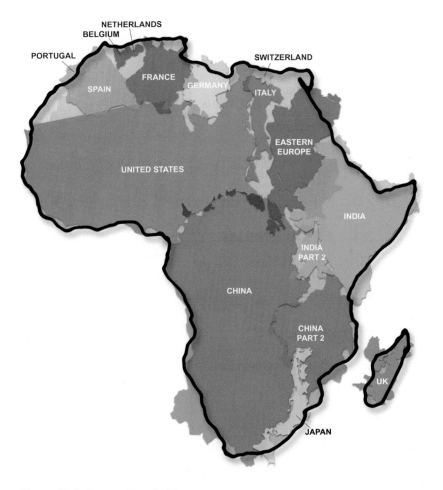

Figure 13-1 The True Size of Africa

> pictogram

A visual aid that conveys its meaning through an image of an actual object.

> word chart

Visual aid that lists words or terms in tabular form in order to clarify information.

> number chart

Visual aid that lists numbers in tabular form in order to clarify information.

> pie chart

A visual aid that divides a circle into wedges, representing percentages of the whole.

those land masses combined. Coincidentally, Figure 13-1 is also a **pictogram**, which is a visual aid that conveys its meaning through images of an actual object.

Word and Number Charts

Word charts and **number charts** are visual depictions of key facts or statistics. Your audience will understand and remember these facts and numbers better if you show them than if you just talk about them. Many speakers arrange the main points of their speech, often in outline form, as a word chart. Other speakers list their main statistics. Charts can depict just words, just numbers, or a combination of the two. Figure 13-2 provides a word-and-number chart that depicts the same data as was implied in the diagram in Figure 13-1.

Pie Charts

Pie charts are shaped as circles with wedges cut into them. They are used to show divisions of any whole: where your tax dollars go, the percentage of the population involved in various occupations, and so on. Pie charts are often

COUNTRY	AREA x 1000 km²
China	9.597
USA	9.629
India	3.287
Mexico	1.964
Peru	1.285
France	633
Spain	506
Papua New Guinea	462
Sweden	441
Japan	378
Germany	357
Norway	324
Italy	301
New Zealand	270
United Kingdom	243
Nepal	147
Bangladesh	144
Greece	132
TOTAL	30.102
AFRICA	30.221

Figure 13-2 Comparative Size of Africa

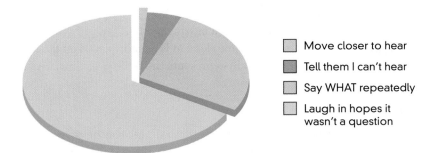

Figure 13-3 When I Can't Hear Someone

made up of percentages that add up to 100 percent. Usually, the wedges of the pie are organized from largest to smallest. The pie chart in Figure 13-3 represents one's person's perception of typical behavioral patterns when one person can't hear what someone else is saying in a noisy room.

Bar and Column Charts

Bar charts compare two or more values by stretching them out in the form of horizontal rectangles. **Column charts**, such as the one shown in Figure 13-4, perform the same function as bar charts but use vertical rectangles.

> bar chart

Visual aid that compares two or more values by showing them as elongated horizontal rectangles.

> column chart

Visual aid that compares two or more values by showing them as elongated vertical rectangles.

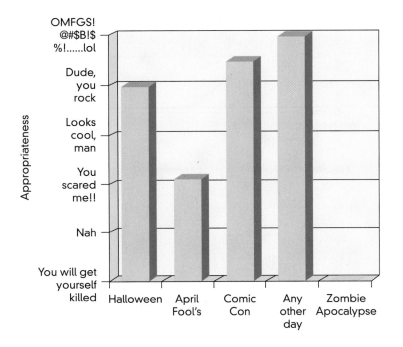

Figure 13-4 Appropriateness to Dress in Zombie Costume

Line Charts

A **line chart** maps out the direction of a moving point; it is ideally suited for showing changes over time. The time element is usually placed on the horizontal axis so that the line visually represents the trend over time. Figure 13-5 is a line chart.

Media for Presenting Visual Aids

Obviously, many types and variations of visual aids can be used in any speech. And a variety of materials can be used to present these aids.

Chalkboards, Whiteboards, and Polymer Marking Surfaces

The major advantage of these write-as-you-go media is their spontaneity. With them you can create your visual aid as you speak, including items generated from audience responses. Along with the odor of whiteboard markers and the squeaking of chalk, a major disadvantage of these media is the difficulty of preparing visual aids on them in advance, especially if several speeches are scheduled in the same room at the same hour.

Flip Pads and Poster Board

Flip pads are like oversized writing tablets attached to a portable easel. Flip pads enable you to combine the spontaneity of the whiteboard (you can write on them as you go) with a portability that enables you to prepare

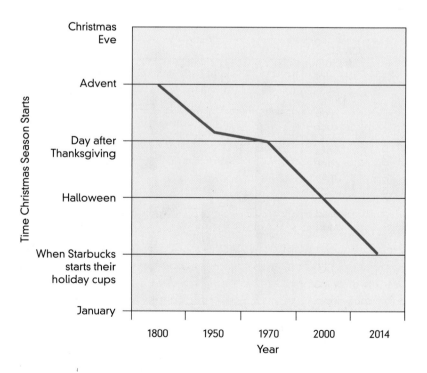

Figure 13-5 Start of Christmas Season

them in advance. If you plan to use your visuals more than once you can prepare them in advance on rigid poster board and display them on the same type of easel. However, flip pads and poster boards are bulky, and preparing professional-looking exhibits on them requires a fair amount of artistic ability.

Handouts

The major advantage of handouts is that audience members can take away the information they contain after your speech. For this reason, handouts are excellent memory and reference aids. The major disadvantage is that they are distracting when handed out during a speech: First, there is the distraction of passing them out, and second, there is the distraction of having them in front of the audience members while you have gone on to something else. It's best, therefore, to pass them out at the end of the speech so audience members can take them when they leave.

Projectors

When your audience is too large to view handheld images, projectors are an ideal tool. Digital projectors allow you to use a screen image directly from a computer screen, making them the most direct way to use computer software presentations. Projectors allow you to use room-sized images, rather than displaying images on screens that are too small for audiences to see well, such as laptops.

Other Electronic Media

A wide range of other electronic media are available as presentation aids. Audio and video files can supply information that could not be presented any other way. For example, you might include a brief YouTube clip to show the audience what divers found in an underwater shipwreck, if that's what your speech is about. But in most cases, you should use video and audio clips sparingly. The general rule when using these media is: *Don't let them get in the way of the direct, person-to-person contact that is the primary advantage of public speaking.*

Rules for Using Visual Aids

It's easy to see that each type of visual aid and each medium for its presentation has its own advantages and disadvantages. Remember that no matter which visual aid you use, you need to talk to your audience, not to your visual aid. Some speakers become so wrapped up in their props that they turn their backs on their audience and sacrifice all their eye contact. Here are some additional guidelines for making your visual aids work for you.

Simplicity

Keep your visual aids simple. Your goal is to clarify, not confuse. Use only key words or phrases, not sentences. The "rule of seven" states that each exhibit you use should contain no more than seven lines of text, each with no more than seven words. (Figure 13-2 is an exception to this rule, as it was presented as a list that stresses a general impression, rather than a detailed reading of each line.) Keep all printing horizontal. Omit all non-essential details.

Size
Visual aids should be large enough for your entire audience to see them at one time but portable enough for you to get them out of the way when they no longer pertain to the point you are making.

Attractiveness
Visual aids should be visually interesting and as neat as possible. If you don't have the necessary artistic or computer skills, try to get help from a friend or at the computer or audiovisual center on your campus.

Appropriateness
Visuals must be appropriate to all the components of the speaking situation—you, your audience, and your topic—and they must emphasize the point you are trying to make. Don't make the mistake of using a visual aid that looks good but has only a weak link to the point you want to make, such as showing a map of a city transit system while talking about the condition of the individual cars.

Reliability
You must be in control of your visual aid at all times. Test all electronic media in advance, preferably in the room where you will speak. Just to be safe, have non-electronic backups ready in case of disaster. Be conservative when you choose demonstrations: Wild animals, chemical reactions, and gimmicks meant to shock a crowd can often backfire.

Presentation Software

Several specialized programs exist just to produce visual aids. Among the most popular of these programs are Microsoft PowerPoint, Apple's Keynote, and Prezi.

In its simplest form, presentation software lets you build an effective slide show out of your basic outline. You can choose color-coordinated backgrounds and consistent formatting that match the tone and purpose of your presentation. Most presentation software programs contain a clip art library that allows you to choose images to accompany your words. They also allow you to import images from outside sources and to build your own charts. However, you have to avoid making your presentation software redundant with what you're saying—a phenomenon known as "death by PowerPoint." Instead, use presentation software to present examples, illustrations, and key points that help your audience keep track of your ideas.

If you would like to learn more about using PowerPoint, Keynote, and Prezi, there are several Web-based tutorial programs, which you can find easily by typing the name of your preferred program into your favorite search engine.

Become familiar with strategies for effectively practicing a speech.   **OBJECTIVE 13.4**

PRACTICING THE SPEECH

As mentioned earlier, preparation is one of the keys to controlling speech anxiety. And one of the ways to be prepared is to practice. Practicing your speech will result in a smooth and natural delivery. To get to know your material and feel comfortable with your presentation, we recommend that you go through some or all of the following steps:

First, present the speech to yourself. "Talk through" the entire speech, including your examples and forms of support. Don't skip through parts of your speech as you practice by using placeholders such as "This is where I present my statistics" or "This is where I explain about photosynthesis." Make sure you know how you plan to present your statistics and explanations.

Record the speech and listen to it. Because we hear our own voices partially through our cranial bone structure, we are sometimes surprised at what we sound like to others. Video recording has been proven to be an especially effective tool for rehearsals, giving you an idea of what you look and sound like.[10]

Present the speech in front of a small group of friends or relatives.[11] **Present the speech to at least one listener in the room in which you will present the final speech** (or, if that room is not available, a similar room).

In each of these steps, you can critique your speech according to the principles of communication outlined in earlier chapters of this book. For example, as you read in Chapter 6, nonverbal behavior can change, or even contradict, the meaning of the words a speaker utters. If audience members want to interpret how you feel about something, they are likely to trust your nonverbal communication more than the words you speak. If you tell them, "It's great to be here today," but you stand before them slouched over with your hands in your pockets and an expression on your face like you're awaiting your execution, they are likely to discount what you say. If, instead, you approach a subject with genuine enthusiasm, your audience is

Which principles of communication will tell you that your speech is effective?

In *Dead Poets Society*, John Keating (Robin Williams) delivers many unorthodox speeches to his students. His marriage of spontaneity and elocution shows he has extensive experience commanding a classroom.

Q *How much practice do you think you need in order to deliver a speech successfully?*

likely to sense it and to feed off of that enthusiasm. You can show enthusiasm through both the visual and auditory aspects of your delivery.

Visual Aspects of Delivery

As audience members watch your speech, they will take into account the visual aspects of your delivery, including your appearance, movement, posture, facial expression, and eye contact.

Appearance

Appearance is not a presentation variable as much as a preparation variable. Some communication consultants suggest new clothes and new hairstyles for their clients. In case you consider any of these, be forewarned that you should be attractive to your audience but not flashy. Research suggests that audiences like speakers who are similar to them, but they prefer the similarity to be shown conservatively.[12] Speakers, it seems, are perceived to be more credible when they look businesslike. Part of looking businesslike, of course, is looking like you took care in the preparation of your clothes and appearance.

Movement

The way you walk to the front of your audience will express your confidence and enthusiasm. And after you begin speaking, nervous energy can cause your body to shake and twitch, and that can be distressing both to you and to your audience. One way to control involuntary movement is to move voluntarily when you feel the need to move. Don't feel that you have to stand in one spot or that all your gestures need to be carefully planned. Simply get involved in your message, and let your involvement create the motivation for your movement. That way, when you move, you will emphasize what you are saying in the same way you would emphasize it if you were talking to a group of friends.

Movement can also help you maintain contact with all members of your audience. Those closest to you will feel the greatest contact. This creates what is known as the "action zone" in the typical classroom, within the area of the front and center of the room. Movement enables you to extend this action zone, to include in it people who would otherwise remain uninvolved. Without overdoing it, you should feel free to move toward, away from, or from side to side in front of your audience.

Posture

Generally speaking, good posture means standing with your spine relatively straight, your shoulders relatively squared off, and your feet angled out to keep your body from falling over sideways. In other words, rather than standing at military attention, you should be comfortably erect.

Good posture can help you control nervousness by allowing you to breathe properly; when your brain receives enough oxygen, it's easier for you to think clearly. Good posture also increases your audience contact because audience members will feel that you are interested enough in them to stand formally, yet relaxed enough to be at ease with them.

Facial Expression

The expression on your face can be more meaningful to an audience than the words you say. Try it yourself with a mirror. Say, "You're a terrific audience," for example, with a smirk, with a warm smile, with a deadpan expression, and then with a scowl. It just doesn't mean the same thing. But, don't try to fake it. Like your movement, your facial expressions will reflect your genuine involvement with your message.

Eye Contact

Eye contact is perhaps the most important nonverbal facet of delivery. Eye contact not only increases your direct contact with your audience but also can be used to help you control your nervousness. Direct eye contact is a form of reality testing. The most frightening aspect of speaking is the unknown. How will the audience react? Direct eye contact allows you to test your perception of your audience as you speak. By deliberately establishing contact with any apparently bored audience members, you might find that they are interested; they just might not be showing that interest because they don't think anyone is looking.

To maintain eye contact, you should try to meet the eyes of each member of your audience squarely at least once during any given presentation. After you have made definite eye contact, move on to another audience member. You can learn to do this quickly, so you can visually latch on to every member of a good-sized class in a relatively short time.

Auditory Aspects of Delivery

As you read in Chapter 6, your paralanguage—the way you use your voice— says a good deal about you, especially about your sincerity and enthusiasm. Controlling your vocal characteristics will also decrease your nervousness. You can control your voice by recognizing and using appropriate volume, rate, pitch, and articulation.

Volume

The loudness of your voice is determined by the amount of air you push past the vocal folds in your throat. The key to controlling volume, then, is controlling the amount of air you use. The key to determining the right volume is audience contact. Your delivery should be loud enough so that your audience members can hear everything you say but not so loud that they feel you are talking to someone in the next room. Too much volume is seldom the problem for beginning speakers. Usually they either are not loud enough or have a tendency to fade off or mumble at the end of a thought. Keep in mind that words you whisper or scream will be emphasized by their volume.

Rate

> rate
The speed at which a speaker utters words.

There is a range of personal differences in speaking speed, or **rate**. Daniel Webster, for example, is said to have spoken at around 90 words per minute,

A speech impediment left Suze Orman unable to pronounce r's, s's or t's as a child. Today, she is one of the most successful motivational speakers in the world, carefully enunciating her words in short, emphatic bursts that have become her trademark.

Q *What aspects of your voice do you need to be mindful of when delivering a speech?*

whereas one actor who is known for his fast-talking commercials speaks at about 250. Normal speaking speed, however, is between 120 and 150 words per minute. That's about the same rate as a television newscaster would speak. If you talk much more slowly than that, you may lull your audience to sleep. Faster speaking rates are sometimes stereotypically associated with speaker competence,[13] but if you speak too rapidly, you will be unintelligible. Once again, your involvement in your message is the key to achieving an effective rate. If you pause or speed up, your rate will suggest emphasis.

Pitch

The highness or lowness of your voice—**pitch**—is controlled by the frequency at which your vocal folds vibrate as you push air through them. Because taut vocal folds vibrate at a greater frequency, pitch is influenced by muscular tension. This explains why nervous speakers have a tendency occasionally to "squeak," whereas relaxed speakers seem to be more in control.

Pitch will tend to follow rate and volume. As you speed up or become louder, your pitch will have a tendency to rise. If your range in pitch is too narrow, your voice will have a singsong quality. If it is too wide, you may sound overly dramatic. You should control your pitch so that your listeners believe you are talking with them rather than at them. Once again, your involvement in your message should take care of this naturally for you.

> **pitch**
> The highness or lowness of one's voice.

Articulation

The final auditory nonverbal behavior, articulation, is perhaps the most important. For our purposes here, **articulation** means pronouncing all the parts of all the necessary words and nothing else. Careful articulation means using your lips, teeth, tongue, and jaw to bite off your words, cleanly and separately, one at a time.

It is not our purpose to condemn regional or ethnic dialects within this discussion. It is true that a considerable amount of research suggests that regional dialects can cause negative impressions,[14] but our purpose here is to suggest careful, not standardized, articulation. Incorrect articulation is usually nothing more than careless articulation. It is caused by leaving off parts of words (deletion), replacing parts of words (substitution), adding parts to words (addition), or overlapping two or more words (slurring).

The most common mistake in articulation is **deletion**, or leaving off part of a word. The most common deletions occur at the ends of words, especially *-ing* words. *Going, doing,* and *stopping* become *goin', doin',* and *stoppin'*. Parts of words can be left off in the middle, too, as in *terr'iss* for *terrorist, Innernet* for *Internet,* and *asst* for *asked*.

Substitution takes place when you replace part of a word with an incorrect sound. The ending *-th* is often replaced at the end of a word with a single *t,* as when *with* becomes *wit*. The *th-* sound is also a problem at the beginning of words, as *this, that,* and *those* have a tendency to become *dis, dat,* and *dose*. (This tendency is especially prevalent in many parts of the northeastern United States.)

> **articulation**
> The process of pronouncing all the necessary parts of a word.

> **deletion**
> An articulation error that involves leaving off parts of words.

> **substitution**
> The articulation error that involves replacing part of a word with an incorrect sound.

> addition

The articulation error that involves adding extra parts to words.

The articulation problem of **addition** is caused by adding extra parts to words, such as *incentative* instead of *incentive*, *athalete* instead of *athlete*, and *orientated* instead of *oriented*. Sometimes this type of addition is caused by incorrect word choice, as when *irregardless* is used for *regardless*. Another type of addition is the use of "tag questions," such as *you know?* or *you see?* or *right?* at the end of sentences. To have every other sentence punctuated with one of these barely audible superfluous phrases can be annoying. Probably the worst type of addition, or at least the most common, however, is the use of *uh*, *umm*, *like*, and *anda* between words. *Anda* is often stuck between two words when *and* isn't even needed. If you find yourself doing that, you might want just to pause or swallow instead.[15]

> slurring

The articulation error that involves overlapping the end of one word with the beginning of the next.

Slurring is caused by trying to say two or more words at once—or at least overlapping the end of one word with the beginning of the next. Word pairs ending with *of* are the worst offenders in this category. *Sort of* becomes *sorta*, *kind of* becomes *kinda*, and *because of* becomes *becausa*. Word combinations ending with *to* are often slurred, as when *want to* becomes *wanna*. Sometimes even more than two words are blended together, as when *that is the way* becomes *thatsaway*.

Online/Virtual Delivery

Increasingly, people may be asked to deliver online presentations, sometimes referred to as webinars (when they are interactive) and webcasts (when they are one-way). Many of the guidelines for presenting speeches in person apply to online presentations as well, but online presentations often use more visual aids. They also require a greater awareness of all the ingredients of effective online video, such as lighting, framing, and clear audio. Several online sites provide tutorials for giving online presentations, but here are just a few general guidelines:[16]

Try out various webconferencing platforms. Collaborative software such as Go-to-Meeting enables you to see who is online and ensure everyone is literally on the same slide.

Schedule a run-through before the actual event. This will help you ensure the presentation is not too long or too short, and it will enable you to iron out any technical issues or glitches.

Use dynamic visuals. Action shots are better than still images when possible. If you plan to show video, keep it short and on point.

Keep the slides simple. Avoid slides with a lot of text.

Keep it entertaining. Employ stories and/or humor to keep your audience engaged.

Start and end on time. People are busy, and many may have other activities or meetings before or after your presentation; show them respect by sticking to the allotted time.

CHECK YOUR UNDERSTANDING

OBJECTIVE 13.1 Understand the sources and remedies of stage fright.

MANAGING SPEECH ANXIETY

Sources of unhelpful speech anxiety include irrational thinking, which might include a belief in one or more of the following fallacies: the fallacy of catastrophic failure, the fallacy of perfection, the fallacy of absolute approval, and the fallacy of overgeneralization. There are several methods of overcoming unhelpful speech anxiety. The first is to remember that nervousness is natural and you can use it to your advantage. The others include being rational, receiver-oriented, positive, and prepared.

Explain your personal process for overcoming stage fright.

OBJECTIVE 13.2 Distinguish among four different types of speech delivery.

CHOOSING A TYPE OF DELIVERY

There are four types of delivery: extemporaneous, impromptu, manuscript, and memorized. Each has its own advantages and disadvantages for individual speaking situations.

Explain why you chose the type of delivery that you did for a speech you gave or might give in this class.

OBJECTIVE 13.3 Use visual aids effectively.

USING VISUAL AIDS

Visual aids are used to illustrate and support ideas in a speech. They include objects and models, diagrams, word and number charts, pie charts, bar and column charts, and line charts. You can present them through a wide range of media.

For a speech that you gave or will give in this class, explain why you chose the type of visual aids that you did.

Become familiar with strategies for effectively practicing a speech.

PRACTICING THE SPEECH

Methods of practicing your speech include presenting it to yourself, recording it, presenting it to a small group of friends, and presenting it in the room in which it will be given. Visual aspects of delivery that the audience will take into account include appearance, movement, posture, facial expression, and eye contact. Auditory aspects of delivery that the audience will take into account include paralanguage: volume, rate, pitch, and articulation.

Practice your speech using at least three of the methods discussed in this chapter. Describe which method was most effective for you in terms of your preparation.

KEY TERMS

addition p. 326
articulation p. 335
bar chart p. 327
column chart p. 327
deletion p. 335
diagram p. 325
extemporaneous speech p. 322
fallacy of approval p. 319
fallacy of catastrophic failure p. 319
fallacy of overgeneralization p. 319

fallacy of perfection p. 319
helpful speech anxiety p. 318
impromptu speech p. 322
irrational thinking p. 319
line chart p. 328
manuscript speech p. 322
memorized speech p. 323
model (in speeches and
     presentations) p. 325
number chart p. 326

pictogram p. 326
pie chart p. 326
pitch p. 335
rate p. 334
slurring p. 336
substitution p. 335
unhelpful speech anxiety p. 318
visual aids p. 324
visualization p. 321
word chart p. 326

DO YOU SUFFER FROM SPEECH ANXIETY?

If your score is:

6 to 9

You have nerves of steel. You're probably a natural public speaker.

10 to 13

You are the typical public speaker. The strategies discussed in this chapter should help you learn how to improve your skills.

14 to 18

You tend to have significant anxiety about public speaking. You need to consider the strategies outlined in this chapter carefully. Although you will benefit from the tips provided, you should keep in mind that some of the greatest speakers of all time have considered themselves highly anxious.

FOR FURTHER EXPLORATION

For more resources, see the *Essential Communication* website at www .oup.com/us/EC. There you will find a variety of resources: a list of books and articles, links to descriptions of feature films and television shows at the *Now Playing* website, study aids, and a self-test to check your understanding of the material in this chapter.

Speaking to Inform, Persuade, and Entertain

14.1 Distinguish among speeches to inform, persuade, and entertain.

14.2 Explain the techniques of informative speaking, and use them to present an effective informative speech.

14.3 Explain the techniques of persuasive speaking, and use them to present an effective persuasive speech.

14.4 Explain the techniques of speaking to entertain, and use them to present an entertaining speech.

TYPES OF SPEECHES

In this final chapter, we take an in-depth and comparative look at each of the three main types of speaking:

To inform: To enlighten audience members by teaching them something.

To persuade: To move your audience toward a new attitude or behavior.

To entertain: To relax audience members by providing them with a pleasant listening experience.

While there are distinctive differences among the three types of speeches, there is also considerable overlap. A speech designed to inform an audience will almost certainly need to be entertaining enough to hold audience members' interest. And, in order to persuade audience members, you will most likely have to inform them about your arguments. Even a speech designed purely to entertain might change audience attitudes or teach that audience something new.

Informative Speeches

Informative speaking goes on all around you, whether it's a professor giving a lecture, a news anchor detailing the latest budget stalemate, or a friend giving you a play-by-play of the game. There are several types of informative speaking. Basically, speeches are considered informative if their purpose is to describe, explain, or instruct. There are two other characteristics of informative speaking that are of interest to us here.

An Informative Topic Tends to Be Noncontroversial

In an informative speech, the speaker will generally not present information that the audience is likely to disagree with. For example, if you were to give a purely informative talk on the differences between hospital births and home-based midwife births, you would describe what the practitioners of each method believe and do without boosting or criticizing one method over the other. The goal is to present information that is objective and will not engender conflict. If a speaker *does* present a controversial topic, he or she will explain all sides of the issue and will not ask the audience to pick a side.

The Informative Speaker Does Not Intend to Change Audience Attitudes

While the informative speaker seeks a response from the listener, his or her primary intent is not to change attitudes or make the audience members *feel* differently about the topic. For example, an informative speaker might explain how a tablet works but not try to "sell" a specific brand to the audience. Persuasive speaking, on the other hand, often seeks to change audience attitudes.

Persuasive Speeches

Persuasion is the process of motivating someone, through communication, to change a particular belief, attitude, or behavior. It is not the same as coercion or forcing someone to do something. Persuasive speaking can be classified three different ways. First, it can be classified by type of proposition, such as facts (whether something is true or false), value (whether some idea, person, or object has worth), or policy (whether a specific course of action should be taken). Persuasion can also be categorized based on the desired outcome, whether it is to convince an audience of something or to go further and move audience members to behave in a certain way. Finally, persuasion can be classified based on the directness of the appeal, whether it is an outright request or a more indirect one.

Persuasion Is Usually Incremental

Persuasion is a process. When it is successful, it generally succeeds over time, usually in small increments. One persuasive speech may be but a single step in an overall persuasive campaign. The best example of this is the various communications that take place during the months of a political campaign. Candidates watch the opinion polls carefully, adjusting their appeals.

Persuasion Can Be Ethical

Even when they understand the difference between persuasion and coercion, some people are still uncomfortable with the idea of persuasive speaking. They may associate it with pushy salespeople or unscrupulous politicians. And it's true, persuasive speaking can be used by unethical speakers for unethical purposes. However, it is also through persuasion that we may influence others' lives in worthwhile ways. Whether it's convincing a loved one to seek treatment, friends to volunteer for a worthwhile cause, or an employer to hire you for a job, persuasion can be ethical. Persuasion is considered ethical if it is in the best interests of the audience and it does not depend on false or misleading information to change an audience's attitude or behavior.

Speeches to Entertain

When people hear the phrase "speaking to entertain," they often think of stand-up comics and **masters of ceremony** (MCs or emcees) for special events. In fact, speaking to entertain is used in a wide variety of what is known as **special occasion speaking**. This term is reserved for speeches that are not primarily informative or persuasive in nature, and are not

> **persuasion**
> The act of motivating a listener, through communication, to change a particular belief, attitude, value, or behavior.

> What is the main difference between an informative and a persuasive speech?

> **master of ceremonies (MC or emcee)**
> The official host of a staged event.

> **special occasion speaking**
> Speeches that are not primarily informative or persuasive in nature, and are presented as part of an event.

In *The Wolf of Wall Street*, Leonardo DiCaprio plays Jordan Belfort, a spellbinding speaker who uses his persuasive powers for unethical purposes.

Q How can you guard against being influenced by unethical speakers?

presented as part of our jobs or everyday routines. These speeches are presented at a special event, such as a wedding, a memorial service, an awards presentation, a retirement, or a banquet, and they often include humor. Although humor may be used to great effect in informative and persuasive speaking, it is the hallmark of entertainment speaking.

OBJECTIVE 14.2

Explain the techniques of informative speaking, and use them to present an effective informative speech.

TECHNIQUES OF INFORMATIVE SPEAKING

The techniques of informative speaking are based on a number of principles of human communication in general, and public speaking specifically, which help an audience understand and care about your speech. To deliver an effective informative speech, you must define a specific purpose, make it easy for your audience to listen, use clear and simple language, emphasize important points, and generate audience involvement.

Define a Specific Informative Purpose

Any good speech, but especially an informative one, must be based on a purpose statement that is audience oriented, precise, and attainable. An **informative purpose statement** is generally worded to stress audience knowledge, ability, or both:

> *After listening to my speech, my audience will be able to recall the three most important questions to ask when shopping for a smart phone.*

> *After listening to my speech, my audience will be able to identify the four reasons that online memes go viral.*

> *After listening to my speech, my audience will be able to discuss the pros and cons of using drones in warfare.*

Notice that in each of these purpose statements a specific verb such as *recall*, *identify*, or *discuss* points out what the audience will be able to do after hearing the speech. Other key verbs for informative purpose statements include these:

Accomplish	Choose	Explain	Name	Recognize
Analyze	Contrast	Integrate	Operate	Review
Apply	Describe	List	Perform	Summarize

A clear, informative purpose statement will lead to a clear thesis statement, which presents the central idea of your speech. Sometimes your thesis statement will just preview the central idea:

> *Today's smartphones have so many features that it is difficult for the uninformed consumer to make a choice.*

> *Understanding why memes go viral could make you very wealthy someday.*

> *Soldiers and civilians have different views on the morality of drones.*

At other times, the thesis statement will delineate the main points of that speech:

> *When shopping for a smart phone, the informed consumer seeks to balance price, dependability, and user friendliness.*

> *The four basic principles of aerodynamics—lift, thrust, drag, and gravity—can explain why memes go viral.*

> *Drones can save the lives of soldiers but cost the lives of civilians.*

Setting a clear informative purpose will help keep you focused as you prepare and present your informative speech.

> **informative purpose statement**
> A sentence that tells what knowledge your audience will gain by listening to your speech.

Make It Easy for the Audience to Listen

Keep in mind the complex nature of listening, discussed in Chapter 5, and make it easy for your audience members to hear, pay attention, understand, and remember. This means that, as you put your speech together, you should take into consideration techniques that recognize the way human beings process information.

Limit the Amount of Information You Present

You probably won't have enough time to transmit all your research to your audience in one sitting. It's better to make careful choices about the three to five main ideas you want to get across and then develop those ideas fully. Too much information leads to overload, anxiety, and a lack of attention on the part of your audience.

Transition from Familiar to Newer Information

Based on your audience analysis (Chapter 12), you should move members of your audience from information that is likely to be familiar to them to your newer information. For example, if you are giving a speech about how the stock market works, you could compare the daily activity of a broker with that of a salesperson in a retail store, or you could compare the idea of capital growth (a new concept to some listeners) with interest earned in a savings account (a more familiar concept).

Transition from Simple to More Complex Information

Just as you move your audience members from the familiar to the unfamiliar, you can move them from the simple to the complex. An average college audience, for example, might be able to understand the complexities of genetic modification if you begin first with the concept of inherited characteristics.

Use Clear, Simple Language

Another technique for effective informative speaking is to use clear language, which means using precise, simple wording and avoiding jargon. As you plan your speech, make sure you use words that are familiar to your audience. Important ideas do not have to sound complicated. Along with simple, precise vocabulary, you should also strive for a direct, short sentence structure.

Emphasize Important Points

One specific principle of informative speaking is to stress the important points in your speech. This can be done through repetition and the use of signposts.

Repetition

Repetition is one of the age-old rules of learning. Humans are more likely to understand information that is stated more than once. This is especially true in a speaking situation, because, in most cases your audience members cannot go back to reread something they have missed.

Of course, simply repeating something in the same words would likely bore the audience members who actually are paying attention, so effective speakers learn to say the same thing in more than one way. Kathy Levine, a student at Oregon State University, used this technique in her speech on contaminated dental water:

> The problem of dirty dental water is widespread. In a nationwide 20/20 investigation, the water used in approximately 90% of dental offices is dirtier than the water found in public toilets. This means that 9 out of 10 dental offices are using dirty water on their patients.[1]

Redundancy can be effective when you use it to emphasize important points.[2] It is ineffective, however, when used with obvious, trivial, or boring points or when repeated to excess. There is no sure rule for making certain you have not overemphasized a point. You just have to use your best judgment.

How can you determine the right amount of repetition to emphasize your most important points?

Signposts

Another way to emphasize important material is by using **signposts**: words or phrases that emphasize the importance of what you are about to say. You can state, simply enough, "What I'm about to say is important," or you can use some variation of that statement: "But listen to this … ," or "The most important thing to remember is … ," or "The three keys to this situation are…."

> **signpost**
> A word or phrase that emphasizes the importance of what you are about to say.

Generate Audience Involvement

The final technique for effective informative speaking is to get your audience involved in your speech. **Audience involvement** is the level of commitment and attention that listeners devote to a speech. Educational psychologists have long known that the best way to teach people something is to have them do it. Social psychologists have added to this rule by proving, in many studies, that participating in an interaction increases audience comprehension of, and agreement with, the message being presented.

There are many ways to encourage audience involvement in your speech. One way is to follow the rules for good delivery by maintaining enthusiasm, energy, and eye contact. Other methods include having your audience actually do something during your speech or holding a question-and-answer period.

> **audience involvement**
> The level of commitment and attention that listeners devote to a speech.

Use Audience Participation

Having your listeners actively do something during your speech through **audience participation** is one way to increase their involvement in your message. For example, if you were giving a demonstration on isometric exercises (muscle-building exercises, which don't require too much room for movement), you could have the entire audience stand up and do one

> **audience participation**
> Having your listeners actually do something during your speech.

When asked at the Miss Teen USA pageant why a fifth of Americans could not locate the United States on a world map, Caitlin Upton provided an awkward and incoherent response, making it clear she had not listened to the question.

Q *How can you recover after responding ineffectively to an audience member's question?*

or two sample exercises. If you were explaining how to fill out a federal income-tax form, you could give each class member a sample form to fill out as you explain it. Outlines and checklists can be used in a similar manner for just about any speech. Figure 14-1 shows how one student used audience participation to demonstrate the various restrictions that were once placed on voting rights.

Have a Question-and-Answer Period

Another way to increase audience involvement that is nearly always appropriate if time allows is to answer questions at the end of your speech. You should encourage your audience to ask questions. The following suggestions may increase your effectiveness in answering them:

> **Listen to the substance of the question.** Don't zero in on irrelevant details. Instead, listen for the big picture, the basic, overall question that is being asked. If you are not really sure what the substance of a question is, ask the questioner to paraphrase it. Don't be afraid to let the questioners do their share of the work.

Voting is something that a lot of us may take for granted. Today, the only requirements for voting are that you are a U.S. citizen aged 18 or older who has lived in the same place for at least 30 days and that you have registered. But it hasn't always been that way. Americans have had to struggle for the right to vote. I'd like to illustrate this by asking everyone to please stand.

[Wait, prod class to stand.]

I'm going to ask some questions. If you answer no to any question, please sit down.

Have you resided at the same address for at least one year? If not, sit down. Residency requirements of more than 30 days weren't abolished until 1970.

Are you white? If not, sit down. The 15th Amendment gave non-whites the right to vote in 1870, but many states didn't enforce it until the late 1960s.

Are you male? If not, sit down. The 19th Amendment only gave women the right to vote in 1920.

Do you own a home? If not, sit down. Through the mid-1800s only property owners could vote.

Are you Protestant? If not, sit down. That's right. Religious requirements existed in the early days throughout the country.

Source: New York Public Interest Research Group, Brooklyn College chapter. (2004). Voter registration project.

Figure 14-1 Using Audience Participation

Paraphrase confusing or quietly asked questions. Use the active listening skills described in Chapter 5. You can paraphrase the question in just a few words: "If I understand your question, you are asking _____. Is that right?"

Avoid defensive reactions to questions. Even if the questioner seems to be calling you a liar or stupid or biased, try to listen to the substance of the question and not to the possible personality attack.

Answer the question briefly. Then check the questioner's comprehension of your answer by observing his or her nonverbal response or by asking, "Does that answer your question?"

Explain the techniques of persuasive speaking, and use them to present an effective persuasive speech.

TECHNIQUES OF PERSUASIVE SPEAKING

> **persuasive speaking**
Reason-giving discourse that involves proposing claims and backing up those claims with proof.

> **proof**
Statements explaining why your claims are true, along with evidence that backs up those claims.

> **speech to change attitudes**
Persuasion designed to change the way audiences think about a topic.

> **speech to change behavior**
Persuasion designed to change audience actions.

The guidelines for informative speaking also form the foundation for persuasive speaking. **Persuasive speaking** has been defined as "reason-giving discourse." Its principal technique involves proposing claims and then backing up those claims with **proof**. Proof includes statements of reasons explaining why your claims are true, along with evidence in the form of the supporting material discussed in Chapter 12.

Preparing an effective persuasive speech isn't easy, but it can be made easier by observing some simple guidelines. These include writing a persuasive purpose statement, structuring the message carefully and strategically, avoiding fallacies, adapting to your audience, and establishing common ground and credibility.

Set a Specific Persuasive Purpose

Just as an informative speech should have a clear purpose statement, a persuasive speech should have one as well. Remember that your objective in a persuasive speech is to move the audience to a specific, attainable attitude or behavior.

In a **speech to change attitudes**, the purpose statement should stress an attitude:

After listening to my speech, my audience members will agree that steps should be taken to save whales from extinction.

In a **speech to change behavior**, the purpose statement will stress behavior:

After listening to my speech, my audience members will sign my petition.

Your purpose statement should always be specific, attainable, and worded from the audience's point of view. "The purpose of my speech is to save the whales" is not a purpose statement that has been carefully thought out. Your audience members wouldn't likely be able to jump into the ocean and save the whales, even if they wanted to. However, they might be able to support a specific piece of legislation.

A clear, specific purpose statement will help you stay on track throughout all the stages of preparing your persuasive speech. Because the main purpose of your speech is to have an effect on your audience, you have a continual test that you can use for every idea and every piece of evidence. The question you ask is "Will this help me to get the audience members to think/feel/behave in the manner I have described in my purpose statement?" If the answer is "yes," you forge ahead.

Structure Your Speech Strategically

One of the keys to delivering a speech that is persuasive is structuring your message carefully. A sample structure of the body of a persuasive speech is outlined in Figure 14-2. With this structure, if your objective is to change attitudes, you concentrate on the first two components: establishing the problem and describing the solution. If your objective is to change behavior, you add the third component, describing the desired audience reaction.

There are, of course, other structures for persuasive speeches. However, the steps outlined in Figure 14-2 can easily be applied to most persuasive topics.

Describe the Problem

In order to convince an audience that something should be changed, you have to show members that a problem exists and that it affects them in some way. For example, if your thesis were "This town needs a shelter for homeless families," you would need to show that there are, indeed, homeless families (perhaps through the use of statistics) and that the plight of these homeless families is serious (perhaps using an effective anecdote). However, it's not enough to prove that a problem exists. Your next challenge is to show your listeners that the problem affects them in some way.[3]

If your prespeech analysis shows that audience members may not feel sympathetic to your topic, you will need to explain why your topic is, indeed, a problem that they should recognize. For example, in a speech about the plight of the homeless, you might need to establish that most

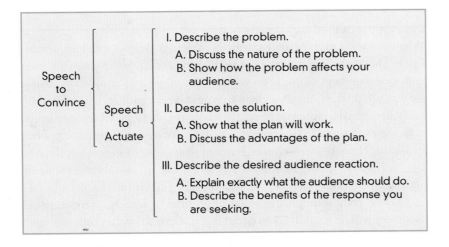

Figure 14-2 Sample Structure for a Persuasive Speech

homeless people are not lazy, able-bodied drifters who choose to panhandle and steal instead of work. You could cite respected authorities, give examples, and maybe even show photographs to demonstrate that some homeless people are hardworking but unlucky parents and innocent children who lack shelter owing to forces beyond their control.

Describe the Solution

Your next step in persuading your audience members is to convince them that there is an answer to the problem you have just introduced. Skeptical listeners might agree with the desirability of your solution but still not believe that it has a chance of succeeding. In the speech about shelters for the homeless discussed previously, you would need to prove that the establishment of a shelter can help unlucky families get back on their feet—especially if your audience analysis shows that some listeners might view such a shelter as a way of coddling people who are too lazy to work.

You also need to describe in specific terms how your solution will lead to the desired changes. This is the step in which you paint a vivid picture of the benefits of your proposal. In the speech proposing a shelter for homeless families, the benefits you describe would probably include these:

1. Families will have a safe place to stay, free of the danger of living on the street.
2. Parents will have the resources that will help them find jobs: an address, phone, clothes washers, and showers.
3. The police won't have to apply antivagrancy laws (such as prohibitions against sleeping in cars) to people who aren't the intended target of those laws.
4. The community (including your listeners) won't need to feel guilty about ignoring the plight of unfortunate citizens.

Describe the Desired Audience Response

When you want to go beyond a strategy to change attitudes and use a strategy to change behavior, you need to describe exactly what you want your audience members to do. Then you need to make it as simple as possible for them to do it. If you want them to vote in a referendum, tell them when and where to go to vote and how to go about registering, if necessary (some activists even provide transportation). If you're asking them to support a legislative change, *you* write the letter or draft a petition and ask them to sign it. If you're asking for a donation, give audience members a stamped, addressed envelope and simple forms that they can return easily.

While your solution might be important to society, your audience members will be most likely to adopt it if you can show that they will get a personal payoff. Explain that saying "no" to a second drink before driving will not only save lives but also help your listeners avoid expensive court costs, keep their insurance rates low, and prevent personal humiliation. Show how helping to establish and staff a homeless shelter can lead to personal feelings of satisfaction and provide an impressive demonstration of community service on a job-seeking résumé.

Use Monroe's Motivated Sequence

Describing the problem and the solution makes up the basic structure for any persuasive speech. However, the best persuasive speeches do far more than the basic minimum. They use the **Motivated Sequence** mentioned in Chapter 12 and described in Figure 14-3.[4] To use the motivated sequence, break the problem down into an attention step and a need step, and break the solution down into a satisfaction step, a visualization step, and an action step. In a speech on organ donation, the motivated sequence might break down as follows:

> **> motivated sequence**
> A five-step persuasive organizational pattern.

I. The attention step draws attention to your subject.
   Someday, someone you know may be on an organ donation list; it might even be you.

II. The need step establishes the problem.
    There is a lack of life-saving organs.

III. The satisfaction step proposes a solution.
     Organ donation benefits both the donor's family and the recipient.

IV. The visualization step describes the results of the solution.
    Donating an organ could be one of the greatest gifts you could ever give.

V. The action step is a direct appeal for the audience to do something.
   Sign an organ donor card today.

STEP	FUNCTION	IDEAL AUDIENCE RESPONSE
❑ 1. Attention	to get audience to listen	"I want to hear what you have to say."
❑ 2. Need	to get audience to feel a need or desire	"I agree. I have that need/desire."
❑ 3. Satisfaction	to tell audience how to fill need or desire	"I see your solution will work."
❑ 4. Visualization	to get audience to see benefits of solution	"This is a great idea."
❑ 5. Action	to get audience to take action	"I want it."

Figure 14-3 The Five Steps of Monroe's Motivated Sequence

Structure Your Argument Carefully

In its purest form, argumentation provides an audience with a series of statements, backed up with support, which then lead to the conclusion the speaker is trying to establish. A **claim** is an expressed opinion that the speaker would like the audience to accept. The primary components of arguments are claims, subclaims, evidence, and then reasoning that links them all together.

Claims and Subclaims

Although you are likely to make claims in any kind of speech, they are most important in persuasive speeches. Within a persuasive speech, several claims and subsidiary claims, or subclaims, are usually advanced. These are organized according to the rules of outlining discussed in Chapter 12.

For example, in a speech on the health hazards of fast food, one claim might be backed up as follows:

A. Soft drinks are bad for you.
1. Soft drinks contain empty calories, which are stored within the body as fat.
2. The sugar in soft drinks rots your teeth.
3. Soft drinks actually make you thirsty.

Some subclaims will need further subclaims to back them up:

3. Soft drinks make you thirsty.⁵
   a. Sugared drinks are absorbed more slowly than water.
   b. You need fluid to digest sugar, so sugar actually causes you to lose fluid.
   c. Caffeine is a mild diuretic, so it increases water loss.

The structure of every argument is different. Even the *same* argument might be structured differently for different audiences. A claim that will be accepted at face value by one audience may need a number of subclaims with another audience.

Take the following proposition:

We should do away with the tolls on our local bridge.

If you were speaking to an audience of residents of your town who were uniformly fed up with the inconvenience of those tollbooths, you might be able to advance the following claim without subclaims backing it up:

A. The traffic delays caused by the tollbooths are bad for the community.

However, were you to advance the same argument to a group of state legislators, some of whom had no experience with the tollbooths or the delays they cause, you might have to back up your claim with subclaims:

> claim
An expressed opinion that the speaker would like the audience to accept.

A. The traffic delays caused by the tollbooths are bad for the community.
1. The delays harm local businesses.
2. The delays cause a waste of fuel.
3. The delays increase air pollution.

For the same proposition with a third audience—one concerned about the income produced by the tolls—you might have to add a second claim:

B. The same revenue could be generated through taxes.

For yet another audience, you might have to back up that claim with subclaims:

B. The same revenue could be generated through taxes.
1. Only a slight increase in real estate taxes would be necessary.
2. Residents would be willing to pass such a tax proposal, because they hate the traffic tie-ups.

Evidence

Evidence is supporting material that the speaker uses to prove any type of claim. All of the forms of support discussed in Chapter 12 can be used to back up your persuasive arguments. Your objective is to find the perfect example, description, analogy, anecdote, statistic, or quotation to establish the truth of your claim in the minds of your specific audience.

> **evidence**
> Supporting material that the speaker uses to prove a type of claim.

The Toulmin Model

In its most basic form, a model of argument proposed by philosopher Stephen Toulmin calls for every claim to be supported not only with evidence but with a **warrant** that ties the claim and evidence together.[6] A warrant, in this sense, is a statement that justifies the use of evidence for a particular claim. The Toulmin model is demonstrated in Figure 14-4.

The point of the Toulmin model is to help you examine every claim to determine if it requires evidence to back it up, and then to examine all of the evidence to see if a warrant is needed to justify the claim. Sometimes neither the evidence nor the warrant needs to be stated out loud. For example, a typical college audience would accept the following claim today: *Cigarette smoking is dangerous to your health.*

After all, such an audience would be familiar with the research linking smoking to respiratory and heart diseases. However, if you were speaking to a group of tobacco company executives, you might need evidence to back up that claim and a warrant to prove that the evidence is justified in light of the claim. If you check your arguments by applying the Toulmin model to each claim you make, you increase the chances that your audience will believe what you say.

> **warrant**
> In the Toulmin Model, this is used to tie the claim and evidence together.

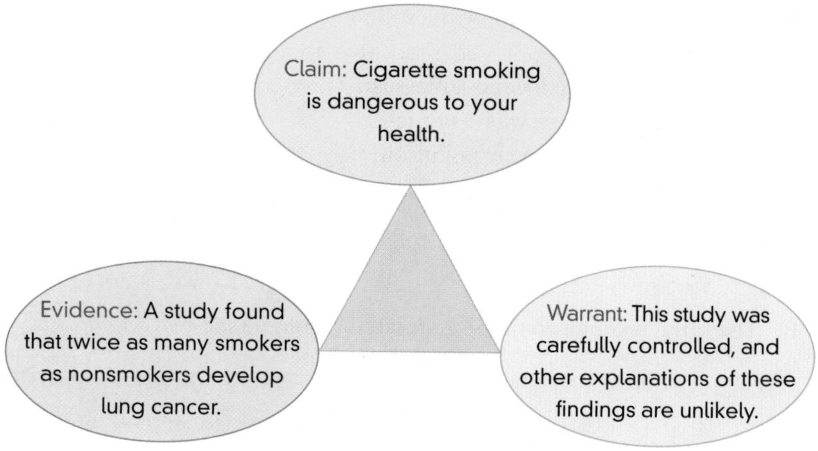

Figure 14-4 The Toulmin Model

Avoid Fallacies

Not only is it important to organize your argument carefully, it's also essential to ensure that the claims and arguments you make within the speech are logical and sound. A **fallacy** (from the Latin word meaning "false") is an error in logic. Although the original meaning of the term implied purposeful deception, most logical fallacies are not recognized as such by those who use them. Scholars have devoted lives and volumes to the description of various types of logical fallacies.[7] Here are some of the most common ones to keep in mind and avoid when building your persuasive argument:[8]

Ad Hominem

In an **ad hominem fallacy** the speaker attacks the integrity of a person in order to weaken the argument. Consider this one: "All this talk about 'family values' is hypocritical. Take Senator _____, who made a speech about the 'sanctity of marriage' last year. Now it turns out he was having an affair with his secretary, and his wife is suing him for divorce." Although the senator certainly seems to be a hypocrite, his behavior doesn't necessarily weaken the merits of family values.

Reductio ad Absurdum

A **reductio ad absurdum fallacy** unfairly attacks an argument by extending it to such extreme lengths that it looks ridiculous. "If we allow the administration to raise tuition this year, soon they will be raising it every year, and before we know it only the wealthiest students will be able to go to school here." This extension of reasoning doesn't make any sense: One tuition increase doesn't mean that others will occur. This policy might be unwise or unfair, but the *ad absurdum* reasoning doesn't prove it.

> **fallacy**
> An error in logic.

> ***ad hominem* fallacy**
> Fallacious reasoning that attacks the integrity of a person to weaken his or her position.

> ***reductio ad absurdum* fallacy**
> Fallacious reasoning that unfairly attacks an argument by extending it to such extreme lengths that it looks ridiculous.

Either-Or

An **either-or fallacy** sets up false alternatives, suggesting that, if the inferior one must be rejected, then the other must be accepted. "Either we outlaw alcohol in city parks or there will be no way to get rid of drunks." This reasoning overlooks the possibility that there may be other ways to control public drunkenness besides banning all alcoholic beverages.

> **either-or fallacy**
Fallacious reasoning that sets up false alternatives, suggesting that if the inferior one must be rejected, then the other must be accepted.

Post Hoc Ergo Propter Hoc

A **post hoc fallacy** mistakenly assumes that one event causes another because they occur sequentially. For example, one critic of education pointed out that the increase in sexual promiscuity among adolescents began about the same time that the courts prohibited prayer in public schools. A causal link in this case may exist: Decreased emphasis on spirituality could contribute to promiscuity. But it would take evidence to establish a *definite* connection between the two phenomena.

> *post hoc* **fallacy**
Fallacious reasoning that mistakenly assumes that one event causes another because they occur sequentially.

Argumentum ad Verecundiam

An **argumentum ad verecundiam fallacy** involves relying on the testimony of someone who is not an authority in the case being argued. Relying on experts is not a fallacy, of course. A professional athlete could be the best person to comment on what it takes to succeed in organized sports. But an *ad verecundiam* fallacy occurs when the athlete tells us why we should buy a certain kind of automobile. When considering endorsements and claims, it's smart to ask yourself whether the source is qualified to make them.

> *argumentum ad verecundiam fallacy*
Fallacious reasoning that tries to support a belief by relying on the testimony of someone who is not an authority on the issue being argued.

Argumentum ad Populum

An **argumentum ad populum fallacy** is based on the notion that, just because many people favor an idea, you should, too (bandwagon appeal). Sometimes, of course, the mass appeal of an idea can be a sign of its merit. If most of your friends have enjoyed a film or a new book, there is probably a good chance that you will, too. But in other cases widespread acceptance of an idea is no guarantee of its validity. In the face of almost universal belief to the contrary, Galileo reasoned accurately that the earth is not the center of the universe, and he suffered for his convictions. The lesson here is simple to comprehend but often difficult to follow: When faced with an idea, don't just follow the crowd. Consider the facts carefully and make up your own mind.

> *argumentum ad populum fallacy*
Fallacious reasoning based on the dubious notion that because many people favor an idea, you should, too.

Adapt to Your Specific Audience

In a persuasive speech, you should appeal to the values of your audience whenever possible, even if they are not *your* strongest values. This does not mean you should pretend to believe in something. It does mean, however, that you have to stress those values that are felt most forcefully by the members of your audience.[9]

In addition, you should use audience analysis (Chapter 12) to predict the type of response you are likely to get. Sometimes you have to

How's your logic?

Identify the logical fallacies used in the following examples:

1. We have to keep controversial speakers from campus or there will be violent protests.
2. If we don't convict these defendants we might as well put out a sign that says "criminals welcome here."
3. I'm going to try that new McDonald's megaburger. Beyoncé says she loves it.
4. Motorcyclists should not be required to wear helmets. In a survey of 2,500 bikers, 98 percent of the respondents said they opposed such laws.
5. Of course, Louie thinks marijuana should be legalized. Louie is a college dropout who hasn't held a job in more than a year.
6. Most people believe we have too much freedom of speech. It is time to consider revoking the First Amendment.
7. President Barack Obama's policies caused the attack on the U.S. Embassy at Bengazi. It happened, after all, during his administration.

The answers appear on p. 367. ●

> **target audience**
The subgroup you must persuade to reach a goal.

pick out one part of your audience—a **target audience** comprising the subgroup you must persuade to reach your goal—and aim your speech mostly at those members. Some of your audience members might be so opposed to what you are advocating that you have no hope of reaching them. Still others might already agree with you, so you don't need to persuade them. A middle portion of your audience members might be undecided or uncommitted, and they would be the most productive target for your appeals.

Establish Common Ground and Credibility

> **common ground**
Similarities between yourself and your audience members.

Establishing **common ground**—stressing as many similarities as possible between yourself and your audience members—helps prove that you understand your audience and gives the audience a reason to listen to you. By showing areas of agreement, you make it easier for the audience to consider settling your one disagreement—the one related to the attitude or behavior you would like them to change.

> **credibility**
The believability of a speaker or other source of information.

Establishing common ground also builds some credibility with the audience. **Credibility** refers to the believability of a speaker. It isn't an objective quality; rather, it is a perception in the minds of the audience. Members of an audience form judgments about the credibility of a speaker based on their perception of many characteristics, including competence, character, and charisma.[10]

Competence refers to the speaker's expertise on the topic. Sometimes this competence can come from personal experience that leads your

In the film *Milk*, civil and human rights leader Harvey Milk (Sean Penn) receives a death threat just moments before speaking. In spite of this, he delivers a stirring and persuasive message by establishing common ground with his audience.

Q *In what ways might you establish common ground with your audience despite facing challenges?*

Why must an audience trust you to be persuaded by your message?

audience to regard you as an authority on the topic. For example, if everyone in the audience knows you've earned big profits in the stock market, they will probably take your investment advice seriously. The other way to be seen as competent is to be well prepared for speaking with a speech that is well researched, organized, and presented.

Character involves the audience's perception of your honesty and impartiality. You should try to find ways to talk about yourself that demonstrate your integrity.

Charisma is the audience's perception of your enthusiasm (how you deliver your remarks) and likeability (which includes how friendly and genuine you are). History and research have shown that audiences are more likely to be persuaded by a charismatic speaker than by a less charismatic one who delivers the same information.

OBJECTIVE 14.4

Explain the techniques of speaking to entertain, and use them to present an entertaining speech.

TECHNIQUES OF SPEAKING TO ENTERTAIN

Informative and persuasive speaking are the usual foci of public speaking classes. Both are enhanced, however, with a consideration of entertainment, and specifically the use of humor. According to the experts, in an informative or persuasive speech, "Humor can show that you have a complete mastery of your subject."[11] It can also make a dull message more interesting, and therefore more effective.[12] Of course, humor is not appropriate for all speeches. Appropriateness, in fact, is one of the three rules to consider before using humor in a speech.

Follow the Rules of Humor

It is easiest to discuss humor by borrowing examples from professional comedians and professional speakers. A word of caution is appropriate: The goal of this discussion is not to make you a professional entertainer. We take professionals as examples only because it pays to learn from the best. From professionals we learn that the requirements for humor include levity, originality, and appropriateness.

Comics Aziz Ansari and Amy Schumer became wildly popular by using their unique and edgy humor.

Q *How can you use humor in ways that will entertain but not offend your audience?*

Levity

Levity is the quality of being light. A speech to entertain does not take itself too seriously. It deals with the serious in an absurd manner or with the absurd in a serious manner. For example, when the Internal Revenue Service was found to have targeted conservative groups for special scrutiny in late 2012, Seth Myers, "Weekend Update" anchor of *Saturday Night Live*, reported the story this way:

> President Obama, this week, denied that he knew about the Inspector General's report detailing the IRS's increased scrutiny of conservative groups. So nothing to worry about, America—There's just a bunch of stuff happening that the President doesn't know about. The President also condemned the IRS for targeting conservative groups for extra scrutiny, saying, "Public service is a solemn privilege." In response, Joe Biden quietly deflated his whoopee cushion.[13]

Originality

Routines such as SNL's "Weekend Update" have become classics. Classic routines, however, are usually not the most effective tactics for an amateur speaker. Anecdotes of your own about strange experiences, strange people, or unique insights into everyday occurrences are the best ingredients for a speech to entertain. Original in this sense does not mean "brand-new." It means "firsthand" or "derived from the source." Take Ellen DeGeneres's observations about air travel:

> The only bad thing about being a comedian is that I have to fly these little commuter airlines to obscure places, little eight-seater planes with an open cockpit, where you can see the pilot reading a manual called "So You Want to Fly a Plane."
>
> The seats recline about an inch, all except for the guy in front of me, whose seat comes back so far I could do dental work on him.
>
> I'm scared of flying. First of all, I don't think we have to go that high in the air. I think they're showing off, those pilots.
>
> And the food is the tiniest little food I've ever seen. I guess they figure everything's relative: You get that high up, you look out the window and then back at your food and you say, "Well, it's as big as that house down there."
>
> Salads are always two pieces of dead lettuce. Salad dressing comes in that astronaut package, so as soon as you open it, it goes on your neighbor's lap. "Could I just dip my lettuce in that? That's a lovely skirt—what is that, silk?"[14]

Somewhere beneath the surface there are two lessons here: First, original anecdotes don't have to be on original topics. Stories on the frustrations of air travel are as common as news stories about crime, but DeGeneres manages to put her own stamp on her observations. Second, original anecdotes are not original in the sense of being "brand-new." They are tested, tried, and true. A comedian who does a "bit" knows it is funny. Comedians generally do not get up in front of an audience with an unproved product. This second lesson is probably the more important one. Test out your humorous anecdotes first.

Appropriateness

Humor must be appropriate to the audience, the speaker, and the occasion. Be careful telling Polish jokes to the Kasimir Pulaski Social Group, or drunk jokes at an Alcoholics Anonymous meeting. Sarah Silverman, for example, is known for delivering shocking jokes juxtaposed with an innocent look. So it might not seem inappropriate for her to say something like this to a late-night audience:

> "I understand that the doctor had to spank me when I was born, but I really don't see any reason why he had to call me a whore."[15]

In most other speaking situations, this same comment would likely be considered inappropriate.

Sometimes humor can be derived from making an inappropriate observation seem more appropriate through the use of a euphemism. David Letterman provided an example:

> One of the reservoirs that supplies about 20 percent of the drinking water here in New York City is going to be closed for a couple of weeks because they found traces of "organic matter" in it. Man, I'll be honest with you, when I read this, it scared the organic matter out of me.[16]

Use the Most Effective Type of Humor

There are many techniques of humor. Physical humor, for example, includes such things as pies in the face, dressing in outlandish outfits, and walking into walls. But physical humor is usually not of much use to the average public speaker. There are several more cerebral techniques that can make your own experiences or insights entertaining, including humorous description, exaggeration, incongruity, **word play**, and satire.

Humorous Description

Humorists have to be sensitive to the scenes in life that sound funny when they are recounted later. They look at life more observantly than everyone else, and point out things that are, upon examination, a little out of whack. For example, when the second Hobbit movie opened in 2013, Craig Ferguson, host of *The Late Late Show With Craig Ferguson*, made fun of the movie this way:

> A big movie opened today—"The Hobbit: The Desolation of Smaug." I want to see it because I love movies about tiny people. In fact, I'll

Would it ever be appropriate to use humor during a eulogy?

> word play
Technique that allows you to create humor by manipulating language.

see anything that stars Tom Cruise. It's hard to believe it's already been a year since the last "Hobbit" movie. Maybe because that last one felt like it was 11 months long. That last "Hobbit" movie was so long, people were growing their own corn to pop.[17]

Of course, humor in that passage does not just rely on description—there is also a suggestion of exaggeration.

Exaggeration

Magnifying description beyond the truth is **exaggeration**, and it is one of the most effective humorous techniques. Consider this example opening a speech:

> In order to prepare today's speech I read 27 books, interviewed 36 experts, ran 14 carefully controlled experiments, and surveyed the entire population of Tanzania. I worked on the speech for over a year, taking only short breaks for sustenance and catnaps. During that time I have lost considerable weight as well as my entire life's savings, and my wife has run off with a used-car salesman from Peoria. I am proud to tell you, though, that it was all worth it, for today I am fully prepared to explain to you *Why Ice Floats*. . . .

> exaggeration
Magnifying description beyond truth.

Incongruity

Statements that are out of place or inconsistent are **incongruities**, and they can also inject humor into a speech. Conan O'Brien used this type of humor when he introduced himself to the graduating class at Dartmouth College:

> Though some of you may see me as a celebrity, you should know that I once sat where you sit. Literally. Late last night I snuck out here and sat in every seat. I did it to prove a point: I am not bright and I have a lot of free time.[18]

> incongruity
Statement that is out of place or inconsistent.

Word Play

A **play on words** allows you to create humor by manipulating language. One way is to place an unexpected ending on a familiar expression:

> Where there's a will, there's a lawsuit.

Another way is to change a word or two in a familiar expression:

> You can lead a man to college, but you can't make him think.

Or just use a common word or expression in an unexpected way:

> I get so tired of putting my cat out at night. I wish he would stop playing with matches.

Steve Martin used a play on words this way:

> I like a woman with a head on her shoulders. I hate necks.[19]

> play on words
Manipulation of language to create humor.

A *pun* is a special type of play on words. It uses a word that sounds like another word but has a different meaning. For example, here's a classic:

I wondered why the baseball was getting bigger. Then it hit me.

Puns should be handled carefully in a speech. They are usually clever rather than funny. They "fool" people rather than entertain. They make people groan, rather than laugh. Therefore, they are a high risk. People have a tendency to think that puns are the lowest form of humor, unless they think of them first, of course. Still, puns can be used sparingly for humorous effect as long as they do not interfere with your message.

Satire

> satire
Humor based on an exposé of human vice or folly.

Humor based on an exposé of human vice or folly is known as **satire** and is considered a much higher form of humor than puns. When Jay Leno learned that the French government, in an attempt to keep the French language pure, had banned American English words that had worked their way into the French language (words such as *le cheeseburger, le bulldozer,* and *le chewing gum*), he announced that we would henceforth exclude the following French words from American English:[20]

FRENCH WORD	WILL NOW BE CALLED
Bidet	Doggy drinking fountain
Hors d'oeuvres	Greasy overpriced Ritz crackers
Maitre'd	Dork in the bad tux
Résumé	Falsified job history
Paté	Gag! What the hell is this?

Satire, as much as any other type of humor, must be handled carefully. It should be appropriate to the speaker, the audience, and the occasion.

No matter what type of humor you use, most professionals would advise you to not try too hard to be funny. If you try too hard, you might reveal a desperation that will make your audience uncomfortable. Professionals advise you to be light, be original, and be appropriate, but let the funny take care of itself. If you do get a laugh, do not talk over it. Wait until the laughter has started to die down before you resume speaking. If you do not get a laugh, keep going as though nothing has happened.

CHECK YOUR UNDERSTANDING

OBJECTIVE 14.1 Distinguish among speeches to inform, persuade, and entertain.

TYPES OF SPEECHES

There are three major types of speeches that, while distinctive, also share aspects in common. A speech to inform seeks to impart knowledge, but it may also be entertaining. A speech to persuade seeks to change audience attitudes or behavior, but it may also be informative and/or entertaining. A speech to entertain uses humor and seeks to relax the audience, but it may also be informative or persuasive in some respects.

Describe the characteristics of your current speech assignment. Which type of speech will it be, based on those characteristics?

OBJECTIVE 14.2 Explain the techniques of informative speaking, and use them to present an effective informative speech.

TECHNIQUES OF INFORMATIVE SPEAKING

To deliver an effective informative speech, you must define a specific purpose, make it easy for your audience to listen, use clear and simple language, emphasize important points through devices like repetition and signposts, and generate audience involvement through audience participation and question-and-answer periods.

Describe the techniques of informative speaking that seem easiest and hardest for you to implement. Why do you think some of the techniques are more difficult than others?

OBJECTIVE 14.3 Explain the techniques of persuasive speaking, and use them to present an effective persuasive speech.

TECHNIQUES OF PERSUASIVE SPEAKING

Preparing an effective persuasive speech starts with the preparation of a persuasive purpose statement. A purpose statement for a speech to change attitudes will stress an attitude; a purpose statement for a speech to change behavior will state the behavior you want to elicit from your audience. In either type, a speech to persuade should be structured strategically. If your objective is to change attitudes, concentrate on establishing a problem and describing a solution. If your objective is to change behavior, also describe the behavior you would like your audience to adopt.

It's also important to ensure that you structure your arguments carefully. The Toulmin model can be used to ensure that every claim you make is supported not only with evidence but with a warrant that ties the claim and evidence together. You should also strive to avoid fallacies in your arguments, adapt your appeals, and establish common ground and credibility with your specific audience.

Explain the aspects of persuasive speaking that might make it more challenging than informative speaking.

OBJECTIVE 14.4 Explain the techniques of speaking to entertain, and use them to present an entertaining speech.

TECHNIQUES OF SPEAKING TO ENTERTAIN

While all types of speeches may include humor, a speech to entertain relies most heavily on the device. Humor must be handled carefully. It requires levity, originality, and appropriateness. Types of humor include humorous description, exaggeration, incongruity, word play, and satire.

Describe speaking situations that might lend themselves to the use of humor. In what situations might humor not be appropriate?

KEY TERMS

HOW'S YOUR LOGIC?

Give yourself one point for each correct answer. Then score yourself as follows:

6–7 You're as logical as Mr. Spock on *Star Trek* (which is to say, very logical). Don't forget to use emotional appeals in your persuasive speech.

4–5 You're about average. Review the section on fallacies one more time.

0–3 Oops. Review the section on fallacies, and find some additional guidelines on fallacies online!

Answers to the logical fallacies assessment on page 358:

1. either-or
2. reduce to the absurd
3. appeal to authority
4. bandwagon
5. ad hominem
6. bandwagon
7. false cause

FOR FURTHER EXPLORATION

For more resources, see the *Essential Communication* website at www .oup.com/us/EC. There you will find a variety of free resources: "Media Room" clips from popular films and television shows to further illustrate important concepts, a list of books and articles, links to descriptions of feature films and television shows at the *Now Playing* website, study aids, and a self-test to check your understanding of the material in this chapter.

INFORMATIVE SPEECH

The following informative speech was presented by Nick Gilyard, a student at Western Kentucky University. He won fourth place at the National Individual Events tournament of the American Forensic Association in April 2014. With this speech, Nick demonstrates how informative and persuasive speaking may sometimes overlap (as mentioned in Chapter 14). Nick seeks to inform his audience about an important study—one that provides significant data on same-sex relationships. Nick does not, however, primarily seek to change attitudes or behavior, as shown in his purpose statement:

> *After listening to my speech, my listeners will understand the key findings from Esther Rothblum's research into the impact of gay civil unions.*

This leads to his thesis statement:

> *Esther Rothblum's study on legal same-sex unions helps us understand this important social phenomenon.*

Nick divides his speech into three main points. His organization is shown in the following outline (numbers in parentheses correspond to paragraphs of the speech):

INTRODUCTION (1–4)
BODY (5–15)
  I. Rothblum's study was carefully set up and designed. (5–7)
    1. Rothblum had an unprecedented study sample. (6)
    2. Rothblum's study design was ideal for long-term study. (7)
  II. Rothblum's study resulted in interesting findings. (8–10)
    1. Same-sex couples reported higher levels of happiness in their relationships than straight couples. (9)
    2. Legal recognition helps couples, gay or straight, sustain a long-term relationship. (10)
  III. Rothblum's study has important implications. (11–15)
    1. Codifying observations as scientifically valid holds great social and legal significance. (12–13)
    2. The civil union population is not representative of minority same-sex couples. (14–15)
CONCLUSION (16)

As you read the speech, notice how Nick structures these points and their related subpoints (as discussed in Chapter 12) while he follows the various guidelines for informative speaking discussed in Chapter 14.

THE TRUTH ABOUT ADAM AND CHRIS

Nick Gilyard

1. Adam and Chris aren't that different from most couples these days. They met online, fell in love and now they blog about it. Their blog, "Tales of the Engayged" showcases the obstacles two gay men encounter getting married in Alabama. They face questions like, how do you fill out a form that only has labels for bride and groom; who picks the color scheme; and are there two bachelor parties?

2. However, like any couple the tougher questions come after the honeymoon. Unfortunately, while straight couples have decades of research to guide their long-term relationships, gay couples get a different response from researchers: "We don't know."

3. Esther Rothblum, a professor at San Diego University, is seeking a better answer. Back in 2000 when Vermont first legalized same sex civil unions, she and a team of researchers took advantage of a unique research opportunity. Their revolutionary study collected data from nearly 1,000 same sex couples concerning division of responsibilities, intimacy, and relationship satisfaction.

4. Ten years later 750 couples remain in the cohort, providing a decade of data. And the National Institute[s] of Health has bestowed 1 million dollars to continue research for another 10 years. Considering the Pew Research Center reports that 71,000 same sex marriages have occurred in America and it's currently legal in seventeen states, it is imperative that we better understand the longest running and most thorough research on long term same sex relationships. So let's first discuss the study itself, next unveil the results, before finally proposing implications and answers.

5. Having a wedding, gay or straight, involves countless hours of planning, preparation, and pinterest. Similarly, Rothblum's study required the proper set up and design.

6. According to the 2006 edition of the *Lesbian and Gay Psychology Review*, 2,473 same-sex couples from all over the nation travelled to Vermont for civil unions in the summer of 2000. Because civil union certificates are treated as public information, these certificates gave researchers access to names, addresses and other specific information about the couples. This was exciting because researchers no longer had to rely on convenience samples, like questionnaires at the local gay bar. They now had access to a more representative nationwide sample. Of the roughly 2500

Nick's introduction gains attention, establishes the relevance of his topic, and provides his thesis statement.

Nick uses a simple human story to transition to more complex technical information throughout this speech.

Statistics are used as supporting material.

Nick establishes his credibility by showing his in-depth knowledge of the topic. What other devices could he have used to establish his credibility?

Again, Nick transitions from simple to more complex information.

Statistics and a citation build Nick's credibility on this topic.

same-sex couples who had civil unions, a whopping 42% were willing to participate.

7. Next, Rothblum compared civil union couples to heterosexual married siblings and their spouses. The inclusion of siblings allowed researchers to compare gay and heterosexual couples of similar ages, family and religious backgrounds. Respondents completed self-report questionnaires with 35 variables including emotional scales seeking to measure levels of commitment, intimacy and equality in the relationship. The researchers published their findings in 2004 and then conducted follow-up surveys in 2008. Dr. Rothblum told ABC News on July 3, 2013 that these participants will always be the longest legally recognized gay couples in the US.

8. Adam nearly had a heart attack when his partner Chris casually mentioned he always thought Adam would take his last name. Likewise Dr. Rothblum's study produced shocking results, and while we can't discuss them all, let's focus on gender norms and breaking up.

9. First, one of the most notable findings was that by nearly every measure, same-sex couples reported higher levels of happiness in their relationships than straight couples. Gay couples reported far less conflict and higher levels of intimacy and affection. Rothblum hypothesizes that gender roles may be partially responsible. She explains that gay relationships tend to be more egalitarian because they don't divide work along traditional gender lines. Same-sex couples have to talk to one another before deciding who takes out the trash and who does the dishes, leading to chores based on preference. In this way same-sex couples can serve as a controlled experiment helping us to see which aspects of marital difficulty are truly rooted in gender.

10. Next, in addition to research concerning staying together, Rothblum also explored why same sex couples break up. The follow up study revealed the breakup rate among non civil unioned gay couples was almost 10 percent, compared to less than 4 percent of gay couples with a civil union. While committed couples are more likely to get a civil union, Rothblum believes it's more complex than that. Her data indicates that legal recognition is the glue that helps couples, gay or straight, sustain a long-term relationship. As one participant responded, "Having a civil union has been good for us. Relationships can be hard, and having at least one formal barrier makes you think twice about splitting up."

Here, Nick develops the next subpoint.

This transition previews the next main point, while establishing that Nick will make it easy for the audience to listen by limiting the amount of information he presents.

Here, Nick develops the next subpoint.

A quotation is used to relate complex information to something simpler.

11. When Adam and Chris tie the knot this fall their lives will forever change. Similarly, Rothblum's work will forever change how we view same sex relationships. Let's explore two implications of her study, concerning hindsight bias and minority voices.

12. With a one million dollar price tag, some have questioned the need for studies such as this. It is tempting to think, well of course same sex couples will split the workload or of course marriage helps couples stay together. But colloquial knowledge is not the same as scientific study. The *Huffington Post* on February 22, 2013 cautions that hindsight bias is a pleasing but dangerous mental error.

13. We tend to undervalue scientific findings that reveal something we suspected through personal experience. However, even if Rothblum's work only confirms stereotypes that we have encountered, codifying those observations as scientifically valid holds great social and legal significance. After all, Supreme Court justices don't make decisions based on anecdote.

14. Finally, when Dr. Rothblum published her findings she explained that the civil union population and therefore her sample is not representative of minority same-sex couples. In the follow-up study, she notes gay couples who have gotten civil unions, domestic partnerships and now even marriages are overwhelmingly white European American.

15. Unfortunately, legal progress has not outpaced stigma in minority communities so these couples often choose family support over legal recognition of their relationship, sacrificing participation in studies such as this one. Over the last decade, Rothblum has made great strides to learn more about how long-term gay relationships work. And while her findings with predominantly white Americans may be applicable to my relationship, until minority communities more fully embrace gay couples, we'll have to wait a little longer for that answer.

16. In the absence of traditional wedding norms Adam and Chris are figuring out what works for them one step at a time. Perhaps future gay couples will look back on their wedding as a guide. Hopefully Dr. Rothblum's study, results, and implications will offer helpful guidance once the wedding is over and their married life begins.

17. Thank you. I have time for a few questions.

Nick transitions to the final main point.

This is the first subpoint.

This is the second subpoint.

Nick's conclusion reviews his main points, restates his thesis, and provides a closing statement.

Nick invites questions from his audience and waits for them.

PERSUASIVE SPEECH

The following persuasive speech was presented by Curt Casper when he was a student at Hastings College. He won second place for this speech at the Interstate Oratorical Association annual contest hosted by James Madison University in 2011.

Curt used a simple problem-effect-solution organizational structure, as seen in his outline, as presented on page 297. He collected his supporting material from a wide range of sources, as seen in his bibliography:

American Association of Suicidology. (2009). *Survivors of Suicide Fact Sheet.* American Association of Suicidology.

American Foundation for Suicide Prevention. (2011). *For the Media.* Retrieved March 15, 2011, from American Foundation for Suicide Prevention: http://www.afsp.org/media

American Foundation for Suicide Prevention. (2011). *Out of the Darkness Community Walks.* (EABnet.) Retrieved March 15, 2011, from SOS-walk.org: http://www.sos-walk.org/sos/index.htm

Belau, D. (2011, March 16). LOSS Team. (C. Casper, Email)

Caruso, K. (2011). *Suicide Survivors: Coping with Rumors and Gossip.* Retrieved March 15, 2011, from Suicide.org: http://www.suicide.org/suicide-survivors-coping-with-rumors-and-gossip.html

Cerel, J., & Jordan, J. R., & Duberstein, P. R. (2008) The Impact of Suicide on the Family. *Crisis Intervention and Suicide Prevention, 29* (1), 38–44.

Evans, D. (2011, February 28). Accidental Death Becomes Suicide When Insurers Dodge Payouts. *Bloomberg Markets Magazine.*

Gearing, R. E., & Lizardi, D. (2009, October). Religion and Suicide. *Journal of Religion and Health, 48* (3), 332–41.

Hudenko, D., & Crenshaw, D. (2010, October 5). *The Relationship between PTSD and Suicide.* Retrieved March 15, 2011, from National Center for PTSD: http://www.ptsd.va.gov/professional/pages/ptsd-suicide.asp

Harvard Mental Health. (2009, November). Supporting Survivors of Suicide Loss. *Harvard Mental Health Letter, 4,* 5.

Hopkins, K. (2010, July 15). Suicides, Attempts Spike Again in Western Alaska Villages. *Anchorage Daily News.*

Insurance.com. (2007, May 17). *Will Mental Illness Affect Your Life Insurance Cost?* Retrieved March 15, 2011, from insurance.com: http://www.insurance.com/life-insurance/health-and-life-insurance/will-mental-illness-affect-your-life-insurance-cost.aspx

Johnson, C. (2011, March 15). Compensability Clauses. (C. Casper, Interviewer)

KHAS-TV. (2011, April 17). Suicide Coverage. (C. Casper, Interviewer)

National Endowment for Financial Education. (2011). *Surviving a Suicide Loss: A Financial Guide*. American Foundation for Suicide Prevention.

Patania, J. (2011, March 16). Program Assistant for American Association of Suicidology. (C. Casper, Interviewer)

University of Nebraska Public Policy Center. (2010). *2010 Nebraska State Suicide Prevention Summit*. Hastings: University of Nebraska-Lincoln.

As you read Curt's speech, notice how he follows the techniques of persuasive speaking outlined in Chapter 14. Take special notice of how carefully he describes the problem, the solution, and the desired audience response.

SURVIVOR SUPPORT

Curt Casper

1. It is the four-year anniversary since my dad decided to drive in front of a train, dying by suicide. My family has never been the same. My little brother Blake, who was ten at the time, has now been in more than a dozen different homes and has been diagnosed with post-traumatic stress syndrome 3 times. While there was initial help from friends and relatives, the support system quickly went away and there was nowhere my family could turn to for help.

2. Three days before my dad killed himself, I received a hug asking for help. I refused to see the pain that my dad was suffering and kept it to myself. Six months later, I wanted to drive in front of a train, because I blamed myself.

3. My brother and I are not alone. Jill Pantania of the American Association of Suicidology recently told me, "there are 6 million people in the US that currently mourn the death of a loved one by suicide. And that number grows by 190,000 each year."

4. Our society is suffering from a mental health stigma. We cannot change this stigma until we stop suicide survivors from suffering alone. Suicide survivors include friends, families and loved ones who are left behind to deal with a suicide. The *Harvard Mental Health* newsletter of November 2009 notes that the death of a loved

Curt begins with a startling statement about his personal experience. This sets the tone for the speech, and helps establish his personal credibility.

Curt expands on his personal experience with another powerful statement. In Monroe's Motivated Sequence, this would be called the attention step.

Curt backs up a series of claims with warrants and evidence.

Here, Curt states his thesis, defines a key term ("suicide survivors"), and provides statistics.

one because of suicide leads to a higher risk for several types of psychiatric disorders. According to the *Hampton Roads Survivors of Suicide* website, "Survivors are 5 times more likely to commit suicide themselves." In other words, suicide isn't the end of a problem for anyone—it's often the starting point for more crises. We all have to become the support that survivors so desperately need.

5. Today, I'd like to tell you how we can all facilitate survivor support. First, though, we need to recognize the reasons suicide survivors do not receive the help they deserve. Second, we need to examine the impact of that lack of help. And then finally, we can consider some possible solutions to give survivors the hope they deserve.

6. The deficiencies in survivor support can be found on both a societal and economic level.

7. First, it can take a while to get over a suicide because our society refuses to use the word "suicide." The website *Suicide.org* says we as a society make up excuses for the suicide, like *it was his time to go;* yet we don't use the word "suicide."

8. This negative connotation regarding suicide is furthered by religious doctrine, because some religions believe that suicide is a one-way ticket to hell. This is confirmed in the essay "Religion and Suicide," published in the *Journal of Religion and Health* in 2009.

9. There are even guidelines in place restricting the use of the word in the media, according to the *American Foundation for Suicide Prevention.* For instance, KHAS-TV said in a personal correspondence on April 14, 2011 that they did not cover a student's death in December because it was suicide, yet in March they covered a student's death because she died from a skiing accident and not from suicide. These guidelines are in place to prevent other suicides. However, these same guidelines implicitly affirm the messages of guilt and stigma for the family and other survivors.

10. Second, as the *National Endowment for Financial Education* states, "someone getting over a suicide will face financial turmoil." Life insurance companies do not provide benefits if a suicide occurs within 24 months of signing with the company. This is known as the "suicide clause." In some cases, this makes it difficult to pay for the funeral arrangements and other financial obligations. For example, one mother in Nebraska lost her husband to suicide ten months after signing with the insurance company. She could not even afford to send her son, who witnessed his father shooting himself, to counseling. In other cases the money *is* received, but it

A transition takes the form of a preview of main points.

Here is another transition in the form of a preview of two subpoints.

Curt backs up his first subpoint with information from a website . . .

. . . and a printed essay . . .

. . . and an example that he found in an email interview.

Curt introduces his second subpoint with a citation, and then he backs it up with an example.

is received in one large sum, and survivors feel guilty about receiving it. They might not want to touch the money, or they might just waste it, rather than saving it for a time of need.

11. With an understanding of the causes that undermine survivor support, we can consider the impact of this lack of support, including profound grief and post traumatic stress disorder on the part of the survivor.

12. First, a suicide causes more grief than most normal deaths, as there are unanswered questions. Survivors wonder *why* and *what could I have done*, which can lead to depression and further suicides, as noted by the *Journal of Crisis Intervention and Suicide Prevention* in 2008. For example, a small community in Alaska, Yukon-Kuskwim Delta, saw 9 people between the age of 17 and 22 commit suicide within only a few weeks of each other. According to the *Anchorage Daily News* of July 15, 2010, there was a chain reaction as each person was affected by the previous death. Alaska is not alone; my campus experienced the suicide cycle back in December.

13. Second, because denial and shock are often the first emotions felt by survivors, it can take years for bereavement, creating a condition known as Post Traumatic Stress Disorder, or PTSD. On average, it takes four and a half years after a suicide before a survivor seeks help. I learned that from Dr. Dan Belau, a Mental Health Advocate, in personal correspondence during March, 2011. According to Dr. Belau, PTSD leads to nightmares and flashbacks, ultimately making it difficult for a survivor to effectively function in society. We have all seen the effects of post traumatic stress on soldiers fighting overseas, but often people don't realize that we are at war *here* with suicide.

14. *The National Center for PTSD* website, which I accessed in October 2010, says there is a "direct link between survivors of suicide and PTSD." Even small events, like seeing someone else's dad come to watch your sports event or come to a birthday party can result in a paralysis of emotions for survivors—even many years after the initial suicide.

15. I was eventually able to get help and I no longer blame myself. I have not contemplated suicide since I got the help I needed. However, many survivors simply do not get help. Survivor support solutions can and should be facilitated on two levels: through survivor-supporters and through survivors themselves.

16. First, our lawmakers could be survivor-supporters by easing the red tape on insurance policies. Insurance Agent Caleb Johnson, in a personal interview on March 15th, 2011 says, "A simple solution

This is a clearly stated transition from Curt's first to his second main point.

Here, Curt supplies examples from research and personal experience.

This is Curt's next subpoint.

Although Curt words this example as a generality, his audience knows he is referring to personal experience here, which provides a transition to his next personal statement.

Here is a transition in the form of a preview of final subpoints.

Curt develops his first subpoint with a quotation.

would be to set a standard that insurance companies give back the premiums that were paid before the suicide." If someone is willing to spend money on insurance, they should know their loved ones would be taken care of if a suicide occurs. If you wanted to become a survivor supporter, you could encourage insurance reform by sending a brief email about this issue to your local lawmakers.

17. On a more personal level, if you have a friend who is a survivor, just be there for them by giving them a list of resources. I've prepared a CD with this type of resources, such as inexpensive but effective councilors, along with a list of websites that can help supporters and survivors. I'd be glad to give you a copy of this CD after my speech.

18. As a survivor supporter, you need to use the word "suicide" when talking to survivors. This will ease their grief, because it will help make suicide visible. While attending an Active Minds Conference, I was able to see a display of 1,100 backpacks that represents the number of collegiate suicides annually. The display entitled Send Silence Packing travels across the nation to show the effects suicide has on all. There are stories of survivors who have dealt with a suicide in each backpack. In addition, the cool part is, you can get the backpacks in your communities—that information will also be available at the end of my speech.

19. Second, I urge survivors to share their stories to help others in similar situations. I use my story, because I know I cannot change what happened to my dad, but by sharing my story I can help other families.

20. The first step is for survivors to realize that they are not at fault for what happened. Yes, the grief is going to be difficult to handle, but it can get easier. We as a community of survivors need to be there for each other. I am currently a member of a LOSS team, which is a group of individuals who are survivors and want to help other survivors. When there is a suicide in the area, the team is dispatched to the family. Dr. Dan Belau, the mental health advocate I mentioned earlier, told me, "the time it takes for a survivor to seek help changes from four and a half years to 39 days" when resources like the LOSS team are provided.

21. Finally, survivors, remember it's never too late to request the help you deserve. If it takes four and a half years to get the courage and seek unsolicited help, how long might it take before we come to terms with the event? Survivor support cannot be rushed; there is no statute of limitations on grief.

Curt uses a direct statement of his next subpoint.

Curt develops his next subpoint with a descriptive anecdote.

20. LOSS stands for Local Outreach to Suicide Survivors. Curt felt the acronym was intuitive and did not require an explanation. Do you agree?

22. I realize this is a tough topic to talk about. That's why I have created this CD with a list of resources that can help you and survivors. Please take one of these. In fact, take a few of them so you can give them to others, because while a survivor will never know the reasons why a suicide occurs, having a better understanding of how to deal with the loss will help ease the grieving mind.

23. I have seen firsthand how a suicide can destroy a family. In light of the four year anniversary of my father's death, I hope that my brother, Blake and the rest of my family will be able to pick up the pieces and begin to rebuild our family. And, while the road to recovery will still be tough and has been tough, I know my dad would have wanted us to move on and know that everything is okay.

Curt picks up the CD here so audience members can see it, making his desired response as easy as possible for the audience to follow.

Curt uses powerful personal experience as supporting material in this conclusion.

SPEECH TO ENTERTAIN

The following speech to entertain was presented by Hananiah Wiggins, a student at Illinois State University. With it, he won second place in After Dinner Speaking at the 2014 National Individual Events Tournament of the American Forensic Association. The AFA defines After Dinner Speaking as "An original, humorous speech by the student, designed to exhibit sound speech composition, thematic coherence, direct communicative public speaking skills, and good taste. The speech should not resemble a nightclub act, an impersonation, or comic dialogue. Audio-visual aids may or may not be used to supplement and reinforce the message. Minimal notes are permitted. Maximum time limit is 10 minutes."[1]

Hananiah's speech demonstrates the overlap among speech types. The primary objective of this speech is to entertain. Much of it, however, is a parody of a more formal persuasive speech, and Hananiah does make important points along the way.

Hananiah organizes his speech as follows (numbers in parentheses correspond to paragraphs of the speech):

INTRODUCTION (1–6)
BODY (7–25)
  I. There are two primary causes of not taking black studies seriously. (8–14)
      1. We don't view black studies as a legitimate field in higher education. (9–11)
      2. We have a false sense of knowledge about black culture. (12–14)
  II. There are two primary effects of not taking black studies seriously. (15–20)
      1. Black students feel devalued. (16–18)
      2. All students gain inaccurate knowledge about black culture. (19–20)
  III. There are two primary solutions for not taking black studies seriously. (21–25)
      1. More black studies programs are needed. (22–23)
      2. There needs to be recognition that black studies are for more than just black people. (23–25)
CONCLUSION (26)

THE MLK PARTY

Hananiah Wiggins

1. This past January, while I was Facebook chatting my mom the 11 reasons why we shouldn't be Snapchat friends, I got an invite to a Martin Luther King Day party. First thought, "Shots on a Monday? Clutch. Second thought, I can wear my MLK Costume! It's just me in a suit. This is it."

2. So I went back to the invite to check the deets. I wanted to see if it would be appropriate to bring my famous Coretta Scott King crab legs. It wasn't. The white host had a different menu in mind. He said to honor the date and Black History Month he would be making fried chicken, kool aid and serving ice-cold watermelon. Which is AWFUL, because everyone knows white people can't make kool aid. It just tastes like blue water.

3. Perhaps the most disturbing part of the invitation was the following sentence: "Lets all pretend to be black studies majors for a day" to which I responded, "Offensive white man said what now?"

4. However, he wasn't the only one who's been looking at black studies recently. Insidehighered.com, on May 9th 2012, in its article "The Trouble with Black Studies," states black studies was undeniably a product of radical activism in the late 1960s and early '70s. So, post slavery, pre-Destiny's Child, administrators established courses only as a concession to student protesters who had a strongly politicized notion of the field's purpose.

5. However, since the creation of black studies America has continuously delegitimized it as a field in education. Putting down black studies not only demeans an entire race of people and their culture, but promotes that it is okay to be ignorant to the cultures of others. For many people like me black studies is a way to not only learn about my culture but to see it being appreciated longer than just the cold ass 28.25 days of February.

6. We need to take black studies more seriously as a field in education. So today, let's look at the causes, effects and solutions to our delegitimizing black studies.

7. Obviously, I went to the party. I had some things to say. Thing the first, January is not Black History Month. Second, MLK Day isn't even held on his BIRTHDAY. That's really great, white people. I'm pretty sure honoring this famous black man by changing his birthday so we get a three-day weekend means racism is dead.

Hananiah's introduction catches the audience's attention with a clever incongruity...

...and word play with "deets" for "details" and another incongruity with the blue water statement.

Satire sets the mood and tone for the overall speech. The party was ridiculous and deserves to be ridiculed.

Hananiah cites legitimate research but throws in a humorous angle.

A serious point ends with the comic description, "cold ass 28.25 days of February."

Here, Hananiah previews the main points.

This represents more humor derived from satire.

8. Causes there are two, first we don't view black studies as a legitimate field in higher education and second, we have a false sense of knowledge about black culture.

9. First, we don't view black studies as a legitimate field in higher education. In the U.S, there is an attitude that black studies is not necessary because it can be combined in other fields. The *Chronicle of Higher Education* on April 30th, 2012 published an article tagged, "The Most Persuasive Case for Eliminating Black Studies: Just Read the Dissertations."

10. In the article Naomi Schaefer Riley devalues many dissertations written by the top young minds in the black studies field, noting that they seemed to be stuck in the year 1963 and that while there were many problems going on in the black community, none of them could be solved with the field of black studies.

11. However, *Mother Jones* on May 8th 2012 states that Naomi Riley didn't even read the dissertations. Seriously. She just went by the titles to tell her what she needed to know. Which was sort of like me watching the Oscars without seeing any of the movies this year. I thought Beasts of the Southern Wild was a porno.

12. Second, we have a false sense of knowledge about black culture and black history. When it comes to black culture and history, many individuals believe they know everything they need to know as long as they have the basic information. For example, Martin Luther King Jr. gave a really important speech, Rosa Parks wouldn't give up her seat on a bus, and Madea—that's a man.

13. Fabio Rojas, in his 2007 book *From Black Power to Black Studies*, states that when it comes to this information a lot of things are generalized. However, people assume they know everything about an entire race. This cannot only make someone look racist and ignorant but can leave us with shallow info and no exciting details.

14. For example, did you know Rosa Parks was a really talented ballet dancer? Is that true? I don't know. But that's the problem; we don't know ANYTHING beyond the surface level details.

15. When I got to the party I was so irate I dropped my tray of Fredrick Douglas deviled eggs all over the statue of Malcom X twerking on Madame CJ Walker. I was gonna give the host a piece of my mind but I got distracted. Watching a girl dressed up as Harriet Tubman do a kegstand takes a lot of concentration. Effects there are two, first black students feel devalued and second we teach inaccurate knowledge about black culture.

Hananiah previews the subpoints of the first main point.

Here, Hananiah lapses into serious points . . .

. . . that set up a witty analogy and humorous exaggeration.

Hananiah develops the second subpoint under the first main point with a humorous description.

This represents humorous description/incongruity.

Here, more exaggeration/ humorous description leads to a preview of the subpoints for the second main point.

16. First, Black students (hello) feel devalued. The *Huffington Post* on July 31st of 2013 suggests black students may have a harder time succeeding in school because of our constant need to legitimize our place at school. When a black student enters a predominantly white university aka most universities we feel out of place by not seeing people who look like us or reflect the educational community we grew up in. Let's put this into perspective: Imagine you are a white person, good job. Now picture you being dropped into the heart of Niger, Africa and everyone just stares at you for being different. My Niger is my 100 level math class I attend daily.

17. I know I feel alienated constantly and it forced me to create an imaginary best friend. His name is Timothy [points out Timothy]. He loves carrots but he hates asparagus.

18. Higher education works when it provides a safe, healthy environment where we can exchange ideas. When we devalue black studies, we delegitimize a culture, and ultimately leave an entire group of people out of the conversation.

19. Second, we teach inaccurate knowledge about black culture. As the previously cited Fabio Rojas book stated, we have a generalized view when it comes to black studies. The education becomes so generalized that we lose important information, and facts can be changed when people receive this information. Dr. Paul Lehman of the University of Oklahoma, on January 1st 2013, in his online blog, states that we need to have more of an accurate representation of black culture reflected in our society. Without this accurate representation we will just continue to fall into a cycle of inaccurate information. [Start to walk away] Timothy! Come here! Sorry he's shy.

20. Well, obviously I was lost when it came to fixing this party faux pas, so I did the only logical thing. I called my grandmother, Bigma. Bigma was outraged and we came to the conclusion that those kids were being pretty racist but also clever. We never would have thought to call the post party hookup session getting underground railroaded.

21. Solutions there are two, first we need to fight! For our right! To have black studies. And second, remember, black studies are for more than just black people.

22. First, we need to take control of our own education. Maybe you're dedicated to a different field and don't have time to major in black studies, so educate yourself. To help I've designed a handout that ranges from easy to hard questions concerning black studies.

Solid evidence leads to humorous wording of a serious analogy.

This is an incongruous reference to an imaginary friend.

Hananiah provides a concise summary of the first subpoint.

Here, Hananiah makes a serious point, followed by comic relief.

Here, Hananiah uses word play/exaggeration.

Hananiah previews the final main point and subpoints.

Hananiah involves an audience member in a risqué joke that is appropriate for his audience of college students.

This particular handout also has my phone number on it so (go to audience member) hey … Call me, we can … Study.

23. First, we need to fight for black studies. In order for black studies to be seen as more legitimate we need to see black studies more in all universities. According to the Testing and Education Reference Center updated now—seriously, they update by the minute—of all the universities in America with all of the undergrad programs available, there are only 199 black studies programs, with an even fewer number offering degrees. If we want to treat black studies equally then there needs to be more programs here.

24. Second, remember black studies are for more than just black people. People of all races should take classes that don't necessarily pertain to their specific background, because that is how we get rid of ignorance and false information. I am currently taking a History of Asia class and a Movement course. I am not Asian, nor do I like to move, but I am educated! *Salon.com*, on May 11th 2012, in its article "Dear White Men Defending Black Studies," states people of other races should feel comfortable not only defending black studies, but feel comfortable taking those classes as well.

25. While the concept of this party may seem funny and pretty ridiculous it actually happened. This party almost caused a civil war within my department and alienated a lot of people by making them feel unsafe and even embarrassed of their own culture in their university. I personally know the party host and do not believe he is racist—he's just ignorant to black culture. Knowing more about other cultures cannot hurt us but only help us to have real merited opinions.

26. Today we have looked at the causes, effects and solutions to us not taking black studies seriously as a legitimate field in education. After my Big Momma talked to everyone, they realized they were actually being pretty racist. We decided that to make things even, on March 3rd I would host a "white people" party to celebrate Bill Nye the Science Guy's birthday, and I would serve stereotypical white people food, like Thai, Indian, Vietnamese, Mexican and Korean food, because everyone knows white people looooove "ethnic food." But after that, no more offensive parties. From now on, we will only celebrate holidays that have no link to anyone's real cultural background and traditions, like St. Patrick's Day.

1. American Forensic Association, "Event Descriptions," at http://www.afa-niet.org, accessed June 29, 2014.

Hananiah develops the first subpoint of the third and final main point, including some humorous exaggeration.

The development of the second subpoint begins with an analogy/humorous description.

Hananiah sums up with a serious point.

Hananiah concludes by reviewing the main points, and he leaves the audience with a humorous closing statement.

NOTES

CHAPTER 1

1. Gergen, K. J. (1991). *The saturated self: Dilemmas of identity in contemporary life*. New York: Basic Books, p. 158.

2. Shannon, C. E., & Weaver, W. (1949). *The mathematical theory of communication*. Urbana: University of Illinois Press.

3. See, for example, Dunne, M., & Ng, S. H. (1994). Simultaneous speech in small group conversation: All-together-now and one-at-a-time? *Journal of Language and Social Psychology, 13*, 45–71.

4. The issue of intentionality has been a matter of debate by communication theorists. For a sample of the arguments on both sides, see Greene, J. O. (Ed.). (1997). *Message production: Advances in communication theory*. Mahwah, NJ: Erlbaum; Motley, M. T. (1990). On whether one can(not) communicate: An examination via traditional communication postulates. *Western Journal of Speech Communication, 54*, 1–20; Bavelas, J. B. (1990). Behaving and communicating: A reply to Motley. *Western Journal of Speech Communication, 54*, 593–602; and Stewart, J. (1991). A postmodern look at traditional communication postulates. *Western Journal of Speech Communication, 55*, 354–379.

5. For an in-depth look at this topic, see Cunningham, S. B. (2012). Intrapersonal communication: A review and critique. In S. Deetz (Ed.), *Communication yearbook* 15 (pp. 597–620). Newbury Park, CA: Sage.

6. John, J. (1953). The distribution of free-forming small group size. *American Sociological Review, 18*, 569–570.

7. For a thorough review of this topic, see Spitzberg, B. H., & Cupach, W. R. (1989). *Handbook of interpersonal competence research*. New York: Springer-Verlag.

8. See Wiemann, J. M., Takai, J., Ota, H., & Wiemann, M. (1997). A relational model of communication competence. In B. Kovacic (Ed.), *Emerging theories of human communication*. Albany: SUNY Press. These goals, and the strategies used to achieve them, needn't be conscious. See Fitzsimons, G. M., & Bargh, J. A. (2003). Thinking of you: Nonconscious pursuit of interpersonal goals associated with relationship partners. *Journal of Personality and Social Psychology, 84*, 148–164.

9. For a discussion of the trait versus state assessments of communication, see Infante, D. A., Rancer, A. S., & Womack, D. F. (1996). *Building communication theory* (3rd ed., pp. 159–160). Prospect Heights, IL: Waveland Press. For a specific discussion of trait-versus-state definitions of communication competence, see Cupach, W. R., & Spitzberg, B. H. (1983). Trait versus state: A comparison of dispositional and situational measures of interpersonal communication competence. *Western Journal of Speech Communication, 47*, 364–379.

10. See O'Keefe, B. J. (1988). The logic of message design: Individual differences in reasoning about communication. *Communication Monographs, 55*, 80–103.

11. See, for example, Heisel, A. D., McCroskey, J. C., & Richmond, V. P. (1999). Testing theoretical relationships and nonrelationships of genetically based predictors: Getting started with communibiology. *Communication Research Reports, 16*, 1–9; and McCroskey, J. C., & Beatty, K. J. (2000). The communibiological perspective: Implications for communication in instruction. *Communication Education, 49*, 1–6.

12. Rubin, R. B., Graham, E. E., & Mignerey, J. T. (1990). A longitudinal study of college students' communication competence. *Communication Education, 39*, 1–14.

13. See, for example, Martin, R. (1992). Relational cognition complexity and relational communication in personal relationships. *Communication Monographs, 59*, 150–163; Stacks, D. W., & Murphy, M. A. (1993). Conversational sensitivity: Further validation and extension. *Communication Reports, 6*, 18–24; and Vangelisti, A. L., & Draughton, S. M. (1987). The nature and correlates of conversational sensitivity. *Human Communication Research, 14*, 167–202.

14. Research summarized in Hamachek, D. E. (1987). *Encounters with the self* (2nd ed., p. 8). Fort Worth, TX: Holt, Rinehart and Winston. See also Daly, J. A., Vangelisti, A. L., & Daughton, S. M.

(1995). The nature and correlates of conversational sensitivity. In M. V. Redmond (Ed.), *Interpersonal communication: Readings in theory and research* (pp. 271–283). Fort Worth, TX: Harcourt Brace.

15. Adapted from the work of R. P. Hart as reported in Knapp, M. L. (1984). *Interpersonal communication and human relationships.* Boston: Allyn & Bacon, 1984, pp. 342–344. See also Hart, R. P., & Burks, D. M. (1972). Rhetorical sensitivity and social interaction. *Speech Monographs, 39,* 75–91; and Hart, R. P., Carlson, R. E., & Eadie, W. F. (1980). Attitudes toward communication and the assessment of rhetorical sensitivity. *Communication Monographs, 47,* 1–22.

16. Johnson, S. (2009, June 5). How Twitter will change the way we live." *Time.*

17. Lengel, R. H., & Daft, R. L. (1988). The selection of communication media as an executive skill. *Academy of Management Executive, 2,* 225–232.

18. Miss Seattle insists she doesn't hate Seattle after Twitter rant. (2012, March 7). *ABC News.* Retrieved from http://abcnews.go.com/blogs/headlines/2012/03/miss-seattle-insists-she-doesnt-hate-seattle-after-twitter-rant/.

19. Bauerlein, M. (2009, September 4). Why Gen-Y Johnny can't read nonverbal cues. *Wall Street Journal.* Retrieved from http://online.wsj.com/article/SB10001424052970203863204574348493483201758.html.

20. Watts, S. A. (2007). Evaluative feedback: Perspectives on media effects. *Journal of Computer-Mediated Communication, 12.* Retrieved from http://jcmc.indiana.edu/v12/issue2/watts.html. See also Turnage, A. K. (2007). Email behaviors and organizational conflict. *Journal of Computer-Mediated Communication, 13*(1), article 3. Retrieved from http://jcmc.indiana.edu/v13/issue1/turnage.html.

21. LeBlanc, J. C. (2012, October 20). *Cyberbullying and suicide: A retrospective analysis of 21 cases.* American Academy of Pediatrics National Conference, New Orleans. Retrieved from https://aap.confex.com/aap/2012/webprogram/Paper18782.html.

22. National Crime Prevention Council. (2007). Executive research summary "teens and cyberbullying." Retrieved from http://www.ncpc.org.

23. Caplan, S. E. (2005). A social skill account of problematic Internet use. *Journal of Communication, 55,* 721–736; Schiffrin, H., Edelman, A., Falkenstein, M., & Stewart, C. (2010). Associations among computer-mediated communication, relationships, and well-being. *Cyberpsychology, Behavior, and Social Networking, 13,* 1–14; Morrison, C. M., & Gore, H. (2010). The relationship between excessive Internet use and depression: A questionnaire-based study of 1,319 young people and adults. *Psychopathology, 43,* 121–126.

24. Ibid. (Caplan, 2005).

25. See, for example, Lenhart, A., Madden, M., Smith, A., & Macgill, A. (2007). Teens creating content. *Pew Internet & American Life Project.* Retrieved from http://www.pewinternet.org/Reports/2007/Teens-and-Social-Media/3-Teens-creating-content/18-Videos-are-not-restricted-as-often-as-photos.aspx?r=1.

26. Strayer, D. L., Drews, F. A., Crouch, D. J., & Johnston, W. A. (2005). Why do cell phone conversations interfere with driving? In W. R. Walker & D. Herrmann (Eds.), *Cognitive technology: Transforming thought and society* (pp. 51–68). Jefferson, NC: McFarland & Company Inc.

27. U.S. Department of Transportation, National Highway Safety Administration. (2010, September). *Traffic safety facts.* Retrieved from http://www.distraction.gov/research/PDF-Files/Distracted-Driving-2009.pdf.

28. Adapted from McCroskey, J. C., & Wheeless, L. R. (1976). *Introduction to human communication* (pp. 3–10). Boston: Allyn & Bacon.

29. Smith, J. L., Ickes, W., & Hodges, S. (Eds.). (2010). *Managing interpersonal sensitivity: Knowing when—and when not—to understand others.* Hauppauge, NY: Nova Science Publishers.

30. For a detailed rationale of the position argued in this section, see Stamp, G. H., & Knapp, M. L. (1990). The construct of intent in interpersonal communication. *Quarterly Journal of Speech, 76,* 282–299. See also Stewart, J. (1991). A postmodern look at traditional communication postulates. *Western Journal of Speech Communication, 55,* 354–379.

31. For a thorough discussion of communication difficulties, see Coupland, N., Giles, H., & Wiemann, J. M. (Eds.). (1991). *"Miscommunication" and problematic talk.* Newbury Park, CA: Sage.

CHAPTER 2

1. Hamachek, D. (1992). *Encounters with the self* (3rd ed., pp. 5–8). Fort Worth, TX: Holt, Rinehart and Winston. See also Campbell, J. D., & Lavallee, L. F. (1993). Who am I? The role of self-concept confusion

in understanding the behavior of people with low self-esteem. In R. F. Baumeister (Ed.), *Self-esteem: The puzzle of low self-regard* (pp. 3–20). New York: Plenum Press.

2. Baumeister, R. F. (2005). *The cultural animal: Human nature, meaning, and social life*. New York: Oxford University Press; and Baumeister, R. F., Campbell, J. D., Krueger, J. I., & Vohs, K. D. (2003). Does high self-esteem cause better performance, interpersonal success, happiness, or healthier lifestyles? *Psychological Science in the Public Interest, 4*, 1–44.

3. Vohs, K. D., & Heatherton, T. F. (2004). Ego threats elicit different social comparison process among high and low self-esteem people: Implications for interpersonal perceptions. *Social Cognition, 22*, 168–191.

4. See also Keltikangas, J. (1990). The stability of self-concept during adolescence and early adulthood: A six-year follow-up study. *Journal of General Psychology, 117*, 361–369.

5. López-Guimerà, G., Levine, M. P., Sánchez-Carracedo, D., & Fauquet, J. (2010). Influence of mass media on body image and eating disordered attitudes and behaviors in females: A review of effects and processes. *Media Psychology, 13*, 387–416.

6. Duvall, S. (2011, November 17). *Top 10 countries celebrating female obesity*. Retrieved from http://www.toptenz.net/top-10-countries-celebrating-female-obesity.php.

7. Alberts, J. K., Kellar-Guenther, U., & Corman, S. R. (1996). That's not funny: Understanding recipients' responses to teasing. *Western Journal of Communication, 60*, 337–357.

8. Katzer, C., Fetchenhauer, D., & Belschak, F. (2009). Cyberbullying: Who are the victims? A comparison of victimization in Internet chatrooms and victimization in school. *Journal of Media Psychology: Theories, Methods, and Applications, 21*, 25–36.

9. Holmes, J. G. (2002). Interpersonal expectations as the building blocks of social cognition: An interdependence theory perspective. *Personal Relationships, 9*, 1–26.

10. Rosenthal, R., & Jacobson, L. (1968). *Pygmalion in the classroom*. New York: Holt, Rinehart and Winston.

11. Hyperprolactinemia diagnosis and treatment: A patient's guide. (2011, February). *Hormone Health Network*. Retrieved from http://vsearch.nlm.nih.gov/vivisimo/cgi-bin/query-meta?v%3Aproject=medlineplus&query=estrogen+and+testosterone&x=-1171&y=-97.

12. Bem, S. L. (1974). The measurement of psychological androgyny. *Journal of Consulting and Clinical Psychology, 42*, 155–162.

13. Choi, Y. S., Gray, H. M., & Ambady, N. (2005). The glimpsed world: Unintended communication and unintended perception. In R. R. Hassin, J. S. Uleman, & J. A. Bargh (Eds.), *The new unconscious* (pp. 309–333). New York: Oxford University Press.

14. Versalle, A., & McDowell, E. E. (2004–2005). The attitudes of men and women concerning gender differences in grief. *Omega: Journal of Death and Dying, 50*, 53–67.

15. Summarized in Hamachek, D. E. (1982). *Encounters with others*. New York: Holt, Rinehart and Winston (pp. 23–30).

16. For a review of these perceptual biases, see Hamachek, D. (1992). *Encounters with the self* (3rd ed.). Fort Worth, TX: Harcourt Brace Jovanovich. See also Bradbury, T. N., & Fincham, F. D. (1990). Attributions in marriage: Review and critique. *Psychological Bulletin, 107*, 3–33. For information on the self-serving bias, see Shepperd, J., Malone, W., & Sweeny, K. (2008). Exploring causes of the self-serving bias. *Social and Personality Psychology Compass, 2/2*, 895–908.

17. See, for example, Kanouse, D. E., & Hanson, L. R. (1972). Negativity in Evaluations. In E. E. Jones, D. E. Kanouse, H. H. Kelley, R. E. Nisbett, S. Valins, & B. Weiner (Eds.), *Attribution: Perceiving the causes of behavior* (pp. 47–62). Morristown, NJ: General Learning Press.

18. See, for example, Baron, P. (1974). Self-esteem, ingratiation, and evaluation of unknown others. *Journal of Personality and Social Psychology, 30*, 104–109; and Walster, E. (1965). The effect of self-esteem on romantic liking. *Journal of Experimental and Social Psychology, 1*, 184–197.

19. Henningsen, D., Henningsen, M., McWorthy, E., McWorthy, C., & McWorthy, L. (2011). Exploring the effects of sex and mode of presentation in perceptions of dating goals in video-dating. *Journal of Communication, 61*(4), 641–658.

20. Stiff, J. B., Dillard, J. P., Somera, L., Kim, H., & Sleight, C. (1988). Empathy, communication, and prosocial behavior. *Communication Monographs, 55*, 198–213.

21. Goffman, E. (1959). *The presentation of self in everyday life*. Garden City, NY: Doubleday; and

Goffman, E. (1971). *Relations in public*. New York: Basic Books.

22. Cupach, W. R., & Metts, S. (1994). *Facework*. Thousand Oaks, CA: Sage. See also Brown, P., & Levinson, S. C. (1987). *Politeness: Some universals in language usage*. Cambridge, England: Cambridge University Press.

23. Sharkey, W. F., Park, H. S., & Kim, R. K. (2004). Intentional self-embarrassment. *Communication Studies, 55*, 379–399.

24. Urciuoli, B. (2009). The political topography of Spanish and English: The view from a New York Puerto Rican neighborhood. *American Ethnologist, 10*, 295–310.

25. Stewart, J., & Logan, C. (1998). *Together: Communicating interpersonally* (5th ed., p. 120). New York: McGraw-Hill, 1998.

26. Leary, M. R., & Kowalski, R. M. (1990). Impression management: A literature review and two-component model. *Psychological Bulletin, 107*, 34–47.

27. Chovil, N. (1991). Social determinants of facial displays. *Journal of Nonverbal Behavior, 15*, 141–154.

28. Snyder, M. (1979). Self-monitoring processes. In L. Berkowitz (Ed.), *Advances in experimental social psychology*. New York: Academic Press; and Snyder, M. (1983, March). The many me's of the self-monitor. *Psychology Today*, p. 34f.

29. The following discussion is based on material in Hamachek, D. (1992). *Encounters with the self* (3rd ed., pp. 24–26). Fort Worth, TX: Holt, Rinehart and Winston.

30. Coleman, L. M., & DePaulo, B. M. (1991). Uncovering the human spirit: Moving beyond disability and "missed" communications. In N. Coupland, H. Giles, & J. M. Wiemann (Eds.), *"Miscommunication" and problematic talk* (pp. 61–84). Newbury Park, CA: Sage.

31. Siibak, A. (2009). Constructing the self through the photo selection: Visual impression management on social networking websites. *Cyberpsychology: Journal of Psychosocial Research on Cyberspace, 3*, article 1. Retrieved from http://www.cyberpsychology.eu/view.php?cisloclanku=2009061501&article=1

32. Hancock, J. T., & Durham, P. J. (2001). Impression formation in computer-mediated communication revisited: An analysis of the breadth and intensity of impressions. *Communication Research, 28*, 325–347.

CHAPTER 3

1. Kroeber, A. L., & Kluckhohn, C. (1952). *Culture: A critical review of concepts and definitions*. Harvard University, Peabody Museum of American Archeology and Ethnology Papers 47.

2. Samovar, L. A., & Porter, R. E. (2007). *Communication between cultures* (6th ed.). Belmont, CA: Wadsworth.

3. Tajfel, H., & Turner, J. C. (1986). The social identity theory of inter-group behavior. In S. Worchel & L. W. Austin (Eds.), *Psychology of intergroup relations*. Chicago: Nelson-Hall.

4. Ten things everyone should know about race. (2003). *Race: The power of an illusion*. Public Broadcasting System, California Newsreel. Retrieved from http://www.pbs.org/race/000_About/002_04-background-01-x.htm.

5. Interview with Jonathan Marks. (2003). *Race: The power of an illusion*. California Newsreel, Public Broadcasting System. Retrieved http://www.pbs.org/race/000_About/002_04-background-01-08.htm.

6. Bonam, C. M., & Shih, M. (2009). Exploring multiracial individuals' comfort with intimate interracial relationships. *Journal of Social Issues, 65*, 87–103.

7. For a summary of research on this subject, see Bradac, J. J. (1990). Language attitudes and impression formation. In H. Giles & W. P. Robinson (Eds.), *Handbook of language and social psychology* (pp. 387–413). Chichester, England: Wiley. See also S. H. Ng & J. J. Bradac, *Power in language: Verbal communication and social influence*. Newbury Park, CA: Sage.

8. Bailey, R. W. (2003). Ideologies, attitudes, and perceptions. *American Speech, 88*, 115–143.

9. Birdwhistell, R. L. (1970). *Kinesics and context*. Philadelphia: University of Philadelphia Press, pp. 30–31.

10. Andersen, P., Lustig, M., & Anderson, J. (1987, November). *Changes in latitude, changes in attitude: The relationship between climate, latitude, and interpersonal communication predispositions*. Paper presented at the annual convention of the Speech Communication Association, Boston; and Andersen, P., Lustig, M., & Andersen, J. (1988, November). *Regional patterns of communication in the United States: Empirical tests*. Paper presented at the annual convention of the Speech Communication Association, New Orleans.

11. What is LGBTQ? (nd). Iknowmine.org., sponsored by Alaska Native Tribal Health Consortium,

Community Health Services. Retrieved from http://www.iknowmine.org/for-youth/what-is-glbt.

12. Federal Bureau of Investigation. (2012, December 10). *Hate crimes accounting: Annual report.* Retrieved from http://www.fbi.gov/news/stories/2012/december/annual-hate-crimes-report-released/annual-hate-crimes-report-released.

13. All of the statements by Anderson Cooper in this paragraph are from: Sullivan, A. (2012, July 2). Anderson Cooper: "The fact is, I'm gay." *The Dish.* Retrieved from http://dish.andrewsullivan.com/2012/07/02/anderson-cooper-the-fact-is-im-gay/.

14. Potter, J. E. (2002). Do ask, do tell. *Annals of Internal Medicine, 137*(5), 341–343, quote on p. 342.

15. Milevsky, A., Shifra Niman, D., Raab, A., & Gross, R. (2011). A phenomenological examination of dating attitudes in ultra-orthodox Jewish emerging adult women. *Mental Health, Religion & Culture, 14,* 311–322.

16. U.S. religious landscape survey. Religious beliefs and practices: Diverse and politically relevant. (2008, June). *The Pew Forum on Religion & Public Life.* Retrieved from http://religions.pewforum.org/pdf/report2-religious-landscape-study-full.pdf.

17. Bartkowski, J. P., Xiaohe, X., & Fondren, K. M. (2011). Faith, family, and teen dating: Examining the effects of personal and household religiosity on adolescent romantic relationships. *Review of Religious Research, 52,* 248–265.

18. Reiter, M. J., & Gee, C. B. (2008). Open communication and partner support in intercultural and interfaith romantic relationships: A relational maintenance approach. *Journal of Social & Personal Relationships, 25,* 539–559.

19. Colaner, C. (2009). Exploring the communication of evangelical families: The association between evangelical gender role ideology and family communication patterns. *Communication Studies, 60,* 97–113. doi:10.1080/10510970902834833ß.

20. Fitch, V. (1985). The psychological tasks of old age. *Naropa Institute Journal of Psychology, 3,* 90–106.

21. Gergen, K. J., & Gergen, M. M. (2000). The new aging: Self construction and social values. In K. W. Schae & J. Hendricks, (Eds.), *The societal impact of the aging process* (pp. 281–306). New York: Springer.

22. Bailey, T. A. (2010). Ageism and media discourse: Newspaper framing of middle age. *Florida Communication Journal, 38,* 43–56.

23. Frijters, P., & Beatoon, T. (2012). The mystery of the U-shaped relationship between happiness and age. *Journal of Economic Behavior & Organization, 82,* 525–542.

24. Ryan, E. B., & Butler, R. N. (1996). Communication, aging, and health: Toward understanding health provider relationships with older clients. *Health Communication, 8,* 191–197.

25. Harwood, J. (2007). *Understanding communication and aging: Developing knowledge and awareness.* Newbury Park, CA: Sage, p. 79.

26. Kroger, J., Martinussen, M., & Marcia, J. E. (2010). Identity status change during adolescence and young adulthood: A meta-analysis. *Journal of Adolescence, 33,* 683–698.

27. Galanaki, E. P. (2012). The imaginary audience and the personal fable: A test of Elkind's theory of adolescent egocentrism. *Psychology, 3,* 457–466.

28. Myers, K. K., & Sadaghiani, K. (2010). Millennials in the workplace: A communication perspective on Millennials' organizational relationships and performance. *Journal of Business and Psychology, 25*(2), 225–238.

29. Lucas, K. (2011). The working class promise: A communicative account of mobility-based ambivalences. *Communication Monographs, 78,* 347–369.

30. Stuber, J. M. (2006). Talk of class. *Journal of Contemporary Ethnography, 35,* 285–318. Quote appears on p. 306.

31. Kim, Y. K., & Sax, L. J. (2009). Student–faculty interaction in research universities: Differences by student gender, race, social class, and first-generation status. *Research in Higher Education, 50,* 437–459.

32. Kaufman, P. (2003). Learning to not labor: How working-class individuals construct middle-class identities. *Sociological Quarterly, 44,* 481–504.

33. National Youth Violence Prevention Resource Center. (2007, December 20). Gangs fact sheet. Retrieved from http://www.safeyouth.org/scripts/facts/gangs.asp.

34. Triandis, H. C. (1995). *Individualism and collectivism.* Boulder, CO: Westview.

35. Cai, D. A., & Fink, E. L. (2002). Conflict style differences between individualists and collectivists. *Communication Monographs, 69,* 67–87.

36. Wu, S., & Keysar, B. (2007). Cultural effects on perspective taking. *Psychological Science, 18,* 600–606.

37. Hall, H. T. (1959). *Beyond culture.* New York: Doubleday.

38. Yuan-shan, C., Chun-yin Doris, C., & Miao-Hsia, C. (2011). American and Chinese complaints: Strategy use from a cross-cultural perspective. *Intercultural Pragmatics, 8*, 253–275.

39. Bin "Robin" Luo, profiled in Adler, R. B., Rodman, G., & du Pré, A. (2014) *Understanding human communication* (12th ed.). New York: Oxford University Press. Quote appears on p. 82.

40. Hofstede, G. (2001). *Culture's consequences: Comparing values, behaviors, institutions, and organizations across nations* (2nd ed.). Thousand Oaks, CA: Sage.

41. Ibid.

42. Dailey, R. M., Giles, H., & Jansma, L. L. (2005). Language attitudes in an Anglo-Hispanic context: The role of the linguistic landscape. *Language & Communication, 25*(1), 27–38.

43. Basso, K. (2012). "To give up on words": Silence in Western Apache culture. In L. Monogahn, J. E. Goodman, & J. M. Robinson (eds.), *A cultural approach to interpersonal communication: Essential readings* (2nd ed., pp. 73–83). Malden, MA: Blackwell.

44. Hofstede, G. (2001). *Culture's consequences.*

45. Ibid.

46. What about Taiwan? (nd). *The Hofstede Centre.* Retrieved from http://geert-hofstede.com/taiwan.html.

47. The androgyny revolution. (2007, December 12). *The Yale Globalist.* Retrieved from http://tyglobalist.org/in-the-magazine/theme/the-androgyny-revolution/.

48. Arasaratnam, L. A. (2006). Further testing of a new model of intercultural communication competence. *Communication Research Reports, 23*, 93–99.

49. Adapted from Chen, G. M., & Starosta, W. J. (2000). The development and validation of the intercultural sensitivity scale. *Human Communication, 3*, 2–14.

50. Pettigrew, T. F., & Tropp, L. R. (2000). Does intergroup contact reduce prejudice? Recent meta-analytic findings. In S. Oskamp (Ed.), *Reducing prejudice and discrimination: Social psychological perspectives* (pp. 93–114). Mahwah, NJ: Erlbaum.

51. Pettigrew, T. F., & Tropp, L. R. (2006). A meta-analytic test of intergroup contact theory. *Journal of Personality and Social Psychology, 90*, 751–783.

52. Kassing, J. W. (1997). Development of the intercultural willingness to communicate scale. *Communication Research Reports, 14*, 399–407.

53. Amichai-Hamburger, Y., & McKenna, K. Y. A. (2006). The contact hypothesis reconsidered: Interacting via the Internet. *Journal of Computer-Mediated Communication, 11.* Retrieved from http://jcmc.indiana.edu/vol11/issue3/amichai-hamburger.html.

54. Iyer, P. (1990). *The lady and the monk: Four seasons in Kyoto.* New York: Vintage, 129–130.

55. See, for example, Otten, M., & Banaji, M. R. (2012). Social categories shape the neural representation of emotion: Evidence from a visual face adaptation task. *Frontiers in Integrative Neuroscience, 6*, 9.

56. Sinclair, S., Lowery, B. S., Hardin, C. D., & Colangelo, A. (2005). Social tuning of automatic racial attitudes: The role of affiliative motivation. *Journal of Personality and Social Psychology, 89*(4), 583.

57. Kim, M. S., Hunter, J. E., Miyahara, A., Horvath, A. M., Bresnahan, M., & Yoon, H. (1996). Individual- vs. culture-level dimensions of individualism and collectivism: Effects on preferred conversational styles. *Communication Monographs, 63*, 28–49.

58. Berger, C. R. (1979). Beyond initial interactions: Uncertainty, understanding, and the development of interpersonal relationships. In H. Giles & R. St. Clair (Eds.), *Language and social psychology* (pp. 122–144). Oxford, England: Blackwell.

59. Carrell, L. J. (1997). Diversity in the communication curriculum: Impact on student empathy. *Communication Education, 46*, 234–244.

60. Oberg, K. (1960). Cultural shock: Adjustment to new cultural environments. *Practical Anthropology, 7*, 177–182.

61. Ibid.

62. Chang, L. C.-N. (2011). My culture shock experience. *ETC: A Review of General Semantics, 68*(4), 403–405.

63. Kim, Y. Y. (2008). Intercultural personhood: Globalization and a way of being. *International Journal of Intercultural Relations, 32*, 359–368.

64. Kim, Y. Y. (2005). Adapting to a new culture: An integrative communication theory. In W. B. Gudykunst (Ed.), *Theorizing about intercultural communication* (pp. 375–400). Thousand Oaks, CA: Sage.

65. Kim, Y. Y. (2008). Intercultural personhood.

CHAPTER 4

1. Wang, W. S. Y. (1982). Language and derivative systems. In W. S. Y. Wang (Ed.), *Human communication: Language and its psychobiological basis* (p. 36). San Francisco: Freeman.

2. Adapted from O'Brien, J., & Kollock, P. (2001). *The production of reality* (3rd ed., p. 66). Thousand Oaks, CA: Pine Forge Press.

3. Henneberger, M. (1999, January 29). Misunderstanding of word embarrasses Washington's new mayor. *New York Times*. Retrieved from http://www.nyt.com.

4. Duck, S. (1993). Steady as she goes: Maintenance as a shared meaning system. In D. J. Caharg & L. Stafford (Eds.), *Communication and relational maintenance* (pp. 49–60). San Diego: Academic Press.

5. Gaudin, S. (2011, March 25). OMG! Text shorthand makes the Oxford English Dictionary. *Computerworld*. Retrieved from http://www.computerworld.com/s/article/9215079/OMG_Text_shorthand_makes_the_dictionary.

6. Pearce, W. B., & Cronen, V. (1980). *Communication, action, and meaning*. New York: Praeger. See also Barge, J. K. (2004). Articulating CMM as a practical theory. *Human Systems: The Journal of Systemic Consultation and Management, 15*, 193–204; and Griffin, E. M. (2006). *A first look at communication theory* (6th ed.). New York: McGraw-Hill.

7. Laham, S. M., Koval, P., & Alter, A. L. (2012). The name-pronunciation effect: Why people like Mr. Smith more than Mr. Colquhoun. *Journal of Experimental Social Psychology, 48*(3), 752–756.

8. Fryer, R. G., & Levitt, S. D. (2004). The causes and consequences of distinctively black names. *Quarterly Journal of Economics, 119*, 767–805.

9. For a summary of research on this subject, see Bradac, J. J. (1990). Language attitudes and impression formation. In H. Giles & W. P. Robinson (Eds.), *Handbook of language and social psychology* (pp. 387–412). Chichester, England: Wiley.

10. Segrest Purkiss, S. L., Perrewé, P. L., Gillespie, T. L., Mayes, B. T., & Ferris, G. R. (2006). Implicit sources of bias in employment interview judgments and decisions. *Organizational Behavior and Human Decision Processes, 101*(2), 152–167.

11. Hosoda, M., Nguyen, L. T., & Stone-Romero, E. F. (2012). The effect of Hispanic accents on employment decisions. *Journal of Managerial Psychology, 27*(4), 347–364; Hosoda, M., & Stone-Romero, E. (2010). The effects of foreign accents on employment-related decisions. *Journal of Managerial Psychology, 25*(2), 113–132.

12. Miller, C., & Swift, K. (1991). *Words and women*. New York: Harper Collins (p. 27).

13. For a discussion of racist language, see Bosmajian, H. A. (1983). *The language of oppression*. Lanham, MD: University Press of America.

14. Mader, D. C. (1992, May). *The politically correct textbook: Trends in publishers' guidelines for the representation of marginalized groups*. Paper presented at the annual convention of the Eastern Communication Association, Portland, ME (p. 5).

15. For a review of the relationship between power and language, see Liska, J. (1992). Dominance-seeking language strategies: Please eat the floor, dogbreath, or I'll rip your lungs out, O.K.? In S. A. Deetz (Ed.), *Communication yearbook 15* (pp. 427–456). Newbury Park, CA: Sage. See also Burrell, N. A., & Koper, R. J. (1994). The efficacy of powerful/powerless language on persuasiveness/credibility: A meta-analytic review. In R. W. Preiss & M. Allen (Eds.), *Prospects and precautions in the use of meta-analysis* (pp. 235–255). Dubuque, IA: Brown & Benchmark.

16. Parton, S., Siltanen, S. A., Hosman, L. A., & Langenderfer, J. (2002). Employment interview outcomes and speech style effects. *Journal of Language and Social Psychology, 21*, 144–161.

17. Ng, S. H., & Bradac, J. J. (1993). *Power in language: Verbal communication and social influence*. Newbury Park, CA: Sage. See also Reid, S. A., & Ng, S. H. (1999). Language, power, and intergroup relations. *Journal of Social Issues, 55*, 119–139.

18. See, for example, Bell, R. A., & Healey, J. G. (1992). Idiomatic communication and interpersonal solidarity in friends' relational cultures. *Human Communication Research, 18*, 307–335; and Bell, R. A., Buerkel-Rothfuss, N., & Gore, K. E. (1987). Did you bring the yarmulke for the cabbage patch kid? The idiomatic communication of young lovers. *Human Communication Research, 14*, 47–67.

19. Cassell, J., & Tversky, D. (2005). The language of online intercultural community formation. *Journal of Computer-Mediated Communication, 10*, Article 2. Retrieved from http://www.justinecassell.com/publications/JCMC.Cassell.Tversky.pdf.

20. Ulaby, Neda. (2006, February 18). OMG: IM slang is invading everyday English. *NPR, Weekend Edition*. Retrieved from http://www.npr.org/templates/story/story.php?storyId=5221618.

21. Kubanyu, E. S., Richard, D. C., Bower, G. B., & Muraoka, M. Y. (1992). Impact of assertive and accusatory communication of distress and anger: A verbal component analysis. *Aggressive Behavior, 18*, 337–347.

22. Motley, M. T., & Reeder, H. M. (1995). Unwanted escalation of sexual intimacy: Male and female

perceptions of connotations and relational consequences of resistance messages. *Communication Monographs, 62,* 356–382. See also Katz, J., & Tirone, V. (2010). Going along with it: Sexually coercive partner behavior predicts dating women's compliance with unwanted sex. *Violence Against Women, 16*(7), 730–742.

23. Labov, T. (1992). Social and language boundaries among adolescents. *American Speech, 4,* 339–366.

24. UCLA slang. (nd). University of California Los Angeles Department of Linguistics. Retrieved from http://www.cs.rpi.edu/~kennyz/doc/humor/slang.humor.

25. Kakutani, M. (2000, July 2). Computer slang scoffs at wetware. *Santa Barbara News-Press,* p. D1.

26. Levitt, A., Sher, K. J., & Bartholow, B. D. (2009). The language of intoxication: Preliminary investigations. *Alcoholism: Clinical and Experimental Research, 33,* 448–454. See also Levitt, A., Schlauch, R. C., & Bartholow, B. D. (2013). Gender differences in natural language factors of subjective intoxication in college students: An experimental vignette study. *Alcoholism: Clinical and Experimental Research.* First published online July 10, 2013.

27. Morrison, B. (2000, September 26). What you won't hear the pilot say. *USA Today,* p. A1.

28. Eisenberg, E. M. (Ed.). (2007). *Strategic ambiguities: Essays on communication, organization and identity.* Thousand Oaks, CA: Sage.

29. For detailed discussions of the relationship between gender and communication, see Canary, D. J., & Emmers-Sommer, T. M. (1997). *Sex and gender differences in personal relationships.* New York: Guilford; Wood, J. (1994). *Gendered lives: Communication, gender, and culture.* Belmont, CA: Wadsworth; and Pearson, J. C. (1994). *Gender and communication* (2nd ed.). Madison, WI: Brown & Benchmark.

30. Sehulster, J. R. (2006). Things we talk about, how frequently, and to whom: Frequency of topics in everyday conversation as a function of gender, age, and marital status. *The American Journal of Psychology, 119,* 407–432.

31. Clark, R. A. (1998). A comparison of topics and objectives in a cross section of young men's and women's everyday conversations. In D. J. Canary & K. Dindia (Eds.), *Sex differences and similarities in communication: Critical essays and empirical investigations of sex and gender in interaction* (pp. 303–310). Mahwah, NJ: Erlbaum.

32. Wood, J. T. (2001). *Gendered lives: Communication, gender, and culture* (4th ed.). Belmont, CA: Wadsworth, p. 141.

33. Mehl, M. R., Vazire, S., Ramírez-Esparza, S., Slatcher, R. B., & Pennebaker, J. W. (2007, July). Are women really more talkative than men? *Science, 317,* 82.

34. For a summary of research on the difference between male and female conversational behavior, see Giles, H., & Street, R. L., Jr. (1985). Communication characteristics and behavior. In M. L. Knapp & G. R. Miller (Eds.), *Handbook of interpersonal communication* (pp. 205–261). Beverly Hills, CA: Sage; and Kohn, A. (1988, February). Girl talk, guy talk. *Psychology Today, 22,* 65–66.

35. Haas, A., & Sherman, M. A. (1982). Conversational topic as a function of role and gender. *Psychological Reports, 51,* 453–454.

36. Fox, A. B., Bukatko, D., Hallahan, M., & Crawford, M. The medium makes a difference: Gender similarities and differences in instant messaging. *Journal of Language and Social Psychology, 26,* 389–397.

37. Eisenegger, C., Haushofer, J., & Fehr, E. (2011). The role of testosterone in social interaction. *Trends in Cognitive Sciences, 15* (1), 263–271. See also Baker, S. (2007, January 1). The sex hormone secrets. *Psychology Today.* Retrieved from http://www.psychologytoday.com/articles/200612/the-sex-hormone-secrets.

38. Jones, A. C., & Josephs, R. A. (2006). Interspecies hormonal interactions between man and the domestic dog (Canis familiaris). *Hormones and Behavior, 50* (3), 393–400.

39. Pennebaker, J. W., Groom, C. J., Loew, D., & Dabbs, J. M. (2004). Testosterone as a social inhibitor: Two case studies of the effect of testosterone treatment on language. *Journal of Abnormal Psychology, 113*(1), 172.

40. Chen, C. P., Cheng, D. Z., & Luo, Y.-J. (2011). Estrogen impacts on emotion: Psychological, neuroscience and endocrine studies. *Science China Life, 41*(11), 1049–1062.

41. Dabbs, J. M., & Dabbs, M. G. (2000). *Heroes, rogues and lovers: On testosterone and behavior.* New York: McGraw-Hill.

42. U.S. Department of Health and Human Services. (2010), *How common is PMS?* Premenstrual syndrome (PMS) fact sheet. Retrieved from http://womenshealth.gov/publications/our-publications/fact-sheet/premenstrual-syndrome.cfm#e.

43. Yong, E. (2009, April 7). Do testosterone and oestrogen affect our attitudes to fairness, trust, risk and altruism? *Discover*. Retrieved from https://blogs.discovermagazine.com/notrocketscience/2009/04/07/do-testosterone-and-oestrogen-affect-our-attitudes-to-fairness-trust-risk-and-altruism/.

44. See, for example, Geddes, D. (1992). Sex roles in management: The impact of varying power of speech style on union members' perception of satisfaction and effectiveness. *Journal of Psychology, 126*, 589–607.

CHAPTER 5

1. Gabric, D., & McFadden, K. L. (2001). Student and employer perceptions of desirable entry-level operations management skills. *Mid-American Journal of Business, 16* (1), 51–59; Landrum, R. E., & Harrold, R. (2003). What employers want from psychology graduates. *Teaching of Psychology, 30*, 131–133.

2. Ceraso, S. (2011, April 25). "I listen with my eyes": Deaf architecture and rhetorical space. *Humanities, Arts, Science, and Technology Alliance and Collabatory.* Retrieved from http://www.hastac.org/blogs/stephceraso/i-listen-my-eyes-deaf-architecture-and-rhetorical-space.

3. Powers, W. L., & Witt, P. L. (2008). Expanding the theoretical framework of communication fidelity. *Communication Quarterly, 56*, 247–267; Fitch-Hauser, M., Powers, W. G., O'Brien, K., & Hanson, S. (2007). Extending the conceptualization of listening fidelity. *International Journal of Listening, 21*, 81–91; Powers, W. G., & Bodie, G. D. (2003). Listening fidelity: Seeking congruence between cognitions of the listener and the sender. *International Journal of Listening, 17*, 19–31.

4. Thomas, T. L., & Levine, T. R. (1994). Disentangling listening and verbal recall: Related but separate constructs? *Human Communication Research, 21*, 103–127.

5. Nichols, R. G. (1948). Factors in listening comprehension. *Speech Monographs, 15*, 154–163.

6. Cowan, N., & AuBuchon, A. M. (2008). Short-term memory loss over time without retroactive stimulus interference. *Psychonomic Bulletin and Review, 15*, 230–235.

7. Ames, D., Maissen, L. B., & Brockner, J. (2012, June). The role of listening in interpersonal influence. *Journal of Research in Personality, 46*, 345–349.

8. Brownell, J. (1990). Perceptions of effective listeners: A management study. *Journal of Business Communication, 27*, 401–415.

9. Rautalinko, E., Lisper, H., & Ekehammar, B. (2007). Reflective listening in counseling: Effects of training time and evaluator social skills. *American Journal of Psychotherapy, 61*, 191–209.

10. Langer, E. (1990). *Mindfulness*. Reading, MA: Addison-Wesley.

11. Burgoon, J. K., Berger, C. R., & Waldron, V. R. (2000). Mindfulness and interpersonal communication. *Journal of Social Issues, 56*, 105–127. Langer, *Mindfulness*, p. 90.

12. Nichols, R. G. (1987, September). Listening is a ten-part skill. *Nation's Business, 75*, 40.

13. Vangelisti, A. L., Knapp, M. L., & Daly, J. A. (1990). Conversational narcissism. *Communication Monographs, 57*, 251–274.

14. McComb, K. B., & Jablin, F. M. (1984). Verbal correlates of interviewer empathic listening and employment interview outcomes. *Communication Monographs, 51*, 367.

15. Hansen, J. (2007). *24/7: How cell phones and the Internet change the way we live, work, and play.* New York: Praeger. See also Turner, J. W., & Reinsch, N. L. (2007). The business communicator as presence allocator: Multicommunicating, equivocality, and status at work. *Journal of Business Communication, 44*, 36–58.

16. Hemp, P. (2009, December 4). Death by information overload. *Harvard Business Review* online. Retrieved from http://www.ocvets4pets.com/archive17/Death_by_Information_Overload_-_HBR.org.pdf.

17. Drullman, R., & Smoorenburg, G. F. (1997). Audiovisual perception of compressed speech by profoundly hearing-impaired subjects. *Audiology, 36*, 165–177.

18. *Listen to this: Hearing problems can stress relationships.* (2008). Retrieved from http://www.hearingcarecenter.org/listen-to-this-hearing-problems-can-stress-relationships. See also Shafer, D. N. (2007). Hearing loss hinders relationships. *ASHA Leader, 12*, 5–7.

19. Agrawal, Y., Platz, E. A., & Niparko, J. K. (2008). Prevalance of hearing loss and differences by demographic characteristics among U.S. adults. Data from the National Health and Nutrition Examination Survey, 1999–2004. *Journal of the American Medical Association, 168*, 1522.

20. National Institute on Deafness and Other Communication Disorders. (2008, August). *Quick statistics.* Bethesda, MD: U.S. Department of Health and Human Services.

21. Kline, N. (1999). *Time to think: Listening to ignite the human mind.* London: Ward Lock, p. 21.

22. Imhof, M. (2003). The social construction of the listener: Listening behaviors across situations, perceived listener status, and cultures. *Communication Research Reports, 20,* 357–366.

23. Zohoori, A. (2013). A cross-cultural comparison of the HURIER Listening Profile among Iranian and U.S. students. *International Journal of Listening, 27,* 50–60.

24. Imhof, M. (2003). The social construction of the listener.

25. Ophir, E., Nass, C., & Wagner, A. D. (2009). Cognitive control in media multitaskers. *Proceedings of the National Academy of Sciences, 106*(37), 15583–15587.

26. Turkle, S. (2011). *Alone together: Why we expect more from technology and less from each other.* New York: Basic Books.

27. Turkle, S. (2012, April 21). The flight from conversation. *New York Times.* Retrieved from http://www.nytimes.com/2012/04/22/opinion/sunday/the-flight-from-conversation.html?pagewanted=all&_r=0.

28. Huerta-Wong, J. E., & Schoech, R. (2010). Experiential learning and learning environments: The case of active listening skills. *Journal of Social Work Education, 46,* 85–101.

29. Sprague, J., & Stuart, D. (1992). *The speaker's handbook* (3rd ed., p. 172). Fort Worth, TX: Harcourt Brace Jovanovich.

30. Segrin, C., & Domschke, T. (2011). Social support, loneliness, recuperative processes, and their direct and indirect effects on health. *Health Communication, 26,* 221–232.

31. Tanis, M. (2007). Online support groups. In A. Joinson, K. McKenna, T. Postmes, & U. Reips (Eds.), *Oxford handbook of Internet psychology* (pp. 137–152). Oxford: Oxford University Press.

32. For a comprehensive discussion of the patterns described here, see Burleson, B. R. (2002, Winter). Psychological mediators of sex differences in emotional support: A reflection on the mosaic. *Communication Reports, 15,* 71–79.

33. Burleson, Psychological mediators.

34. Beehr, T. A., Bowling, N. A., & Bennett, M. M. (2010). Occupational stress and failures of social support: When helping hurts. *Journal of Occupational Health Psychology, 15,* 45–49.

35. Young, R. W., & Cates, C. M. (2004). Emotional and directive listening in peer mentoring. *International Journal of Listening, 18,* 21–33.

CHAPTER 6

1. For a survey of the issues surrounding the definition of nonverbal communication, see Knapp, M., & Hall, J. A. (2010). *Nonverbal communication in human interaction* (6th ed., Chapter 1). Belmont, CA: Wadsworth.

2. Keating, C. F. (2006). Why and how the silent self speaks volumes. In V. Manusov & M. L. Patterson (Eds.), *Sage handbook of nonverbal communication* (pp. 321–340). Thousand Oaks, CA: Sage.

3. Manusov, F. (1991, Summer). Perceiving nonverbal messages: Effects of immediacy and encoded intent on receiver judgments. *Western Journal of Speech Communication, 55,* 235–253.

4. See Smith, S. W. (1994). Perceptual processing of nonverbal relational messages. In D. E. Hewes (Ed.), *The cognitive bases of interpersonal communication* (pp. 349–388). Hillsdale, NJ: Erlbaum.

5. See, for example, Rosenthal, R., Hall, J. A., Matteg, M. R. D., Rogers, D., & Archer, D. (1979). *Sensitivity to nonverbal communication: The PONS test.* Baltimore, MD: Johns Hopkins University Press.

6. Hall, J. A. (1979). Gender, gender roles, and nonverbal communication skills. In R. Rosenthal (Ed.), *Skill in nonverbal communication: Individual differences* (pp. 32–67). Cambridge, MA: Oelgeschlager, Gunn, and Hain.

7. Research supporting these claims is cited in Burgoon, J. K., & Hoobler, G. D. (2002). Nonverbal signals. In M. L. Knapp & J. A. Daly (Eds.), *Handbook of interpersonal communication* (3rd ed., pp. 240–299). Thousand Oaks, CA: Sage.

8. Jones, S. E., & LeBaron, C. D. (2002). Research on the relationship between verbal and nonverbal communication: Emerging interactions. *Journal of Communication, 52,* 499–521.

9. Rourke, B. P. (1989). *Nonverbal learning disabilities: The syndrome and the model.* New York: Guilford Press.

10. Cross E. S., & Franz, E. A. (2003, March-April). *Talking hands: Observation of bimanual gestures as a facilitative working memory mechanism.* Paper presented at the 10th annual meeting of the Cognitive Neuroscience Society, New York.

11. Kleinke, C. R. (1977). Compliance to requests made by gazing and touching experimenters in field settings. *Journal of Experimental Social Psychology, 13*, 218–233.

12. Argyle, M. F., Alkema, F., & Gilmour, R. (1971). The communication of friendly and hostile attitudes: Verbal and nonverbal signals. *European Journal of Social Psychology, 1*, 385–402.

13. Buller, D. B., & Burgoon, J. K. (1994). Deception: Strategic and nonstrategic communication. In J. Daly & J. M. Wiemann (Eds.), *Interpersonal communication* (pp. 191–223). Hillsdale, NJ: Erlbaum.

14. Burgoon, J. K., Buller, D. B. Guerrero, L. K., & Feldman, C. M. (1994). Interpersonal deception: VI. Effects on preinteractional and international factors on deceiver and observer perceptions of deception success. *Communication Studies, 45*, 263–280; and Burgoon, J. K., Buller, D. B., & Guerrero, L. K. (1995). Interpersonal deception: IX. Effects of social skill and nonverbal communication on deception success and detection accuracy. *Journal of Language and Social Psychology, 14*, 289–311.

15. Riggio, R. G., & Freeman, H. S. (1983). Individual differences and cues to deception. *Journal of Personality and Social Psychology, 45*, 899–915.

16. Vrij, A. (2006). Nonverbal communication and deception. In V. Manusov & M. L. Patterson (Eds.), *Sage handbook of nonverbal communication* (pp. 341–359). Thousand Oaks, CA: Sage.

17. DePaulo, B. M., Lindsay, J. J., Malone, B. E., Muhlenbruck, L., Charlton, K., & Cooper, H. (2003). Cues to deception. *Psychological Bulletin, 129*, 74–118; and Vrig, A., Edward, K., Roberts, K. P., & Bull, R. (2000). Detecting deceit via analysis of verbal and nonverbal behavior. *Journal of Nonverbal Behavior, 24*, 239–263.

18. Dunbar, N. E., Ramirez, A., Jr., & Burgoon, J. K. (2003). The effects of participation on the ability to judge deceit. *Communication Reports, 16*, 23–33.

19. Vrig, A., Akehurst, L., Soukara, S., & Bull, R. (2004). Detecting deceit via analyses of verbal and nonverbal behavior in children and adults. *Human Communication Research, 30*, 8–41.

20. Millar, M. G., & Millar, K. U. (1998). The effects of suspicion on the recall of cues to make veracity judgments. *Communication Reports, 11*, 57–64.

21. Matsumoto, D. (2006). Culture and nonverbal behavior. In V. Manusov & M. L. Patterson (Eds.), *Sage handbook of nonverbal communication (pp. 219–235).* Thousand Oaks, CA: Sage.

22. Edman, P., Friesen, W. V., & Ellsworth, P. (1972). *Emotion in the human face: Guidelines for research and an integration of findings.* Elmsford, NY: Pergamon.

23. Maurer, R. E., & Tindall, J. H. (1983). Effect of postural congruence on client's perception of counselor empathy. *Journal of Counseling Psychology, 30*, 158–163.

24. Myers, M. B., Templer, D., & Brown, R. (1984). Coping ability of women who become victims of rape. *Journal of Consulting and Clinical Psychology, 52*, 73–78. See also Rubenstein, C. (1980, August). Body language that speaks to muggers. *Psychology Today, 20*, 20; and Meer, J. (1984, May). Profile of a victim. *Psychology Today, 24*, 76.

25. Ekman, P. (1985). *Telling lies: Clues to deceit in the marketplace, politics, and marriage.* New York: Norton, 1985, pp. 109–110.

26. Ekman, P., & Friesen, W. V. (1974). Nonverbal behavior and psychopathology. In R. J. Friedman & M. N. Katz (Eds.), *The psychology of depression: Contemporary theory and research* (pp. 203–232). Washington, DC: J. Winston.

27. Sutton, R., & Rafaeli, A. (1988). Untangling the relationship between displayed emotions and organizational sales: The case of convenience stores. *Academy of Management Journal, 31*, 463.

28. Akechi, H., Senju, A., Uibo, H., Kikuchi, Y., Hasegawa, T., & Hietanen, J. K. (2013). Attention to eye contact in the West and East: Autonomic responses and evaluative ratings. *Plos ONE, 8*(3), 1–10.

29. Starkweather, J. A. (1961). Vocal communication of personality and human feeling. *Journal of Communication, II*, 69; and Scherer, K. R., Koiwunaki, J., & Rosenthal, R. (1972). Minimal cues in the vocal communication of affect: Judging emotions from content-masked speech. *Journal of Psycholinguistic Speech, I*, 269–285. See also Cox, F. S., & Olney, C. (1985, November). *Vocalic communication of relational messages.* Paper presented at the annual meeting of the Speech Communication Association, Denver, CO.

30. Burns, K. L., & Beier, E. G. (1973). Significance of vocal and visual channels for the decoding of emotional meaning. *Journal of Communication, 23,* 118–130. See also Hegstrom, T. G. (1979). Message impact: What percentage is nonverbal? *Western Journal of Speech Communication, 43,* 134–143; and McMahan, E. M. (1976). Nonverbal communication as a function of attribution in impression formation. *Communication Monographs, 43,* 287–294.

31. Bennett, J. (2010). The beauty advantage. *Newsweek* (July 19). Retrieved from http://www.newsweek.com/2010/07/19/the-beauty-advantage.html.

32. Guerrero, L. K., & Hecht, M. L. (2008). *The nonverbal communication reader: Classic and contemporary readings* (3rd ed.). Long Grove, IL: Waveland Press.

33. Brand, R., Bonatsos, A., D'orazio, R., & Deshong, H. (2001). What is beautiful is good, even online: Correlations between photo attractiveness and text attractiveness in men's online dating profiles. *Computers in Human Behavior, 28,* 166–170.

34. Abdala, K. F., Knapp, M. L., & Theune, K. E. (2002). Interaction appearance theory: Changing perceptions of physical attractiveness through social interaction. *Communication Theory, 12,* 8–40.

35. McDermott, L. A., & Pettijohn, T. F., II. (2011). The influence of clothing fashion and race on the perceived socioeconomic status and person perception of college students. *Psychology & Society, 4,* 64–75.

36. Dishman, L. (2011, September 15). Does causal dress hurt your income? *PayScale Career News.* Retrieved from http://www.payscale.com/career-news/2011/09/dress-for-success.

37. Roberts, S., Owen, R. C., & Havlicek, J. (2010). Distinguishing between perceiver and wearer effects in clothing color-associated attributions. *Evolutionary Psychology, 8*(3), 350–364.

38. Rehman S. U., Nietert P. J., Cope D. W., & Kilpatrick, A. O. (2005). What to wear today? Effect of doctor's attire on the trust and confidence of patients. *The American Journal of Medicine, 118,* 1279–1286.

39. Hoult, T. F. (1954). Experimental measurement of clothing as a factor in some social ratings of selected American men. *American Sociological Review, 19,* 326–327.

40. Gulledge, N., & Fischer-Lokou, J. (2003). Another evaluation of touch and helping behaviour. *Psychological Reports, 92,* 62–64.

41. Kraus, M. W., Huang, C., & Keltner, D. (in press). Tactile communication, cooperation, and performance: An ethological study of the NBA. *Emotion.*

42. Gulledge & Fischer-Lokou (2003). Another evaluation.

43. Martin, B. S. (2012). A stranger's touch: Effects of accidental interpersonal touch on consumer evaluations and shopping time. *Journal of Consumer Research, 39,* 174–184.

44. Hart, S., Field, T., Hernandez-Reif, M., & Lundy, B. (1998). Preschoolers' cognitive performance improves following massage. *Early Child Development and Care, 143,* 59–64. For more about the role of touch in relationships, see Keltner, D., *Born to be good: The science of a meaningful life.* New York: Norton, pp. 173–198.

45. Montagu, A. (1972). *Touching: The human significance of the skin.* New York: Harper & Row, p. 93.

46. Chan, Y. K. (1999). Density, crowding, and factors intervening in their relationship: Evidence from a hyper-dense metropolis. *Social Indicators Research, 48,* 103–124.

47. Hall, E. (1969). *The hidden dimension.* Garden City, NY: Anchor Books, pp. 113–130.

48. Hackman, M., & Walker, K. (1990). Instructional communication in the televised classroom: The effects of system design and teacher immediacy. *Communication Education, 39,* 196–206. See also McCroskey, J. C., and Richmond, V. P. (1992). Increasing teacher influence through immediacy. In V. P. Richmond & J. C. McCroskey (Eds.), *Power in the classroom: Communication, control, and concern* (pp. 101–119). Hillsdale, NJ: Erlbaum.

49. Conlee, C., Olvera, J., & Vagim, N. The relationships among physician nonverbal immediacy and measures of patient satisfaction with physician care. *Communication Reports, 6,* 25–33.

50. Mehrabian, A. (1976). *Public places and personal spaces: The psychology of work, play, and living environments.* New York: Basic Books, p. 69.

51. Sadalla, E. (1987). Identity and symbolism in housing. *Environment and Behavior, 19,* 569–587.

52. Sommer, R. (1969). *Personal space: The behavioral basis of design.* Englewood Cliffs, NJ: Prentice-Hall, p. 78.

53. Maslow, A. H., & Mintz, N. L. (1956). Effects of esthetic surroundings. *Journal of Psychology, 41,* 247–254.

54. See, for example, Hill, O. W., Block, R. A., & Buggie, S. E. (2000). Culture and beliefs about time: Comparisons among black Americans, black Africans,

and white Americans." *Journal of Psychology, 134*, 443–457.

55. Ballard, D. I., & Seibold, D. R. (2000). Time orientation and temporal variation across work groups: Implications for group and organizational communication. *Western Journal of Communication, 64*, 218–242.

56. Ekman, P., & Friesen, W. (1975). *Unmasking the face*. New York: Prentice Hall.

57. Ekman, P., Friesen, W. V., & Baer, J. (1984). The international language of gestures. *Psychology Today, 18*, 64–69.

58. Hall, *The Hidden Dimension*.

59. Ibid.

60. Hall, J. A., Carter, J. D., & Horgan, T. G. (2001). Status roles and recall of nonverbal cues. *Journal of Nonverbal Behavior, 25*, 79–100.

61. Hall, J. A. (2006). Women and men's nonverbal communication. In V. Manusov & M. L. Patterson (Eds.), *The SAGE handbook of nonverbal communication* (pp. 201–218). Thousand Oaks, CA: Sage.

62. Carlson, E. N. (2013). Overcoming barriers to self-knowledge: Mindfulness as a path to seeing yourself as you really are. *Perspectives on Psychological Science, 8*, 173–186.

CHAPTER 7

1. For a discussion of the characteristics of impersonal and interpersonal communication, see Bochner, A. P. (1984). The functions of human communication in interpersonal bonding. In C. C. Arnold & J. W. Bowers (Eds.), *Handbook of rhetorical and communication theory*. Boston: Allyn and Bacon, p. 550; Trenholm S. , & Jensen, A. *Interpersonal communication*. Belmont, CA: Wadsworth, p. 37; and Stewart, J., Zediker, K. E., & Witteborn, S. (2007). *Together: Communicating interpersonally: A social construction approach*. New York: Oxford University Press.

2. See Dillard, J. P., Solomon, D. H., & Palmer, M. T. (1999). Structuring the concept of relational communication. *Communication Monographs, 66*, 46–55.

3. Frei, J. R., & Shaver, P. R. (2002). Respect in close relationships: Prototype, definition, self-report assessment, and initial correlates. *Personal Relationships, 9*, 121–139.

4. See Rossiter, C. M., Jr. (1974). Instruction in metacommunication. *Central States Speech Journal, 25*, 36–42, and Wilmot, W. W. (1980). Metacommunication: A reexamination and extension. In *Communication Yearbook 4*. New Brunswick, NJ: Transaction Books.

5. Nguyen, M., Bin, Y., & Campbell, A. (2012). Comparing online and offline self-disclosure: A systematic review. *Cyberpsychology, Behavior & Social Networking, 15*, 103–111.

6. Rosenfeld, L. B., & Kendrick, W. L. (1984). Choosing to be open: Subjective reasons for self-disclosing. *Western Journal of Speech Communication, 48* (Fall), 326–343.

7. Altman, I., & Taylor, D. A. (1973). *Social penetration: The development of interpersonal relationships*. New York: Holt, Rinehart and Winston.

8. Luft, J. (1969). *Of human interaction*. Palo Alto, CA: National Press.

9. Summarized in Pearson, J. (1989). *Communication in the family*. New York: Harper & Row, pp. 252–257.

10. Eisenberg, E. M., & Witten, M. G. (1987). Reconsidering openness in organizational communication. *Academy of Management Review, 12*, 418–428.

11. Rosenfeld, L. B., & Gilbert, J. R. (1989). The measurement of cohesion and its relationship to dimensions of self-disclosure in classroom settings. *Small Group Behavior, 20*, 291–301.

12. Kraut, R., Patterson, M., Lundmark, V., Kiesler, S., Mukophadhyay, T., & Scherlis, W. (1998). Internet paradox: A social technology that reduces social involvement and psychological well-being? *American Psychologist, 53*, 1017–1031.

13. Przybylski, A. K., & Weinstein, N. (2013). Can you connect with me now? How the presence of mobile communication technology influences face-to-face conversation quality. *Journal of Social and Personal Relationships, 30*, 237–246.

14. Jin, B., & Peña, J. F. (2010). Mobile communication in romantic relationships: Mobile phone use, relational uncertainty, love, commitment, and attachment styles. *Communication Reports, 23*, 39–51.

15. Pempek, T. A., Yermolayeva, Y. A., & Calvert, S. L. (2009). College students' social networking experiences on Facebook. *Psychology, 30*, 227–238.

16. Lenhart, A., Madden M., & Smith A. (2010). *Teens and social media*. Pew Internet & American Life Project. Retrieved from http://www.pewinternet.org/Reports/2007/Teens-and-Social-Media/1-Summary-of-Findings.aspx?r=1.

17. Hales, K. D. (2012, May). *Multimedia use for relational maintenance in romantic couples*. Paper presented at the annual meeting of the International

Communication Association, Phoenix, AZ. Quotes here appear on pages 14 and 15.

18. Teng, C., Chen, M., Chen, Y., & Li, Y. (2012). Loyalty due to others: The relationships among challenge, interdependence, and online gamer loyalty. *Journal of Computer-Mediated Communication, 17*, 489–500.

19. Steinkuehler, C. A., & Williams, D. (2006), Where everybody knows your (screen) name: Online games as "third places." *Journal of Computer-Mediated Communication, 11*, 885–909.

20. Baiocco, R., Laghi, F., Schneider, B. H., Dalessio, M., Amichai-Hamburger, Y., Coplan, R. J., Koszycki, D., & Flament, M. (2011). Daily patterns of communication and contact between Italian early adolescents and their friends. *Cyberpsychology, Behavior, and Social Networking* (Impact Factor: 1.84), *14*(7–8), 467–471.

21. Kirkpatrick, D. (1992). Here comes the payoff from PCs. *Fortune, March 23*, 93–102.

22. Cissna, K. N. L., & Seiburg, E. (1995). Patterns of interactional confirmation and disconfirmation. In M. V. Redmond (Ed.), *Interpersonal communication: Readings in theory and research* (pp. 301–317). Fort Worth, TX: Harcourt Brace.

23. Ibid.

24. For a discussion of reactions to disconfirming responses, see Vangelisti, A. L., & Crumley, L. P. (1998). Reactions to messages that hurt: The influence of relational contexts. *Communication Monographs, 64*, 173–196. See also Cortina, L. M., Magley, V. J., Williams, J. H., & Langhout, R. D. (2001). Incivility in the workplace: Incidence and impact. *Journal of Occupational Health Psychology, 6*, 64–80.

25. See Wilmot, W. W. (1987). *Dyadic communication.* New York: Random House, pp. 149–158; and Andersson, L. M., & Pearson, C. M. (1999). Tit for tat? The spiraling effect of incivility in the workplace. *Academy of Management Review, 24*, 452–471. See also Olson, L. N., & Braithwaite, D. O. (2004). "If you hit me again, I'll hit you back": Conflict management strategies of individuals experiencing aggression during conflicts. *Communication Studies, 55*, 271–286.

26. Wilmot, W. W., & Hocker, J. L. (2007). *Interpersonal conflict* (7th ed., pp. 21–22). New York: McGraw-Hill.

27. Ibid., pp. 23–24.

28. Gottman, J. M., Driver, J., & Tabares, A. (2002). Building the sound marital house: An empirically

derived couple therapy. In A. S. Gurman & N. S. Jacobson (Eds.), *Clinical handbook of couple therapy* (3rd ed., pp. 373–400). New York: Guilford Press.

29. Gibb, J. (1961). Defensive communication. *Journal of Communication, 11*, 141–148. See also Eadie, W. F. (1982). Defensive communication revisited: A critical examination of Gibb's theory. *Southern Speech Communication Journal, 47*, 163–177.

30. For a review of research supporting the effectiveness of "I" language, see Proctor, R. F. II, and Wilcox, J. R. (1993). An exploratory analysis of responses to owned messages in interpersonal communication. *Et Cetera: A Review of General Semantics, 50*, 201–220. See also Proctor, R. F. II (1989). Responsibility or egocentrism? The paradox of owned messages. *Speech Association of Minnesota Journal, 16*, 59–60.

CHAPTER 8

1. Demir, M., & Özdemir, M. (2010). Friendship, need satisfaction and happiness. *Journal of Happiness Studies, 11*, 243–259.

2. Buote, V. M., Pancer, S., Pratt, M. W., Adams, G., Birnie-Lefcovitch, S., Polivy, J., & Wintre, M. (2007). The importance of friends: Friendship and adjustment among 1st-year university students. *Journal of Adolescent Research, 22*, 665–689.

3. Demir, M., Özdemir, M., & Marum, K. (2011). Perceived autonomy support, friendship maintenance, and happiness. *Journal of Psychology, 145*, 537–571.

4. Deci, E., La Guardia, J., Moller, A., Scheiner, M., & Ryan, R. (2006). On the benefits of giving as well as receiving autonomy support: Mutuality in close friendships. *Personality & Social Psychology Bulletin, 32*, 313–327.

5. Danby, S., Thompson, C., Theobald, M., & Thorpe, K. (2012). Children's strategies for making friends when starting school. *Australasian Journal of Early Childhood, 37*, 63–71.

6. Hashim, I. M., Mohd-Zaharim, N., & Khodarahimi, S. (2012). Perceived similarities and satisfaction among friends of the same and different ethnicity and sex at workplace. *Psychology, 3*, 621–625.

7. Nelson, P., Thorne, A., & Shapiro, L. (2001). I'm outgoing and she's reserved: The reciprocal dynamics of personality in close friendships in young adulthood. *Journal of Personality, 79*, 1113–1147.

8. Specher, S. (1998). Insiders' perspectives on reasons for attraction to a close other. *Social Psychology Quarterly, 61*, 287–300.

9. See, for example, Roloff, M. E. (1981). *Interpersonal communication: The social exchange approach.* Beverly Hills, CA: Sage.

10. Becker, J. H., Johnson, A., Craig, E. A., Gilchrist, E. S., Haigh, M. M., & Lane, L. T. (2009). Friendships are flexible, not fragile: Turning points in geographically close and long-distance friendships. *Journal of Social & Personal Relationships, 26,* 347–369. Quote appears on p. 347.

11. Johnson, A., Haigh, M. M., Craig, E. A., & Becker, J. H. (2009). Relational closeness: Comparing undergraduate college students' geographically close and long-distance friendships. *Personal Relationships, 16,* 631–646.

12. Manago, A., Taylor, T., & Greenfield, P. (2012). Me and my 400 friends: The anatomy of college students' Facebook networks, their communication patterns, and well-being: Interactive media and human development. *Developmental Psychology, 48,* 369–380. Quote appears on p. 375.

13. Migliaccio, T. (2009). Men's friendships: Performances of masculinity. *Journal of Men's Studies, 17,* 226–241.

14. Hall, J. A. (2011). Sex differences in friendship expectations: A meta-analysis. *Journal of Social and Personal Relationships, 28,* 723–747.

15. Bello, R. S., Brandau-Brown, F. E., Zhang, S., & Ragsdale, J. (2010). Verbal and nonverbal methods for expressing appreciation in friendships and romantic relationships: A cross-cultural comparison. *International Journal of Intercultural Relations, 34,* 294–302.

16. Hall, J. A., Sex differences in friendship expectations.

17. Ibid.

18. Bleske-Rechek, A., Somers, E., Micke, C., Erickson, L., Matteson, L., Stocco, C., Schumacher, B., & Ritchie, L. (2012). Benefit or burden? Attraction in cross-sex friendship. *Journal of Social and Personal Relationships, 29,* 569–596.

19. Hall, J. A. (2011). Sex differences in friendship expectations: A meta-analysis. *Journal of Social and Personal Relationships, 28,* 723–747.

20. Ibid.

21. Baiocco, R., Laghi, F., Di Pomponio, I., & Nigito, C. S. (2012). Self-disclosure to the best friend: Friendship quality and internalized sexual stigma in Italian lesbian and gay adolescents. *Journal of Adolescence, 35,* 381–387.

22. Ibid.

23. Russell, E. M., DelPriore, D. J., Butterfield, M. E., & Hill, S. E. (2013). Friends with benefits, but without the sex: Straight women and gay men exchange trustworthy mating advice. *Evolutionary Psychology, 11*(1), 132–147.

24. Quinn, B. (2011, May 8). Social network users have twice as many friends online as in real life. *The Guardian.* Retrieved from http://www.theguardian.com/media/2011/may/09/social-network-users-friends-online.

25. Whitty, M., & Joinson, A. (2009). *Truth, lies & trust on the Internet.* New York: Routledge.

26. Chan, D. K.-S., & Cheng, G. H.-L. (2004). A comparison of offline and online friendship qualities at different stages of relationship development. *Journal of Social and Personal Relationships, 21,* 305–320.

27. Walther, J. B. (1996). Computer-mediated communication: Impersonal, interpersonal, and hyperpersonal interaction. *Communication Research, 23,* 3–43; Okdie, B. M., Guadagno, R. E., Bernieri, F. J., Geers, A. L., & Mclarney-Vesotski, A. R. (2011). Getting to know you: Face-to-face versus online interactions. *Computers in Human Behavior, 27,* 153–159.

28. Ranney, J. D., & Troop-Gordon, W. (2012). Computer-mediated communication with distant friends: Relations with adjustment during students' first semester in college. *Journal of Educational Psychology, 104*(3), 848–861.

29. Cacioppo, J. T., Cacioppo, S., Gonzaga, G. C., Ogburn, E. L., & VanderWeele, T. J. (2013). Marital satisfaction and break-ups differ across on-line and off-line meeting venues. *Proceedings of the National Academy of Sciences, 110*(25), 10135–10140.

30. Guerrero, L. K., Farinelli, L., & McEwan, B. (2009). Attachment and relational satisfaction: The mediating effect of emotional communication. *Communication Monographs, 76,* 487–514.

31. Tabak, B., McCullough, M., Luna, L., Bono, G., & Berry, J. (2012). Conciliatory gestures facilitate forgiveness and feelings of friendship by making transgressors appear more agreeable. *Journal of Personality, 80,* 503–536.

32. Davis, J. R., & Gold, G. J. (2011). An examination of emotional empathy, attributions of stability, and the link between perceived remorse and forgiveness. *Personality & Individual Differences, 50,* 392–397.

33. Bello, R. S., Brandau-Brown, F. E., Zhang, S., & Ragsdale, J. D. (2010). Verbal and nonverbal

methods for expressing appreciation in friendships and romantic relationships: A cross-cultural comparison. *International Journal of Intercultural Relations, 34,* 294–302.

34. van der Horst, M., & Coffe, H. (2012). How friendship network characteristics influence subjective well-being. *Social Indicators Research, 107,* 509–529.

35. Rawlins, W. K., & Holl, M. (1987). The communicative achievement of friendship during adolescence: Predicaments of trust and violation. *Western Journal of Speech Communication, 51,* 345–363.

36. Deci, E., La Guardia, J., Moller, A., Scheiner, M., & Ryan, R. (2006). On the benefits of giving as well as receiving autonomy support: Mutuality in close friendships. *Personality & Social Psychology Bulletin, 32,* 313–327.

37. Minow, M. (1998). Redefining families: Who's in and who's out? In K. V. Hansen & A. I. Garey (Eds.), *Families in the U.S.: Kinship and domestic policy* (pp. 7–19). Philadelphia: Temple University Press. (Originally published in the *University of Colorado Law Review,* 1991, *62,* 269–285.)

38. Galvin, K. M. (2006). Diversity's impact of defining the family: Discourse-dependence and identity. In R. L. West & L. H. Turner (Eds.), *The family communication sourcebook* (pp. 3–20). Thousand Oaks, CA: Sage.

39. Trace the evolution of this model by exploring McLeod, M. J., & Chaffee, S. H. (1972). The construction of social reality. In J. Tedeschi (Ed.), *The social influence process* (pp. 177–195). Mahwah, NJ: Lawrence Erlbaum; Ritchie, L. D., & Fitzpatrick, M. A. (1990), Family communication patterns: Measuring interpersonal perceptions of interpersonal relationships. *Communication Research, 17,* 523–544; and Koerner, A. F., & Fitzpatrick, M. A. (2006). Family communication patterns theory: A social cognitive approach. In D. O. Braithwaite & L. A. Baxter (Eds.), *Engaging theories in family communication: Multiple perspectives* (pp. 50–65). Thousand Oaks, CA: Sage.

40. Young, S. L. (2009). The function of parental communication patterns: Reflection-enhancing and reflection-discouraging approaches. *Communication Quarterly, 57,* 379–394.

41. Hamon, J. D., & Schrodt, P. (2012). Do parenting styles moderate the association between family conformity orientation and young adults' mental

well-being? *Journal of Family Communication, 12,* 151–166.

42. Koerner, A. F., & Fitzpatrick, M. A. (2002). Understanding family communication patterns and family functioning: The roles of conversation orientation and conformity orientation. *Communication Yearbook, 26,* 37–68.

43. For background on this theory, see Baumrind, D. (1991). The influence of parenting styles on adolescent competence and substance use. *The Journal of Early Adolescence, 11,* 56–95.

44. Hamon, J. D., & Schrodt, P. (2012). Do parenting styles moderate the association between family conformity orientation and young adults' mental well-being? *Journal of Family Communication, 12,* 151–166. Quote appears on p. 162.

45. Ibid.

46. Ibid.

47. Stewart, R. B., Kozak, A. L., Tingley, L. M., Goddard, J. M., Blake, E. M., & Cassel, W. A. (2001). Adult sibling relationships: Validation of a typology. *Personal Relationships, 8,* 299–324.

48. Riggio, H. (2006). Structural features of sibling dyads and attitudes toward sibling relationships in young adulthood. *Journal of Family Issues, 27,* 1233–1254.

49. Scharf, M., Shulman, S., & Avigad-Spitz, L. (2005). Sibling relationships in emerging adulthood and in adolescence. *Journal of Adolescent Research, 20,* 64–90.

50. Riggio, H. (2006). Structural features of sibling dyads and attitudes toward sibling relationships in young adulthood. *Journal of Family Issues, 27,* 1233–1254.

51. Myers, S. A., & Goodboy, A. K. (2010). Relational maintenance behaviors and communication channel use among adult siblings. *North American Journal of Psychology, 12,* 103–116.

52. Livingston, G. (2013, September 4). At grandmother's house we stay. *PewResearch Center's Social & Demographic Trends.* Retrieved from http://www.pewsocialtrends.org/2013/09/04/at -grandmothers-house-we-stay/.

53. Brenner, J., & Smith, A. (2013, August 5). 72% of online adults are social networking site users. *Pew Research Center's Internet Project.* Retrieved from http://www.pewinternet.org/Reports/2013/social -networking-sites.aspx.

54. Siibak, A., & Tamme, V. (2013). "Who introduced granny to Facebook?" An exploration of everyday family interactions in web-based communication environments. *Northern Lights: Film & Media Studies Yearbook, 11*, 71.

55. Breheny, M., Stephens, C., & Spilsbury, L. (2013). Involvement without interference: How grandparents negotiate intergenerational expectations in relationships with grandchildren. *Journal of Family Studies, 19*, 174–184.

56. Feiler, B. (2013). *The secrets of happy families: Improve your mornings, rethink family dinner, fight smarter, go out and play, and much more.* New York: HarperCollins. Quote appears on p. 141.

57. Mansson, D. H. (2012). A qualitative analysis of grandparents' expressions of affection for their young adult grandchildren. *North American Journal of Psychology, 14*, 207–219.

58. Geurts, T., van Tilburg, T., & Poortman, A. (n.d.). The grandparent-grandchild relationship in childhood and adulthood: A matter of continuation? *Personal Relationships, 19*, 267–278.

59. Duke, M. P., Lazarus, A., & Fivush, R. (2008). Knowledge of family history as a clinically useful index of psychological well-being and prognosis: A brief report. *Psychotherapy Theory, Research, Practice, Training, 45*, 268–272.

60. Duke, M. P. (20013, March 23). The stories that bind us: What are the twenty questions? *The Blog.* Retrieved from http://www.huffingtonpost.com/marshall-p-duke/the-stories-that-bind-us-_b_2918975.html.

61. Guerrero, L. K., Farinelli, L., & McEwan, B. (2009). Attachment and relational satisfaction: The mediating effect of emotional communication. *Communication Monographs, 76*, 487–514.

62. Young, S. L., The function of parental communication patterns.

63. Information in this paragraph is from Petronio, S. (2010). Communication privacy management theory: What do we know about family privacy regulation? *Journal of Family Theory & Review, 2*, 175–196.

64. Baraldi, C., & Iervese, V. (2010). Dialogic mediation in conflict resolution education. *Conflict Resolution Quarterly, 27*, 423–445.

65. Strom, R. E., & Boster, F. J. (2011). Dropping out of high school: Assessing the relationship between supportive messages from family and educational attainment. *Communication Reports, 24*, 25–37.

66. Feiler, B., *The secrets of happy families.*

CHAPTER 9

1. Ahmetoglu, G., Swami, V., & Chamorro-Premuzic, T. (2010). The relationship between dimensions of love, personality, and relationship length. *Archives of Sexual Behavior, 34*, 1181–1190.

2. Malouff, J. M., Schutte, N. S., & Thorsteinsson E. B. (2013). Trait emotional intelligence and romantic relationship satisfaction: A meta-analysis. *American Journal of Family Therapy, 42*, 53–66.

3. Erickson, E. H. (1963). *Childhood and society* (2nd ed.). New York: Norton.

4. Floyd, K., Hess, J. A., Miczo, L. A., Halone, K. K., Mikkelson, A. C., & Tusing, K. (2005). Human affection exchange: VIII. Further evidence of the benefits of expressed affection. *Communication Quarterly, 53*, 285–303.

5. Bond, B. J. (2009). He posted, she posted: Gender differences in self-disclosure on social network sites. *Rocky Mountain Communication Review, 6*(2), 29–37.

6. MacGeorge, E. L., Graves, A. R., Feng, B., Gillihan, S. J., & Burleson, B. R. (2004). The myth of gender cultures: Similarities outweigh differences in men's and women's provision of and responses to supportive communication. *Sex Roles, 50*, 143–175.

7. Information in this paragraph is from Hall, E., Travis, M., Anderson, S., & Henley, A. (2013). Complaining and Knapp's relationship stages: Gender differences in instrumental complaints. *Florida Communication Journal, 41*, 49–61.

8. Elliott, S., & Umberson, O. (2008). The performance of desire: Gender and sexual negotiation in long-term marriages. *Journal of Marriage and Family, 70*, 391–406.

9. Balsam, K. F., Beauchaine, T. P., Rothblum, E. D., & Solomon, S. E. (2008). Three-year follow-up of same-sex couples who had civil unions in Vermont, same-sex couples not in civil unions, and heterosexual married couples. *Developmental Psychology, 44*, 102–116.

10. Gottman, J., Levenson, R., & Swanson, C. (2003). Observing gay, lesbian and heterosexual couples' relationships: Mathematical modeling of conflict interaction. *Journal of Homosexuality, 45*, 65–91.

11. Chapman, G. (2010). *The five love languages: The secret to love that lasts.* Chicago: Northfield Publishing.

12. Chapman, G. (1995). *The five love languages: How to express heartfelt commitment to your mate.* Chicago: Northfield Publishing, p. 17. See also Egbert, N., & Polk, D. (2006). Speaking the language of relational maintenance: A validity test of Chapman's (1992) five love languages. *Communication Research Reports, 23*(1), 19–26.

13. Frisby, B. N., & Booth-Butterfield, M. (2012). The "how" and "why" of flirtatious communication between marital partners. *Communication Quarterly, 60,* 465–480.

14. Merolla, A. J. (2010). Relational maintenance during military deployment: Perspectives of wives of deployed US soldiers. *Journal of Applied Communication Research, 38*(1), 4–26.

15. Haas, S. M., & Stafford, L. (2005). Maintenance behaviors in same-sex and marital relationships: A matched sample comparison. *Journal of Family Communication, 5,* 43–60.

16. Ibid.

17. Soin, R. (2011). Romantic gift giving as chore or pleasure: The effects of attachment orientations on gift giving perceptions. *Journal of Business Research, 64,* 113–118.

18. Guéguen, N. (2010). The effect of a woman's incidental tactile contact on men's later behavior. *Social Behavior and Personality: An International Journal, 38,* 257–266.

19. Floyd, K., Boren, J. P., & Hannawa, A. F. (2009). Kissing in marital and cohabiting relationships: Effects of blood lipids, stress, and relationship satisfaction. *Western Journal of Communication, 73,* 113–133.

20. Knapp, M. L., & Vangelisti, A. L. (2009). *Interpersonal communication and human relationships* (6th ed.). Boston: Allyn and Bacon.

21. Canary, D. J., & Stafford, L. (Eds.). (1994). *Communication and relational maintenance.* San Diego: Academic Press. See also Lee, J. (1998). Effective maintenance communication in superior-subordinate relationships. *Western Journal of Communication, 62,* 181–208.

22. Wilson, S. R., Kunkel, A. D., Robson, S. J., Olufowote, J. O., & Soliz, J. (2009). Identity implications of relationship (re)definition goals: An analysis of face threats and facework as young adults initiate, intensify, and disengage from romantic relationships. *Journal of Language and Social Psychology, 28,* 32–61.

23. Baxter, L. A. (1987). Symbols of relationship identity in relationship culture. *Journal of Social and Personal Relationships, 4,* 261–280.

24. Fox, J., Warber, K. M., & Makstaller, D. (2013). The role of Facebook in romantic relationship development: An exploration of Knapp's relational stage model. *Journal of Social and Personal Relationships, 30,* 771–794.

25. Dunleavy, K., & Booth-Butterfield, M. (2009). Idiomatic communication in the stages of coming together and falling apart. *Communication Quarterly, 57,* 416–432.

26. Brown, B. (2010). *The gifts of imperfection.* Center City, MN: Hazelden.

27. Knapp, M. L. (1984). *Interpersonal communication and human relationships.* Boston, MA: Allyn & Bacon.

28. See, for example, Baxter, L. A., & Montgomery, B. M. (1998). A guide to dialectical approaches to studying personal relationships. In B. M. Montgomery & L. A. Baxter (Eds.), *Dialectical approaches to studying personal relationships (pp. 1–16).* Mahwah, NJ: Erlbaum; and Ebert, L. A., & Duck, S. W. (1997). Rethinking satisfaction in personal relationships from a dialectical perspective. In R. J. Sternberg & M. Hojjatr (Eds.), *Satisfaction in close relationships.* New York: Guilford.

29. Summarized by Baxter, L. A. (1994). A dialogic approach to relationship maintenance. In D. J. Canary & L. Stafford (Eds.), *Communication and relational maintenance* (pp. 233–254). San Diego: Academic Press.

30. Ibid.

31. Morris, D. (1971). *Intimate behavior.* New York: Kodansha Globe, pp. 21–29.

32. VanLear, C. A. (1991). Testing a cyclical model of communicative openness in relationship development. *Communication Monographs, 58,* 337–361.

33. Adapted from Baxter & Montgomery, A guide to dialectical approaches, pp. 1–16.

34. Siffert, A., & Schwarz, B. (2011). Spouses' demand and withdrawal during marital conflict in relation to their subjective well-being. *Journal of Social and Personal Relationships, 28,* 262–277.

35. Serota, K. B., Levine, T. R., & Boster, F. J. (2010). The prevalence of lying in America: Three studies of

self-reported lies. *Human Communication Research,* *36*(1), 2–25.

36. Harrell, E. (2009, August 19). Why we lie so much. *Time.* Retrieved from http://www.time.com/time/health/article/0,8599,1917215,00.html.

37. McCornack, S. A., & Levine, T. R. (1990). When lies are uncovered: Emotional and relational outcomes of discovered deception. *Communication Monographs, 57,* 119–138.

38. Guthrie, J., & Kunkel, A. (2013). Tell me sweet (and not-so-sweet) little lies: Deception in romantic relationships. *Communication Studies, 64*(2), 141–157.

39. Kaplar, M. E., & Gordon, A. K. (2004). The enigma of altruistic lying: Perspective differences in what motivates and justifies lie telling within romantic relationships. *Personal Relationships, 11,* 489–507.

40. Bryant, E. (2008). Real lies, white lies and gray lies: Towards a typology of deception. *Kaleidoscope: A Graduate Journal of Qualitative Communication Research, 7,* 723–748.

41. Bavelas, J. B. (2009). Equivocation. In T. T. Reis & S. Sprecher (Eds.), *Encyclopedia of human relationships* (Vol. 1, pp. 537–539). Thousand Oaks, CA: Sage. Retrieved from http://web.uvic.ca/psyc/bavelas/2009Equivocation.pdf.

42. Gunderson, P. R., & Ferrari, J. R. (2008). Forgiveness of sexual cheating in romantic relationships: Effects of discovery method, frequency of offense, and presence of apology. *North American Journal of Psychology, 10,* 1–14.

43. Jang, S. A., Smith, S. W., & Levine, T. R. (2002). To stay or to leave? The role of attachment styles in communication patterns and potential termination of romantic relationships following discovery of deception. *Communication Monographs, 69,* 236.

44. Bippus, A. M., Boren, J. P., & Worsham, S. (2008). Social exchange orientation and conflict communication in romantic relationships. *Communication Research Reports, 25,* 227–234.

45. Meyer, J. R. (2004). Effect of verbal aggressiveness on the perceived importance of secondary goals in messages. *Communication Studies, 55,* 168–184.

46. Zacchilli, T. L., Hendrick, C., & Hendrick, S. S. (2009). The romantic partner conflict scale: A new scale to measure relationship conflict. *Journal of Social and Personal Relationships, 26,* 1073–1096.

47. Gottman, J. M., & Levenson, R. W. (2002). A two-factor model for predicting when a couple will divorce: Exploratory analyses using 14-year longitudinal data. *Family Process, 41*(1), 83–96; Gottman, J. M., Coan, J., Carrere, S., & Swanson, C. (1998). Predicting marital happiness and stability from newlywed interactions. *Journal of Marriage and the Family, 60*(1), 5–22. Retrieved from http://www.jstor.org/pss/353438; Carrere, S., Buehlman, K. T., Gottman, J. M., Coan, J. A., & Ruckstuhl, L. (2000). Predicting marital stability and divorce in newlywed couples. *Journal of Family Psychology, 14*(1), 42–58; Gottman, J. M. (1991). Predicting the longitudinal course of marriages. *Journal of Marital and Family Therapy, 17*(1), 3–7; Gottman, J. M., & Krokoff, L. J. (1989). The relationship between marital interaction and marital satisfaction: A longitudinal view. *Journal of Consulting and Clinical Psychology, 57,* 47–52; Carrere, S., & Gottman, J. M. (1999). Predicting divorce among newlyweds from the first three minutes of a marital conflict discussion. *Family Process, 38*(3), 293–301.

48. Gottman, J. (1994). *Why marriages succeed or fail: And how you can make yours last.* New York: Simon & Schuster.

49. Gottman, J. M. (2009). *The marriage clinic.* New York: Norton.

50. Rusbult, C. E., & Martz, J. M. (1995). Remaining in an abusive relationship: An investment analysis of nonvoluntary dependence. *Personality and Social Psychology Bulletin, 21,* 558–571.

51. Arriaga, X. B., Capezza, N. M., Goodfriend, W., Ray, E. S., & Sands, K. J. (2013). Individual well-being and relationship maintenance at odds: The unexpected perils of maintaining a relationship with an aggressive partner. *Social Psychological and Personality Science, 4,* 676–684.

52. Are you in a violent relationship? (2013). *The Center for Prevention of Abuse.* Retrieved from http://www.centerforpreventionofabuse.org/violent-relationship.php.

53. Domestic violence and abusive relationships safety plan. (2012). *University of Maryland Sexual Assault and Relational Violence Response Team.* Retrieved from http://www.umbc.edu/uhs/documents/resources/SARVRT_DV_RV_Safety_Plan-Fall_2012_Updates.pdf.

54. Domestic violence against women: Recognize patterns, seek help. (2014). *Mayo Clinic.* Retrieved from http://www.mayoclinic.org/healthy-living/adult

-health/in-depth/domestic-violence/art-20048397
?pg=1.

55. The problem. What is battering? (2009). *National Coalition Against Domestic Violence.* Retrieved from http://www.ncadv.org/learn/TheProblem_100.html.

CHAPTER 10

1. Morreale, S. P., & Pearson, J. C. (2008). Why communication education is important: The centrality of the discipline in the 21st century. *Communication Education, 57*(2), 224–240.

2. National Association of Colleges and Employers. (2013, October). *Job outlook 2014* (survey). Bethlemen, PA: Author.

3. Calandra, B. (2002, September). Toward a silver-tongued scientist. *The Scientist, 16*, 42.

4. Crispin, G., & Mehler, M. (2010). Impact of the Internet on source of hires. *CareerXRoads.* Retrieved from http://www.careerxroads.com/news/impactoftheinternet.doc.

5. Dodds, P. S., Muhamad, R., & Watts, D. J. (2003). An experimental study of search in global social networks. *Science, 301*, 827–829.

6. Rosen, J. (2010, July 25). The end of forgetting. *New York Times Magazine*, pp. 30–35.

7. Tullier, M. (2002). The art and science of writing cover letters: The best way to make a first impression. *Monster.com.* Retrieved from http://resume.monster.com/coverletter/coverletters.

8. Graham, A. (2011, January 14). You won't land a job if you can't follow directions. *Forbes.* Retrieved from http://www.forbes.com/sites/work-in-progress/2011/01/14/you-wont-land-a-job-if-you-cant-follow-directions/.

9. Moss, C. (2013, September 28). 14 weird, open-ended job interview questions asked at Apple, Amazon and Google. *Business Insider* [online blog]. Retreived from http://www.businessinsider.com/weird-interview-questions-from-apple-google-amazon-2013-9?op=1#ixzz37PdzyCTk. See also: Top 25 oddball interview questions for 2014. *Glassdoor.* Retrieved from http://www.glassdoor.com/Top-25-Oddball-Interview-Questions-LST_KQ0,34.htm.

10. Rabin, M., & Schrag, J. L. (1999). First impressions matter: A model of confirmatory bias. *The Quarterly Journal of Economics, 14*, 37–82.

11. Mitchell, N. R. (nd). Top 10 interview tips from an etiquette professional. *Experience* [online blog]. Retrieved from http://www.experience.com/entry-level-jobs/jobs-and-careers/interview-resources/top-10-interview-tips-from-an-etiquette-professional/. Quote appears in paragraph 7.

12. Blue, G. M. (2014). 4 tips for conducting a job interview using Skype. *Inc.* Retrieved from http://www.inc.com/guides/201103/4-tips-for-conducting-a-job-interview-using-skype.html.

13. Lunenberg, F. C. (2010). Formal communication channels: Upward, downward, horizontal, and external. *Focus on Colleges, Universities, and Schools, 4,* 3. Retrieved from http://www.nationalforum.com/Electronic%20Journal%20Volumes/Lunenberg,%20Fred%20C,%20Formal%20Comm%20Channels%20FOCUS%20V4%20N1%202010.pdf.

14. Managers' shoptalk. *Working Woman*, February 1985 (p. 22).

15. Katz, D., & Kahn, R. (1978). *The social psychology of organizations* (2nd ed.). New York: Wiley, p. 239.

16. Peters, T. J., & Waterman, R. H., Jr. (1982). *In search of excellence: Lessons from America's best-run companies.* New York: Harper & Row, p. 267.

17. Lunenberg, "Formal communication channels," p. 4.

18. See, e.g., Kassing, J. W. (2000). Investigating the relationship between superior-subordinate relationship quality and employee dissent. *Communication Research Reports, 17*, 58–70.

19. Schuster, L. (1982, April 20). Wal-Mart chief's enthusiastic approach infects employees, keeps retailer growing. *Wall Street Journal*, p. 21.

20. Klaus, P. (2007). *The hard truth about soft skills.* New York: Collins Business; Solomon, M. (1993). *Getting praised, raised and recognized.* Englewood Cliffs, NJ: Prentice-Hall.

21. Spillan, J. E., Mino, M., & Rowles, M. S. (2002, Fall). Sharing organizational messages through effective lateral communication. *Qualitative Research Reports in Communication*, 96–104.

22. Adapted from Goldhaber, G.M. (1993). *Organizational Communication* 6th ed., Madison, Wis.: Brown & Benchmark, pp. 174–175.

23. Goleman, C. (2006). *Social intelligence: The new science of human relationships.* New York: Bantam Dell.

24. Millennial Branding and American Express release new study on Gen Y workplace expectations. (2013, September 3). *Millennial branding.* Retrieved from http://millennialbranding.com/2013/09/gen-workplace-expectations-study/.

25. Fleming, P., & Sturdy, A. (2009). "Just be yourself!": Towards neo-normative control in organisations? *Employee Relations, 31*, 569–583.

26. Ragins, B. R. (2008). Disclosure disconnects: Antecedents and consequences of disclosing invisible stigmas across life domains. *Academy of Management Review, 33,* 194–215. See also Ragins, B. R., Singh, R., & Cornwell, J. M. (2007). Making the invisible visible: Fear and disclosure of sexual orientation at work. *Journal of Applied Psychology, 92,* 1103–1118.

27. Cross-cultural communiation tips for effective diversity management. (nd). *Hcareers.* Retrieved from http://www.hcareers.com/us/resourcecenter/tabid/306/articleid/507/.

28. Rosh, L., & Offermann, L. (2013, October). Be yourself, but carefully. *Harvard Business Review.* Retrieved from http://hbr.org/2013/10/be-yourself-but-carefully/ar/1.

29. Parker, T. (2013, October 25). 30 non-Americans on the American norms they find weird. *Thought Catalogue* [online forum]. Retrieved from http://thoughtcatalog.com/timmy-parker/2013/10/30-non-americans-on-the-weirdest-things-that-are-norms-to-americans/.

30. Kang, J. (2010). Ethical conflict and job satisfaction of public relations practitioners. *Public Relations Review, 36,* 152–156.

31. Zaslow, J. (2010, January 6). Before you gossip, ask yourself this…. *Moving On.* Retrieved from: http://online.wsj.com/article/SB10001424052748704160504574640111681307026.html.

32. Ibid.

33. "New hires—Stand out at work." Published May 2010 in OfficePro. Retrieved from http://web.ebscohost.com.libproxy.sbcc.edu:2048/bsi/detail?vid=4&hid=9&sid=079bf30df37c-4ad6-897ec1626aa9bb49%40sessionmgr14&bdata=JnNpdGU9YnNpLWxpdmU%3d#db=buh&AN=50544049.

34. Nikravan, L. (2014, January 10). Employees behaving badly. *Talent Management.* Retrieved from http://talentmgt.com/articles/view/employees-behaving-badly/1

35. Chandler, N. (nd). 10 tips for managing conflict in the workplace. *HowStuffWorks.* Retrieved from http://money.howstuffworks.com/business/starting-a-job/10-tips-for-managing-conflict-in-the-workplace1.htm#page=1.

36. Goleman, D. (2007, October 7). E-mail is easy to write (and to misread). *New York Times.* Retrieved from http://www.nytimes.com/2007/10/07/jobs/07pre.html?_r=0.

37. Leaping lizards! OfficeTeam survey reveals managers' most embarrassing moment at work. (2011, January 18). *OfficeTeam.* Retrieved from http://officeteam.rhi.mediaroom.com/WorkMishaps.

38. Saks, A. M. (2006). Antecedents and consequences of employee engagement. *Journal of Managerial Psychology, 21*(7), 600–619.

39. Grynderup, M. B., Mors, O., Hansen,Å. M., Andersen, J. H., Bonde, J. P., Kærgaard, A., Kærlev, L., Mikkelsen, S., Rugulies, R. E., Thomsen, J. F., & Kolstad, H. A. (2012). A two-year follow-up study of risk of depression according to work-unit measures of psychological demands and decision latitude. *Scandinavian Journal of Work, Environment & Health, 38,* 527–536.

40. Sorensen, S. (2013, June 20). How employee engagement drives growth. *Gallup Business Journal.* Retrieved from http://businessjournal.gallup.com/content/163130/employee-engagement-drives-growth.aspx.

41. Lapin, R. (2008). *Working with difficult people.* London: Dorling Kindersley.

42. Warnell, M. (2014, January 20). How to handle a bad boss: 7 strategies for "managing up." *Forbes.* Retrieved from http://www.forbes.com/sites/margiewarrell/2014/01/20/6-strategies-to-hanhandldling-a-bad-boss/.

43. Leaving a job professionally: Wrapping up your current position before moving on. (2010). *Claros Group.* Retrieved from http://www.clarosgroup.com/leavingjob.pdf.

44. Cain, S. (2013). *Quiet: The power of introverts in a world that can't stop talking.* New York: Broadway, p. 53.

45. Drucker, P. (1997). Foreword. In F. Hesselbein, M. Goldsmith, & R. Beckhard (Eds.), *The leader of the future: New visions, strategies, and practices for the next era.* San Francisco: Jossey-Bass, p. xi.

46. Aristotle. (1958). *Politics.* New York: Oxford University Press, Book 7.

47. Flaum, J. P. (2010). When it comes to business, nice guys finish first. *Green Peak Partners.* Retrieved from http://greenpeakpartners.com/resources/pdf/6%208%2010%20Executive%20study%20GP%20commentary%20article_Final.pdf.

48. Ibid.

49. For a discussion of situational theories, see Wilson, G. L. (2002). *Groups in context* (6th ed.). New York: McGraw-Hill, pp. 190–194.

50. Fiedler, F. E. (1967). *A theory of leadership effectiveness.* New York: McGraw-Hill.

51. Hersey, P., & Blanchard, K. (2001). *Management of organizational behavior: Utilizing human resources* (8th ed.). Upper Saddle River, NJ: Prentice Hall.

52. For a detailed discussion of leadership emergence, see Bormann, E. G. G., & Bormann, N. C. (1997). *Effective small group communication* (6th ed.). New York: Pearson Custom Publishing.

53. Hackman, M. Z., & Johnson, C. E. (2004). *Leadership: A communication perspective.* Long Grove, IL: Waveland. See also Anderson, C., & Kilduff, G. J. (2009). Why do dominant personalities attain influence in face-to-face groups? The competence-signaling effects of trait dominance. *Journal of Personality and Social Psychology, 96,* 491–503.

54. Bormann, *Small group communication.* For a succinct description of Bormann's findings, see Rothwell, *In mixed company,* p. 165.

55. Agho, A. O. (2009). Perspectives of senior-level executives on effective followership and leadership. *Journal of Leadership & Organizational Studies, 16,* 159–166.

56. Kelley, R. E. (2008). Rethinking followership. In R. E. Riggio, I. Chaleff, & J. Lipman-Blumen (Eds.), *The art of followership: How great followers create great leaders and organizations* (pp. 5–16). San Francisco: Jossey-Bass.

57. Kelley, 2008, p. 8

58. Kellerman, B. (2008). *Followership: How followers are creating change and changing leaders.* Boston, MA: Harvard Business Press.

59. The following types of power are based on the categories developed by French, J. R., & Raven, B. (1968). The basis of social power. In D. Cartright & A. Zander (Eds.), *Group dynamics.* New York: Harper & Row, p. 565.

60. Rothwell, J. D. (2013). *In mixed company: Communicating in small groups* (8th ed.). Boston: Cengage Learning.

CHAPTER 11

1. For a more detailed discussion of the advantages and disadvantages of working in groups, see Beebe, S. A., & Masterson, J. T. (2003). *Communicating in small groups: Principles and practices* (9th ed.). Needham Heights, MA: Allyn & Bacon.

2. Marby, E. A. (1999). The systems metaphor in group communication. In L. R. Frey (Ed.), *Handbook of group communication theory and research* (pp. 71–91). Thousand Oaks, CA: Sage.

3. Rothwell, J. D. (2004). *In mixed company: Small group communication* (5th ed.). Belmont, CA: Wadsworth, pp. 29–31.

4. Is your team too big? Too small? What's the right number? (2006, June 14). *Knowledge@Wharton.* Retrieved from http://knowledge.wharton.upenn.edu/article.cfm?articleid=1501.

5. Lowry, P., Roberts, T. L., Romano, N. C., Jr., Cheney, P. D., & Hightower, R. T. (2006). The impact of group size and social presence on small-group communication. *Small Group Research, 37,* 631–661.

6. Hackman, J. (1987). The design of work teams. In J. Lorsch (Ed.), *Handbook of organizational behavior* (pp. 315–342). Englewood Cliffs, NJ: Prentice Hall.

7. Lutgen-Sandvik, P., Riforgiate, S., & Fletcher, C. (2011). Work as a source of positive emotional experiences and the discourses informing positive assessment. *Western Journal of Communication, 75,* 2–27.

8. National Association of Colleges and Employers. (2013, October). *Job outlook 2014.* Bethlehem, PA: Author; Robles, M. M. (2012). Executive perceptions of the top 10 soft skills needed in today's workplace. *Business Communication Quarterly, 75,* 453–465.

9. Jones, B. (2009). The burden of knowledge and the death of the Renaissance man: Is innovation getting harder? *Review of Economic Studies, 76* (1).

10. State of California, Employment Development Department. (1995). Professional occupations in multimedia. *California Occupational Guide* (No. 2006). Sacramento, CA: Author, p. 4. See also Reagan & Associates. (1997). *A labor market analysis of the interactive digital media industry: Opportunities in multimedia.* San Francisco: Author, pp. 15–29.

11. LaFasto, F., & Carson, C. (2001). *When teams work best: 6,000 team members and leaders tell what it takes to succeed.* Thousand Oaks, CA: Sage. Larson, C. E., & LaFasto, F. M. J. (1989). *Teamwork: What must go right, what can go wrong.* Thousand Oaks, CA: Sage.

12. Kirschner, F., Paas, F., & Kirschner, P. A. (2010). Superiority of collaborative learning with complex tasks: A research note on alternative affective explanation. *Computers in Human Behavior, 27,* 53–57.

13. Tuckman, B. (1965). Developmental sequence in small groups. *Psychological Bulletin, 63,* 384–399.

14. Gouran, D. S., Hirokawa, R. Y., Julian, K. M., & Leatham, G. B. (1992). The evolution and current

status of the functional perspective on communication in decision-making and problem-solving groups. In S. A. Deetz (Ed.), *Communication yearbook 16* (pp. 573–600). Newbury Park, CA: Sage. See also Wittenbaum, G. M., Hollingshead, A. B., Paulus, P. B., Hirokawa, R. Y., Ancona, D. G., Peterson, R. S., Jehn, K. A., & Yoon, K. (2004). The functional perspective as a lens for understanding groups. *Small Group Research, 35,* 17–43.

15. Mayer, M. E. (1998). Behaviors leading to more effective decisions in small groups embedded in organizations. *Communication Reports, 11,* 123–132.

16. Bales, R. F., & Strodbeck, P. L. (1951). Phases in group problem solving. *Journal of Abnormal and Social Psychology, 46,* 485–495.

17. See, for example, Pavitt, C. (2003). Do interacting groups perform better than aggregates of individuals? *Human Communication Research, 29,* 592–599; Wittenbaum, G. M. (2004). Putting communication into the study of group memory. *Human Communication Research, 29,* 616–623; and Frank, M. G., Feely, T. H., Paolantonio, N., & Servoss, T. J. (2004). Individual and small group accuracy in judging truthful and deceptive communication. *Group Decision and Negotiation, 13,* 45–54.

18. Rae-Dupree, J. (2008, December 7). Innovation is a team sport. *New York Times.* Retrieved from http://www.nytimes.com/2008/12/07/business/worldbusiness/07iht-innovate.1.18456109.html?_r=0.

19. Adler, R. B., Elmhorst, J. M., & Lucas, K. (2013). *Communicating at work: Principles and practices for business and the professions* (11th ed.). New York: McGraw-Hill, pp. 215–216.

20. Fisher, B. A. (1970). Decision emergence: Phases in group decision making. *Speech Monographs, 37,* 53–66.

21. Frantz, C. R., & Jin, K. G. (1995). The structure of group conflict in a collaborative work group during information systems development. *Journal of Applied Communication Research, 23,* 108–127.

22. Bohm, D. (1996). *On dialogue* (L. Nichol, Ed.). London: Routledge & Kegan Paul.

23. See, example.g., Powell, A., Piccoli, G., & Ives, B. (2004). Virtual teams: A review of current literature and directions for future research. *ACM SIGMIS Database, 35,* 6–16. See also Walther, J. B., & Bazarova, N. (2008). Validation and application of electronic propinquity theory to computer-mediated communication in groups. *Communication Research, 35,* 622–645.

24. Schaefer, R. A. B., & Erskine, L. (2012). Virtual team meetings: Reflections on a class exercise exploring technology choice. *Journal of Management Education, 36,* 777–801.

25. Berry, G. R. (2011). Enhancing effectiveness on virtual teams. *Journal of Business Communication, 48,* 186–206.

26. Capdeferro, N., & Romero, M. (2012). Are online learners frustrated with collaborative learning experiences? *International Review of Research in Open & Distance Learning, 13,* 26–44.

27. Nunamaker, J. F., Jr., Reinig, B. A., & Briggs, R. O. (2009). Principles for effective virtual teamwork. *Communications of the ACM, 52*(4), 113–117.

28. Dewey, J. (1910). *How we think.* New York: Heath.

29. Poole, M. S. (1991). Procedures for managing meetings: Social and technological innovation. In R. A. Swanson & B. O. Knapp (Eds.), *Innovative meeting management* (pp. 53–109). Austin, TX: 3M Meeting Management Institute. See also Poole, M. S., & Holmes, M. E. (1995). Decision development in computer-assisted group decision making. *Human Communication Research, 22,* 90–127.

30. Lewin, K. (1951). *Field theory in social science.* New York: Harper & Row, pp. 30–59.

31. Hastle, R. (1983). *Inside the jury.* Cambridge, MA: Harvard University Press.

32. Waller, B. M., Hope, L., Burrowes, M., & Morrison, E. R. (2011). Twelve (not so) angry men: Managing conversational group size increases perceived contribution by decision makers. *Group Processes & Intergroup Relations, 14,* 835–843.

33. Rothwell, J. D. (2013). *In mixed company* (8th ed.). Boston: Wadsworth-Cengage, pp. 139–142.

34. Janis, I. (1982). *Groupthink: Psychological studies of policy decisions and fiascoes.* Boston: Houghton Mifflin. See also Baron, R. S. (2005). So right it's wrong: Groupthink and the ubiquitous nature of polarized group decision making. In M. P. Zanna (Ed.), *Advances in experimental social psychology* (Vol. 37, pp. 219–253). San Diego: Elsevier Academic Press.

35. Janis, I. L. (1972). *Victims of groupthink: A psychological study of foreign-policy decisions and fiascoes.* Boston: Houghton Mifflin.

36. Peralta, E., Memmott, M., & Coleman, K. (2012, July 12). Paterno, others slammed in report for failing to protect Sandusky's victims. *National Public Radio.*

37. Adapted from Rothwell, J. D. (2013). *In mixed company* (8th ed.). Boston: Wadsworth-Cengage, pp. 139–142, see note 49.

38. van Knippenberg, D., van Ginkel, W. P., & Homan, A. C. (2013, July). Diversity mindsets and the performance of diverse teams. *Organizational Behavior and Human Decision Processes, 121,* 183–193.

CHAPTER 12

1. Kangas Dwyer, K., & Davidson, M. M. (2012, April-June). Is public speaking really more feared than death? *Communication Research Reports, 29,* 99–107. This study found that public speaking was selected more often as a common fear than any other fear, including death. However, when students were asked to select a top fear, students selected death most often.

2. For example, see Kopfman, J. E., & Smith, S. (1996, February). Understanding the audiences of a health communication campaign: A discriminant analysis of potential organ donors based on intent to donate. *Journal of Applied Communication Research, 24,* 33–49.

3. Stutman, R. K., & Newell, S. E. (1984, Fall). Beliefs versus values: Silent beliefs in designing a persuasive message. *Western Journal of Speech Communication, 48*(4), 364.

4. Kelley, M. (2012). The new catch-22: Unemployment discrimination. In *Winning Orations, 2006* (p. 49). Mankato, MN: Interstate Oratorical Association. Kelley was coached by Craig Brown and Darren Epping.

5. Hallum, E. (1998). Untitled. In *Winning Orations, 1998* (p. 4). Mankato, MN: Interstate Oratorical Association. Hallum was coached by Clark Olson.

6. Monroe, A. (1935). *Principles and types of speech.* Glenview, IL: Scott, Foresman.

7. Adapted from an example given by Vaughn Kohler at http://vaughnkohler.com/wp-content/uploads/2013/01/Monroe-Motivated-Sequence-Outline-Handout1.pdf, accessed May 23, 2013.

8. Graham, K. (1976, April). The press and its responsibilities. *Vital Speeches of the Day, 42*(13), 395.

9. Hamilton, S. (2000). Cruise ship violence. In *Winning Orations, 2000* (p. 92). Mankato, MN: Interstate Oratorical Association. Hamilton was coached by Angela Hatton.

10. Anderson, G. (2009). Don't reject my homoglobin. In *Winning Orations, 2009* (p. 33). Mankato, MN: Interstate Oratorical Association. Anderson was coached by Leah White.

11. Hobbs, E. (2006). Untitled. In *Winning Orations, 2006* (p. 45). Mankato, MN: Interstate Oratorical Association. Hobbs was coached by Kevin Minch and Kris Stroup.

12. Ibid.

13. Wideman, S. (2006). Planning for peak oil: Legislation and conservation. In *Winning Orations, 2006* (p. 7). Mankato, MN: Interstate Oratorical Association. Wideman was coached by Brendan Kelly.

14. Herbert, B. (2007). Hooked on violence. *New York Times,* April 26.

15. Sherriff, D. (1998, April 1). Bill Gates too rich. Posted on CRTNET discussion group.

16. Elsesser, K. (2010). "And the gender-neutral scar goes to. . . ." *New York Times,* March 4.

17. Remarks by Aaron Sorkin at Syracuse University's Commencement, May 13, 2012.

18. Khanna, R. (2000). Distortion of history. In *Winning Orations, 2000* (p. 46). Mankato, MN: Interstate Oratorical Association. Khanna was coached by Alexis Hopkins.

19. Notebaert, R. C. (1998). Leveraging diversity: Adding value to the bottom line. *Vital Speeches of the Day,* November 1, 47.

20. McCarley, E. (2009). On the importance of drug courts. In *Winning Orations, 2009* (p. 36). Mankato, MN: Interstate Oratorical Association.

21. Ibid.

CHAPTER 13

1. Some recent literature specifically refers to Public Speaking Anxiety, or PSA. See, for example, Bodie, G. D. (2010, January). A racing heart, rattling knees, and ruminative thoughts: Defining, explaining, and treating public speaking anxiety. *Communication Education 59*(1), 70–105.

2. See, e.g., Borhis, J., & Allen, M. (1992, January). Meta-analysis of the relationship between communication apprehension and cognitive performance. *Communication Education, 41*(1), 68–76.

3. Daly, J. A. Vangelisti, A. L. & Weber, D. J. (1995, December). Speech anxiety affects how people prepare speeches: A protocol analysis of the preparation process of speakers. *Communication Monographs, 62,* 123–134.

4. Researchers generally agree that communication apprehension has three causes: genetics, social learning, and inadequate skills acquisition. See, e.g.,

Finn, A. N. (2009). Public speaking: What causes some to panic? *Communication Currents, 4*(4), 1–2.

5. See, e.g., Sawyer, C. R. & Behnke, R. R. (1997, Summer). Communication apprehension and implicit memories of public speaking state anxiety. *Communication Quarterly, 45*(3), 211–222.

6. Adapted from Ellis, A. (1977). *A new guide to rational living.* North Hollywood, CA: Wilshire Books. G. M. Philips listed a different set of beliefs that he believed contributes to reticence. The beliefs are: (1) an exaggerated sense of self-importance. (Reticent people tend to see themselves as more important to others than others see them.) (2) Effective speakers are born, not made. (3) Skillful speaking is manipulative. (4) Speaking is not that important. (5) I can speak whenever I want to; I just choose not to. (6) It is better to be quiet and let people think you are a fool than prove it by talking (they assume they will be evaluated negatively). (7) What is wrong with me requires a (quick) cure. See Keaten, J. A., Kelly, L., & Finch, C. (2000, April). Effectiveness of the Penn State program in changing beliefs associated with reticence." *Communication Education, 49*(2), 134.

7. Behnke, R. R., Sawyer, C. R., & King, P. E. (1987, April). The communication of public speaking anxiety. *Communication Education, 36*, 138–141.

8. Honeycutt, J. M., Choi, C. W., & DeBerry, J. R. (2009, July). Communication apprehension and imagined interactions. *Communication Research Reports, 26*(2), 228–236.

9. Behnke R. R. & Sawyer, C. R. (1999, April). Milestones of anticipatory public speaking anxiety. *Communication Education, 48*(2), 165.

10. Hinton, J. S., & Kramer, M. W. (1998, April). The impact of self-directed videotape feedback on students' self-reported levels of communication competence and apprehension. *Communication Education, 47*(2), 151–161. Significant increases in competency and decreases in apprehension were found using this method.

11. Research has confirmed that speeches practiced in front of other people tend to be more successful. See, e.g., Smith, T. E., & Frymier, A. B. (2006, February). "Get real": Does practicing speeches before an audience improve performance? *Communication Quarterly, 54*, 111–125.

12. See, e.g., Rosenfeld, L. R., & Civikly, J. M. (1976). *With words unspoken.* New York: Holt, Rinehart and Winston, p. 62. Also see Chaiken, S. (1979). Communicator physical attractiveness and persuasion. *Journal of Personality and Social Psychology, 37*, 1387–1397.

13. A study demonstrating this stereotype is Street, R. L., Jr., & Brady, R. M. (1982, December). Speech rate acceptance ranges as a function of evaluative domain, listener speech rate, and communication context. *Speech Monographs, 49*, 290–308.

14. See, e.g., Mulac, A., & Rudd, M. J. (1977). Effects of selected American regional dialects upon regional audience members. *Communication Monographs, 44*, 184–195. Some research, however, suggests that nonstandard dialects do not have the detrimental effects on listeners that was once believed. See, e.g., Johnson, F. L., & Buttny, R. (1982, March). White listeners' responses to "sounding black" and "sounding white": The effect of message content on judgments about language. *Communication Monographs, 49*, 33–39.

15. Smith, V., Siltanen, S. A., & Hosman, L. A. (1998, Fall). The effects of powerful and powerless speech styles and speaker expertise on impression formation and attitude change. *Communication Research Reports, 15*(1), 27–35. In this study, a powerful speech style was defined as one without hedges and hesitations such as *uh* and *anda*.

16. Examples include http://www.slideshare.net/GoTo Webinar/webinar-organizerchecklist, http://www .techsoup.org/support/articles-and-how-tos/10-steps -for-planning-a-successful-webinar,andhttp://www .inc.com/kevin-daum/10-tips-for-giving-great-online -presentations.html.

CHAPTER 14

1. Levine, K. (2001). The dentist's dirty little secret. In *Winning Orations 2001.* Mankato, MN: Interstate Oratorical Association, p. 77. Levine was coached by Trischa Goodnow.

2. Cacioppo, J. T., & Petty, R. E. (1979). Effects of message repetition and position on cognitive response, recall, and persuasion. *Journal of Personality and Social Psychology, 37*, 97–109.

3. Stallings, H. (2009). Prosecution deferred is justice denied. *Winning Orations 2009.* Mankato, MN: Interstate Oratorical Association. Stallings was coached by Randy Richardson and Melanie Conrad.

4. Monroe, A. (1935). *Principles and types of speech.* Glenview, IL: Scott, Foresman.

5. Baar, K. (1995). You may be thirstier than you feel. *New York Times*, August 2.

6. Toulmin, S. E. (1964). *The uses of argument.* New York: Cambridge University Press.

7. There are, of course, other classifications of logical fallacies than those presented here. See, e.g., Warnick, B., & Inch, E. (1994). *Critical thinking and communication: The use of reason in argument* (2nd ed., pp. 137–161). New York: Macmillan.

8. Sprague, J., & Stuart, D. (1992). *The speaker's handbook* (3rd ed., p. 172). Fort Worth, TX: Harcourt Brace Jovanovich.

9. For an example of how one politician failed to adapt to his audience's attitudes, see Hostetler, M. J. (1998, Winter). Gov. Al Smith confronts the Catholic question: The rhetorical legacy of the 1928 campaign. *Communication Quarterly, 46*(1), 12–24. Smith was reluctant to discuss religion, attributed bigotry to anyone who brought it up, and was impatient with the whole issue. He lost the election. Many years later, John F. Kennedy dealt with "the Catholic question" more reasonably and won.

10. DeVito, J. A. (1986). *The communication handbook: A dictionary.* New York: Harper & Row, pp. 84–86.

11. Dunn, D. H. (1983). The serious business of using jokes in public speaking. *Business Week*, September 5, p. 93.

12. See Markiewicz, D. (1974, September). Effects of humor on persuasion. *Sociometry, 37*, 407–422.

13. Seth Myers, "Weekend Update," *Saturday Night Live*, Season 38, ep. 21, May 18th, 2012.

14. DeGeneres, E. (1994). HBO *Comedy Showcase*, shown in its syndicated version over WNBC-TV, July 17, 1994.

15. Best joke ever: Sarah Silverman and the art of the non-dirty joke. *Timothy McSweeny's Internet Tendency.* Retrieved April 14, 2014, from http://www.mcsweeneys.net/articles/sarah-silverman-and-the-art-of-the-non-dirty-joke.

16. *The Late Show with David Letterman*, CBS Television Network, Friday, September 7, 1994.

17. Craig Ferguson, *The Late Late Show With Craig Ferguson*, CBS Television Network, December 12, 2013.

18. Conan O'Brien, Commencement Address, Dartmouth College, June 11, 2011.

19. Martin, S. (1978). *Wild and crazy guy* [record]. Burbank, CA: Warner Brothers.

GLOSSARY

ad hominem fallacy Fallacious reasoning that attacks the integrity of a person to weaken his or her position.

addition The articulation error that involves adding extra parts to words.

affect blend The combination of two or more expressions, each showing a different emotion.

affinity The degree to which we like or appreciate others.

all-channel network A communication network pattern in which group members are always together and share all information with one another.

altruistic lie Deception intended to be nonmalicious, or even helpful, to the person to whom it is told.

ambushers Receivers who listen carefully to gather information to use in an attack on the speaker.

analogy Extended comparison that can be used as supporting material in a speech.

analytical listening Listening in which the primary goal is to fully understand the message, prior to any evaluation.

androgynous Combining masculine and feminine traits.

anecdote A brief personal story used to illustrate or support a point in a speech.

argumentum ad populum fallacy Fallacious reasoning based on the dubious notion that because many people favor an idea, you should, too.

argumentum ad verecundiam fallacy Fallacious reasoning that tries to support a belief by relying on the testimony of someone who is not an authority on the issue being argued.

articulation The process of pronouncing all the necessary parts of a word.

assertive communication A style that directly expresses the sender's needs, thoughts, or feelings, delivered in a way that does not attack the receiver's dignity.

attending The process of focusing on certain stimuli from the environment.

attitude Predisposition to respond to an idea, person, or thing favorably or unfavorably.

attribution The process of attaching meaning.

audience analysis A consideration of characteristics including the type, goals, demographics, beliefs, attitudes, and values of listeners.

audience involvement The level of commitment and attention that listeners devote to a speech.

audience participation Having your listeners actually do something during your speech.

authoritarian An approach in which parents are strict and demanding and expect unquestioning obedience.

authoritative An approach in which parents are firm, clear, and strict, but encourage children to communicate openly with them.

avoidance spiral A communication pattern in which the parties slowly reduce their dependence on one another, withdraw, and become less invested in the relationship.

bar chart Visual aid that compares two or more values by showing them as elongated horizontal rectangles.

basic speech structure The division of a speech into introduction, body, and conclusion.

behavioral interview A formal meeting (in person or via communication technology) to exchange information about an applicant's past performance as it relates to the job at hand.

belief An underlying conviction about the truth of an idea, often based on cultural training.

breadth The range of topics about which an individual discloses.

breakout groups A strategy used when the number of members is too large for effective discussion. Subgroups simultaneously address an issue and then report back to the group at large.

cause-effect pattern Organizing plan for a speech that demonstrates how one or more events result in another event or events.

certainty Messages that dogmatically imply that the speaker's position is correct and that the other person's ideas are not worth considering.

chain network A communication network in which information passes sequentially from one member to another.

channel Medium through which a message passes from sender to receiver.

chronemics The study of how humans use and structure time.

citation Brief statement of supporting material in a speech.

claim An expressed opinion that the speaker would like the audience to accept.

coculture The perception of membership in a group that is part of an encompassing culture.

coercive power The power to influence others by the threat or imposition of unpleasant consequences.

cognitive complexity The ability to construct a variety of frameworks for viewing an issue.

cohesiveness The totality of forces that causes members to feel themselves part of a group and makes them want to remain in that group.

collectivistic culture A culture in which members focus on the welfare of the group as a whole, rather than being concerned mostly about personal success.

column chart Visual aid that compares two or more values by showing them as elongated vertical rectangles.

common ground Similarities between yourself and your audience members.

communication The process of creating meaning through symbolic interaction.

communication climate The emotional tone of a relationship as it is expressed in the messages that the partners send and receive.

communication competence Ability to maintain a relationship on terms acceptable to all parties.

compromise An approach to conflict resolution in which both parties attain at least part of what they seek through self-sacrifice.

conclusion (of a speech) The final structural unit of a speech, in which the main points are reviewed and final remarks are made to motivate the audience to act or help listeners remember key ideas.

confirming response A message that expresses respect and valuing of the other person.

conflict stage A stage in problem-solving groups when members openly defend their positions and question those of others.

conformity A family communication pattern in which members are expected to adhere to an established set of rules, beliefs, and values.

connection power Influence granted by virtue of a member's ability to develop relationships that help the group reach its goal.

contempt Reflects the speaker's negative attitude or opinion toward another person.

content message Communicates information about the subject being discussed.

contextually interpersonal communication Any communication that occurs between two individuals.

control The social need to influence others.

controlling communication Messages in which the sender tries to impose some sort of outcome on the receiver, usually resulting in a defensive reaction.

convergence Accommodating one's speaking style to another person, usually a person who is desirable or has higher status.

conversation A family communication pattern in which members are encouraged to communicate openly about rules and expectations.

credibility The believability of a speaker or other source of information.

critical listening Listening in which the goal is to evaluate the quality or accuracy of the speaker's remarks.

criticism Personal, all-encompassing, and accusatory messages.

culture The language, values, beliefs, traditions, and customs people share and learn.

decoding The process in which a receiver attaches meaning to a message.

defensive listeners Receivers who perceive a speaker's comments as an attack.

defensiveness Striking back when one feels attacked by another.

deletion An articulation error that involves leaving off parts of words.

demographics Audience characteristics that can be analyzed statistically, such as age, gender, education, and group membership.

depth The level of personal information a person reveals on a particular topic.

descriptive communication Messages that focus on the speaker's thoughts and feelings instead of judging the listener.

developmental model (of relational maintenance) Proposes that relationships develop, maintain stability, and come apart in stages that reflect different levels of intimacy.

diagram A line drawing that shows the most important components of an object.

dialectical model (of relational maintenance) A model claiming that, throughout their lifetime, people in virtually all interpersonal relationships must deal with equally important, simultaneous, and opposing forces such as connection and autonomy, predictability and novelty, and openness versus privacy.

dialogue A process in which people let go of the notion that their ideas are more correct or superior to those of others and instead seek to understand an issue from many different perspectives.

directly aggressive message An expression of the sender's thoughts or feelings, or both, that attacks the position and dignity of the receiver.

disconfirming response A message that expresses a lack of caring or respect for another person.

disfluency A nonlinguistic verbalization such as *um, er, ah.*

disinhibition The tendency to transmit messages without considering their consequences.

divergence A linguistic strategy in which speakers emphasize differences between their communicative style and that of others in order to create distance.

downward communication Messages from supervisors to the people they supervise.

dyad A two-person unit.

dyadic communication Two-person communication.

either-or fallacy Fallacious reasoning that sets up false alternatives, suggesting that if the inferior one must be rejected, then the other must be accepted.

emblems Deliberate nonverbal behaviors with precise meanings, known to virtually all members of a cultural group.

emergence stage A stage in problem-solving groups when members back off from their dogmatic positions.

emergent leader A member who assumes leadership roles without being appointed by higher-ups.

emotive language Language that conveys the sender's attitude rather than simply offering an objective description.

empathy The ability to project oneself into another person's point of view, so as to experience the other's thoughts and feelings.

encoding The process of putting thoughts into symbols, most commonly words.

environment Both the physical setting in which communication occurs and the personal perspectives of the parties involved.

equality Conveyed when communicators show that they believe others have just as much worth as human beings as they do.

equivocal words Language with more than one likely interpretation.

equivocation A vague statement that can be interpreted in more than one way.

escalatory conflict spirals A pattern in which disconfirming messages reinforce one another, often leading to a full-blown argument.

ethnicity A social construct that refers to the degree to which a person identifies with a particular group, usually on the basis of nationality, culture, religion, or some other unifying perspective.

ethnocentrism The attitude that one's own culture is superior to that of others.

euphemism A pleasant-sounding term used in place of a more direct but less pleasant one.

evaluative communication Statements interpreted as judgmental; often described as accusatory "you" language, as in, "You are so inconsiderate."

evidence Supporting material that the speaker uses to prove a type of claim.

exaggeration Magnifying description beyond truth.

example A specific case that is used to demonstrate a general idea.

expert power The ability to influence others by virtue of one's perceived expertise on the subject in question.

extemporaneous speech A speech that is planned in advance but presented in a direct, conversational manner.

fabrication A message in which the speaker deliberately misleads another person in a mean-spirited or manipulative way.

face The socially approved identity that a communicator tries to present.

facework Verbal and nonverbal behavior designed to create and maintain a communicator's face and the face of others.

factual statement A statement that can be verified as being true or false.

fallacy An error in logic.

fallacy of approval The irrational belief that it is vital to win the approval of virtually every person a communicator deals with.

fallacy of catastrophic failure The irrational belief that the worst possible outcome will probably occur.

fallacy of overgeneralization Irrational belief in which (1) conclusions (usually negative) are based on limited evidence or (2) communicators exaggerate their shortcomings.

fallacy of perfection The irrational belief that a worthwhile communicator should be able to handle every situation with complete confidence and skill.

family People who share affection and resources as a family and who think of themselves and present themselves as a family, regardless of their genetic commonality.

feedback The discernible response of a receiver to a sender's message.

flaming Sending angry and/or insulting emails, text messages, and posts.

focus group A procedure used in market research by sponsoring organizations to survey potential users or the public at large regarding a new product or idea.

force field analysis A method of problem analysis that identifies the forces contributing to resolution of the problem and the forces that inhibit its resolution.

formal outline A consistent format and set of symbols used to identify the structure of ideas.

formal role A role assigned to a person by group members or an organization, usually to establish order.

forum A discussion format in which audience members are invited to add their comments to those of the official discussants.

gatekeepers Producers of mass messages who determine what messages will be delivered to consumers, how those messages will be constructed, and when they will be delivered.

gender A socially constructed set of expectations about what it means to be "masculine" or "feminine."

general purpose One of three basic ways a speaker seeks to affect an audience: to entertain, inform, or persuade.

Gibb categories Types of supportive and defensive communication patterns that affect the climate of our relationships.

group A small collection of people whose members interact with one another, usually face-to-face, over time in order to reach goals.

group goals Goals that a group collectively seeks to accomplish.

groupthink A group's collective striving for unanimity that discourages realistic appraisals of alternatives to its chosen decision.

haptics The study of touch.

hearing The process wherein sound waves strike the eardrum and cause vibrations that are transmitted to the brain.

helpful speech anxiety A moderate level of apprehension about speaking before an audience that helps improve the speaker's performance.

high-context culture A culture that relies heavily on subtle, often nonverbal cues to maintain social harmony.

hinting Saying something to bring about a desired response without asking for it directly.

horizontal communication Messages between members of an organization with equal power.

hypothetical example Example that asks an audience to imagine an object or event.

identity management Strategies used by communicators to influence the way others view them.

immediacy The degree of interest and attraction we feel toward and communicate to others; usually expressed nonverbally.

impromptu speech A speech given "off the top of one's head," without preparation.

incongruity Statement that is out of place or inconsistent.

indirect communication Hinting at a message instead of expressing thoughts and feelings directly.

individual goals Individual motives for joining a group.

individualistic culture A culture in which members focus on the value and welfare of individual members, as opposed to a concern for the group as a whole.

inferential statement Conclusion arrived at from an interpretation of evidence.

informal roles Roles usually not explicitly recognized by a group that describe functions of group members, rather than their positions. These are sometimes called "functional roles."

informational interview A structured meeting in which you seek answers from a source whose knowledge can help enhance your success.

informative purpose statement A sentence that tells what knowledge your audience will gain by listening to your speech.

in-groups Groups with which we identify.

insensitive listeners Receivers who fail to recognize the thoughts or feelings that are not directly expressed by a speaker, instead accepting the speaker's words at face value.

insulated listeners Receivers who ignore undesirable information.

interpersonal communication Communication in which the parties consider one another as unique individuals rather than as objects.

intimacy A state of closeness between people that can be manifested physically, intellectually, emotionally, and via shared activities.

intrapersonal communication Communication that occurs within a single person.

introduction (of a speech) The first structural unit of a speech, in which the speaker captures the audience's attention and previews the main points to be covered.

irrational thinking Beliefs that have no basis in reality or logic; one source of unhelpful speech anxiety.

jargon The specialized vocabulary that is used as a kind of shorthand by people with common backgrounds and experience.

Johari window A model that describes the relationship between self-disclosure and self-awareness.

kinesics The study of body movement, gesture, and posture.

language A collection of symbols, governed by rules and used to convey messages between individuals.

legitimate power The ability to influence a group owing to one's position in a group.

line chart Visual aid consisting of a grid that maps out the direction of a trend by plotting a series of points.

linear communication model A characterization of communication as a one-way event in which a message flows from sender to receiver.

listening Process wherein the brain reconstructs electro-chemical impulses generated by hearing into representations of the original sound and gives them meaning.

listening fidelity The degree of congruence between what a listener understands and what the message sender was attempting to communicate.

low-context culture A culture in which people use language primarily to express thoughts, feelings, and ideas as directly as possible.

manipulators Movements in which one part of the body grooms, massages, rubs, holds, fidgets, pinches, picks, or otherwise manipulates another part.

manuscript speech A speech that is read word for word from a prepared text.

mass communication The transmission of messages to large, usually widespread audiences via broadcast (such as radio and television), print (such as newspapers, magazines, and books), multimedia (such as DVD), online, and other forms of media such as recordings and movies.

master of ceremonies (MC or emcee) The official host of a staged event.

mediated communication Messages sent to one person or to many via a medium such as telephone, email, or instant messaging.

memorized speech A speech learned and delivered by rote without a written text.

message A sender's planned and unplanned words and nonverbal behaviors.

metacommunication Messages (usually relational) that refer to other messages; communication about communication.

mindful listening Active, high-level information processing.

mindless listening Passive, low-level information processing.

model (in speeches and presentations) Replica of an object being discussed. Usually used when it would be difficult or impossible to use the actual object.

monochronic The use of time that emphasizes punctuality, schedules, and completing one task at a time.

motivated sequence A five-step organizational pattern for persuasive speeches.

narration Presentation of speech-supporting material as a story with a beginning, middle, and end.

networking The strategic process of deliberately meeting people and maintaining contacts.

neutrality A defense-arousing behavior in which the sender expresses indifference toward a receiver.

noise External, physiological, and psychological distractions that interfere with the accurate transmission and reception of a message.

nominal leaders People who have been officially designated as being in charge of a group.

nonassertion The inability or unwillingness to express one's thoughts or feelings.

nonverbal communication Messages expressed by other than linguistic means.

norms Shared values, beliefs, behaviors, and procedures that govern a group's operation.

number chart Visual aid that lists numbers in tabular form in order to clarify information.

omission A type of deception in which one person withholds information that another person deserves to know.

opinion statement A statement based on the speaker's beliefs.

organizational communication Communication that occurs within a structured collection of people in order to meet a need or pursue a goal.

orientation stage A stage in problem-solving groups when members become familiar with one another's position and tentatively volunteer their own.

out-groups Groups of people that we view as different from us.

panel discussion A discussion format in which participants consider a topic more or less conversationally, without formal procedural rules. Panel discussions may be facilitated by a moderator.

paralanguage Nonlinguistic means of vocal expression: rate, pitch, tone, and so on.

paraphrasing Feedback in which the receiver rewords the speaker's thoughts and feelings to verify understanding, demonstrate empathy, or help others solve their problems.

passive aggression An indirect expression of aggression, delivered in a way that allows the sender to maintain a facade of kindness.

perceived self The person we believe ourselves to be in moments of candor. It may be identical with or different from the presenting and ideal selves.

perception checking A three-part method for verifying the accuracy of interpretations, including a description of the sense data, two possible interpretations, and a request for confirmation of the interpretations.

permissive An approach in which parents are open to dialogue but do not require children to follow many rules.

persuasion The act of motivating a listener, through communication, to change a particular belief, attitude, value, or behavior.

persuasive speaking Reason-giving discourse that involves proposing claims and backing up those claims with proof.

phonological rules Linguistic rules governing how sounds are combined to form words.

pictogram A visual aid that conveys its meaning through an image of an actual object.

pie chart A visual aid that divides a circle into wedges, representing percentages of the whole.

pitch The highness or lowness of one's voice.

play on words Manipulation of language to create humor.

polychronic The use of time that emphasizes flexible schedules in which multiple tasks are pursued at the same time.

***post hoc* fallacy** Fallacious reasoning that mistakenly assumes that one event causes another because they occur sequentially.

power The ability to influence others' thoughts and/or actions.

power distance The degree to which members of a group are willing to accept a difference in power and status.

pragmatic rules Rules that govern how people use language in everyday interaction.

prejudice An unfairly biased and intolerant attitude toward others who belong to an out-group.

presenting self The image a person presents to others, which may be identical to or different from the perceived and ideal selves.

problem census A technique used to equalize participation in groups when the goal is to identify important issues or problems. Members first put ideas on cards, which are then compiled by a leader to generate a comprehensive statement of the issue or problem.

problem orientation A supportive style of communication in which the communicators focus on working together to solve their problems instead of trying to impose their own solutions on one another.

problem-solution pattern Organizing pattern for a speech that describes an unsatisfactory state of affairs and then proposes a plan to remedy the problem.

procedural norms Norms that describe rules for the group's operation.

proof Statements explaining why your claims are true, along with evidence that backs up those claims.

provisionalism A supportive style of communication in which the sender expresses a willingness to consider the other person's position.

proxemics The study of how people and animals use space.

pseudolisteners Receivers who imitate true listening but whose minds are elsewhere.

public communication Communication that occurs when a group becomes too large for all members to contribute. It is characterized by an unequal amount of speaking and by limited verbal feedback.

purpose statement A complete sentence that describes precisely what a speaker wants to accomplish.

qualitatively interpersonal communication Interaction in which people treat one another as unique individuals, regardless of the context in which the interaction occurs or the number of people involved.

race A social construct originally created to explain biological differences among people whose ancestors originated in different regions of the world.

rate The speed at which a speaker utters words.

receiver One who notices and attends to a message.

***reduction ad absurdum* fallacy** Fallacious reasoning that unfairly attacks an argument by extending it to such extreme lengths that it looks ridiculous.

referent power The ability to influence others by virtue of the degree to which one is liked or respected.

reflected appraisal The influence of others on one's self-concept.

reinforcement stage A stage in problem-solving groups when members endorse the decision they have made.

relational listening A listening style that is driven primarily by the goal of building emotional closeness with the speaker.

relational maintenance The process of keeping stable relationships operating smoothly and satisfactorily.

relational message Conveys the social relationship between two or more individuals.

relative words Words that gain their meaning by comparison.

remembering The act of recalling previously introduced information, short-term and long-term.

residual message The part of a message a receiver can recall after short- and long-term memory loss.

respect The degree to which we hold others in esteem.

responding Providing observable feedback to another person's behavior or speech.

reward power The ability to influence others by the granting or promising of desirable consequences.

roles The patterns of behavior expected of group members.

rule An explicit, officially stated guideline that governs group functions and member behavior.

salience How much weight we attach to a particular person or phenomenon.

satire Humor based on an exposé of human vice or folly.

selection interview A formal meeting (in person or via communication technology) to exchange information that may occur when you are being considered for employment or being evaluated for promotion or reassignment.

selective listeners Receivers who respond only to messages that interest them.

self-concept The relatively stable set of perceptions each individual holds of himself or herself.

self-disclosure The process of deliberately revealing information about oneself that is significant and that would not normally be known by others.

self-esteem The part of the self-concept that involves evaluations of self-worth.

self-fulfilling prophecy A prediction or expectation of an event that makes the outcome more likely to occur than would otherwise have been the case.

self-monitoring The process of paying close attention to one's own behavior and using these observations to shape the way one behaves.

self-serving bias The tendency to interpret and explain information in a way that casts the perceiver in the most favorable manner.

semantic rules Rules that govern the meaning of language as opposed to its structure.

sender The originator of a message.

sex A biological category (male, female, and intersex).

significant other A person whose opinion is important enough to affect one's self-concept strongly.

signpost A word or phrase that emphasizes the importance of what you are about to say.

situational leadership A theory that argues that the most effective leadership style varies according to leader-member relations, the leader's power, and the task structure.

slang Language used by a group of people whose members belong to a similar coculture or other group.

slurring The articulation error that involves overlapping the end of one word with the beginning of the next.

small group communication Communication within a group that is small enough for every member to participate actively with all other members.

social exchange theory A model that suggests that we stay with people who can give us rewards that are greater than or equal to the costs we encounter in dealing with them.

social intelligence The capacity to effectively negotiate complex social relationships and environments.

social loafing Lazy behavior that some members use to avoid doing their share of the work.

social media Digital communication channels used primarily for personal reasons, often to reach small groups of receivers.

social norms Group norms that govern the way members relate to one another.

social penetration model A model describing how intimacy can be achieved via the breadth and depth of self-disclosure.

social roles Emotional roles concerned with maintaining smooth personal relationships among group members. Also termed *"maintenance functions."*

space pattern Organizing plan for a speech that arranges points according to their physical location.

special occasion speaking Speeches that are not primarily informative or persuasive in nature, and are presented as part of an event.

specific purpose The precise effect that the speaker wants to have on an audience. Expressed in the form of a purpose statement.

speech to change attitudes Persuasion designed to change the way audiences think about a topic.

speech to change behavior Persuasion designed to change audience actions.

spiral Reciprocal communication pattern in which each person's message reinforces the other's.

spontaneity Supportive communication behavior in which the sender expresses a message without any attempt to manipulate the receiver.

stage hogs Receivers who are more concerned with making their point than with understanding the speaker.

statistics The arrangement or organization of numbers to show how a fact or principle is true for a large percentage of cases.

stereotyping The perceptual process of applying exaggerated beliefs associated with a categorizing system.

stonewalling A form of avoidance in which one person refuses to engage with the other.

strategy Gibb's term for manipulative behavior.

substitution The articulation error that involves replacing part of a word with an incorrect sound.

superiority A type of communication that suggests one person is better than another.

supportive listening The reception approach to use when others seek help for personal dilemmas.

symbol An arbitrary sign used to represent a thing, person, idea, event, or relationship in a way that makes communication possible.

sympathy Compassion for another's situation.

symposium A discussion format in which participants divide the topic in a manner that allows each member to deliver in-depth information without interruption.

syntactic rules Rules that govern the ways in which symbols can be arranged as opposed to the meanings of those symbols.

target audience The subgroup you must persuade to reach a goal.

task norms Group norms that govern the way members handle the job at hand.

task roles Roles group members take on in order to help solve a problem.

task-oriented listening A listening style that is primarily concerned with accomplishing the task at hand.

team A group that has clear and inspiring shared goals, a results-driven structure, competent team members, unified commitment, a collaborative climate, external support and recognition, and principled leadership.

territory Fixed space that an individual assumes some right to occupy.

testimony Supporting material that proves or illustrates a point by citing an authoritative source.

thesis statement A complete sentence describing the central idea of a speech.

time pattern Organizing plan for a speech based on chronology.

topic pattern Organizing plan for a speech that arranges points according to logical types or categories.

trait theories of leadership The belief that it is possible to identify leaders by personal traits, such as intelligence, appearance, or sociability.

transactional communication model A characterization of communication as the simultaneous sending and receiving of messages in an ongoing, irreversible process.

transition Phrase that connects ideas in a speech by showing how one relates to the other.

uncertainty avoidance The cultural tendency to seek stability and honor tradition instead of welcoming risk, uncertainty, and change.

understanding The act of interpreting a message by following syntactic, semantic, and pragmatic rules.

unhelpful speech anxiety Intense level of apprehension about speaking before an audience, resulting in poor performance.

upward communication Messages from team members to supervisors.

value A deeply rooted belief about a concept's inherent worth.

virtual groups People who interact with one another via mediated channels, without meeting face-to-face.

visual aids Graphic devices used in a speech to illustrate or support ideas.

visualization A technique for behavioral rehearsal (e.g., for a speech) that involves imagining the successful completion of the task.

warrant In the Toulmin Model, this is used to tie the claim and evidence together.

Web 2.0 A term used to describe how the Internet has evolved from a one-way medium into a combination of mass and interpersonal communication.

wheel network A communication network in which a gatekeeper regulates the flow of information from all other members.

win-win problem solving A means of resolving conflict in which the goal is a solution that satisfies both people's needs.

word chart Visual aid that lists words or terms in tabular form in order to clarify information.

word play Technique that allows you to create humor by manipulating language.

working outline Constantly changing organizational aid used in planning a speech.

PHOTOGRAPHS

Page 2 Francisco Romero/Getty Images; **5** © iStock.com/EdStock; **7** © iStock.com/ferrantraite; **20** © iStock.com/Juanmonino; **20** © iStock.com/pearleye; **23** AP Photo/Danny Moloshok; **23** © Featureflash/Shutterstock; **28** © photo.ua/Shutterstock; **32** © Helga Esteb/Shutterstock; **35** © Mary Evans/Interfoto/The Image Works; **37** © s_bukley/Shutterstock; **37** © Helga Esteb/Shutterstock; **42** © iStock.com/mattjeacock; **46** Everett Collection / Shutterstock.com; **46** Rex Features via AP Images; **50** © iStock.com/tacojim; **52** © iStock.com/MTMCOINS; **56** AP Photo/Tony Dejak; **64** © iStock.com/EdStock; **69** AP Photo/Carolyn Kaster; **69** AP Photo/Pablo Martinez Monsivais; **74** Luis Davilla/Getty Images; **79** AP Photo/Detroit News, Dale G. Young; **81** Photo by John Shearer/Invision/AP; **100** © nikitabuida/Shutterstock; **102** ZUMA Press, Inc. / Alamy; **105** AP Photo/Mary Altaffer; **110** © Bryan Solomon/Shutterstock; **110** © Stocksnapper/Shutterstock; **110** © iStock.com/Zeffss1; **110** © iStock.com/david franklin; **110** © Hector Sanchez/Shutterstock; **110** © Richard Peterson/Shutterstock; **110** © Oleksandr Rybitskiy/Shutterstock; **124** Dorling Kindersley/Getty Images; **127** AP Photo/Marcio Jose Sanchez; **128** Bravo/Getty Images; **136** Stockton PD/Rex Features; **137** AP Photo/Ben Margot; **139** © iStock.com/shipfactory; **139** © iStock.com/Deborah Cheramie; **139** © Dirk Ott/Shutterstock; **139** © iStock.com/skynesher; **140** VIEW Pictures Ltd / Alamy; **142** © Champion studio/Shutterstock; **142** © Stocksnapper/Shutterstock; **142** © Ecoimages/Shutterstock; **142** © auremar/Shutterstock; **142** © Aaron Amat/Shutterstock; **146** Photo by Dan Harr/Invision/AP; **150** © iStock.com/skodonnell; **153** Photo by John Shearer/Invision/AP; **162** © iStock.com/youngvet; **174** © iStock.com/mamadela; **177** AF Archive / Alamy; **179** ZUMA Press, Inc. / Alamy; **179** ZUMA Press, Inc. / Alamy; **188** AF Archive /Alamy; **194** © Alis Photo/Shutterstock; **196** Photo by Andy Kropa/Invision/AP; **200** ZUMA Press, Inc. / Alamy; **200** ZUMA Press, Inc. / Alamy; **203** Photo by Matt Sayles/Invision/AP; **213** PjrStudio/Alamy; **213** Pictoral Press Ltd/Alamy; **224** © iStock.com/skodonnell; **246** C20TH Fox/Ronald Grant Archive/Alamy; **246** AF Archive / Alamy; **251** epa european pressphoto agency b.v./Alamy; **255** Robert Clay/Alamy; **260** Jutta Klee/Getty Images; **263** AF archive / Alamy; **269** Michele K. Short/© FX Networks/courtesy Everett Collection; **273** Patrick Wymore/TM and Copyright © 20th Century Fox Film Corp. All rights reserved./Courtesy Everett Collection; **279** FOX/Getty Images; **279** AP Photo/Matt Sayles; **282** Everett Collection Historical/Alamy; **288** © design56/Shutterstock; **292** Photos 12/Alamy; **302** ZUMA Press, Inc. / Alamy; **308** Keith Bernstein/© HBO/courtesy Everett Collection; **310** Nate Shron/Getty Images; **316** Aigars Reinholds/Alamy; **320** Photoshot/Everett Collection; **323** AP Photo/Matt Sayles; **323** John Shearer/Invision/AP; **324** Jim Goldstein/Alamy; **334** © Albert H. Teich/Shutterstock; **340** © kldy/Shutterstock; **348** AP Photo/Miss Universe, Patrick Prather; **359** © Focus Features/Courtesy Everett Collection; **360** AP Photo/Matt Sayles; **360** John Davisson/Invision/AP

TEXT, TABLES, AND FIGURES

Page 86 Harvard Dialect Survey, which concluded in 2003 (Vaux, Bert and Scott Golder. 2003. The Harvard Dialect Survey. Cambridge, MA: Harvard University Linguistics Department). http://www4.uwm.edu/FLL/linguistics/dialect/staticmaps/q_50.html; **92** Brownlow, S., Rosamond, J. A., & Parker, J. A. (2003). Gender-linked linguistic behavior in television interviews. Sex Roles, 49(3), 121–132. Springer. Retrieved from http://www.springerlink.com/index/w501725035716337.pdf. Mehl, M. R., & Pennebaker, J. W. (2003). The sounds of social life: A psychometric analysis of students' daily social environments and natural conversations. Journal of Personality and Social Psychology, 84(4), 857–870. doi:10.1037/0022–3514.84.4.857; **113** Adapted with the authors' permission from: Bodie, G. D., Worthington, D. L., & Gearhart, C. G. (2013). The Revised Listening Styles Profile (LSP-R): Development and validation. Communication Quarterly, 61, 72–90. doi: 10.1080/01463373.2012.720343.; **126** Adapted from Stewart, J., & D'Angelo, G. (1980). Together: communicating interpersonally (2nd ed.). Reading, MA: Addison-Wesley, p. 22. Copyright © 1993 by McGraw-Hill. Reprinted/adapted by permission.; **132** Based on material from Ekman, P. (1981). Mistakes when deceiving. In T. A. Sebok & R. Rosenthal (Eds.), The Clever Hans phenomenon: Communication with horses, whales, apes and people (pp. 269–278). New York: New York Academy of Sciences.; **252** Adapted from Bass & Stodgill's Handbook of Leadership, 3rd. ed., by Bernard M. Bass. Copyright © 1990 by The Free Press.; **277** Adapted from Brilhart, J., & Galanes, G. Adapting problem-solving methods. *Effective group discussion* (10th ed.), p. 291. Copyright © 2001. Reprinted by permission of McGraw-Hill Companies, Inc.; **394** New York Public Interest Research Group, Brooklyn College chapter. (2004). Voter registration project.; **369** Courtesy of Nick Gilyard; **374** Courtesy of Curt Casper; **380** Courtesy of Hananiah Wiggins.